EFFECTIVE PROGRAMS
FOR LATINO STUDENTS

EFFECTIVE PROGRAMS FOR LATINO STUDENTS

Edited by

Robert E. Slavin
Margarita Calderón
Johns Hopkins University

LEA LAWRENCE ERLBAUM ASSOCIATES, PUBLISHERS
2001 Mahwah, New Jersey   London

Lawrence Erlbaum Associates, Inc., Publishers
10 Industrial Avenue
Mahwah, New Jersey 07430

Library of Congress Cataloging-in-Publication Data

Effective programs for Latino students : edited by Robert E. Slavin, Margarita Calderón.
   p. cm.
   Includes bibliographical references (p.) and index.
   ISBN 0-8058-3412-5 (cloth : alk. paper) — ISBN 0-8058-3413-3 (pbk. : alk. paper)
   1. Hispanic American students—Education.   2. Education, Bilingual—United States. I.
Slavin, Robert E.   II. Calderón, Margarita.
LC2669 .E44 2000
371.829′68073—dc21   00-027034
                                                        CIP

Books published by Lawrence Erlbaum Associates are printed on acid-free paper,
and their bindings are chosen for strength and durability.

Printed in the United States of America
10 9 8 7 6 5 4 3 2 1

Contents

Preface

At the very heart of the American ethos is the idea that immigrants to the United States are able to build a better life for their children and grandchildren, by means of their own hard work and sacrifice and with the help of a public school system dedicated to helping every child, regardless of home background, language, or culture, achieve his or her full potential. Although the ethos of the common school contains as much myth as reality, it is nevertheless the case that the great majority of middle-class Americans whose families came to the United States in the past century can tell a story of parents, grandparents, or great-grandparents who came to the United States with nothing, struggled with linguistic and cultural barriers, but saw their children or grandchildren succeed in school and thereby achieve economic security. The school is the ladder by which the children of immigrants climb out of poverty into the mainstream. This is precisely the story of one of the editors of this book, whose grandfather came to New York from Argentina with no money, no English, and no trade. The other editor is herself a first-generation immigrant from Mexico.

Today, the descendents of the Italians, Poles, Greeks, Jews, and other immigrants of the early 20th century have long since achieved the American dream. At the turn of the 21st century, it is now immigrants from Asia and, especially, from the Americas who are enriching the United States with their energies, their cultural strengths, and their determination to build a better life for their children.

The largest group of immigrants by far is Spanish-speaking people from Mexico, the Caribbean, Central America, and South America. These Latino, or Hispanic, people have come to the United States for many generations and were in fact well established in parts of what is now the United States long before the *Mayflower* reached Plymouth Rock. However, the pace of Latino immigration has so accelerated in the past quarter century that a large proportion of Latinos in the United States today are first, second, or third generation. As recently as 1973, Latinos were only 6% of all U.S. school children, but increased to 12% by 1993. By 2010, Latinos will be the largest minority group in the United States, surpassing African Americans.

Will the public schools serve Latinos as the ladder to prosperity, as they have earlier immigrants? Answers to this question are complex. Of course, hundreds of thousands of Latino students are doing well in school and are graduating into the middle class; their accomplishments are only obscured in the statistics because of the educational problems of more recent immigrants. Some Latino groups, such as those from Cuba and South America, and middle-class families from all countries, are making particularly rapid progress into the mainstream. Yet there is also a large group of Latinos whose children are not making acceptable progress, even across several generations. For these families, the school is not serving as a ladder, but as a barrier. Although dropout rates for White and African American students have diminished sharply over the past 20 years, they remain shockingly high for Latino students, even second- and third-generation students who are fully proficient in English. Achievement levels for Latino students have risen since the early 1970s, but remain far below those of Whites and Asians, on average.

The persistent problems of many Latino groups in school, as well as a growing backlash against immigrants in some parts of the United States, have led to ferocious controversies. As of this writing, Proposition 227 in California, banning most native-language instruction, is being implemented (and, often, openly or covertly ignored) throughout our largest state. Anti-bilingual legislation is being proposed in many states. In this climate, educators concerned about Latino students have to take a position on the barricades, but at the same time they must recognize that language of instruction is not the only issue of importance. After many years of both Spanish bilingual and English-only schools, it is clear that neither type of school is routinely producing academic excellence for Latino students on a broad scale. There are islands of excellence, of course, but schools serving Latino students need effective programs that build on the children's linguistic and social assets. They need programs based on high-quality research, capable of being replicated and adapted to local circumstances and needs.

The purpose of this book is to present the current state of the art with respect to programs for Latino students. It is intended for educators, policymakers, and researchers who want to use research to inform the decisions they make about how to help Latino students succeed in elementary and secondary schools, and beyond. The chapters in this book use a variety of research methods, and the solutions they propose are extremely diverse. What binds them together, however, is a shared belief that Latino students can succeed at the highest levels if they are given the quality of instruction they deserve, and a shared belief that reform of schools serving many Latino students is both possible and essential. This is a book filled with statistics and description and reviews of research, but even more it is a book filled with optimism about what schools for Latino students can be, and what these students will achieve.

Some of the chapters of this book grew out of the Hispanic Dropout Project, commissioned by New Mexico Senator Jeff Bingaman and led by Walter Secada of the University of Wisconsin. The book was assembled and edited under funding from the Office of Educational Research and Evaluation, U.S. Department of Education (grant R-117D-40005). However, any opinions expressed are those of the chapter authors, and do not necessarily represent the positions or policies of the U.S. Department of Education.

1

Effective Programs for Latino Students in Elementary and Middle Schools

Olatokunbo S. Fashola
Robert E. Slavin
Margarita Calderón
Johns Hopkins University

Richard Durán
University of California at Santa Barbara

Education has always been the means by which children of immigrants to the United States enter the economic mainstream of our society. As a nation of immigrants, we have always taken pride in the idea (if not the reality) that our schools should give children from all cultures and backgrounds a fair chance to succeed in school and thereby in society.

In recent years, however, many have begun to question the effectiveness of schools for children from nonmainstream cultures. In particular, there is great concern about the education of children from families that originated in Latin America. Latino (or Hispanic) children are one of the fastest growing groups in our schools. In 1973 they represented less than 6% of all public school children; by 1993 they were almost 12% of all students (National Center for Education Statistics [NCES], 1995). Although other immigrant groups have also experienced substantial increases, Latino students are by far the largest group in absolute numbers.

Of course, Latino students are highly diverse; it is inappropriate to make generalizations about students from Mexican, Puerto Rican, Cuban, or South American backgrounds, those whose families have been in the United States for hundreds of years and those whose families arrived a month ago, those who have entered the growing Latino middle class and those who are struggling in poverty, and so on. For example, Mexi-

1

can American and Central American children drop out at almost three times the rate of Cuban American and South American children, who are near the national average dropout rate (General Accounting Office, 1994). Nevertheless, it is worthwhile to consider the characteristics of Latino students as a whole.

On average, Latino students perform much worse in elementary and secondary school than Anglo students on measures of academic achievement. On the National Assessment of Educational Progress (NAEP), Latino students have been gradually increasing their scores over the past two decades, especially in reading, and have significantly reduced the gap between their performance and that of non-Hispanic Whites, or Anglos (NCES, 1994), although the gap grew somewhat over the 1991–1994 period. However, the average performance of Latino students remains significantly below that of Anglos at all grade levels and in all subjects tested. For example, Latino students are about 2 years below Anglos in reading at age 13 years. In science, the average Latino 13-year-old scores at about the level of Anglo 9-year-olds.

The dropout rate among Latino students is extremely high. In 1991, approximately 35.3% of Latinos ages 16–24 years were out of school without a high school degree, compared to 8.9% of Anglos and 13.6% of African Americans (NCES, 1993). The comparison with African American dropout rates is particularly telling; Latino students' academic performance and socioeconomic status are similar to those of African Americans, but their dropout rate is 2½ times higher. Worse, although dropout rates have been falling for Anglo and African American students, they have been rising since the 1980s among Latino students. Part of this relates to increasing immigration rates; dropout rates are especially high among Latinos born outside of the United States (43%). However, even among U.S.-born Latinos in the second generation or beyond, dropout rates averaged 24%, still far higher than that for Anglos and almost twice that for African Americans. In fact, second-generation Latinos' dropout rate is higher than that of first generation native-born Latinos (17%).

Latino students face two major barriers to educational success: low socioeconomic status and language. By any measure, Latino students are far more likely than Anglo students to come from homes in poverty and to have parents who have limited education. Forty percent of Latino children are living in poverty, almost twice the rate for all U.S. children (NCES, 1995). Latino students from low-income families perform less well and are far more likely to drop out than are those from middle- or upper-income families (Knapp & Woolverton, 1995), but even within income categories, Latino students are much more likely to drop out than are other students. Middle-income Latino students, for example, are almost three times more likely to drop out than middle-income White or African American students, and they are about as likely to drop out as low-income African American students (NCES, 1993).

Clearly, low socioeconomic status alone does not explain the educational difficulties of Latino students. A second key factor is language. Of an estimated 2.3 million limited English proficient students in grades K–12, about 75% speak Spanish (Fleishman & Hopstock, 1993; U.S. Department of Education, 1992). Limited English proficient students of all nationalities perform significantly lower than fully English proficient students (Council of Chief State School Officers, 1990; Durán, 1994a). Further, about half of all limited English proficient students were born outside of the United States, and immigrant status (highly correlated with language) is a key predictor of school success (General Accounting Office, 1994).

Clearly, there is a crisis in the education of Latino students, and this crisis is not fully explained by recent immigration status or even limited English proficiency, as second-generation Latinos are likely to be proficient in English. There are many islands of excellence among schools serving many Latino children, but far too many of these children are placed at risk by schools and community institutions unable to build on the cultural, personal, and linguistic strengths these children are likely to bring with them to school (Vasquez, 1993).

BEYOND LANGUAGE OF INSTRUCTION

Discussion of appropriate education for Latino students has focused for many years on the question of the appropriate language of instruction for limited English proficient students. Research on this topic has generally found that limited English proficient, Spanish-dominant students who are taught to read Spanish and then transitioned to English ultimately become better readers in English than do students taught to read only in English (August & Hakuta, 1997; Garcia, 1991; Willig, 1985; Wong-Fillmore & Valdez, 1986). An influential study by Ramirez, Yuen, and Ramey (1991) added to this conclusion a caution about bilingual programs that transition students to English-only instruction too early or too abruptly—such programs produced results no better than those produced by English immersion strategies.

Despite the research evidence, there is a sustained assault on native-language instruction under way at this writing, most exemplified by the passage of Proposition 227 in California. Proposition 227 is intended to substantially curtail the use of bilingual education, and although many schools are finding loopholes to enable them to continue their bilingual programs, many others have moved to English-only models.

Proposition 227 and other political movements heighten the debate about language of instruction, which is certain to continue, but there is another question that is at least as important for Latino English language learners: How can we ensure that students will succeed in school, whichever language is used to teach them? (See, for example, Garcia, 1994.) If Spanish-dominant students are taught in Spanish, they must succeed in Spanish. There is no reason to believe that children failing to read well in Spanish will later become good readers and successful students in English. On the contrary, research consistently supports the commonsense expectation that the better students in Spanish bilingual programs read Spanish, the better their English reading will be (Garcia, 1991; Hakuta & Garcia, 1989). Clearly, the quality of instruction in Spanish is a key factor in the success of students in bilingual programs, and must be a focus of research and professional development in the education of these children.

Further, it is important to note that most Latino students are taught in English. The majority are fully proficient in English when they enter school, and among those who are not, only about half participate in bilingual programs, due to such factors as local policies against native-language instruction, shortages of fully bilingual teachers, parental preferences for English-only instruction, lack of adequate concentrations of limited English proficient students in a given school to justify a bilingual program, or other factors. In addition, even in schools with bilingual programs, Spanish instruction is typically given only in some subjects and only for a few years. For these reasons, a large proportion of Latino students will always be taught most or all subjects entirely in English (with English as a second language [ESL] instruction as a supplement for students who need it). As is true of bilingual education, the quality of classroom instruction, ESL instruction, and the integration of the two are essential in determining the success of Latino students.

Without minimizing the importance of the debate over language of instruction, it is time to move beyond this debate, to ask what instructional programs are most effective for Latino students regardless of their language proficiency and regardless of availability of native-language instruction.

The purpose of this report is to present research on the effectiveness of instructional programs for Latino students in the elementary and middle grades (K–8). This is a critical period in students' development. Although dropout usually takes place during the secondary years, the processes that lead to dropout begin much earlier. Low achievement, retention in grade, and other school success indicators as early as third grade can predict high school dropout with a high degree of reliability (Ekstrom, Goertz, Pollack, & Rock, 1986; Lloyd, 1978; Rumberger, 1987).

Further, for many students, intervention in high school is too late. Census data cited by Rumberger (1995) show that almost half of Latino males who dropped out of school did so before they completed their first year of high school. During elementary and middle school, students largely define themselves as learners. Failure in the early grades ultimately leads to low academic self-esteem, frustration, truancy, delinquency, and dropout (Finn, 1989).

FOCUS OF THE REVIEW

The focus of this review is on the identification of programs that have been shown to be effective in rigorous evaluations, that are replicable across a broad range of elementary and middle schools, and that have been successfully evaluated or at least frequently applied to schools serving many Latino students. There are many articles and books on general principles of effective practice for Latino students and for bilingual education (e.g., Council of Chief State School Officers, 1990; Durán, 1994a, 1994b; Howe, 1994; Leighton, Hightower, & Wrigley, 1995; Losey, 1995; Milk, 1993; Vasquez, 1993) and descriptions of outstanding schools for Latino or bilingual students (e.g., Fleischman & Hopstock, 1993; Gutierrez, Larson, & Kreuter, 1996; Jiménez, García, & Pearson, 1995). The reader is encouraged to seek out these and other writings on effective practices. However, the focus of this review is on specific strategies that schools could select to improve achievement outcomes for Latino students. Other compendia list promising programs (e.g., Leighton et al., 1995; National Diffusion Network, 1995), but unlike these, this review applies consistent standards to evaluate the likely effectiveness and replicability of programs available to educators committed to transforming schools and classrooms to meet the needs of Latino students. Two reviews, by Herman (1999) and by Slavin and Fashola (1998), have reviewed programs using consistent standards of effectiveness, but have not focused on Latino students.

The criteria applied in this review are described in the following sections.

Effectiveness

Programs were considered to be effective if evaluations compared students who participated in the program to similar students in matched comparison or control schools and found the program students to perform significantly better on fair measures of academic performance. Such evaluations were required to demonstrate that experimental and control students were initially equivalent on measures of academic performance, language proficiency, and other measures, and were similar in other ways. "Fair measures" were ones assessing objectives pursued equally by experimental and control groups; for example, a curriculum-specific measure would be fair only if the control group were implementing the same curriculum.

Many studies of innovative programs used evaluations that compared gains made by program students on standardized tests, usually expressed in percentiles or normal curve equivalents (NCEs), to "expected" gains derived from national norming samples. This design, widely used in evaluations of Chapter 1/Title I and Chapter VII/Title VII programs, is prone to error and generally overstates program impacts (Slavin & Madden, 1991). In studies of limited English proficient students that use standardized tests in English, this design is particularly prone to error, as low pretests among LEP students are likely to be due to lack of English language skills, not lack of content knowledge. As students learn English they are likely to appear to make more rapid progress than an English-proficient norming group. Programs evaluated using NCE gains or other alternatives to experimental–control comparisons are discussed as promising if their outcomes are particularly striking, but such data are not considered conclusive.

In this review, we exclude after-the-fact comparisons of experimental and control groups chosen after outcomes are known.

Replicability

The best evidence that a program is replicable in other schools is that it has in fact been replicated elsewhere, especially if there is evidence that the program was evaluated and found to be effective in sites beyond its initial pilot locations. The existence of an active dissemination effort is also a strong indication of replicability. Programs are considered low in replicability if they have been used in a small number of schools and appear to depend on conditions (e.g., charismatic principals, magnet schools, extraordinary resources) unlikely to exist on a significant scale elsewhere.

Evaluation or Application With Latino Students

Ideally, the programs emphasized in this review are ones that have been successfully evaluated in schools serving many Latino students. However, it would be foolish to exclude programs known to be effective with non-Latino populations if they have promise for Latino students. Therefore, programs were included if they had strong evidence of effectiveness and replicability and had been disseminated to schools with many Latino students, even if the reported evaluations did not include Latino students.

LITERATURE SEARCH PROCEDURES

The broadest possible search was carried out for programs that had been evaluated and/or applied to Latino students. In addition to searches of the Education Resource and Information Center (ERIC) system and of education journals, we obtained reports on promising programs listed by the National Diffusion Network (NDN) and by Title VII grantees. The NDN was a part of the U.S. Department of Education that identified promising programs, disseminated information about them through a system of state facilitators, and provided "developer/demonstrator" grants to help developers prepare their products for dissemination and then to carry out a dissemination plan. To be listed by NDN a program must have presented evidence of effectiveness to a Program Effectiveness Panel (PEP), or formerly to the Joint Dissemination Review Panel (JDRP). PEP or JDRP panel members reviewed the data for educationally significant effects. However, the evaluation requirements for PEP/JDRP were generally low, and more than 500 programs of all kinds approved, mostly on the basis of NCE gain designs.

SELECTION FOR REVIEW

Ideally, programs emphasized in this review would be those that were specifically designed for use with Latino students, present rigorous evaluation evidence in comparison to control groups showing significant and lasting impacts on the achievement of Latino students, have active dissemination programs that have implemented the program in many schools serving Latino students, and have evidence of effectiveness in dissemination sites, ideally from studies conducted by third parties. To require all of these conditions would limit this review to two programs, our own Success for All/*Éxito Para Todos* program and the Spanish adaptation of Reading Recovery, *Descubriendo La Lectura*. To include a much broader range of programs, we have had to compromise on one or more criteria. For example, we have included programs that have excellent data that show positive effects for Latino students even if the program has not been widely replicated (as long as there is no obvious reason it could not be replicated). We have included programs that have excellent outcome data and evidence of replicability with non-Latino students if the program has been replicated in areas with large Latino populations. We have included programs that have shakier evidence of effectiveness if they are particularly well known, widely replicated, and appropriate to the needs of Latino students. Thus, our listing of a program in this review does not mean that we believe the program to be highly effective, replicable, and uniquely adapted to the needs of Latino students. Instead, among the hundreds of programs we have reviewed, these were the ones we felt to be most appropriate to be considered by elementary and middle schools serving many Latino students. We have tried to present the evidence that school and district staff would need to begin a process leading to an informed choice from among effective and promising programs capable of being replicated.

EFFECT SIZES

The outcomes of the evaluations summarized in this review are quantified as *effect sizes*. These are computed as the difference between experimental and control group means divided by the control group's standard deviation (Glass, McGaw, & Smith, 1981). To give a sense of scale, an effect size of $+1.0$ would be equivalent to 100 points on the SAT scale, two stanines, 15 points of IQ, or about 21 NCEs. In general, an effect size of $+.25$ or more would be considered educationally significant. When means and standard deviations are not known, they can usually be estimated from t-tests, Fs, chi-squares, or exact p values. If effect sizes cannot be computed, study outcomes are still included if they meet all other inclusion criteria. Because of differences between measures, experimental designs, and other factors, effect sizes should be interpreted with caution. For example, effect sizes are almost always higher on experimenter-made tests closely aligned with program curricula than on more general standardized tests (Rosenshine & Meister, 1994). However, effect sizes do provide a useful indication of programs' effects on student achievement that can be compared (with caution) across studies and programs.

SCHOOLWIDE REFORM PROGRAMS

Some of the most promising programs for Latino students are programs designed to reform the entire school, touching on everything from curriculum and instruction to school organization and assessment. Most of these are adaptations or applications of national programs (see Herman, 1999) not originally designed for Latino or LEP students but modified or redesigned for this purpose in schools with many such children.

Success for All/*Éxito Para Todos*

The schoolwide reform program that has been most extensively evaluated in schools serving many Latino students is Success for All, a comprehensive reform program for elementary schools serving many children placed at risk (Slavin, Madden, Dolan, & Wasik, 1996). Success for All provides schools with innovative curricula and instructional methods in reading, writing, and language arts from kindergarten to Grade 6, with extensive professional development. The curriculum emphasizes a balance between phonics and meaning in beginning reading and extensive use of cooperative learning throughout the grades. Recently, programs in mathematics, social studies, and science have been added to Success for All, making up a program called Roots and Wings (Slavin & Madden, in press a).

One-to-one tutoring, usually from certified teachers, is provided to children who are having difficulties in learning to read, with an emphasis on first graders. Family support services provided in each school build positive home–school relations and solve problems such as truancy, behavior problems, or needs for eyeglasses or health services. A program facilitator works with all teachers on continuing professional development and coaching, manages an assessment program to keep track of student progress, and ensures close coordination among all program components.

In schools with Spanish bilingual programs, Success for All (or *Éxito Para Todos*, in Spanish) uses a beginning reading curriculum called *Lee Conmigo*, which applies instructional strategies similar to those used in the English program (Reading Roots), but uses a curriculum sequence and materials appropriate to Spanish language and Latino culture. Beginning at the second grade level, students use *Alas Para Leer* (Reading Wings) an adaptation of Bilingual Cooperative Integrated Reading and Composition (BCIRC). *Alas*/BCIRC uses Spanish novels or basals in a comprehensive cooperative learning approach to reading, writing, and language arts. *Alas* and BCIRC also use cooperative learning activities to help students transition from Spanish to English reading at the point of transition mandated by district policies.

A different adaptation of Success for All is made in schools with many limited English proficient students but no native-language instruction. In these schools, the English curriculum is used, but there is a close coordination between ESL and classroom reading programs to infuse effective ESL strategies into the reading approach. ESL teachers usually provide classroom reading instruction and, often, tutoring to LEP children.

Research on the Success for All program in general has taken place in 77 schools in 12 districts throughout the United States. In each case, Success for All schools were matched with similar comparison schools. Students were pretested to establish comparability and then individually posttested each year on scales from the Woodcock Reading Mastery Test and the Durrell Oral Reading Test. Results show consistent, substantial positive effects of the program, averaging an effect size (ES) of about +.50 at each grade level. For the most at-risk students, those in the lowest 25% of their grades, effect sizes have averaged more than a full standard deviation (ES = +1.00 or more). In grade-equivalent terms, differences between Success for All and control students have averaged 3 months in the first grade, increasing to more than a full grade equivalent by fifth grade (Slavin & Madden, in press b; Slavin, Madden, Dolan, & Wasik, 1996). Follow-up studies have found that this difference maintains into sixth and seventh grades, after students have left the program schools.

Chapter 6 in this book reviews research on Success for All with Latino students, and this research is briefly summarized here. For Latino students, the effects of Success for All have been particularly positive (Slavin & Madden, 1999). Bilingual schools using Éxito Para Todos in Philadelphia found substantial differences between Success for All and control schools on scales from the Spanish Woodcock, with an effect size at the end of second grade of +1.81 (almost a full grade equivalent higher). A study in two California bilingual schools (Dianda & Flaherty, 1995) also found very positive effects of Success for All/Éxito Para Todos. At the end of first grade, Success for All students exceeded control students by an effect size of +1.03, or about 5 months. Dianda and Flaherty (1995) also reported an effect size of +1.02 for Spanish-dominant LEP students in a sheltered English adaptation of Success for All in a third California school. Incidentally, a 5-year study of the ESL adaptation of Success for All to limited English proficient Cambodian students in Philadelphia also found extremely positive outcomes, averaging an effect size of +1.44 and a grade equivalent difference of almost 3 years by the end of fifth grade (Slavin & Madden, 1999).

As of fall 1999, Success for All is in use in more than 1,500 schools in 48 states, of which more than one third have significant numbers of Latino students. Over 750,000 children benefit from this program. A training staff in 16 regional training programs disseminates the program nationally (see Slavin & Madden, in press b).

Accelerated Schools

Accelerated Schools (Hopfenberg & Levin, 1993; Levin, 1987) is an approach to school reform built around three central principles. One is *unity of purpose*, a common vision of what the school should become, agreed to and worked toward by all school staff, parents, students, and community. A second is *empowerment coupled with responsibility*, which means that staff, parents, and students find their own way to transform themselves, with freedom to experiment but also a responsibility to carry out their decisions. *Building on strengths* means identifying the strengths of students, of staff, and of the school as an organization, and then using these as a basis for reform. One of the key ideas behind Accelerated Schools is that rather than remediating students' deficits, students who are placed at risk of school failure must be accelerated, given the kind of high-expectations curriculum typical of programs for gifted and talented students.

The school implements these principles by establishing a set of "cadres," which include a steering committee and work groups focused on particular areas of reform. The program has no specific instructional approaches and provides no curriculum material; instead, school staff are encouraged to search for methods that help them realize their vision. However, there is an emphasis both on reducing all uses of remedial activities and on adopting constructivist, engaging teaching strategies (such as project-based learning).

Accelerated Schools began in schools near its home at Stanford University, and from the outset has been used in many schools serving Latino students.

The evaluation evidence on Accelerated Schools is quite limited and largely anecdotal. The program's developers state that the program takes 5 years to fully implement and that it is unfair to evaluate program outcomes until that much time has passed. No evaluation evidence has yet been reported from schools in the program this long. However, data from a few individual schools earlier in their implementations have been reported.

There have been three evaluations of individual Accelerated Schools, all including significant numbers of Latino students (but none separately reporting results for these students). McCarthy and Still (1993) reported on one Texas school with a large Latino majority that showed gains over time in its fifth-grade standardized test scores (other grades were not mentioned). A similar comparison school showed losses over the same period.

Another Texas evaluation of Accelerated Schools was reported by Knight and Stallings (1995). This study compared a school with a 25% Latino population to a matched comparison school over a 2-year period. On standardized tests in reading the Accelerated School students gained more than the comparison students in Grades 1–3, but not 4–5. In language, the Accelerated School scored better in Grades 1–2, but the control schools did as well or better in 3–5. On a statewide accountability test, Accelerated School students passed at a higher rate than comparison students on math and reading tests in Grade 3, but the opposite was true in Grade 5. On a writing measure students in the Accelerated School performed slightly higher at both grade levels.

In a Sacramento school with students speaking 13 languages, Chasin and Levin (1995) reported gains on standardized tests for sixth graders but did not mention changes in other grades. These gains are difficult to attribute to the program, as the school's population also increased substantially over the same period.

More than 1,000 schools in 37 states are currently involved in the Accelerated Schools network, and there are four regional training sites for the program in addition to the original training site at Stanford.

School Development Program

The School Development Program (SDP) (Comer, 1980, 1988; Comer, Haynes, Joyner, & Ben-Avie, 1996) is a comprehensive approach to school reform in elementary and middle schools. The program's focus is on building a sense of common purpose among school staff, parents, and community, and engaging school staff and others in a planning process intended to change school practices to improve student outcomes.

Each SDP school creates three teams that take particular responsibility for moving the reform agenda forward. A School Planning and Management Team, made up of representatives of teachers, parents, and administration, develops and monitors implementation of a comprehensive school improvement plan. A Mental Health Team, principally composed of school staff concerned with mental health such as school psychologists, social workers, counselors, and selected teachers, plans programs focusing on prevention, building positive child development, positive interpersonal relations, and so on.

The third major component of the SDP is a Parent Program, designed to build a sense of community among school staff, parents, and students.

The Parent Program incorporates existing parent participation activities (such as the PTA) and implements further activities to draw parents into the school, to increase opportunities for parents to provide volunteer services, and to design ways for the school to respect and celebrate the ethnic backgrounds of its students.

The three teams in SDP schools work together to create comprehensive plans for school reform. The main focus is on mental health and parent involvement, but schools are also encouraged to examine their instructional programs and to look for ways to serve children's academic needs more effectively.

The SDP was originally designed especially to meet the needs of African American children and families, but large numbers of Latino students also attend SDP schools, especially in California and Texas.

Evaluations of the effects of SDP have taken place in a number of locations. The first was a longitudinal evaluation of the first two SDP schools in New Haven, Connecticut, which showed marked improvements in student performance on standardized tests over a 14-year period (Comer, 1988). A later independent evaluation following first graders in two SDP schools also showed positive effects (Stringfield & Herman, 1995). Other evaluations comparing SDP to matched control schools have found mixed, inconsistent effects, with substantial site-to-site variation. Outcomes emphasized by the program, such as self-concept and school climate, have been more consistently associated with the program than have achievement gains (Becker & Hedges, 1992; Haynes, 1991, 1994). Formal research on the SDP has not taken place in districts with significant Latino populations, but documentation of achievement gains over time is being gathered in San Diego, California, Dallas, Texas, and Dade County, Florida, schools that serve many Latino students.

The SDP is currently involved with more than 700 schools, mostly elementary and middle, in 22 states. It has regional training programs in several states.

Consistency Management & Cooperative Discipline/*Disciplina Consistente y Cooperativa*

Consistency Management & Cooperative Discipline (CMCD) (Freiberg, Prokosch, & Treister, 1990) is a schoolwide reform program designed to improve discipline in inner-city schools at grade levels K–6, to provide an appropriate environment for learning and improve academic achievement. CMCD emphasizes shared responsibility for classroom discipline between students and teachers, turning classrooms into communities of ownership, where the teachers and students together make the rules for classroom management. The idea is that if students have a hand in creating and enforcing the rules, then acting up to defy the teacher would not work anymore, "because (students) would also be breaking their own laws" (Freiberg et al., 1990).

CMCD exists as a stand-alone program, or can be used along with other innovative programs directed at improving curriculum and instruction. Teachers initially assess the needs of their classrooms in the spring. During the summer, they attend various workshops on CMCD, and also work with facilitators from their own schools. During the school year, teachers return for workshops and follow-up sessions.

CMCD provides a framework of regulations, which schools adapt to fit their needs. The main components or themes of CMCD that exist at every school are prevention, caring, cooperation, organization, and community. At the initial implementation stages of CMCD, the teachers engage in a series of interviews and assessment sessions, whose goals are to evaluate the school's strengths and weaknesses and adapt the program to fit their school.

Although CMCD was not originally specifically designed for Latino children, it has primarily been evaluated in inner-city schools in Houston that serve Latino students and have many bilingual classes (Freiberg, Stein, & Huang, 1995). Other participants were predominantly African American. The main evaluation of CMCD followed five CMCD and five matched control schools in Houston over a period of 5 years. Two of the CMCD schools and three control schools had significant proportions of Latino students. Eighty-three percent qualified for free or reduced-price lunches. Discipline problems and mobility rates were high.

The first study (Freiberg et al., 1990) was an evaluation of the five schools after the first 2 years of implementation. This study showed that the students of teachers from the five program schools who had attended at least seven sessions of CMCD outperformed students in the comparison schools, with minimal effect sizes ranging from +.09 to +.29 on the Metropolitan Achievement Test (MAT-6).

The second evaluation involved the comparison of one of the CMCD schools with its control school (Freiberg et al., 1995). Although both schools had equal scores on the ITBS composite pretest, the experimental group outperformed the control group on the composite MAT-6 for the next 3 years, with effect sizes ranging from +.44 to +.95. The treatment group outscored the comparison group in math (ES = +.15), reading (ES = +.52), and writing (ES = +.84). CMCD students also exceeded control students on the Texas Educational Assessment of Minimal Skills (TEAMS), with effect sizes ranging from +.40 to +1.24 in math, from +.13 to +.40 in reading, and from +.14 to +.45 in writing. Measures of motivation, self-concept, and other measurements of positive attitudes toward school and learning also favored the CMCD school.

Freiberg and Huang (1994) followed an initial cohort of students who entered before the first year the program was implemented (1985–1986) and stayed in their respective schools until they reached the sixth grade (1991–1992). Students who later attended the school, students of teachers who were trained at times other than the initial year of implementation, students who did not have scores from all tests (TEAMS and MAT-6) for all 5 years, and students who were retained at least a year were not included. Because of these restrictions and the high mobility rates, the final number of students who were followed for all 6 years was very small: 27 for the control school and 27 for the experimental school.

Students who had remained in the CMCD program for 6 years showed significantly higher test scores on TEAMS. Adjusting for pretest differences, effect sizes for the differences between the two groups ranged from +.08 to +.99. The students in the program schools also scored consistently higher than the students in the comparison schools on the MAT-6. Students involved in CDMC scored above the 50th percentile on the MAT-6 during all of the years they were assessed, whereas the scores of students in the comparison group dropped. Adjusting for pretest differences, effect sizes ranged from +1.13 to +1.23 in reading, +1.44 to +1.51 in math, and +.99 to +1.71 in writing.

The most recent study of CMCD (Freiberg, 1996) compared the performances of students in schools implementing a mathematics program with those in schools implementing a combination of CMCD and the mathematics program. All of the schools involved in this study had a majority of Latino students. The students in the combined program outperformed students involved in the mathematics-only program, with an effect size of +.33.

CMCD currently exists in more than 25 schools in three Texas districts, as well as abroad. It is part of a broader school reform model, Project GRAD, that is used in several schools in Houston, Newark, and Los Angeles, and is preparing for national dissemination (McAdoo, 1998). Project GRAD is described in chapter 2 of this book. A Spanish adaptation of CMCD called *Disciplina Consistente y Cooperativa*, designed specifically for Spanish-speaking English language learners and their families, is also being used and evaluated in many schools.

Goldenberg and Sullivan Program

The goal of Goldenberg and Sullivan's (1995) program is to prepare teachers and principals for school reform by making them active participants in reform efforts before and after the reform movement has begun in the school. Goldenberg and Sullivan (1995) stated that unless teachers feel as though they are a part of the reform planning process, they are likely to feel overwhelmed and ineffective when students do not show positive changes in academic achievement. They stipulated that in order to achieve both positive attitudes and better academic performance, both administrative and curricular issues must be addressed directly. Progress on four factors is needed: goals that are set and shared, indicators that measure success, assistance by capable others, and leadership that supports and pressures. When these goals are implemented properly, the teachers are expected to have better attitudes toward teaching and reform in general, and the students' achievement scores should improve.

Based on this hypothesis, Goldenberg and Sullivan (1995) implemented a school reform effort in a California elementary school. The school studied was primarily Latino, and the students were not performing well academically. At the beginning of the reform effort, Goldenberg and Sullivan (1995) and a number of teachers created an Academic Expectations Committee (which then became the Academic Assessment Committee), whose goal was to facilitate change in the school. This committee implemented the four components felt to be necessary for effective school change. For example, to implement the first factor in language arts, the committee members shared goals, they brought in experts to provide in-service training and seminars to the staff, and grade-level goals specifying products and process were established. For example, in the first grade, although they expected the students to be able to read, they also expected some of the students to exhibit emergent literacy characteristics such as pseudo-reading (guessing at words using pictures and other cues).

The committee developed indicators that measured success, such as book placement and performance assessment rubrics. It measured different aspects of students' literacy such as self-reading, attitudes toward reading and writing, competencies in writing summaries, and writing original story endings.

The third factor, assistance by more capable others, included making various groups of people (such as mentor teachers, administrators, outside experts, and fellow teachers) accountable to one another. This was implemented by forming work groups that were grade specific and subject specific across grades, and were ongoing throughout the year.

The final component, leadership that supports and pressures, involved having committee members and administrators following through with the goals, reminding the teachers of their responsibilities to fulfill the goals, providing support for anyone in need, and seeking better ways to attain the goals if the teachers were experiencing difficulty.

With the four elements implemented, Goldenberg and Sullivan (1995) documented improvements in school climate in general. Teachers felt that they were in better positions to teach because of the level of student support from each other and from the administration. The goal of higher academic achievement was also attained. Both English-dominant students who took the California Assessment Project (CAP) and the California Learning Assessment System (CLAS) tests and Spanish-dominant children who took the Spanish Assessment of Basic Education (SABE) showed improvements from the onset of the project. Students in both groups were given a pretest in spring 1990, and then assessed again in spring 1993.

Before the project began, the schools' mean scores on the CAP were below those of both the district and the state. By the third year, the treatment students had surpassed students in the district on the CAP/CLAS in reading, and were close to the statewide scores. In writing, the students had outscored the district, but not the state.

With the Latino students, the treatment students remained below those of other school districts during the first year on the SABE on reading, but surpassed them for the second, third, and fourth years of implementation.

This was a school-specific study, so there is no dissemination information available. The project directors emphasize that the model should be adapted to the school-specific situations in which it is being implemented.

CLASSROOM INSTRUCTIONAL PROGRAMS

Most of the programs currently available to schools for replication are classroom instructional programs, often focusing on a single subject. For example, the National Diffusion Network (1995) listed more than 500 replicable programs with some evidence of effectiveness, and the great majority of these were classroom innovations. The following sections discuss replicable classroom programs that have been researched and/or extensively applied with Latino students.

Cooperative Learning Methods

Cooperative learning refers to a broad range of instructional methods in which students work together to learn academic content. Research comparing cooperative learning and traditional methods has found positive effects on the achievement of elementary and secondary school students, especially when two key conditions are fulfilled. First, groups must be working toward a common goal, such as the opportunity to earn recognition or rewards based on group performance. Second, the success of the groups must depend on the individual learning of all group members, not on a single group product (Slavin, 1995).

Cooperative learning methods are widely used throughout the United States and other countries with all kinds of schools and children, and the research on these methods has equally involved a broad diversity of schools and students. There are two cooperative methods, however, that were specifically designed for use in Spanish bilingual programs, and many more, although not specifically intended for this purpose, have been researched and used in schools serving many Latino students (Calderón, 1991, 1994a, 1994b; McGroarty, 1993; Slavin, 1990). These are described in the following sections.

Bilingual Cooperative Integrated Reading and Composition

Bilingual Cooperative Integrated Reading and Composition, or BCIRC (Calderón, 1994a; Calderón, Hertz-Lazarowitz, & Slavin, 1998; Calderón, Tinajero, & Hertz-Lazarowitz, 1992), is an adaptation of Cooperative Integrated Reading and Composition (CIRC) (Stevens, Madden, Slavin, & Farnish, 1987) for application in bilingual classrooms. The original CIRC model, used in Grades 2–8, involves a series of activities derived from research on reading comprehension and writing strategies (Stevens et al., 1987). Students work in four-member heterogeneous learning teams. After the teacher introduces a story from a basal text or trade book, students work in their teams on a prescribed series of activities relating to the story. These include partner reading, where students take turns reading to each other in pairs; "treasure hunt" activities, in which students work together to identify characters, settings, problems, and problem solutions in narratives; and summarization activities. Students write "meaningful sentences" to show the meaning of new vocabulary words, and write compositions that relate to their reading. The program includes a curriculum for teaching main idea, figurative language, and other comprehension skills, and includes a home reading and book report component. The writing/language arts component of CIRC uses a cooperative writing process approach in which students work together to plan, draft, revise, edit, and publish compositions in a variety of genres. Students master language mechanics skills in their teams, and these are then added to editing checklists to ensure their application in students' own writing. Teams earn recognition based on the performance of their members on quizzes, compositions, book reports, and other products (Madden et al., 1996).

BCIRC adds to the CIRC structure several adaptations to make it appropriate to bilingual settings. It is built around Spanish reading materials in the younger grades and then uses transitional reading materials as students begin to transition from Spanish to English. The age of transition depends on district policies; materials to accompany Spanish basals and novels have been developed though the sixth grade, but most such materials are used in transitional bilingual education programs only through the third or fourth grades. In addition, effective ESL strategies designed to engage students in negotiating meaning in two languages and increase authentic oral communication are built into the training program.

The original CIRC program has been evaluated in three studies in elementary schools (Stevens et al., 1987; Stevens & Slavin, 1995) and in one study in two middle schools (Stevens & Durkin, 1992). In each case, CIRC students made significantly greater gains than control students on standardized tests of reading achievement. Two studies in Israel, one in Hebrew and one in Arabic, also found positive effects of CIRC compared to traditional methods (Hertz-Lazarowitz, Lerner, & Schaedel, 1996; Schaedel et al., 1996).

A 4-year study of BCIRC was conducted in 24 Grade 2–4 bilingual classes in El Paso, Texas (Calderón, 1994a; Calderón et al., 1998). Experimental and control classes were carefully matched. Students transitioned from mostly Spanish instruction in second grade to mostly English instruction in fourth grade. At the end of second grade, BCIRC students scored significantly better than controls on the Spanish TAAS (Texas Assessment of Academic Skills) in both reading (ES = +.43) and writing (ES = +.47). In third grade, students were tested on the English Norm-referenced Assessment Program for Texas (NAPT), and again BCIRC students outperformed controls in reading (ES = +.59) and language (ES = +.29). Finally, fourth graders in BCIRC scored higher than controls in NAPT reading (ES = +.19), but not language. However, these differences were depressed by the transfer of students out of the bilingual classes into English-only classes, which happened with four times as many BCIRC as control students. Students who were moved out of the bilingual classes early tended to be the highest achievers, so deleting them from the sample reduced the apparent experimental–control differences.

CIRC is used in several hundred schools nationally, and BCIRC is used in more than a hundred, including Success for All programs with bilingual programs that use an adaptation of BCIRC. Training programs for CIRC and BCIRC exist at Johns Hopkins University in Baltimore and El Paso, and additional trainers in both models are located in many parts of the United States.

Complex Instruction/Finding Out/*Descubrimiento*

Complex Instruction is the name given to a set of cooperative learning approaches developed and researched by Elizabeth Cohen (1994a) and her associates at Stanford University. From its inception, the program has focused on Spanish bilingual classes. It was first built around a discovery-oriented science and mathematics program called Finding Out/*Descubrimiento*, developed by DeAvila and Duncan (1980). Finding Out/*Descubrimiento* provides students with a series of activity cards in English and Spanish that direct them to do experiments, take measurements, solve problems, and so on. Students work in small, heterogeneous groups to do experiments and answer questions intended to evoke high-level thinking. As it relates to bilingual education, a major focus of the program is to get students to use complex, sophisticated language to express, debate, and defend their ideas, thereby building language fluency first in their home language and then in English. Whenever possible, each group contains monolingual Spanish, monolingual English, and bilingual children, who freely translate ideas for each other. Complex Instruction adds to Finding Out/*Descubrimiento* a group structure, in which students take on specified roles (e.g., facilitator, checker, reporter) and learn group process skills, such as active listening, maintaining a positive group atmosphere, and ensuring equal participation. The program also emphasizes building positive expectations for all students—for example, by giving low-status children opportunities to be the group expert and constantly reinforcing the idea that all children have different abilities, each of which is worthy of respect (Cohen, 1994a).

The evaluations of Complex Instruction/Finding Out/*Descubrimiento* have not generally met the standards established in this review. Most have reported positive correlations between the frequency of students' talking and working together and gains in student achievement (Cohen, 1994b; Cohen & Intili, 1981; Cohen, Lotan, & Leechor, 1989; Stevenson, 1982). This could be taken as an indication that better implementers of the program get better results, but it does not indicate that the children are performing better than they would have without the program. Similarly, reports of NCE gains in the program classes (Cohen, 1994b) are inadequate indicators of program impacts. Still, the accumulation of imperfect but supportive evidence and the clear focus on improving the higher order thinking of students in bilingual programs makes this program appealing.

The Complex Instruction program at Stanford provides materials and professional development to support program adoption in elementary and middle schools, and it is used in many schools, particularly in California.

Student Teams-Achievement Divisions and Teams-Games-Tournament

Two related cooperative learning programs developed at Johns Hopkins University are among the most thoroughly evaluated of all cooperative methods, and have been extensively disseminated in schools with Latino children. These are Student Teams-Achievement Divisions (STAD) and Teams-Games-Tournament (TGT) (Slavin, 1994, 1995). In STAD, students work in four-member, heterogeneous learning teams. First the teacher provides the lesson content through direct instruction. Then students work in their teams to help each other master the content, using study guides, worksheets, or other material as a basis for discussion, tutoring, and assessment among students. Following this, students take brief quizzes, on which they cannot help each other. Teams can earn recognition or privileges based on the improvement made by each team member over his or her own past record. TGT is the same as STAD except that students play academic games with members of the other teams to add points to an overall team score. Both programs emphasize the use of group goals (in this case, recognition) in which teams can only achieve success if each team member can perform well on an independent assessment. This motivates team members to do a good job of teaching and assessing each other.

Both STAD and TGT have been extensively evaluated in comparison to control groups in a wide variety of subjects. Across 26 such studies of at least 4 weeks duration, there was a median effect size of +.32 for STAD; in 7 studies of TGT, the median effect size was +.38 (Slavin, 1995). One study in Riverside, California (Kagan, Zahn, Widaman, Schwarzwald, & Tyrell, 1985), evaluated STAD and TGT with Latino students, and this study found no experimental–control differences in spelling for this group. However, two studies with significant numbers of

Latino students did find positive effects of STAD, although they did not separately analyze results for Latino students. These were a study in Harrisburg, Pennsylvania (Stevens, Slavin, & Farnish, 1991), in which elementary school students were taught to find the main ideas of paragraphs, and a study of spelling in San Diego, California (Tomblin & Davis, 1985), which found nonsignificant positive effects of the program.

STAD and TGT are used in hundreds of classrooms nationwide. A training program at Johns Hopkins University and certified trainers throughout the United States provide professional development in these methods.

Jigsaw

Jigsaw (Aronson, Blaney, Stephan, Sikes, & Snapp, 1978) is a cooperative learning technique in which students work in small groups to study text, usually social studies or science. In this method, each group member is assigned to become an "expert" on some aspect of a unit of study. After reading about their area of expertise, the experts from different groups meet to discuss their topic, and then return to their groups and take turns teaching their topics to their groupmates. In a variation of Jigsaw called Jigsaw II (Slavin, 1994), students are given topics in a common reading, such as a text chapter, biography, or short book. After they have read the material, discussed it with their counterparts in other groups, and shared their topics with their own group, they take a quiz on all topics, as in STAD.

Jigsaw was first used with Latino students, and much of the research on this topic has involved schools in the Southwest serving many Latino students. The first brief Jigsaw evaluation (Lucker, Rosenfield, Sikes, & Aronson, 1976) found positive effects of the program for "minority students" (Latino and African American students analyzed together), but not for Anglos. A study in bilingual classes (Gonzales, 1981) and one in majority Latino schools (Tomblin & Davis, 1985) found no achievement benefits. Outcomes for Jigsaw II have been more positive (Mattingly & VanSickle, 1991; Ziegler, 1981), but these studies have involved few Latinos.

Jigsaw is widely used nationwide. Training in numerous Jigsaw variations is provided by Spencer Kagan and his colleagues (Kagan, 1995), among others.

Learning Together

David Johnson and Roger Johnson's (1994) Learning Together models of cooperative learning are among the most widely used of all cooperative learning models. In these methods, students work in small groups on common assignments, typically creating a single group product. All group members are evaluated based on this product. In some applications of this method, groups may earn recognition or grades based either on overall group performance or on the sum of individual performances.

Many evaluations of Learning Together models have been very brief and artificial, but among those of at least 4 weeks duration, evidence supports the achievement effects of forms of the Learning Together model that incorporate group goals and individual accountability (i.e., group success depends on the sum of individual performances). One year-long study of Learning Together took place in bilingual classes in southern California, and this study found positive program effects on a standardized test of language but not on tests of reading, spelling, or math (Martinez, 1990).

The Johnsons' methods are widely used throughout the world. Trainers in these methods are located at the University of Minnesota and in many other parts of the United States.

Group Investigation

Group Investigation is a form of project-based learning developed by Yael Sharan and Shlomo Sharan (1992) and their colleagues in Israel. In this method, students form their own two to six-member groups. The groups choose topics from a unit being studied by the entire class, break these topics into individual tasks, and carry out activities necessary to prepare and present group reports. Studies of Group Investigation have generally supported the effectiveness of this approach, especially on higher order skills (Sharan & Shachar, 1988). An adaptation of this approach was implemented by Margarita Calderón in two-way bilingual schools in El Paso.

CURRICULUM-SPECIFIC PROGRAMS: READING, WRITING, AND LANGUAGE ARTS

There are many well-evaluated and replicable programs designed for use in specific grades and subjects. In reading, two programs described earlier, Success for All/*Lee Conmigo* and CIRC/BCIRC, have documented positive effects with Latino as well as non-Latino students, and three additional programs are described in this section. In writing and language arts, effective methods generally include some form of writing process, in which students work together to plan, draft, revise, edit, and publish compositions. A general review of writing process models (Hillocks, 1984) found consistently positive effects on quality of students' writing.

CIRC and BCIRC, described earlier, use process writing methods and have adapted them specifically to Spanish bilingual education. Other approaches to writing successfully that have been researched and/or disseminated with Latino students are described later in this chapter.

Direct Instruction

Direct Instruction (DISTAR) (Bereiter & Engelmann, 1966), is an early elementary school program originally designed to extend the Direct Instruction early childhood curriculum (Bereiter & Engelmann, 1966) into the elementary grades as part of a federal program called Follow Through, which funded the development and evaluation of programs to continue the positive effects of early childhood programs. The primary goal of both the early childhood program and DISTAR was to provide low socioeconomic status (low-SES) children with opportunities to succeed academically by utilizing a scripted program that stresses structured direct instruction. Revisions of DISTAR have been disseminated in recent years under the titles of Reading Mastery/Math Mastery and Direct Instruction.

Teachers involved in DISTAR have specific instructions on how to teach each of the units presented to the students, as well as what units to teach them. Students initially begin with DISTAR in either kindergarten or first grade. Progress in DISTAR is usually monitored by evaluating academic performance of students in the program, using both criterion-referenced and norm-referenced measures. The DISTAR curriculum was not specifically written for Latino students, but it has been used and evaluated among Latino children.

The most comprehensive evaluation of DISTAR compared the results of nine Follow Through programs that also had early childhood education programs. Each program was compared to control groups that were not implementing Follow Through (Abt Associates, 1977). The total number of subjects was 9,255 for the Follow Through (experimental group) and 6,485 for the non-Follow Through students.

All of the children were from similar socioeconomic backgrounds. The study evaluated the effects of the programs on academic achievement, cognitive achievement, and self-esteem, as measured by performance on norm-referenced tests such as MAT, Ravens Progressive Matrices, Coopersmith Self-Esteem Inventory, and the Intellectual Achievement Responsibility Scale. Programs were clustered in three groups in terms of their overall goals for the children. The first cluster of programs stressed individualized, child-initiated activities, and focused on the development of the whole child. Examples of these programs included the Open Education

Model, Tucson Early Education Model, Cognitively Oriented Curriculum, Responsive Education Model, and the Bank Street College Model.

The second cluster of programs stressed direct instruction, with the specific goal of developing and improving students' academic skills. These two programs were the Behavior Analysis model and the Direct Instruction model. The final cluster included programs whose goals were to improve specific areas related to the performance of the children. These programs were the Florida Parent Education Model and the Language Development (Bilingual) Model.

Direct Instruction and Behavior Analysis were the only models that showed substantial effects both when compared to non-Follow Through programs and when compared to other programs. Other programs evaluated showed either effects of zero or negative effects when all three of the skills (basic, cognitive, or affective) were measured. The Direct Instruction group did better than all of the other groups on the MAT language (ES = +.84) and mathematics computation (ES = +.57). Direct Instruction students also scored somewhat higher in reading comprehension (ES = +.07) and mathematics problem solving (ES = +.17), and were also higher in self-esteem.

Becker and Gersten (1982) studied the lasting effects of Direct Instruction on students in fifth and sixth grades. This study followed up students who had been in DISTAR in Grades 1–3 in five sites. The students were matched with control groups based on income level, gender, primary home language, and mother's education level, and these factors were used as covariates. One of these sites (Uvalde, Texas) consisted primarily of Latino students. Students in this site were pretested in spring 1975, using all subtests of the MAT, and also the Language Acquisition Scale test. This study was then replicated using posttest scores in 1976. Overall results show that DISTAR students outperformed non-DISTAR students on the overall Wide Range Assessment Test (WRAT) (ES = +.53) and on all of the subtests of the MAT. The Uvalde students outperformed their control-group counterparts on all of the WRAT tests (ES = +.47) and on the MAT in 1975 (ES = +.03 to +.33) and in 1976 (ES = +.04 to +.52).

Gersten (1985) addressed the use of Direct Instruction in second-language learning in a study that assessed the longitudinal progress of low-income English language learners in Grades 3–6. The program served LEP students in a structured immersion model that included giving students and teachers a structured curriculum designed to ensure their academic success.

The population of this study was predominantly Asian students in two cohorts. Treatment-group students (structured immersion Direct Instruc-

tion) were compared to students who were in traditional bilingual programs. Students were initially pretested using the Language Assessment
Scale (LAS), and the CTBS reading, Total Math, and Total Reading
scores. The students were neither randomly assigned to groups nor
matched at the beginning of the evaluation. Students in the control
group whose baseline scores fell below grade level were not included,
whereas all of the Direct Instruction students, regardless of their baseline
scores, were included. The Language Assessment Scale scores for both
groups were similar. For both of the cohorts, the DISTAR group had
more students at or above grade level than did the comparison groups.

Meyer (1984) investigated the long-term effects of DISTAR on children who had had 3 and 4 years of the program, and compared their
achievements to those of matched control groups. The study involved
three cohorts of students from a New York City elementary school. Students in the Direct Instruction Follow Through school in New York City
were matched with control-group students based on achievement scores
on the MAT, free-lunch eligibility, and ethnicity (African American and
Puerto Rican).

Evaluators compared the two groups of students on high school graduation rate, ninth-grade reading score, ninth-grade math score, student's
application to college, student's acceptance to college, student's special
education placement, and student's school attendance for the previous
year. Students who had been involved in the program in 1968–1969,
1969–1970, or 1970–1971 were followed up in 1981, when they were
high school seniors.

Over the three cohorts, more than 63% of the Direct Instruction students graduated from high school, as opposed to 38% of the control group.
An average of 21% of the Direct Instruction students were retained compared to 33% of the control students. The Direct Instruction students had a
lower dropout rate (28%) than the control group (46%) over the three cohorts. More of the Direct Instruction (34%) group students applied to college than the control group (22%), and more of the Direct Instruction group
students were accepted for admission to college over the three cohorts
(34%) than were the control group students (17%).

The follow-up evaluation also compared ninth-grade mean reading
and math scores in grade equivalents. Overall, students in the Direct Instruction cohort outperformed students in the control group in reading
($ES = +.41$) and in math ($ES = +.29$).

A large number of smaller scale studies of the effectiveness of Direct
Instruction, mostly supporting the program's effectiveness, were summarized by Adams and Engelmann (1996).

As of fall 1998, Direct Instruction is being implemented in more than 150 schools.

Exemplary Center for Reading Instruction

The goal of the Exemplary Center for Reading Instruction (ECRI) (Reid, 1989) is to improve elementary students' reading ability. This program emphasizes such reading-related skills as word recognition, study skills, spelling, penmanship, proofing, and writing skills, leading to improvement in decoding, comprehension, and vocabulary.

ECRI teachers expect all students to excel. The lessons for ECRI are scripted, and incorporate multisensory and sequential methods and strategies of teaching. In a typical lesson, teachers introduce new concepts in lessons using at least seven methods of instruction, teaching at least one comprehension skill, one study skill, and a grammar/creative writing skill. Initially, students are prompted for answers by teachers. As the students begin to master the information presented, fewer and fewer prompts are provided until students can perform independently. ECRI was not originally developed for Latino students, but it has been used among Spanish-speaking and bilingual students. Evaluations of ECRI have included a variety of students, but its effectiveness has also been measured specifically among Latino students.

In one evaluation of ECRI (Reid, 1989), researchers investigated the effects of ECRI on students in Grades 2–7 in Morgan County, Tennessee, and compared them to students in a control group who were using a commercial reading program. Both schools were tested using Stanford Achievement Test reading comprehension and vocabulary subtests. ECRI students outperformed those in the control group, with effect sizes ranging from +.48 to +.90 in reading comprehension and from +.31 to +1.40 in vocabulary. In an evaluation of the effectiveness of ECRI on Latino bilingual students in Oceanside, California, Killeen, Texas, and Calexico, California, Reid (1989) showed NCE gains that ranged from +6.4 to +25.7. ECRI is used in hundreds of schools nationwide, including many serving Latino students.

Reciprocal Teaching

Reciprocal Teaching (Palincsar & Brown, 1984) is a reading program designed to improve the reading comprehension of children in elementary and middle schools that emphasizes cognitive strategies of scaffolding through dialogue.

The main two components of Reciprocal Teaching are comprehension fostering, which includes the four strategies of question generation, summarization, prediction, and clarification, and dialogue, which includes prepared conversations and questions that guide the comprehension process and product. The program uses a scaffolding process, in which teachers are initially more responsible for producing questions, guiding the dialogue, and showing the students how to comprehend text. Eventually, the students become more responsible for the products, creating questions for each other and guiding the dialogue with less teacher input.

A typical Reciprocal Teaching session begins with students reading an initial paragraph of expository material, with the teacher modeling how to comprehend the paragraph. The students then practice the strategies on the next section of the text, and the teacher supports each student's participation through specific feedback, additional modeling, coaching, hints, and explanation. The strategies include commenting and elaborating on summaries of paragraphs, suggesting additional questions, providing feedback on their peers' predictions, and requesting clarification of material not understood.

Although Reciprocal Teaching has several important components that distinguish it from other reading approaches, it is flexible. For example, in some forms of Reciprocal Teaching, the cognitive dialogue precedes the text reading exercise; in other forms, cognitive dialogue takes place while the students are reading the text.

A meta-analysis of the achievement effects of Reciprocal Teaching was carried out by Rosenshine and Meister (1994). Sixteen studies representing different levels of implementation (high, medium, and low) and different methods of teaching were synthesized. High-implementation studies included dialogue, questions, and assessment of student learning strategies, medium-level studies included dialogue but did not include assessments, and low-level studies had neither dialogue nor assessment information.

The meta-analysis investigated how Reciprocal Teaching students performed on standardized and experimenter-made tests as compared to their control-group peers. The overall effect size for performance on standardized tests was $+.32$, but only in two cases did the Reciprocal Teaching students do better than their control-group counterparts. Effect sizes were much higher on the experimenter-made tests (ES $= +.88$). In several cases, effect sizes were lower in studies in which implementations were rated as low in quality, but there were few differences between the outcomes of high- and medium-quality implementations.

Reciprocal Teaching has not been studied in schools serving many Latino students, but it has been widely disseminated in schools including such students.

Profile Approach to Writing

The Profile Approach to Writing (PAW, 1995; Hartfiel, Hughey, Wormuth, & Jacobs, 1985; Hughey & Hartfiel, 1979; Hughey, Wormuth, Hartfiel, & Jacobs, 1985; Jacobs, Zinkgraf, Wormuth, Hartfiel, & Hughey, 1981) is a program that provides professional development in creative writing to students in Grades 3–12. The program emphasizes a process of drafting and revision of compositions, and makes use of a writing profile to assess and guide student writing performance. The profile is a holistic/analytic scale that assesses content, organization, vocabulary use, language use, and mechanics in students' compositions. PAW was not specifically developed for use with Latino students, but has been extensively used and evaluated in schools with many Latino students.

Several evaluations of the Profile Approach to Writing have been carried out by the program developers (Profile Approach to Writing, 1995). One of these compared students in a predominately (55%) Latino middle school in Texas to a control group. Students in the experimental and control group were pre- and posttested on the project's own Composition Profile, the 100-point holistic/analytic scale used in the instructional program. Experimental and control students were similar in scores at pretest. Students in the PAW school gained significantly more than those in the control group (ES = +.69) in a year-long comparison. Other less well-controlled evaluations on district-administered tests also found positive effects of PAW in middle and high schools not serving significant numbers of Latino students.

A methodological limitation of the main experimental–control comparison is the fact that it used the project's own evaluation instrument, which teachers and students had been using all year. However, holistic/analytic writing comparisons of this kind are common in many writing performance measures and are widely accepted by writing curriculum experts. The replicability of PAW has been amply demonstrated. The program is in use in more than 1,000 schools and has certified trainers in seven states.

Multicultural Reading and Thinking

Multicultural Reading and Thinking (McRAT) is a writing program that trains teachers to improve students' academic achievement by adding multicultural themes to all areas of the curriculum in Grades 3–8. The program, developed by the Arkansas Department of Education (Arkansas Department of Education, 1992; Quellmalz, 1987; Quellmalz & Hoskyn, 1988), is intended to make students better readers and writers by adding multicultural and problem-solving components to all areas of the curriculum. McRAT does not exist as a stand-alone program, but works with the existing school curriculum. It strives to teach children to think critically about what they read in class, so that they can apply these critical processes to their writing and to real-life situations in which people of different backgrounds have to learn to work and live together. Specific skills that the children are taught include analysis, comparison, inference/interpretation, and evaluation, and these skills are used in all areas of the curriculum.

In the study that evaluated the effects of McRAT on achievement, students represented a range of socioeconomic status backgrounds, achievement levels, and ethnic backgrounds. This evaluation (Arkansas Department of Education, 1992) studied the effects of McRAT on achievement scores in the specific cognitive areas that the students were taught in the program; McRAT students were compared to matched control students.

The students in the treatment group were 32% minority, 15% gifted and talented, and 25% Title I students. In the control group, the students were 30% minority, 15% gifted and talented, and 10% Title I students. Students in both the experimental and control groups were using the same curriculum, the only difference being that students in the experimental group had McRAT-trained teachers. Students in this sample included 234 fourth-, fifth-, and sixth-grade McRAT students, and 106 fourth-, fifth-, and sixth-grade non-McRAT students. Teachers in the treatment group were in either their first or second years of McRAT implementation. Students in both groups were assessed using an assessment measure created by the project in September and again in May. The McRAT students outperformed the control students in the areas of analysis (ES = +.41), inference (ES = +.57), comparison (ES = +.65), and evaluation (ES = +.45). McRAT joined the National Diffusion Network in 1993, is currently used in 136 school districts, involves 450 teachers, and is also being disseminated nationally. It has not been used extensively with Latino students as yet.

CURRICULUM-SPECIFIC PROGRAMS: MATHEMATICS

Five mathematics programs met the inclusion standards applied in this review.

Comprehensive School Mathematics Program

The Comprehensive School Mathematics Program (CSMP, 1995) is a math program for grades K–6 that emphasizes problem solving rather than drill and practice lessons. CSMP strives to teach children the mathematical thinking skills and concepts that they need to use when approached with new math problems. The contents of the CSMP curriculum range from basic skills such as addition and subtraction to more abstract skills such as probability, statistics, and classification using higher order thinking skills, understanding of concepts, and algorithmic thinking. The program incorporates the use of calculators and computers.

CSMP uses different types of "languages" for performing different types of mathematical functions. For example, the language of strings is used to gather data, the language of arrows places the different components of the mathematical problem into sets, and the language of a minicomputer allows the children to compute different problems using an abacus. Students also use manipulatives, such as tiles and blocks, to solve their problems. Although not originally designed for use with Latino students, CSMP has been applied in many districts with large Latino populations, including bilingual schools.

The materials used in CSMP were developed in classrooms in the Carbondale, Illinois, and University City, Missouri, school districts, both of which are integrated (20–50% African American) middle-class communities. Disproportionately high numbers of both high- and low-performing students were included in the program development. After the initial pilot testing, the materials were tested nationwide. CSMP was developed, evaluated, and initially disseminated by CEMREL, a former education laboratory in St. Louis.

Two research designs were used to evaluate CSMP (Comprehensive School Mathematics Program, 1995). The first design controlled for teacher effects: Teachers taught the regular curriculum during the first year and the CSMP curriculum during the second year. In the second design, CSMP classes were matched with a control group studying the regular curriculum. In both designs, students were given a problem-solving test called Mathematics Applied to Novel Situations (MANS).

The CSMP students outscored the control students in the second, third, and sixth grades, with effect sizes of $+1.26$, $+.22$, and $+.30$, respectively. In the fourth and fifth grades, the non-CSMP students outperformed the CSMP students, with effect sizes of $-.16$ and $-.32$, respectively.

CSMP, which has been an NDN program since 1978, is now disseminated by another educational laboratory (MCREL, in Aurora, Colorado) and has been used in 550 schools throughout 35 states.

Cognitively Guided Instruction

Cognitively Guided Instruction (CGI) (Carey, Fennema, Carpenter, & Franke, 1993; Carpenter, Fennema, Peterson, Chiang, & Loef, 1989) is a mathematics program designed to develop student problem solving in the early elementary grades. CGI was created to teach the teachers of first-grade students about problem-solving processes that their students use when solving simple arithmetic and complex mathematics problems and to train the teachers to create curricula consistent with new understandings of how children learn. Following extensive training, CGI teachers create units and themes to last the entire school year. The Cognitively Guided Instruction model was not specifically created for Latino students, but has been used among students of various ethnicities and SES levels.

In an evaluation of CGI (Carpenter et al., 1989), 40 teachers were randomly assigned to either a control or a treatment group. CGI as well as control teachers had volunteered to participate in a summer in-service program that would last 4 weeks, and also to be observed in their classrooms during instruction in mathematics during the following year. Teachers in both of the groups were involved in problem-solving workshops, but one was a CGI workshop, and the other was a generic problem-solving workshop. Teachers in the CGI workshop, for instance, learned that they should closely relate problem solving to basic skills competency, and that problem solving should be the main focus of the mathematics lessons. They also learned that students should use prior knowledge when solving problems and be able to link what they already know to new problems that they may be solving. Teachers in the CGI workshop learned about teaching children conceptual problem solving, and the teachers were familiarized with curricular materials available for instruction. Finally, CGI teachers were asked to write a mathematics curriculum, based on what they had learned at the CGI workshops, that would span the academic year.

Teachers in the control groups also participated in problem-solving exercises for a similar amount of time. The teachers learned about the general concept of problem solving, but did not discuss how to understand how children solve problems or how to write a curriculum that would help children to solve problems based on this information.

All students were given the Iowa Test of Basic Skills (ITBS) level 6 as a pretest in September, and the computation subtest of the ITBS level 7 was used as the written posttest of computation in April–May. Interviews were also conducted with the students.

Student achievement results showed that CGI students outscored their control group counterparts in computations (specifically in number facts) and in problems that involved complex addition/subtraction. Interviews also found that treatment students also had better attitudes toward math and felt more confident that they could perform complex mathematics.

A second study of CGI evaluated the effectiveness of the program among low-income minority students (Villaseñor & Kepner, 1993). Twelve experimental and 12 control teachers were randomly assigned to CGI and control classes in Milwaukee, Wisconsin. Minority populations ranged from 57% to 99%, primarily Latino or African American. A 14-item arithmetic word-problem test focusing on higher level cognitive processes (Carpenter et al., 1989), developed by the creators of CGI, was administered as a pretest in early October, and again as a posttest in late February and early March.

On the pretest, students in the experimental group had a slightly higher mean score than did students in the control group. Controlling for these differences, the experimental students still outscored their control-group counterparts.

CGI is currently being implemented nationally, and training programs for the model have been established in Wisconsin, North Carolina, and Ohio.

Project SEED

Project SEED (Hollins, Smiler, & Spencer, 1994; Johntz, 1966, 1975; Phillips & Ebrahimi, 1993; Project SEED, 1995) is an enrichment mathematics program designed to teach elementary school students, particularly low-income and minority students, to develop confidence in their ability to be successful in all academic work. Project SEED prepares students to be successful in their academic careers, and gives them the grounding to help them face challenging academic situations by using advanced mathematics as a tool. Students participating in Project SEED are taught to improve their mathematics achievement skills and to continue to take classes in abstract and advanced mathematics at a rate that is higher than those of students not involved in the program.

Project SEED hires and trains mathematicians, scientists, and engineers to teach students in the targeted population. Project SEED mathematics specialists then go into the classroom and introduce abstract mathematical concepts using a discovery method based on Socratic questioning and always making students active participants in the lessons. The Project SEED curriculum does not take the place of the regular mathematics curriculum, but is a supplement to it. When the Project SEED mathematics specialists teach the students, the regular classroom teachers remain in the classroom and observe and participate in what is being taught. Students involved in the program are expected to learn using dialogue, choral responses, discussion, and debates. In addition to teaching the students, the Project SEED mathematics specialists conduct workshops with the regular classroom teachers. Part of ongoing staff development includes Project SEED math specialists observing and critiquing each other in the classroom at work and attending internal workshops. Project SEED was not specifically designed to benefit Latino students, but its use among Latino students has been evaluated in various states that have high populations of Latino students.

A study that evaluated the effects of one semester of Project SEED in Detroit (Webster & Chadbourn, 1992) compared the California Achievement Test (CAT) scores of 244 fourth-grade students in SEED classrooms to those of 244 fourth-grade students in SEED schools, but not in SEED classrooms (non-SEED) and to those of 244 fourth grade students neither in SEED schools nor in SEED classrooms (comparison group) during the 1991–1992 academic year. Students in all three groups were matched based on gender, ethnicity, free or reduced-price lunch status, and third-grade CAT scores.

The SEED students outscored comparison group students in total math scores (ES = +.37), math computation (ES = +.38), and math concepts (ES = +.32). The non-SEED students in SEED schools also outscored the comparison students in all three areas with effect sizes of +.17, +.23, and +.13 respectively. When the SEED and non-SEED students were compared, students in the SEED group also outperformed students in the non-SEED groups on math total (ES = +.19), math computation (ES = +.16), and math concepts (ES = +.19).

The effect of one semester of SEED was also evaluated in Dallas in a Project SEED longitudinal evaluation study (Webster & Chadbourn, 1992). The Dallas evaluation consisted of 11 elementary Learning Centers (South Dallas Learning Centers and West Dallas Learning Centers). Students in the South Dallas Learning Centers were 80% African American, and students in the West Dallas Learning Centers were mostly Latino. There was a total of 10,890 Project SEED and matched comparison students. The treatment students were those who had been involved in Project SEED for at least one semester between 1982 and 1991. Students were administered either the Iowa Tests of Basic Skills (ITBS) or the Norm-referenced Assessment Program for Texas (NAPT). The test scores between the control and experimental groups were equivalent at the beginning of the experiment. Students were tested on three ITBS scales: concepts and problem solving, computation, and mathematics total. As with the Detroit study, SEED students significantly outscored the non-SEED students on all scales.

The cumulative effects of Project SEED on students after one, two, and three semesters of involvement were also investigated (Webster &

Chadbourn, 1992). In total, 3,092 students in five different settings were matched with control students on the basis of grade level, total mathematics achievement score, gender, ethnicity, and socioeconomic status, as determined by free lunch program participation. Beginning in the fourth grade, students in the treatment group received either one, two, or three semesters of Project SEED. Students were matched with students in other schools who did not receive SEED instruction but may have received other types of intervention. Students were pretested on the ITBS and, after 1991, the Norm-referenced Achievement Program for Texas (NAPT). In every case except 1 out of 30 comparisons, the Project SEED students significantly outperformed the students in the control groups on the posttests for both the NAPT and the ITBS, and the more semesters that a student had been involved in Project SEED (up to the maximum of three semesters), the greater the cumulative effect of Project SEED.

A follow-up study (Webster & Chadbourn, 1992) sought to evaluate the retention of mathematics skills after students had left Project SEED. This study included a total of 1,215 matched students from the previous study. Students who had been involved in the project for only one semester were followed for 5 years after their involvement, and students who had received three semesters of Project SEED in Grades 4–6 were followed through the 1991–1992 school year. Overall, Project SEED students, regardless of how long they had been in the program, still outscored the non-SEED students on the ITBS/NAPT up to 2 years after Project SEED exposure ended. More specifically, students who had been involved in Project SEED for one semester retained their mathematics skills for at least 2 years after they had left the program, and students who had been involved in the program for three semesters still retained their skills when tested between 2 and 5 years after they had left the program.

In the final Dallas longitudinal follow-up study of Project SEED (Webster & Chadbourn, 1992), results showed that students who had been involved in Project SEED were more likely to enroll in advanced mathematics classes in the 9th, 10th, 11th, and 12th grades than were students who had not been involved in Project SEED.

Project SEED is currently being used in Texas, Michigan, Indiana, Pennsylvania, and California, and is validated by the National Diffusion Network.

Skills Reinforcement Project

The Skills Reinforcement Project (Mills, 1992; SRP, 1984, 1992, 1995) was developed by the Johns Hopkins University Center for Talented Youth (CTY). CTY began as a program for gifted or "highly able" students, but it later added SRP, which is specifically designed for use with minority or low socioeconomic status students who are likely to be underrepresented in advanced mathematics. The program was written to prepare fifth- through eighth-grade students to succeed in advanced level mathematics, with hopes that they would eventually become involved in mathematics and science careers. The program was not specifically designed for Latino students, but many of the students involved in the research have been Latino.

Staff in schools that adopt SRP attend training sessions before the implementation and during the year. SRP schools have a coordinator, who oversees the general management of the program at the school and also oversees teacher training, curriculum development, and program evaluation. In addition to this, SRP schools involve a site director who acts as a facilitator for the program.

Students involved in the SRP program are volunteers. They attend Saturday school during the school year, and then they participate in a 2-week summer residential program. Students are initially assessed, and then teaching is based on the results of this testing. The SRP program provides a balance of individualized instruction and cooperative learning. The content of the SDP curriculum ranges from arithmetic concepts and skills to more advanced areas of study such as algebra, geometry, and statistics.

Research on SRP has been done at two sites in California, at schools with populations of 40% African American, 40% Latino, and 20% other, with a majority of the minority students qualifying for free lunches. The research design for all of the evaluations consisted of pre–post experimental/control comparisons. Student participants in both the control and treatment groups were volunteered by parents, and had to score between the 80th and 95th percentiles on the California Achievement Test. Students who met the criteria were randomly assigned to the SRP and control conditions, where the experimental students received substantial additional mathematics instruction, and the control group students received no extra mathematics instruction. The students were also equivalent on the basis of gender, ethnicity, income level, and mean pretest scores.

In addition to the CAT, the Sequential Tests of Educational Progress II (STEP) were used as a pre- and posttest. The School and College Ability Test (SCAT) was used to assess mathematical reasoning ability.

The first evaluation was done in Pasadena, California (Lynch & Mills, 1990). In this study, 32 SRP and 32 control sixth graders were administered the CAT and the STEP while they were in the sixth grade, and again 9 months later in the fall, when they were in the seventh grade.

Adjusting for pretest differences, SRP students outperformed their control group counterparts (ES = +.41).

A replication study was also done in Pasadena (SRP, 1992). This study involved 38 students: 19 in the control group, and 19 in the experimental group. In this study also, SRP students outscored the control group on both the SCAT (ES = +.72) and the CAT/STEP tests (ES = +.73).

The third evaluation was done in Los Angeles (Mills, Stork, & Krug, 1992). This study involved 54 students: 28 SRP students and 26 students in the control group. Once again, SRP students outscored the students in the control group on the SCAT (ES = +.55) and on the CAT/STEP (ES = +1.35).

It is important to note that the evaluation of SRP does not compare one instructional method to another, but instead compares additional mathematics instruction to no extra instruction. SRP is currently being used in three California school districts.

Maneuvers With Mathematics

Maneuvers With Mathematics (MWM) was founded at the University of Illinois at Chicago (Long, 1993; MWM, 1995; Page, 1989). This program was designed to teach students in Grades 5–8 advanced mathematics problem solving. The goal of MWM is to motivate students to use mathematics in a creative manner, while still learning basic arithmetic skills. MWM trainers attend training sessions in summer institutes.

An emphasis of MWM is on training both the teachers and students to use calculators to solve both simple arithmetic and complex geometry and advanced mathematics problems. Students are shown how math is used every day—for example, in cooking, traveling, building houses, and using money. They use specific books created by MWM that stress problem solving, rechecking answers, and using mathematics in real-life situations. Teacher guides provide alternative ways of presenting topics and concepts to the students. This program was not originally developed for Latino students, but has been used with this population.

The main evaluation of this program was done in 1991. This evaluation involved 617 MWM students matched with 223 control students (MWM, 1991). The students in both groups exceeded the state norms in mobility and in the number of low-income, limited English proficient (LEP) students. At the beginning of the year, students in both groups were administered pretests created by the Second International Mathematics Study (SIMS) and the National Assessment of Educational Progress (NAEP). The same tests were also used as posttests at the end of the school year. Students were not allowed to use calculators on these tests.

Adjusting for pretest differences, the MWM students outperformed the students in the control group (ES = +.47). At each individual grade level, MWM students made better gains than the students in the control groups (ES = +.12, +.54, +.59, and +.86 in the fifth, sixth, seventh, and eighth grades, respectively).

MWM is validated by the National Diffusion Network, and is currently being used in all 50 states nationwide.

CURRICULUM-SPECIFIC PROGRAMS:
EARLY CHILDHOOD

One of the best ways to ensure that students succeed in school is to provide them with high-quality experiences before they enter school. Although studies of long-term impacts of early childhood programs have a long history, there is relatively little research on the effects of such programs on Latino students. In the 1960s, when most of this research was begun, the main populations studied were African American and Anglo students. This section discusses programs that have proven to be effective for preschool students in general. Many of these programs were not designed for Latino students, but some have been evaluated with them and address their needs. In addition to the programs reviewed here, preschool and kindergarten curricula are part of Success for All/*Éxito Para Todos*, discussed earlier.

Head Start

The largest federal investment in early childhood education is Project Head Start (Zigler & Muenchow, 1992; Zigler & Valentine, 1979). Head Start began as one of President Lyndon Johnson's War On Poverty programs in 1965. The goal of Head Start was to provide young children (mainly 4-year-olds) with social and cognitive competence, by addressing certain specific outcomes felt to increase the likelihood that students would succeed when they entered elementary school. It was designed to achieve these outcomes through seven service components: education, parent involvement, mental health, physical health, nutrition, social services, and disabled student services or special needs.

Head Start has served millions of children since its inception in 1965, and its effects have been extensively evaluated. Like Title I, Head Start is a funding source, not a specific program. Thus, it is difficult to evaluate Head Start as a whole, as many different Head Start centers have different curriculum goals. Studies have shown that, overall, the program is effective in helping children adjust to kindergarten and elementary school (McKey et al., 1985), in including parents as participants in their children's education, and in seeing that children are up-to-date on their immunizations. Evaluations of the academic achievements of students who attend Head Start schools and centers generally find positive effects on early cognitive measures (such as IQ tests).

Karweit (1989, 1994) and Stein, Leinhart, and Bickel (1989) reviewed the effects of Head Start programs, and their syntheses found that Head Start showed immediate improvement on cognitive functioning (ES = +.52). After the first year, the effects decreased substantially (ES = +.10), and also decreased further during the second and third years (ES = +.08 and +.02, respectively). Longitudinal studies of the Perry Preschool program, described next, have found positive effects of preschool participation on such outcomes as high graduation and delinquency, but there is little indication at any age that attending Head Start or other early childhood programs increases performance on measures of school achievement, such as reading or math scores.

In recent years, the Latino student population has increased in the elementary schools and among young children receiving early childhood education. Head Start and many other publicly funded preschool programs have proven to be effective in helping both children and their parents get adjusted to schooling systems in the United States. Especially with Spanish-speaking students, Head Start has provided innovative bilingual and English as a second language instruction. One of the requirements of Head Start, for instance, is that if there is at least one child who speaks a second language, then the program is expected to employ at least one person on staff who speaks the language of the child and the parents. This is crucial, as the goal of Head Start is really to work with the whole family for the benefit of the child. Head Start teachers and staff provide bilingual services in all of the seven components, seeking to ensure that the students adjust smoothly to Head Start and eventually to elementary school.

Perry Preschool/High Scope

One of the most extensively researched curriculum-specific early childhood education programs is the Perry Preschool Curriculum (Weikart, Rogers, Adcock, & McClelland, 1971). The creators of the Perry Preschool Curriculum believe in empowering the family, the child, and the teacher, as in Head Start programs, but the Perry Preschool program also has specific academic goals for participants in the program and its developers created a specific curriculum to accomplish these goals. Based on

Piaget's theories of cognition, the Perry Preschool curriculum seeks to increase academic achievement and reduce students' chances of being placed in special education classes by teaching them to become active learners. The teacher acts as a facilitator of knowledge who sets up the classroom in such a way that the student is provided with the opportunity to learn math, science, reading, art, music, social studies, and movement every day. Students choose what they wish to study or work with, but the teacher is expected to be available to answer any questions and clarify any misunderstandings that students may have.

The Perry Preschool model has been evaluated to investigate both short-term and long-term outcomes with at-risk preschoolers. As with other preschool programs, the Perry Preschool program has shown immediate (end-of-the-year) positive effects on cognitive measures such as IQ, but these effects do not maintain into elementary school.

In addition to the cognitive gains made by students who had attended Perry Preschool programs, a longitudinal evaluation of the effects of the Perry Preschool program on at-risk students (Schweinhart & Weikart, 1980; Schweinhart, Weikart, & Larner, 1986a, 1986b) showed that children involved in these programs tended to stay in school longer, had fewer cases of teenage pregnancies and juvenile arrests, were retained less, were less likely to drop out of school, were more literate, were more likely to be employed, and were more likely to attend college or vocational school than students in control groups who had had no preschool experience. Evaluations of the long-term effects of the program on social adjustment showed that when students in three preschool groups (Direct Instruction, High Scope, and nursery) were compared on self-reported delinquency, High Scope students were the least likely to have committed delinquent acts, followed by students who had attended traditional nursery school, and followed by students involved in Direct Instruction.

A 22-year follow-up study done on 95% of the participants involved in the original High Scope study (Schweinhart, Barnes, Weikart, Barnett, & Epstein, 1993) showed that High Scope graduates still had a smaller chance of being arrested than the control group (35%); earned approximately $2,000 per month more than nonprogram members; were more likely to own their own home (36%) than nonprogram participants (13%); and had a higher rate of high school graduation (71%) than the control group students (54%). The High Scope curriculum exists today in all 50 states. The program provides an early elementary curriculum that is also used around the nation. Although the High Scope model has not been studied in schools serving many Latino students, it has been disseminated to such schools.

Early Intervention for School Success

Project Early Intervention for School Success (EISS, 1986; Rogers, 1993) is an early intervention program developed under special funding from the California Legislature to provide low-income children with early education opportunities to help them become successful learners and thinkers. The legislative intent of this program was threefold: first, to establish a system to identify pupils at the ages of 4 to 7 years who may be at-risk; second, to implement appropriate instructional programs to reduce the frequency and severity of learning disability for these pupils in later years; and third, to reduce the likelihood that these pupils will be placed in remedial programs with higher costs. Specific learning areas that this program strives to improve include receptive language, visual motor skills, and academic achievement.

EISS works with early childhood providers in California to teach them effective ways to educate children by training them to use developmentally appropriate curricula. Specifically, the teachers are trained in organization and planning, assessment, strategies, and curriculum. The EISS program does not have its own curriculum, but rather it trains teachers to adjust their own curricula so that the children are being taught content that will benefit them academically, linguistically, culturally, and ethnically. EISS facilitators also train the teachers to be sensitive to the cultural and economic backgrounds of the students. Academic goals of the program include improving the children's receptive language and their visual motor skills.

Although the program was not designed to benefit Latino students only, they represent a substantial portion of the population that has used this program over the years. Spanish-dominant LEP students involved in EISS were analyzed as a subgroup beginning in the 1987–1988 academic year.

To date, two studies have evaluated the effectiveness of EISS. In the first study, which compared control and experimental groups, the effects of EISS on receptive language and visual motor skills were evaluated. The students in the treatment group received the EISS curriculum for a period of 7.2 months between pre- and posttesting. EISS students outperformed the control group on the Peabody Picture Vocabulary Test (PPVT), with effect sizes of $+.31$ in 1989–1990 and $+.29$ in 1990–1991. Visual motor skills, which were measured using the Visual Motor Integrated test (VMI), produced similar outcomes in favor of EISS students, with an effect size of $+.50$ in 1990–1991.

To evaluate the long-term academic achievement effects of EISS on both English- and Spanish-speaking children, a number of different tests were used. The Comprehensive Test of Basic Skills (CTBS-4) and the Stanford Achievement Test (SAT-8) were used for the English-speaking children, and the Aprenda was used for the Spanish-speaking children who had received EISS in kindergarten during the 1989–1990 academic year. When compared to a matched non-EISS group, students maintained large gains (ES = +1.09) the first year after the program, and medium gains (ES = +.65) after being out of the program for 2 years.

EISS also performed a longitudinal study (EISS, 1995) to investigate the long-term effects of the program on achievement, the number of special education placements, and grade retention. This study included 5,095 students in EISS and 6,333 matched students in control schools. Students in the control groups showed a decrease in retention, but not to the same extent as the EISS group, compared to the 2 years before EISS implementation. Observations in the long-term study show that EISS students were retained at a lower rate than the comparison students, the lower rates were sustained through third grade, and significantly fewer students were placed in special education classes by the third or fourth grade.

EISS was recognized as an exemplary program by the National Diffusion Network in 1994, and has served approximately 270,000 students in more than 500 schools in California.

TUTORING PROGRAMS

Reading Recovery/Descubriendo La Lectura

Reading Recovery (RR) was developed in the mid 1970s by New Zealand educator and psychologist Marie M. Clay (1985), who conducted observational research in the mid 1960s that enabled her to design techniques for detecting and intervening with early reading difficulties of children. During the 1988–1989 academic year, Reading Recovery was introduced to the United States by researchers at Ohio State University who had previously received training in New Zealand (Pinnell, DeFord, & Lyons, 1988).

Reading Recovery is an early intervention tutoring program for young readers who are experiencing difficulty in their first year of reading instruction. RR serves the lowest achieving readers (lowest 20%) in first-grade classes by providing the children with supplemental tutoring in addition to their regular reading classes. Children participating in RR receive daily one-to-one 30-min lessons for 12–20 weeks with a teacher trained in the RR method. The lessons consist of a variety of experiences designed to help children develop effective strategies for reading and writing. When the student reaches a stage at which he or she is able to read at or above the average class level and can continue to read without later remedial help, the student is discontinued from the program. Students who are not discontinued are excluded from the program after 60 lessons and may be placed either in special education classes or in some other form of remedial education.

RR tutors are certified teachers who receive an additional year's training in Reading Recovery tutoring. The tutoring model emphasizes "learning to read by reading" (Pinnell, 1989; Pinnell et al., 1988). The lessons are one-to-one tutorial sessions that include reading known stories, reading a story that was read once the day before, writing a story, working with a cut-up sentence, and reading a new book. RR does not have a prescribed set of books that each child must read; teachers involved in the program use a variety of readily available books that the children select as they work on the various components of RR. For the first few tutoring sessions, the teacher and student "roam around the known," reading and writing together in an unstructured, supportive fashion, to build a positive relationship and to give the teacher a broader knowledge of the child and his or her reading skills. After this, the teachers begin to use a structured sequence of activities that include rereading familiar books, analysis of student progress, reading and writing of short messages, and reading new books.

Although RR was not originally created for Latino or LEP students, the program is frequently used with such students in either Spanish or English, depending on the language of instruction in the students' regular reading classes. RR is currently used in states that have high Latino populations, such as Arizona, California, and Texas, and has been evaluated with Latino students.

Descubriendo La Lectura (DLL) is a Spanish adaptation of Reading Recovery (RR), developed and studied in Tucson, Arizona. It is equivalent in all major program aspects to the original program. Students in Spanish bilingual classes whose reading scores fall at the bottom 20% in the first grade are placed in DLL.

The Ohio State group has conducted three longitudinal studies comparing English Reading Recovery to traditional Title I pull-out or in-class methods. The first (pilot) study (Huck & Pinnell, 1986; Pinnell, 1988) of RR involved first-grade students from six inner-city Columbus, Ohio, schools and six matched comparison classes. The lowest 20% of students in each class served as the experimental and control group, respectively. The second longitudinal study (DeFord, Pinnell, Lyons, & Young, 1988;

Pinnell, Short, Lyons, & Young, 1986) involved 32 teachers in 12 schools in Columbus. Again, students in the lowest 20% of their classes were randomly assigned to Reading Recovery or control conditions. Results showed that Reading Recovery students substantially outperformed control students on almost all measures in a series of assessments developed by the program except in tests of letter identification and word recognition, both of which had ceiling effects. With the exception of these, the effects ranged from +.57 to +.72.

An oral reading measure called Text Reading Level was given at the end of first, second, and third grades. On this test, students were asked to read books that got progressively more difficult. The results of this study for Text Reading Level at the end of first grade showed substantial positive effects for both the pilot cohort and the second cohort (ES = +.72 and +.78, respectively). On a follow-up assessment at the end of second grade, the effects diminished (ES = +.29 and +.46, respectively). At the end of third grade, the effect sizes had diminished even further (ES = +.14 and +.25, respectively). The raw experimental–control differences remained about the same over the 3-year period, but due to the increasing standard deviations the effect sizes diminished (Wasik & Slavin, 1993).

A third study of Reading Recovery involved schools in 10 districts throughout the state of Ohio (Pinnell, Lyons, DeFord, Bryk, & Seltzer, 1994). This study compared Reading Recovery to three program variations and a control group. On midyear assessments, Reading Recovery students scored better than control students and better than an RR variation that involved a shorter training period, a group (not one-to-one) version of RR, and an alternative tutoring model. A Gates–McGinitie given in May of first grade showed small and nonsignificant effects, but the following fall RR students scored significantly higher than controls on both Text Reading Level and a dictation test. None of the RR variations were significantly higher than control groups on these measures.

Studies of Reading Recovery conducted by researchers who are not associated with the program find patterns of results similar to those found by the Ohio State researchers. Tests given immediately after the Reading Recovery intervention show substantial positive effects of the program. These effects diminish in size in years after first grade, although some difference is usually still detectable in third grade (Baenen, Bernholc, Dulaney, Banks, & Willoughby, 1995; Center, Wheldall, Freeman, Outhred, & McNaught, 1995; Shanahan & Barr, 1995).

An evaluation of *Descubriendo La Lectura* (DLL) was conducted by Escamilla (1994) in Tucson. The experiment compared 23 DLL students to 23 matched comparison students in a school that did not have DLL. In both cases, students were identified as being in the lowest 20% of their classes based on individually administered tests and teacher judgment.

The outcomes of DLL on Spanish reading measures given at the end of first grade were extremely positive. On six scales of a Spanish Observation Survey adapted from the measures used in evaluations of the English Reading Recovery program, DLL students started out below controls and ended the year substantially ahead of them, with effect sizes (adjusted for pretest differences) ranging from +.97 to +1.71. These scores were also compared to those of a random sample of all students, most of whom were not having reading difficulties, and the DLL students performed above the level of the classes as a whole on all scales. Students were also pre- and posttested on a standardized test, the Aprenda Spanish Achievement Test. On a total reading score, DLL students increased from the 28th to the 41st percentile. Control students increased from the 26th to the 28th percentile, while classes as a whole decreased from the 35th to the 31st percentile.

A much larger study of DLL was carried out in California by Kelly, Gomez-Valdez, Klein, and Neal (1995). This study did not have a low-achieving control group, but did show both that "discontinuation rates" (an indicator of successful program completion) were similar in DLL and in English Reading Recovery, and that end-of-first-grade reading performance of children who participated in DLL was not far below the level of children in general in their schools (most of whom were not at risk for reading failure). Similar results, also lacking appropriate control groups, were reported by Ashdown and Simic (1999).

Reading Recovery is very widely used, and has regional training centers in 18 states, mostly at universities. The training or residency period for RR lasts 1 academic year. Teachers then return to their individual sites to implement the program, staying in contact with the RR network through conferences, newsletters, and other network activities. In 1998, the Reading Recovery Program was used by more than 9,000 schools nationwide.

Helping One Student To Succeed

Helping One Student To Succeed (HOSTS) (Gallegos, 1995; HOSTS Corporation, 1994; Wilbur, 1995) is a model that helps schools create tutoring programs for at-risk students using a mentoring approach. HOSTS schools provide one-to-one, usually after-school tutorial services to Title I students in elementary through high school who are performing below the 30th percentile. This includes LEP students and those who have been retained or are in special education. HOSTS trains community volunteers from businesses and the community, as well as peers and cross-age mentors, to serve as tutors. HOSTS was not created specifically to serve Latino students, but some of the school districts where HOSTS has been most successful have large numbers of Latino students, such as Pasadena, California, and Houston, Texas.

HOSTS helps school staffs choose curriculum materials that are especially tailored to the individual needs of the child receiving services and aligned with what is being taught in the regular classroom. Schools involved in HOSTS have access to thousands of learning materials that have been designed to help the targeted population. The mentor/tutor follows a carefully designed lesson plan generated by the Title I teacher from a comprehensive database that aligns the curriculum of the schools to local objectives or state frameworks.

HOSTS evaluations have not included pre–post, experimental/control group studies. They have measured their student participants' success by looking at NCE scores, NCE gains, and the number of students who pass at grade level.

In a multistate study of HOSTS done for Title I national validation (HOSTS Corporation, 1994), the students in Grades 1, 2, and 3 made substantial NCE spring-to-spring gains (15, 25, and 25 respectively), while the students in other grades also made significant NCE gains. In a spring-to-spring California evaluation that had a 95% population of Hispanic students, students in second, third, and fifth grades had NCE gains of 11.4, 9.5, and 9.9, respectively. These NCE gains exceeded those of the school and the state.

Since its inception in Vancouver, Washington, in 1972, HOSTS has involved over 150,000 students and 100,000 mentors in more than 1000 programs across 41 states.

CATEGORIZATION OF PROGRAMS REVIEWED

As noted earlier, an ideal program for this review would be one that was specifically designed for Latino students (and had Spanish materials available), had been rigorously evaluated many times in elementary or middle schools serving many Latino students, and had been extensively replicated in such schools. However, few programs would meet all of these criteria. Table 1.1 summarizes the degree to which each of the programs reviewed met the various inclusion criteria. The table is only a summary; see the program reviews for more detail on the characteristics, evaluation evidence, and replicability of each program.

TABLE 1.1
Categorization of Programs Reviewed

Program Name	Grades Served	Spanish Bilingual Focus	Meets Evaluation Criteria for Achievement	Evaluated with Latinos	Designed Specifically for Latinos	Widely Replicated
Schoolwide reform programs						
SFA/Éxito Para Todos	K–6	Yes	Yes	Yes	Yes	Yes
Accelerated Schools	K–6	No	Partially	Yes	No	Yes
School Development Program	K–6	No	Partially	Yes	No	Yes
Consistency Management & Cooperative Discipline	K–6	Yes	Yes	Yes	No	Yes
Goldenberg & Sullivan	K–6	No	Yes	Yes	Yes	No
Cooperative learning methods						
CIRC/BCIRC	2–8	Yes	Yes	Yes	Yes	Yes
Complex Instruction/Finding Out/Descubrimiento	1–6	Yes	Partially	Yes	Yes	Yes
STAD/TGT	2–12	No	Yes	Yes	No	Yes
Jigsaw	2–12	No	Partially	Yes	No	Yes
Learning Together	K–12	No	Yes	Yes	No	Yes
Reading/writing/language arts programs						
DISTAR/Reading Mastery	1–3	No	Yes	Yes	Yes	Yes
ECRI	1–10	No	Yes	Yes	No	Yes
Reciprocal Teaching	1–8	No	Yes	Yes	No	Yes
Profile Approach to Writing (PAW)	3–12	No	Yes	Yes	No	Yes
Multicultural Reading and Thinking (McRAT)	3–8	No	Yes	No	No	Yes

(Continued)

TABLE 1.1
(Continued)

Program Name	Grades Served	Spanish Bilingual Focus	Meets Evaluation Criteria for Achievement	Evaluated with Latinos	Designed Specifically for Latinos	Widely Replicated
Mathematics programs						
Comprehensive School Mathematics Program	K–6	No	Yes	Yes	No	Yes
Cognitively Guided Instruction	1	No	Yes	Yes	No	Yes
Project SEED	3–8	No	Yes	Yes	No	Yes
Skills Reinforcement Project	3–8	No	Yes	Yes	No	Yes
Maneuvers With Mathematics	5–8	No	Yes	Yes	No	Yes
Preschool programs						
Perry Preschool/High Scope	Preschool	No	Yes	No	No	Yes
EISS	Preschool–1	No	Yes	Yes	No	Yes
Tutoring programs						
Reading Recovery/*Descubriendo La Lectura*	1	Yes	Yes	Yes	Yes	Yes
HOSTS	1–6	No	Yes	Yes	No	Yes

WHAT FACTORS CONTRIBUTE
TO PROGRAM EFFECTIVENESS?

The programs reviewed in this chapter vary in focus, research designs, measures, and other aspects, and often serve different populations. In addition, we focused on locating programs that have evidence of effectiveness. Those we did not include typically lacked adequate research designs; rarely do we have evidence that a given program was *not* effective, as such evidence is seldom reported. For these reasons we cannot definitively compare effective and ineffective programs and reach firm conclusions about what factors contribute to program success. However, in the course of reviewing hundreds of articles for this and other reports on effective programs for students placed at risk, we have identified a set of conditions that are usually present in programs that work. These are discussed next.

1. Effective programs have clear goals, emphasize methods and materials linked to those goals, and constantly assess students' progress toward the goals. There is no magic in educational innovation. Programs that work almost invariably have a small set of very well-specified goals (e.g., raise mathematics achievement, improve creative writing skills), a clear set of procedures and materials linked to those goals, and frequent assessments that indicate whether or not students are reaching the goals. Effective programs leave little to chance. They incorporate many elements, such as research-based curricula, instructional methods, classroom management methods, assessments, and means of helping students who are struggling, all of which are tied in a coordinated fashion to the instructional goals.

Programs almost always have their strongest impacts on the objectives they emphasize. For example, programs emphasizing complex problem solving in mathematics report stronger impacts on problem solving than on computations; programs emphasizing thinking skills tend to show effects on thinking skills, not reading comprehension. Again, there is no magic in educational innovation. Interventions that are not closely linked to desired outcomes rarely affect these outcomes.

2. Effective and replicable programs have well-specified components, materials, and professional development procedures. There is a belief in many quarters that each school, with the participation of all staff, must develop or codevelop its own reform model, that externally developed programs cannot be successfully replicated in schools that had no hand in developing them. This belief is often traced to the influential Rand Corporation (1978) Change Agent Study, although that study's principal author,

Milbrey McLaughlin (1990), later denied that the Change Agent Study in fact implied that externally developed programs could not work in new schools. Over time, evidence has mounted that reform models that ask teachers to develop their own materials and approaches are rarely implemented at all (see, e.g., Elmore, 1996; Muncey & McQuillan, 1993). Studies of alternative programs implemented under similar conditions find that the more highly structured and focused programs that provide specific materials and training are more likely to be implemented and effective than are less well-specified models (e.g., Bodilly, 1996, 1998; Herman & Stringfield, 1995).

Within the present review, the same observations hold true. Although there are examples of success in models lacking clear structure, the programs with the most consistent positive effects with Latino as well as non-Latino students are those that have definite procedures and materials used in all participating schools. School staffs may be asked to adapt materials to their own needs, and most successful programs have some buy-in procedure to ensure that participating teachers or whole school staffs have made an informed and uncoerced choice to use a given program. The provision of well-specified methods and materials clearly contributes to both the effectiveness of programs and to the ease of replicating programs in additional schools and producing positive outcomes beyond initial pilots.

3. Effective programs provide extensive professional development. A characteristic shared by almost all of the effective programs we identified is the provision of extensive professional development and follow-up technical assistance. Few if any provide the classic half-day, one-time workshops that constitute the great majority of "in-service" programs, especially those usually provided with textbook adoptions. On the contrary, most of the successful programs we identified provide many days of inservice followed by in-class technical assistance to give teachers detailed feedback on their program implementations. Typically, teachers work with each other and with peer or expert coaches to discuss, assess, and refine their implementations. The training provided is rarely on generic strategies from which teachers pick a few ideas to add to their bags of tricks. Instead, training focuses on comprehensive strategies that replace, not just supplement, teachers' current strategies.

4. Effective programs are disseminated by organizations that focus on the quality of implementation. The programs identified in this review that have been associated with consistent positive effects in many settings tend to be ones that are developed and disseminated by active, well-structured organizations that concentrate efforts on ensuring the quality of program

implementation in all schools. These organizations, often based in universities, provide training and materials and typically create support networks among program users. For example, many of the organizations have national and/or regional conferences to keep up participants' skills and commitment, distribute newsletters and other updates, and work to ensure that schools claiming to use the program are in fact doing so with adequate preparation and integrity. Few of the programs are distributed by commercial publishers. DISTAR/Reading Mastery is one exception, but a number of training organizations provide supplemental training in the program beyond that provided by the publisher.

CONCLUSION

The research presented in this review, plus that reported in the scores of programs that did not meet the standards for inclusion applied here, supports two seemingly inconsistent conclusions. First, there is a broad range of replicable programs from which elementary and middle schools can choose to meet the needs of their Latino students. Most of these are backed up by networks of trainers and experienced users, materials, manuals, videos, and other supports, and some have convincing evidence of effectiveness. Anyone who believes that the often dismal performance of many Latino students is inevitable must confront the data from these programs. Anyone who believes that every school must reinvent its own path to reform must confront the evidence of replicability presented by so many programs. Some of the programs (such as Accelerated Schools, the School Development Project, and the Goldenberg and Sullivan program) are designed to help schools develop their own approaches, but this is not the same as asking schools without the support of these experienced and skillful networks to reinvent their practices. Every program requires adaptation to the circumstances, needs, and resources of every school. It would be foolish for schools to ignore the rich and varied set of alternatives available to them to enhance the learning of their Latino and non-Latino students.

Yet this same review also shows the enormous gaps in our knowledge base. Hundreds of articles and dozens of studies have debated the question of native language versus English reading instruction for English language learners, but few studies have compared alternative approaches to instruction in Spanish or English for Latino children, and even fewer studies have examined alternative methods of facilitating transition from Spanish to English reading, whenever that transition takes place. Studies of replicable, effective practices for students in general are few, but studies of such methods specifically designed for Latino or English language learners are even fewer. Not one of the programs that met the rather liberal standards applied in this review would be out of place in a review of research on effective practices for students in general. Five of the six programs that were specifically designed for Latino and English language learners, *Éxito Para Todos*, BCIRC, Finding Out/*Descubrimiento*, *Descubriendo La Lectura*, and *Disciplina Consistente y Cooperativa*, are applications of programs not specifically designed for Latino students: Success for All, CIRC, Complex Instruction, Reading Recovery, and Consistency Management and Cooperative Discipline, respectively.

Even when programs do present convincing evidence of effectiveness, the measures used often give an advantage to the experimental group, as they often emphasize skills or concepts more likely to be taught in the experimental group. This may be why we found more effective programs for teaching creative writing, mathematics problem solving, and critical thinking than we did programs for teaching reading, language arts, or mathematics computations. Traditional control groups are sure to be emphasizing the latter subjects—to do better on them than the control group, an innovative method must be a better way to teach the same material. In contrast, a program teaching creative writing, problem solving, or critical thinking may look effective simply because the control teachers are spending little time on these topics.

Although the number of proven programs and the quality of evidence for students are not always what we'd wish for, there are almost certainly many more effective programs in existence than those we have identified. Programs were seldom rejected from this review because we had evidence that they were *not* effective; instead, most simply lacked even rudimentary evidence to establish their effectiveness. Better evaluations of promising, attractive programs for Latino and other students would probably find many more effective and replicable models to add to our list.

The message of this review is one of hope and urgency. Schools can do a much better job of educating Latino students, using methods and materials that are readily available. There are approaches that are effective and appropriate for bilingual classes, for ESL classes, and for English- dominant Latino students. The existence of these approaches demonstrates that the low achievement of so many Latino students is not inevitable. We need not wait for social or political transformation or conclusive resolution of the question of language of instruction to dramatically improve educational outcomes for Latino students.

Even as the use of bilingual instruction is being debated on the political level, we must move toward a day when schools have available a wide range of replicable programs known to significantly accelerate the achievement of Latino children in Spanish or English, or both. Otherwise, resolution of the debate will mean little. This report takes one step in this direction by summarizing the best evidence on the best programs we have available today, but there is much more remaining to be done.

ACKNOWLEDGMENTS

An earlier version of this chapter was written for the Hispanic Dropout Project. It was partially supported by a grant from the Office of Educational Research and Improvement, U.S. Department of Education (grant R-117D-40005). However, any opinions expressed do not necessarily represent the positions or policies of the U.S. Department of Education. Portions of this chapter are adapted from Fashola and Slavin (1997).

APPENDIX: CONTACTS FOR INFORMATION ON PROGRAMS REVIEWED

Accelerated Schools
Claudette Spriggs
National Center for the Accelerated Schools Project
Stanford University
CERAS 109
Stanford, CA 94305-3084
650-725-7158 or 650-725-1676

Bilingual Cooperative Integrated Reading and Composition (BCIRC)
Success For All Foundation
200 West Towsontown Boulevard
Baltimore, MD 21204-5200
800-548-4998
Web site: www.successforall.net

Cognitively Guided Instruction (CGI)
Elizabeth Fennema or Thomas Carpenter
University of Wisconsin, Madison
Wisconsin Center for Education Research
1025 West Johnson Street
Madison, WI 53706
608-263-4265

Complex Instruction/Finding Out/Descubrimiento
Elizabeth G. Cohen
Stanford University, School of Education

Stanford, CA 94305
415-723-4661 and 415-723-5992

Comprehensive School Mathematics Program (CSMP)
Clare Heidema, Director
McREL–CSMP
2550 South Parker Road, Suite 500
Aurora, CO 80014
303-632-5520
Fax: 303-337-3005
E-mail: cheidema@mcrel.org
Web site: http://www.mcrel.org/products/csmp

Consistency Management and Cooperative Discipline (CMCD)
H. Jerome Freiberg, Katrina Willis
University of Houston
College of Education
Houston, TX 77204-5872
713-743-8663

Direct Instruction/DISTAR/Reading Mastery
Association for Direct Instruction
Brian Wickman
805 Lincoln
Eugene, OR 97401
541-485-1293

Early Intervention for School Success
Dean Hiser
200 Calmus Drive
PO Box 9050
Costa Mesa, CA 92628-9050
714-900-4125

Exemplary Center for Reading Instruction (ECRI)
Ethna R. Reid
Reid Foundation
3310 South 2700 East
Salt Lake City, UT 84109
801-486-5083 or 801-278-2334
Fax: 801-485-0561

Goldenberg and Sullivan
Claude Goldenberg
Department of Teacher Education
CSU Long Beach
1250 Bellflower Blvd.
Long Beach, CA 90840

562-985-5733
Fax: 562-985-1543

Helping One Student to Succeed (HOSTS)
William E. Gibbons, Chairman
Linda Brocksmill
8000 N.E. Parkway Drive, Suite 201
Vancouver, WA 98662-6459
206-260-1995 or 800-833-4678
Fax: 206-260-1783

Jigsaw
Kagan Publishing
Kagan Professional Development
Spencer Kagan
Resources for Teachers
27134 A Paseo Espada #202
San Juan, Capistrano, CA 92675
1-800-WEE-COOP
Web site: http://www.kaganonline.com

Learning Together
Roger T. Johnson and David W. Johnson
The Cooperative Learning Center
60 Peik Hall, University of Minnesota
Minneapolis, MN 55455
612-624-7031

Maneuvers With Mathematics (MWM)
David A. Page or Kathryn B. Chval
University of Illinois at Chicago
851 Morgan Street (m/c 249) SEO 1309
Chicago, IL 60607-7045
312-996-8708

Multicultural Reading and Thinking (McRAT)
Janita Hoskyn, National Consultant
1019 Ronwood Drive
Little Rock, AK 72227
501-225-5809
Fax: 501-445-4137

Profile Approach to Writing (PAW)
Jane B. Hughey or Dixie Copeland
1701 Southwest Parkway, Suite 102
College Station, TX 77840
409-764-9765 Phone or Fax

Project SEED (Berkeley, California)
Helen Smiler, National Projects Coordinator
2530 San Pablo Avenue, Suite K
Berkeley, CA 94702
510-644-3422
Fax: 510-644-0566

Project SEED (Dallas, Texas)
Hamid Ebrahimi, National Director
3414 Oak Grove Avenue
Dallas, TX 75204
214-954-4432

Reading Recovery/*Descubriendo La Lectura*
Dr. Carol A. Lyons, Dr. Gay Su Pinnell, Dr. Diane E. DeFord, Dr. Rogers
Reading Recovery Program
Ohio State University
200 Ramseyer Hall
29 West Woodruff Avenue
Columbus, OH 42310
614-292-7807
Fax: 614-688-3646

Reciprocal Teaching
Anne Marie Palinscar
University of Michigan, Ann Arbor
4204c SEB
610 E. University
Ann Arbor, MI 48109

School Development Program (SDP)
Ed Joyner
Child Study Center
School Development Program
230 South Frontage Road
PO Box 20790
New Haven, CT 06520-7900
203-785-2548
Fax: 203-785-3359

Sheltered English Approach (SEA)
Alice Petrossian
Joanna Junge
Glendale Unified School District
Special Projects
223 North Jackson Street
Glendale, CA 91206
818-241-3111 Ext. 301
Fax: 818-246-3715

Skills Reinforcement Project (SRP)
Elizabeth Jones Stork
Director, IAAY Western Region, and Deputy Director, CAA
Johns Hopkins University, Western Regional Office
206 North Jackson Street, Suite 304
Glendale, CA 91206
818-500-9034
Fax: 818-500-9058

Student Teams-Achievement Divisions (STAD) and
    Teams-Games-Tournament (TGT)
Success for All Foundation
200 West Towsontown Boulevard
Baltimore, MD 21204-5200
800-548-4998
Web site: www.successforall.net

Success For All/Éxito Para Todos
Success for All Foundation
200 West Towsontown Boulevard
Baltimore, MD 21204-5200
800-548-4998
Web site: www.successforall.net

REFERENCES

Abt Associates. (1977). *Education as experimentation: A planned variation model* (Vol. IV). Cambridge, MA: Abt Associates.

Adams, G. L., & Engelmann, S. (1996). *Research on Direct Instruction: 25 years beyond DISTAR.* Seattle, WA: Educational Achievement Systems.

Arkansas Department of Education. (1992). *Multicultural Reading and Thinking (McRAT): Proposal submitted to the Program Effectiveness Panel of the National Diffusion Network.* Washington, DC: U.S. Department of Education.

Aronson, E., Blaney, N., Stephan, C., Sikes, J., & Snapp, M. (1978). *The Jigsaw classroom.* Beverly Hills, CA: Sage.

Ashdown, J., & Simic, O. (1999, April). *Is early literacy intervention effective for ESL students? Evidence from Reading Recovery.* Paper presented at the annual meeting of the American Educational Research Association, Montreal.

August, D., & Hakuta, K. (1997). *Improving schooling for language-minority children: A research agenda.* Washington, DC: National Research Council.

Baenen, N., Bernholc, A., Dulaney, C., Banks, K., & Willoughby, M. (1995). *Evaluation report: WCPSS Reading Recovery 1990–1994.* Raleigh, NC: Wake County Public Schools.

Becker, W. C., & Gersten, R. (1982). A follow-up of Follow Through: The later effects of the direct instruction model on children in fifth and sixth grades. *American Educational Research Journal, 19,* 1, 75–92.

Becker, B. J., & Hedges, L. V. (1992). A review of the literature on the effectiveness of Comer's School Development Program. Unpublished manuscript, Michigan State University, East Lansing.

Bereiter, C., & Engelmann, S. (1966). Teaching disadvantaged children in the preschool. Englewood Cliffs, NJ: Prentice Hall.

Bodilly, S. J. (1996). Lessons from the New American Schools Development Corporation's development phase. Washington, DC: RAND.

Bodilly, S. J. (1998). Lessons from New American Schools' scale-up phase. Washington, DC: RAND.

Calderón, M. (1991). Benefits of cooperative learning for Hispanic students. Texas Research Journal, 2, 39–57.

Calderón, M. (1994a). Cooperative learning for bilingual settings. In R. Rodriguez, N. J. Ramos, & J. A. Ruiz-Escalante (Eds.), Compendium of readings in bilingual education (pp. 95–110). San Antonio, TX: Texas Association for Bilingual Education.

Calderón, M. (1994b, April). Transforming learning and curriculum of language-minority students through cooperative learning. Paper presented at the annual meeting of the American Educational Research Association, New Orleans, MO.

Calderón, M., Hertz-Lazarowitz, R., & Slavin, R. E. (1998). Effects of Bilingual Cooperative Integrated Reading and Composition on students making the transition from Spanish to English reading. Elementary School Journal, 99(2), 153–165.

Calderón, M., Tinajero, J., & Hertz-Lazarowitz, R. (1992). Adapting CIRC to meet the needs of bilingual students. Journal of Educational Issues of Linguistic Minority Students, 10, 79–106.

Carey, D. A., Fennema, E., Carpenter, T. P., & Franke, M. L. (1993). Equity and mathematics education. In W. Secada, E. Fennema, & L. Byrd (Eds.), New directions in equity for mathematics education (pp. 55–91). New York: Teachers College Press.

Carpenter, T. P., Fennema, E., Peterson, P. L., Chiang, C. P., & Loef, M. (1989). Using knowledge of children's mathematics thinking in classroom teaching: An experimental study. American Educational Research Journal, 26(4), 499–531.

Center, Y., Wheldall, K., Freeman, L., Outhred, L., & McNaught, M. (1995). An evaluation of Reading Recovery. Reading Research Quarterly, 30, 240–261.

Chasin, G., & Levin, H. M. (1995). Thomas Edison Accelerated Elementary School. In J. Oakes & K. H. Quartz (Eds.), Creating new educational communities (pp. 130–147). Chicago: University of Chicago Press.

Clay, M. M. (1985). The early detection of reading difficulties. Exeter, NH: Heinemann.

Cohen, E. G. (1994a). Designing groupwork: Strategies for the heterogeneous classroom (2nd ed.). New York: Teachers College Press.

Cohen, E. (1994b). Restructuring the classroom: Conditions for productive small groups. Review of Educational Research, 64(1), 1–35.

Cohen, E. G., & Intili, J. K. (1981). Interdependence and management in bilingual classrooms. Unpublished technical report, Stanford University.

Cohen, E. G., Lotan, R., & Leechor, C. (1989). Can classrooms learn? Sociology of Education, 62, 75–94.

Comer, J. (1980). School power. New York: Free Press.

Comer, J. (1988). Educating poor minority children. Scientific American, 259, 42–48.

Comer, J. P., Haynes, N. M., Joyner, E. T., & Ben-Avie, M. (1996). Rallying the whole village: The Comer process for reforming education. New York: Teachers College Press.

Comprehensive School Mathematics Program. (1995). *Comprehensive School Mathematics Program: Submission to the Program Effectiveness Panel of the National Diffusion Network.* Washington, DC: U.S. Department of Education.

Council of Chief State School Officers. (1990). *School success for limited English proficient students: The challenge and state response.* Washington, DC: Author.

DeAvila, E. A., & Duncan, S. E. (1980). *Finding Out/Descubrimiento.* Corte Madera, CA: Linguametrics Group.

DeFord, Pinnell, G. S., Lyons, C., & Young, P. (1988). *Reading Recovery: Volume IX, Report on the follow-up studies.* Columbus: Ohio State University.

Dianda, M., & Flaherty, J. (1995, April). *Effects of Success for All on the reading achievement of first graders in California bilingual programs.* Paper presented at the annual meeting of the American Educational Research Association, San Francisco, CA.

Durán, R. P. (1994a). Hispanic student achievement. In M. Justiz, R. Wilson, & L. Bjork (Eds.), *Minorities in higher education* (pp. 111–132). Phoenix, AZ: Oryx Press.

Durán, R. P. (1994b). Cooperative learning for language-minority students. In R. DeVillar, C. Faltis, & J. Cummins (Eds.), *Cultural diversity in schools* (pp. 68–81). Albany, NY: SUNY Press.

Early Intervention for School Success. (1986). *Annual report to the California State Legislature.* Sacramento, CA: California State Department of Education.

Early Intervention for School Success. (1995). *Proposal submitted to the Program Effectiveness Panel of the National Diffusion Network.* Washington, DC: U.S. Department of Education.

Ekstrom, R. B., Goertz, M. E., Pollack, J. M., & Rock, D. A. (1986). Who will drop out of high school and why? *Teachers College Record, 87,* 356–373.

Elmore, R. F. (1996). Getting to scale with good educational practice. *Harvard Educational Review, 66,* 1–26.

Escamilla, K. (1994). Descubriendo La Lectura: An early intervention literacy program in Spanish. *Literacy, Teaching, and Learning, 1*(1), 57–70.

Fashola, O. S., & Slavin, R. E. (1997). Promising programs for elementary and middle schools: Evidence of effectiveness and replicability. *Journal of Education for Students Placed at Risk, 2*(3), 251–307.

Fashola, O. S., & Slavin, R. E. (1998). Effective dropout prevention and college attendance programs for students placed at risk. *Journal of Education for Students Placed at Risk, 3*(2), 159–183.

Finn, J. D. (1989). Withdrawing from school. *Review of Educational Research, 59,* 117–142.

Fleischman, H. L., & Hopstock, P. J. (1993). *Descriptive study of services to limited English proficient students.* Arlington, VA: Development Associates.

Freiberg, H. J. (1996). *Consistency management and cooperative discipline: A sample design.* Houston, TX: University of Houston.

Freiberg, H. J., & Huang, S. (1994). *Final report study 2.4: The longitudinal study of the life cycle of improving schools* (year ending October 31, 1993). Philadelphia, PA: National Center on Education in the Inner Cities.

Freiberg, H. J., Prokosch, N., & Treister, E. S., (1990). Turning around five at-risk elementary schools. *School Effectiveness and School Improvement, 1*(1), 5–25.

Freiberg, H. J., Stein, T. A., & Huang, S. (1995). Effects of a classroom management intervention on student achievement in inner-city elementary schools. *Educational Research and Evaluation, 1*(1), 36–66.

Gallegos, G. (1995). *Investing in the future: HOSTS evaluation for the Pasadena Independent School District.* Vancouver, WA: HOSTS Corporation.

Garcia, E. E. (1991). Bilingualism, second language acquisition, and the education of Chicano language minority students. In R. R. Valencia (Ed.), *Chicano school failure and success: Research and policy agendas for the 1990's* (pp. 31–49). New York: Falmer.

Garcia, E. E. (1994, April). *The impact of linguistic and cultural diversity on America's schools: A need for new policy.* Paper presented at the annual meeting of the American Educational Research Association, New Orleans.

General Accounting Office. (1994). *Hispanics' schooling: Risk factors for dropping out and barriers to resuming education.* Washington, DC: GAO.

Gersten, R. (1985). Direct instruction with special education students: A review of evaluation research. *Journal of Special Education, 19*(1), 41–58.

Glass, G. V., McGaw, B., & Smith, M. L. (1981). *Meta-analysis in social research.* Beverly Hills, CA: Sage.

Goldenberg, C., & Sullivan, J. (1995). *Making change happen: The search for coherence.* (Educational Practice Report 13). Santa Cruz, CA: National Center for Research on Cultural Diversity and Second Language Learning.

Gonzales, A. (1981). *An approach to interdependent/cooperative bilingual education measures related to social motives.* Fresno, CA: California State University at Fresno.

Gutierrez, K., Larson, J., & Kreuter, B. (1996). Constructing classrooms as communities of learners: Literacy learning as social practice. In P. Smagorinsky (Ed.), *Culture and literacy: Bridging the gap between community and classroom* (pp. 172–199). Urbana, IL: National Council of Teachers of English.

Hakuta, K., & Garcia, E. E. (1989). Bilingualism and education. *American Psychologist, 44,* 374–379.

Hartfiel, V. F., Hughey, J. B., Wormuth, D. R., & Jacobs, H. C. (1985). *Learning ESL composition.* Rowley, MA: Newberry House.

Haynes, N. M. (1991). *Summary of School Development Program documentation and research.* New Haven, CT: Yale Child Study Center.

Haynes, N. M. (Ed.). (1994). *School Development Program research monograph.* New Haven, CT: Yale Child Study Center.

Herman, R. (1999). *An educator's guide to schoolwide reform.* Arlington, VA: Educational Research Service.

Herman, R., & Stringfield, S. (1995, April). *Ten promising programs for educating disadvantaged students: Evidence of impact.* Paper presented at the annual meeting of the American Educational Research Association, San Francisco, CA.

Hertz-Lazarowitz, R., Lerner, M., & Schaedel, B. (1996). Story-related writing: An evaluation of CIRC in Israel. *Helkat-Lashon* [Journal of Linguistic Education, in Hebrew], *23,* 205–231.

Hillocks, G. (1984). What works in teaching composition: A meta-analysis of experimental treatment studies. *American Journal of Education, 93,* 133–170.

Hollins, E. R., Smiler, H., & Spencer, K. (1994). Benchmarks in meeting the challenges of effective schooling for African American youngsters. In E. R. Hollins, J. E. King, & W. C. Hayman (Eds.), *Teaching diverse populations: Formulating a knowledge base* (pp. 90–113). Albany: State University of New York Press.

Hopfenberg, W. S., & Levin, H. M. (1993). *The Accelerated Schools resource guide.* San Francisco, CA: Jossey-Bass.

HOSTS Corporation. (1994). *Independent evaluations of the HOSTS structured mentoring program in language arts.* Vancouver, WA: Author.

Howe, C. K. (1994). Improving the achievement of Hispanic students. *Educational Leadership, 51*(8), 42–44.

Huck, C. S., & Pinnell, G. S. (1986). *The Reading Recovery project in Columbus, Ohio: Pilot year, 1984–85.* Columbus, OH: Ohio State University.

Hughey, J. B., & Hartfiel, V. F. (1979). *Profile Approach to Writing.* College Station, TX: Profile Writing Program, Inc.

Hughey, J. B., Wormuth, D. R., Hartfiel, V. F, & Jacobs, H. L. (1985). *Teaching ESL composition: Principles and techniques.* Rowley, MA: Newberry House.

Jacobs, H. L., Zinkgraf, S. A., Wormuth, D. R., Hartfiel, V. F., & Hughey, J. B. (1981). *Testing ESL composition: A practical approach.* Rowley, MA: Newberry House.

Jiménez, R. T., García, G. E., & Pearson, P. D. (1995). Three children, two languages, and strategic reading: Case studies in bilingual/monolingual reading. *American Educational Research Journal, 32*(1), 67–97.

Johnson, D. W., & Johnson, R. T. (1994). *Learning together and alone: Cooperative, competitive, and individualistic learning* (4th ed.). Boston: Allyn & Bacon.

Johntz, W. F. (1966). Mathematics and the culturally disadvantaged. *Bulletin of the California Mathematics Council*, January.

Johntz, W. F. (1975). *Project SEED and its implications for mathematics education internationally: The teaching of algebra at the pre-college level.* St. Louis, MO: CEMREL.

Kagan, S. (1995). *Cooperative learning.* Boston, MA: Charlesbridge.

Kagan, S., Zahn, G. L., Widaman, K. F., Schwartzwald, J., & Tyrrell, G. (1985). Classroom structural bias: Impact of cooperative and competitive classroom structures on cooperative and competitive groups. In R. E. Slavin, S. Sharan, S. Kagan, R. Hertz-Lazarowitz, C. Webb, & R. Schmuck (Eds.), *Learning to cooperate, cooperating to learn* (pp. 277–312). New York: Plenum.

Karweit, N. L. (1989). Effective preschool programs for students at risk. In R. E. Slavin, N. L. Karweit, & N. A. Madden (Eds.), *Effective programs for students at risk* (pp. 75–102). Boston, MA: Allyn & Bacon.

Karweit, N. L. (1994). Can preschool alone prevent early reading failure? In R. E. Slavin, N. L. Karweit, & B. A. Wasik (Eds.), *Preventing early school failure* (pp. 58–77). Boston: Allyn & Bacon.

Kelly, P. R., Gomez-Valdez, C., Klein, A. F., & Neal, J. C. (1995, April). *Progress of first and second language learners in an early intervention program.* Paper presented at the annual meeting of the American Educational Research Association, San Francisco, CA.

Knapp, M. S., & Woolverton, S. (1995). Social class and schooling. In J. A. Banks & C. A. M. Banks (Eds.), *Handbook of research on multicultural education* (pp. 548–569). New York, NY: MacMillan.

Knight, S. L., & Stallings, J. A. (1995). The implementation of the Accelerated School model in an urban elementary school. In R. L. Allington & S. A. Walmsley (Eds.), *No quick fix: Rethinking literacy programs in America's elementary schools* (pp. 236–252). New York: Teachers College Press.

Leighton, M. S., Hightower, A. M., & Wrigley, P. G. (1995). *Model strategies in bilingual education: Professional development.* Washington, DC: U.S. Department of Education.

Levin, H. M. (1987). Accelerated schools for disadvantaged students. *Educational Leadership, 44*(6), 19–21.

Lloyd, D. N. (1978). Prediction of school failure from third-grade data. *Educational and Psychological Measurement, 38,* 1193–1200.

Losey, K. M. (1995). Mexican American students and classroom interaction: An overview and critique. *Review of Educational Research, 65,* 283–318.

Long, U. M. (1993). UIC-MWMI: A model middle grades mathematics reform project. *Mathematics Teacher, 86*(3).

Lucker, B., Rosenfield, D., Sikes, J., & Aronson, E. (1976). Performance in the independent classroom: A field study. *American Educational Research Journal, 13,* 115–123.

Lynch, S., & Mills, C. J. (1990). The skills reinforcement project: An academic program for high potential minority youth. *Journal for the Education of the Gifted, 13*(4), 364–79.

Madden, N. A., Slavin, R. E., Farnish, A. M., Livingston, M. A., Calderón, M., & Stevens, R. J. (1996). *Reading Wings: Teacher's manual.* Baltimore, MD: Johns Hopkins University, Center for Research on the Education of Students Placed at Risk.

Maneuvers With Mathematics. (1991). *Proposal submitted to the Program Effectiveness Panel of the National Diffusion Network.* Washington, DC: U.S. Department of Education.

Maneuvers With Mathematics. (1995). *Proposal submitted to the Program Effectiveness Panel of the National Diffusion Network.* Washington, DC: U.S. Department of Education.

Martinez, L. J. (1990). *The effect of cooperative learning on academic achievement and self-concept with bilingual third-grade students.* Unpublished doctoral thesis, United States International University.

Mattingly, R. M., & Van Sickle, R. L. (1991). Cooperative learning and achievement in social studies: Jigsaw II. *Social Education, 55*(6), 392–395.

McAdoo, M. (1998). Project GRAD's strength is in the sum of its parts. *Ford Foundation Report, 29*(2), 8–11.

McCarthy, J., & Still, S. (1993). Hollibrook Accelerated Elementary School. In J. Murphy & P. Hallinger (Eds.), *Restructuring schooling: Learning from ongoing efforts* (pp. 63–83). Newbury Park, CA: Corwin.

McGroarty, M. (1993). Cooperative learning and second language acquisition. In D. D. Holt (Ed.), *Cooperative learning: A response to cultural diversity* (pp. 61–80). Sacramento, CA: California State Department of Education.

McKey, R., Condelli, L., Ganson, H., Barrett, B., McConkey, C., & Plantz, M. (1985). *The impact of Head Start on children, families, and communities* (DHHS Publication No. (OHDS) 85-31193). Washington, DC: Department of Health and Human Services.

McLaughlin, M. W. (1990). The Rand Change Agent Study revisited: Macro perspectives and micro realities. *Educational Researcher, 19*(9), 11–16.

Meyer, L. A. (1984). Long-term academic effects of direct instruction project follow-through. *Elementary School Journal, 84,* 380–394.

Milk, R. D. (1993). Bilingual education and English as a second language: The elementary school. In M. B. Arias & U. Casanova (Eds.), *Bilingual education: Politics, practice and research.* Chicago: University of Chicago Press.

Mills, C. J. (1992). Reflections on recognition and development of academic talent in educationally disadvantaged students. *Exceptionality, 3,* 189–192.

Mills, C. J., Stork, E. J., & Krug, K. (1992). Recognition and development of academic talent in educationally disadvantaged students. *Exceptionality, 3,* 165–180.

Muncey, D. E., & McQuillan, P. J. (1993). Preliminary findings from a five-year study of the Coalition of Essential Schools. *Phi Delta Kappan, 74*(6), 486–489.

National Center for Education Statistics. (1993). *Dropout rates in the United States.* Washington, DC: U.S. Department of Education, NCES.

National Center for Education Statistics. (1994). *The condition of education, 1994.* Washington, DC: U.S. Department of Education, NCES.

National Center for Education Statistics. (1995). *The educational progress of Hispanic students.* Washington, DC: U.S. Department of Education, NCES.

National Diffusion Network. (1995). *Educational programs that work: The catalogue of the National Diffusion Network* (21st ed.). Longmont, CO: Sopris West.

Page, D. A. (1989). *The University of Illinois Arithmetic project: Teacher education materials.* Newton, MA: Education Development Center, Inc.

Palincsar, A. S., & Brown, A. L. (1984). Reciprocal teaching of comprehension fostering and comprehension-monitoring activities. *Cognition and Instruction, 2,* 117–175.

Phillips, H., & Ebrahimi, H. (1993). Equation for success: Project SEED. In G. Cuevas & M. Driscoll (Eds.), *Reaching all students with mathematics* (pp. 127–144). Reston, VA: National Council of Teachers of Mathematics.

Pinnell, G. S. (1988, April). *Sustained effects of a strategy-centered early intervention program in reading.* Paper presented at the annual meeting of the American Educational Research Association, New Orleans.

Pinnell, G. S. (1989). Reading Recovery: Helping at-risk children learn to read. *Elementary School Journal, 90,* 161–182.

Pinnell, G. S., DeFord, D. E., & Lyons, C. A. (1988). *Reading Recovery: Early intervention for at-risk first graders.* Arlington, VA: Education Research Service.

Pinnell, G. S., Lyons, C. A., DeFord, D. E., Bryk, A. S., & Seltzer, M. (1994). Comparing instructional models for the literacy education of high-risk first graders. *Reading Research Quarterly, 29,* 9–40.

Pinnell, G. S., Short, A. G., Lyons, C. A., & Young, P. (1986). *The Reading Recovery project in Columbus, Ohio, Year I: 1985–1986.* Columbus: Ohio State University.

Profile Approach To Writing. (1995). *Profile Approach to Writing: Submission to the Program Effectiveness Panel of the U.S. Department of Education.* Washington, DC: U.S. Department of Education.

Project SEED, Inc. (1995). *Project SEED: Submission to the Program Effectiveness Panel of the U.S. Department of Education.* Berkeley, CA, and Dallas, TX: Author.

Quellmalz, E. S. (1987). Developing reasoning skills. In J. R. Baron & R. J. Sternberg (Eds.), *Teaching thinking skills: Theory and practice* (pp. 207–231). New York: Freeman Press.

Quellmalz, E. S., & Hoskyn, J. A. (1988). Making a difference in Arkansas: The Multicultural Reading and Thinking Project. *Educational Leadership, 45*(7), 52–55.

Ramirez, J. D., Yuen, S. D., & Ramey, D. R. (1991). *Longitudinal study of structured English immersion strategy, early-exit and late-exit transitional bilingual education programs for language-minority children.* San Mateo, CA: Aguirre International.

Rand Corporation. (1978). *Volume VIII: Implementing and sustaining innovations.* Santa Monica, CA: Author.

Reid, E. M. (1989). *Exemplary center for reading instruction: Submission to the Program Effectiveness Panel of the U.S. Department of Education.* Washington, DC: U.S. Department of Education.

Rogers, M. R. (1993). *Increasing prevention of school failure by early intervention for school success of at-risk students kindergarten through grade three.* Practicum Report, Nova University, Tampa, Florida.

Rosenshine, B., & Meister, C. (1994, April). *A comparison of results with standardized tests and experimenter-developed comprehension tests when teaching cognitive strategies.* Paper presented at the annual meeting of the American Educational Research Association, New Orleans.

Rumberger, R. W. (1987). High school dropouts: A review of issues and evidence. *Review of Educational Research, 57,* 101–127.

Rumberger, R. W. (1995). Dropping out of middle school: A multilevel analysis of students and schools. *American Educational Research Journal, 32,* 583–625.

Schaedel, B., Hertz-Lazarowitz, R., Walk, A., Lerner, M., Juberan, S., & Sarid, M. (1996). The Israeli CIRC (ALASH): First year achievements in reading and comprehension. *Helkat-Lashon* (Journal of Linguistic Education, in Hebrew), *23,* 401–423.

Schweinhart, L. J., Barnes, H. V., Weikart, D. P., Barnett, W. S., & Epstein, A. S. (1993). *Significant benefits: The High Scope/Perry Preschool study through age 27.* Monographs of the High Scope Educational Research Foundation, 10. Ypsilanti, MI: High Scope Press.

Schweinhart, L. J., & Weikart, D. P. (1980). *Young children grow up: The effects of the Perry Preschool program on youths through age 15.* Ypsilanti, MI: High Scope Educational Research Foundation.

Schweinhart, L. J., Weikart, D. P., & Larner, M. B. (1986a) Consequences of three preschool curriculum models through age 15. *Early Childhood Research Quarterly, 1,* 15–45.

Schweinhart, L. J., Weikart, D. P., & Larner, M. B. (1986b). Child-initiated activities in early childhood programs may help prevent delinquency. *Early Childhood Research Quarterly, 1,* 303–312.

Shanahan, T., & Barr, R. (1995). *Reading Recovery: An independent evaluation of an early instructional intervention for at risk learners.* Chicago: University of Illinois at Chicago.

Sharan, S., & Shachar, H. (1988). *Language and learning in the cooperative classroom.* New York: Springer.

Sharan, Y., & Sharan, S. (1992). *Expanding cooperative learning through group investigation.* New York: Teachers College Press.

Skills Reinforcement Project. (1984). *Developing mathematical talent in minority and disadvantaged students.* Baltimore, MD: Johns Hopkins University, Center for Talented Youth.

Skills Reinforcement Project. (1992). *Proposal submitted to the Program Effectiveness Panel of the National Diffusion Network.* Washington, DC: U.S. Department of Education.

Skills Reinforcement Project. (1995). *Program description.* Baltimore, MD: Johns Hopkins University, Center for Talented Youth (CTY).

Slavin, R. E. (1990, April). *Cooperative learning and language minority students.* Paper presented at the annual meeting of the American Educational Research Association, Boston.

Slavin, R. E. (1994). *Using Student Team Learning* (4th ed.). Baltimore, MD: Johns Hopkins University, Center for Social Organization of Schools.

Slavin, R. E. (1995). *Cooperative learning: Theory, research, and practice* (2nd ed.). Boston: Allyn & Bacon.

Slavin, R. E., & Fashola, O. S. (1998). *Show me the evidence: Proven and promising programs for America's schools.* Thousand Oaks, CA: Corwin.

Slavin, R. E., & Madden, N. A. (1991). Modifying Chapter 1 program improvement guidelines to reward appropriate practices. *Educational Evaluation and Policy Analysis, 13,* 369–379.

Slavin, R. E., & Madden, N. A. (1995, April). *Effects of Success for All on the achievement of English language learners.* Paper presented at the annual meeting of the American Educational Research Association, San Francisco, CA.

Slavin, R. E., & Madden, N. A. (1999). Effects of bilingual and English as a second language adaptations of Success for All on the reading achievement of students acquiring English. *Journal of Education for Students Placed at Risk, 4*(4), 393–416.

Slavin, R. E., & Madden, N. A. (in press a). Roots & Wings: Effects of whole-school reform on student achievement. *Journal of Education for Students Placed at Risk.*

Slavin, R. E., & Madden, N. A. (in press b). *One million children: Success for All.* Thousand Oaks, CA: Corwin.

Slavin, R. E., Madden, N. A., Dolan, L. J., & Wasik, B. A. (1996). *Every child, every school: Success for All.* Newberry Park, CA: Corwin.

Stein, M. K., Leinhardt, G., & Bickel, W. (1989). Instructional issues for teaching students at risk. In R. E. Slavin, N. L. Karweit, & N. A. Madden (Eds.), *Effective programs for students at risk* (pp. 145–194). Boston: Allyn & Bacon.

Stevens, R. J., & Durkin, S. (1992). *Using Student Team Reading and Student Team Writing in middle schools: Two evaluations* (Report No. 36). Baltimore, MD: Johns Hopkins University, Center for Research on Effective Schooling for Disadvantaged Students.

Stevens, R. J., Madden, N. A., Slavin, R. E., & Farnish, A. M. (1987). Cooperative Integrated Reading and Composition: Two field experiments. *Reading Research Quarterly, 22*, 433–454.

Stevens, R. J., & Slavin, R. E. (1995). Effects of a cooperative approach in reading and writing on academically handicapped and nonhandicapped students. *Elementary School Journal, 95*(3), 241–262.

Stevens, R. J., Slavin, R. E., & Farnish, A. M. (1991). The effects of cooperative learning and direct instruction in reading comprehension strategies on main idea identification. *Journal of Educational Psychology, 83*(1), 8–16.

Stevenson, B. J. (1982). *An analysis of the relationship of student-student consultation to academic performance in differential classroom settings.* Unpublished doctoral dissertation, Stanford University.

Stringfield, S., & Herman, R. (1995, April). *The effects of promising programs on students: Results from the Special Strategies study.* Paper presented at the annual meeting of the American Educational Research Association, San Francisco, CA.

Tomblin, E. A., & Davis, B. R. (1985). *Technical report of the evaluation of the race/human relations program: A study of cooperative learning environment strategies.* San Diego, CA: San Diego City Schools.

U.S. Department of Education. (1992). *The condition of bilingual education in the nation.* Washington, DC: Author.

Vasquez, J. A. (1993). Teaching to the distinctive traits of minority students. In K. M. Cauley, F. Linder, & J. H. McMillan (Eds.), *Annual editions: Educational Psychology 93/94* (pp. 122–126). Guilford, CT: Dushkin.

Villaseñor, J. R. A., & Kepner, H. S. (1993). Arithmetic from a problem solving perspective: An urban implementation. *American Educational Research Journal, 21*(1), 62–69.

Wasik, B. A., & Slavin, R. E. (1993). Preventing early reading failure with one-to-one tutoring: A review of five programs. *Reading Research Quarterly, 28*, 178–200.

Webster, W. J. (1992). *The Evaluation of Project SEED 1990–1991* (EPS91-043-2). Dallas, TX: Dallas Independent School District.

Webster, W. J. (1995). *Executive summary: The evaluation of Project SEED 1991–1994.* Detroit, MI: Detroit Public Schools.

Webster, W. J., & Chadbourn, R. A. (1992). *The evaluation of Project SEED.* Dallas, TX: Dallas Independent School District.

Weikart, D. P., Rogers, L., Adcock, C., & McClelland, D. (1971). *The cognitively oriented curriculum: A framework for preschool teachers*. Urbana: University of Illinois.

Wilbur, J. (1995). A gift of time: HOSTS: Help One Student To Succeed. *Partnerships in Education Journal*, 9(3), 1–5.

Willig, A. C. (1985). A meta-analysis of selected studies on the effectiveness of bilingual education. *Review of Educational Research, 55*, 269–317.

Wong-Filmore L., & Valdez, C. (1986). Teaching bilingual learners. In M. C. Wittrock (Ed.), *Handbook of research on teaching* (3rd ed., pp.   ). New York: Macmillan.

Ziegler, S. (1981). The effectiveness of cooperative learning teams for increasing cross-ethnic friendship: Additional evidence. *Human Organization, 40*(3), 264–268.

Zigler, E., & Muenchow, S. (1992). *Head Start: The inside story of America's most successful educational experiment*. New York: Basic Books.

Zigler, E., & Valentine, J. (Eds.) (1979). *Project Head Start: A legacy of the war on poverty*. New York: Free Press.

2

Effective Dropout Prevention and College Attendance Programs for Latino Students

Olatokunbo S. Fashola
Robert E. Slavin
Johns Hopkins University

A high school diploma is the minimum qualification for full participation in the U.S. economy. A worker without one can find work in only the most menial of occupations. The factory jobs that once allowed workers to make good incomes without a high school degree are diminishing, and the educational requirements for jobs in general are increasing. High school dropouts are seriously at risk. For example, they are four times more likely than high school graduates to be on welfare; in 1996, 27% of dropouts, but only 6% of high school graduates who did not attend college, were on welfare (Educational Testing Service [ETS], 1996; National Center for Educational Statistics [NCES], 1996). Unemployment for workers over age 19 years is twice as high for dropouts than for graduates (NCES, 1995; Rumberger, 1987; Stern, Paik, Caterall, & Nakata, 1989).

For most segments of the U.S. population, high school graduation rates have been steadily increasing over the past two decades. Between 1972 and 1994, the White, non-Latino dropout rate (individuals ages 16–24 years out of school without a degree) has diminished by more than a third, from 12.3% to 7.7%. The African American dropout rate has diminished by more than 40%, from 21.3% to 12.6%. Yet the dropout rate among Latino students has always been high and has only slightly diminished. It was 34.3% in 1972, and 30.0% in 1994 (NCES, 1993, 1996).

Why has the dropout rate among Latino students remained so high? Poverty is one explanation; dropout rates are strongly correlated with parents' socioeconomic status (NCES, 1996). Yet although the socioeconomic status of Latino families is similar to that of African Americans, Latinos' dropout rates are now 2½ times higher than those for African Americans, whose dropout rate is diminishing. Dropout rates for low-income Latinos are almost twice as high as for other low-income students, and among middle-income Latino students dropout rates are more than twice as high as that for other middle-income students. In fact, the dropout rate for middle-income Latinos (23.9%) is about the same as that for low-income African Americans (24.5%) (NCES, 1995).

Recent immigration is another factor in high dropout rates for Latino students. Foreign-born Latinos are far more likely than other students to drop out (43%). Dropout rates for first-generation (17%) and second-generation (24%) Latino students are still higher than those for all African Americans (13%) and Whites (8%). Language is another potential explanation, as students with limited English proficiency are more likely than others to drop out (Rumberger & Larson, 1995; Steinberg, Blinde, & Chan, 1984). Yet the high dropout rates (24%) for second-generation Latinos, who are presumably proficient in English, indicate that other factors must be at work. Fully English proficient Latino students also perform significantly below national norms (McArthur, 1993).

Low achievement is clearly a precursor of dropout, and Latino students do perform below national averages on most skills at all grade levels. However, test scores for Latino students are similar to those of African Americans, and their dropout rates are much higher.

It is important to note that dropout rates are not the same for all Latino subgroups. Mexican American, Central American, Puerto Rican, and Dominican students have high dropout rates, whereas rates for students from Cuba and South America are closer to national averages (General Accounting Office, 1994).

The causes of the high dropout rate among Latinos are certainly complex. The individual factors that lead to dropouts among Latinos are similar to those for other groups: low achievement and disaffection with school, a desire to begin work early, and (for girls) early pregnancy (Fernández & Velez, 1989; Romo & Falbo, 1996). At the group level, some combination of problems with poverty, language, and recent immigration status probably interacts with factors relating to the poorly funded, overburdened, and insensitive schools that many Latinos in barrios and poor rural areas must attend (Mehan, 1996; Orfield & Monfort, 1988; Rumberger, 1995; Velez, 1989).

Whatever the precise reasons for Latino dropout may be, it is clear that this situation is intolerable. To have a segment of our population leaving school in such large numbers is an indictment of our schools and our society. Furthermore, this segment is rapidly growing; Latinos were only 6% of the U.S. population as recently as 1980, have increased to 9% today, and are projected to be almost a quarter of the U.S. population by 2050.

Although it is obviously important to understand the causes and consequences of the Latino dropout rate, we cannot wait until the problem is completely understood to begin solving it. Over the past 10 years a number of programs designed to affect dropout rates and related outcomes have been implemented and evaluated in middle and high schools serving many Latino students. Collectively, these studies show that schools can make a dramatic difference in the dropout rates, school success, and college enrollment rates of at-risk Latino youth.

The purpose of this chapter is to review research on programs of this kind. In the previous chapter, we reviewed evaluations of elementary and middle school programs capable of enhancing the achievement of Latino students. Increasing student achievement and other indicators of school success is certainly one way of reducing dropout rates (see Ekstrom, Goertz, Pollack, & Rock, 1986; Finn, 1989). However, even with the best preventive programs, many students will still be at risk for dropping out, and many will fail to achieve their full potential. Interventions are needed in secondary schools to increase the chances that students will stay in school, complete their high school degrees, and make a successful transition to postsecondary studies or to the workforce.

DROPOUT PREVENTION APPROACHES

The prevention of dropping out among students in general has been a high priority since the 1950s, when high school graduation first became a goal for all students. A wide range of programs has been implemented and evaluated in schools to reduce dropout rates. Increasingly, dropout prevention programs are explicitly focusing on increasing college attendance, as well as achievement and other outcomes.

There are many quite different approaches to dropout prevention, which are often used in combination or with different subgroups in the same schools. One approach is primary prevention, providing students with high-quality elementary and middle school experiences to deal with the key precursors to dropout: low achievement, retention in grade, dislike of school, and related outcomes (see Fashola, Slavin, Calderón, & Durán, 1996). Of course, improving student performance is of value in its own right, but as a dropout prevention strategy, increasing school success at all levels is obviously important. Increasing the quality and attractiveness of the secondary curriculum is another obvious approach to dropout prevention. Secondary whole-school reforms intended to improve the achievement and social development of adolescents would be expected to affect dropout rates as well.

Other approaches to dropout prevention focus on identifying key hurdles to school success and helping students over them. For example, many approaches provide individual or small-group tutoring to help students pass courses, especially such critical "gatekeeper" courses as algebra and English. After-school, summer-school, and Saturday programs are often provided to help students make it through their coursework (see, e.g., Fashola, 1998; Rumberger & Larson, 1994). Recognizing the strong correlation between truancy and dropout, many programs also focus on increasing student attendance.

A recurrent theme in many dropout prevention programs is the importance of personalizing the high school experience for at-risk students, with an expectation that increasing attachments to valued adults in the school or giving students high-status roles in the school will reduce disaffection and dropout. Various mentoring or counseling programs are built around this theme, as is the approach taken in at least a few programs of engaging young adolescents in prosocial activities such as tutoring younger children or volunteering in nursing homes.

Another theme in many dropout prevention programs is giving students a sense of purpose for completing school, in essence making the long-term consequences of high school completion and college attendance more apparent on a day-to-day basis. For example, many dropout prevention programs have a strong link to vocational education, part-time job placements, and internships in local businesses, both to maintain students' interests in school and to give them a clear picture of what life after school might be like and how a diploma helps in the real world (see Hayward & Tallmadge, 1995). Similarly, many programs designed to increase college attendance, including the widely used Upward Bound model, place students on college campuses during the summer to give them a realistic idea of what college life is like and a more concrete experience of a potential future. An important variant of this approach involves providing college scholarships to students who meet certain standards of performance in high school.

Related to dropout prevention strategies are reentry or recovery programs, in which dropouts are encouraged to reenter high school or, more often, to attend special evening or weekend programs to enable them to finish their high school degree while they are working full time. GED programs are of course a variation on this theme.

Dropout prevention programs for Latino students are not very different from those for students in general. Accommodations are often made for Latino culture and for the language difficulties of students who are recent immigrants, but the great majority of Latino high school students are fully proficient in English. Although this review primarily focuses on programs that have been researched and/or widely disseminated among Latino students, it is probably the case that effective dropout prevention programs for non-Latino students are likely to be effective for Latino students who are similar in other ways.

FOCUS OF THE REVIEW

The focus of this review is on the identification of programs that have been shown to have a significant impact on dropouts, college attendance, school performance, or related outcomes in rigorous evaluations, that are replicable across a broad range of secondary schools, and that have been successfully evaluated among or at least frequently applied to schools serving many Latino students. There are many articles and books on the general principles of effective practice for Latino students and for bilingual education (e.g., Council of Chief State School Officers, 1990; Durán, 1994a, 1994b; Howe, 1994; Leighton, Hightower, & Wrigley, 1995; Losey, 1995; Vasquez, 1993) and descriptions of outstanding secondary schools for Latino or bilingual students (e.g., Lockwood, 1996). This book contains several chapters on these topics. However, the focus of this chapter is on specific strategies that schools could select to improve outcomes for Latino students. Other compendia list promising programs (e.g., Leighton et al., 1995; National Diffusion Network, 1995), but unlike these, this chapter applies consistent standards to evaluate the likely effectiveness and replicability of programs available to educators committed to transforming secondary schools and classrooms to meet the needs of Latino students.

The criteria applied in this review are similar to those used in chapter 1, which reviews effective elementary and middle school programs for Latino students. They are described next.

Effectiveness

Programs were considered to be effective if evaluations compared students who participated in the program to similar students in matched comparison or control schools and found the program students to perform significantly better on fair measures of dropout, college attendance, or related measures of school success. Such evaluations were required to demonstrate that experimental and control students were initially equivalent on measures of academic performance, language proficiency, socioeconomic status, and other measures, and were similar in other ways.

Replicability

The best evidence that a program is replicable in other schools is an indication that it has in fact been replicated elsewhere, especially if there is evidence that the program was evaluated and found to be effective in sites beyond its initial pilot locations. The existence of an active dissemination effort is also a strong indication of replicability. Programs are considered low in replicability if they have been used in a small number of schools and appear to depend on conditions (e.g., charismatic principals, magnet schools, extraordinary resources) unlikely to exist on a significant scale elsewhere.

Evaluation or Application with Latino Students

Ideally, the programs emphasized in this review are ones that have been successfully evaluated in schools serving many Latino students. However, programs known to be effective with non-Latino populations were included if they had strong evidence of effectiveness and replicability and had been disseminated to schools with many Latino students, even if the reported evaluations did not include Latino students.

LITERATURE SEARCH PROCEDURES

The broadest possible search was carried out for programs that had been evaluated and/or applied to Latino students. In addition to searches of the ERIC system and of education journals, we obtained reports on promising programs listed by the National Diffusion Network (NDN) and by Title VII grantees. Until its funding was phased out in 1996, the NDN was a part of the U.S. Department of Education that identified promising programs, disseminated information about them through a system of state facilitators, and provided "developer/disseminator" grants to help developers prepare their products for dissemination and then to carry out a dissemination plan. To be listed by NDN, a program had to present evidence of effectiveness to a Program Effectiveness Panel (PEP), or formerly to the Joint Dissemination Review Panel (JDRP). PEP or JDRP panel members reviewed the data for educationally significant effects.

However, the evaluation requirements for PEP/JDRP were low, and more than 500 programs of all kinds were approved, mostly on the basis of pre–post NCE-gain designs.

SELECTION FOR REVIEW

Ideally, programs emphasized in this review would be those that were specifically designed for use with Latino students, present rigorous evaluation evidence in comparison to control groups showing significant and lasting impacts on dropout or related outcomes for Latino students, have active dissemination programs that have implemented the program in many schools serving Latino students, and have evidence of effectiveness in dissemination sites, ideally from studies conducted by third parties. To require all of these conditions would overly limit this review. To include a much broader range of programs, we have had to compromise on one or more criteria. For example, we have included programs with excellent data that show positive effects for Latino students even if such a program has not been widely replicated (as long as there is no obvious reason it could not be replicated). We have included programs with excellent outcome data and evidence of replicability with non-Latino students if such a program has been replicated in areas with large Latino populations. We have included programs with shakier evidence of effectiveness if they are particularly well known, widely replicated, and appropriate to the needs of Latino students. In other words, our listing a program in this review is not necessarily a statement that we believe the program to be highly effective, replicable, and uniquely adapted to the needs of Latino students. Instead, it is an indication that among many dropout prevention programs we could have mentioned, these were the ones we felt to be most appropriate to be considered by secondary schools serving many Latino students. Later in this chapter, Table 2.1 summarizes the degree to which each program reviewed meets our ideal criteria. We have tried to present the evidence that school and district staff would need to begin a process leading to an informed choice from among effective and promising programs capable of being replicated in their settings.

PROGRAM TYPES

Six programs met the inclusion criteria included in this review. These programs (as well as many others that did not meet our standards) fall into two major categories. The first is programs designed to work with the most at-risk students in middle, junior high, or high school to keep them from dropping out. The second category is programs designed to increase the college attendance rates (or college eligibility) of students who may show promise but are at risk of not fulfilling their promise. The college attendance programs also emphasize dropout prevention as a goal, and programs designed strictly as dropout prevention models often report college attendance or eligibility as a valued outcome, but there is a clear distinction in practice between the two types of programs in terms of their emphasis on helping students to take and pass courses that lead to college, familiarizing students with college, assisting students with financial aid applications, and in at least one case (Project GRAD) actually providing college scholarships. In addition to the programs that did meet our evaluation criteria, we also discuss a few additional programs that did not, but that are nonetheless of interest.

DROPOUT PREVENTION PROGRAMS

Two programs primarily designed to increase the high school graduation rates of at-risk Latino students met the standards of this review: the Coca-Cola Valued Youth Program (VYP) and ALAS (Achievement for Latinos through Academic Success).

The Coca-Cola Valued Youth Program

The Coca-Cola Valued Youth Program (1991) is a cross-age tutoring program designed to increase the self-esteem and school success of at-risk middle and high school students by placing them in positions of responsibility as tutors of younger elementary school students. The Valued Youth Program was originally developed by the Intercultural Development Research Association (IDRA) in San Antonio, Texas. The original implementation of the program was funded by Coca-Cola and implemented in collaboration with five school districts in San Antonio between 1984 and 1988, with approximately 525 high school tutors and 1,575 elementary tutees.

The overall goal of the program is to reduce the dropout rates of at-risk students by improving their self-concepts and academic skills. This is done by making them tutors and providing assistance with basic academic skills. The program also emphasizes elimination of nonacademic and disciplinary factors that contribute to dropping out. For example, it attempts to develop student sense of self-control, decrease student truancy, and reduce disciplinary referrals. It also seeks to form home–school partnerships to increase the level of support available to students.

The first goals of improvement of academic skills are met when students agree to serve as tutors. The tutors are required to enroll in a special tutoring class, which allows them to improve their own basic academic skills as well as their tutoring skills. The students who are involved as tutors are paid a minimum wage stipend. The tutors work with three elementary students at a time for a total of about 4 hours per week. They are taught to develop self-awareness and pride, which is expected to make them less likely to exhibit disciplinary problems.

Functions are held to honor and recognize the tutors as role models. They receive T-shirts, caps, and certificates of merit for their efforts.

The main evaluation of the Coca-Cola Valued Youth Program compared 63 VYP tutors to 70 students in a comparison group (Cardenas, Montecel, Supik, & Harris, 1992). The students in four San Antonio schools were matched on the basis of age, ethnicity, lunch eligibility, percentage of students retained in grade, and scores on tests of reading, quality of school life, and self-concept. They were selected (not randomly) into the experimental group based on scheduling and availability, and then the remaining students were placed into the comparison group. Nearly all students in both groups were Latino and limited English proficient (LEP). The control students were somewhat less likely to qualify for free lunch or to have been retained in grade.

Two years after the program began, 12% of the comparison students but only 1% of the VYP students had dropped out. Reading grades were significantly higher for the VYP group, as were scores on a self-esteem measure and on a measure of attitude toward school.

The VYP has been widely replicated throughout the Southwest and elsewhere. In 1990, additional funding was provided by Coca-Cola for sites in California, Florida, New York, and Texas, and the program is now being extended to schools in Idaho, Oregon, and Montana and other schools across the country. Currently, the program is implemented in more than 157 schools in 16 cities across the United States, Puerto Rico, Great Britain, and Brazil. In the 1998–1999 school year, over 3,000 students participated as tutors or tutees.

ALAS

Achievement for Latinos through Academic Success (ALAS; Larson & Rumberger, 1995) is a dropout prevention program for high-risk middle or junior high school Latino students, particularly Mexican American students from high-poverty neighborhoods. This program focused on youth with learning and emotional/behavioral disabilities using a collaborative approach across multiple spheres of influence: home, school, and community. Students served in the program came from primarily Latino Los Angeles communities with high rates of crime, drug use, and gang activity.

The intervention addressed three major forces that influence the life of the adolescent: family, community, and school. Students were provided with social problem solving training, counseling, and recognition for academic excellence. School strategies included remediating the students' deficient social and task-related problem solving skills, maintaining intensive attendance monitoring, providing recognition and bonding activities for the participants, and providing frequent teacher feedback to the parent and the student. Family strategies included use of community resources, parent training in school participation, and training to guide and monitor adolescents. Parents were offered workshops on school participation and teen behavior management. The program also focused on integrating school and home needs with community services, and advocating for the student and parent when necessary. Community strategies included enhancement of collaboration among community agencies for youth and family services, and enhancement of skills and methods for serving the youth and family.

ALAS was evaluated in a junior high school that was 96% Latino, 2% Anglo, and 2% African American, with 70% of the students in the school participating in the school lunch program. Of the cohort of students who entered the seventh grade in 1990, 62% spoke English as a first language, 60% remained in school for Grades 7, 8, and 9, and only 65% of these students had earned enough high school credits in the ninth grade.

ALAS served the most at-risk students in the school. Students who fit this category were identified in one of two ways. One group of students had had an active Individual Education Plan (IEP) from sixth grade, identifying them as learning disabled or severely emotionally disabled using state and federal guidelines. These students are referred to as the Special Education (SE) group. Students with IEPs who entered the seventh grade during fall of 1990 (the first year of implementation) were placed in special education treatment group 1 (SE1, $n = 33$). Students with IEPs who entered the seventh grade during fall of 1991 (the second year of implementation) were placed in special education treatment group 2 (SE2, $n = 44$). Students with IEPs who entered the seventh grade during the third year of the study were placed in the special education control group (SEC, $n = 55$).

Students in the second category were those who were not formally identified for special education but who exhibited characteristics that placed them at risk for dropping out of school. These students were identified using a 6-item teacher rating scale that evaluated students' level of functioning based upon level of motivation, academic potential, grades, social interaction skill, difficulty to teach, and need for special education services. Students in this group were classified as high risk (HR) if they rated below average on four or more of the six categories. Students who spoke no English were excluded from the study. Students who qualified as high risk were randomly assigned to one of two groups. The first group of at-risk students consisted of the high-risk seventh-grade students who entered the seventh grade in the fall of 1990 and received the ALAS treatment (HRT, $n = 46$). The second group consisted of the high-risk seventh-grade students who did not receive the ALAS treatment but served as a control group (HRC, $n = 48$). A low-risk group was also assessed to provide an additional point of comparison. This group of students fit the demographic descriptions of students receiving ALAS.

The full impact of the program was not supposed to have taken effect until the children had been in the program for at least 2 years. Results were reported at the end of the 9th grade, and follow-up assessment was done at the end of the 11th grade.

In this study, "dropout" was defined as not being enrolled in school during the last 20 days of ninth grade, with no requests for student records from another school. Among the special education samples, the second cohort (SE2) had the lowest dropout rate (2%). This was significantly lower than the other two groups. The first special education cohort (SE1) experienced a 12% dropout rate, and although this was less than the dropout rate for the special education control group (16%), the difference was not statistically significant.

Among the high-risk groups, the ALAS students had a much lower dropout rate (2.2%) than the high-risk control group (16.7%). The rate for the high-risk treatment group was even lower than that for the low-risk comparison group (5.1%). In summary, the ALAS program worked well for the students in the treatment groups, and especially well for students in the second special education cohort and the high-risk group. The attrition rates (dropouts plus transfers to other schools) were also lower for the treatment groups than they were for the control groups.

Another variable measured was the number of high school credits earned by the students in the various groups, defined as accumulating enough units by the end of the ninth grade (including summer) to be on track to graduate from high school in 4 or 5 years.

Among the special education cohorts, 54% of the first cohort and 70% of the second cohort had accumulated enough units to graduate, compared to 30% of the special education control group. More of the low-risk students (70%) earned their high school credits than any of the at-risk groups. More of the high-risk treatment students (56%) than the high-risk control students (45%) had enough credits.

ALAS also measured recovery rates as the percentage of students who left the school who then returned. This was another measure of the "holding power" of the ALAS program. Students with the highest recovery rates were those in the treatment groups. Special education cohort 1 (SE1) had a 47% recovery rate, whereas special education cohort 2 (SE2) had a 33% recovery rate. The special education control group had a 4% recovery rate. The high-risk treatment group (HRT) had a 41% recovery rate, the high-risk control group had a 4% recovery rate, and the low-risk control group had a 21% recovery rate.

Attendance was measured as the percent of students absent more than 25% of the time. Among the special education groups, SE1 had slightly fewer students with many absences (40%) than the SEC (43%), but this difference was not significant. The second special education cohort had significantly fewer students with many absences (19%) than either of the other special education groups. The high-risk treatment group had a lower (15%) absenteeism rate than the high-risk control group (38%).

Another measure of academic progress was the percentage of F grades received by the students in six classes in all of the groups. At the end of the ninth grade, the smallest average percentage of failures occurred among the SE2 group (7.3%), followed closely by the SE1 students (8.25%), and then the high-risk treatment group (8.62%). The two control groups had substantially higher numbers of failures (19.24% for HRC and 20.25% for SEC).

In summary, the groups that benefited the most from ALAS through the end of the ninth grade were the special education second cohort and the high-risk treatment group.

A long-term evaluation of some of the study variables was also done on the initial ALAS cohorts, including the special education cohort 1 (SE1), the high-risk treatment cohort (HRT), the high-risk control group (HRC), and the low-risk control group (LRC).

The first variable followed was the number of high school credits earned by the students. By the 11th grade, although students in the two treatment groups (SE1 and HRT) had more credits than those in the high-risk control group, this difference was not significant, and all had fewer credits than the low-risk control group. Comparing the high-risk treatment and the high-risk control students in terms of whether they had sufficient credits to graduate in 1 or 2 years, the high-risk treatment group had more students qualifying in both cases (33% compared to 25.9% were on track to graduate in no more than 1 year, and 66.7% compared to 51.9% were on track to graduate in no more than 2 years). However, the differences between the two groups were not significant.

ALAS has not been disseminated beyond its pilot sites, but provides one effective and well-evaluated model for increasing the school successes and persistence of at-risk Latino students.

COLLEGE ATTENDANCE PROGRAMS

Four programs designed to increase the college attendance rates of Latino students met the standards of this review: Upward Bound, SCORE, AVID, and GRAD. In each of these, reducing dropout and increasing academic achievement (among other outcomes) were also important program goals, but these programs are distinctive in their focus on ensuring that promising Latino and other minority students do what is necessary to attend college.

Upward Bound

The U.S. Department of Education administers a set of six college entrance programs whose main goal is to increase the number of first-generation low socioeconomic status (SES) students attending college by providing them with academic skills and additional resources that they may need in order to make them college eligible. The programs, collectively referred to as TRIO, include Upward Bound, Talent Search, Student Support Services, Educational Opportunity Centers, Training Program for Special Services Staff and Leadership Personnel, and the Ronald McNair Post-Baccaulaureate Achievement program.

Upward Bound is the oldest and largest of the TRIO programs, and it has been evaluated the most thoroughly. Upward Bound targets 13- to 19-year-old students whose family income is under 150% of the poverty level, and/or students who are potential first-generation college students. To be eligible for Upward Bound, students must have completed the eighth grade, met the socioeconomic criteria, and plan to attend college. Students are usually recommended into the program by a guidance or academic counselor. Students with behavioral and emotional problems are usually screened out of the pool of applicants.

Once enrolled in Upward Bound, students are provided extra instruction, usually after school and on Saturdays, in mathematics, laboratory science, foreign language, English, and composition, and are also provided with instruction in study skills, academic or personal counseling, exposure to cultural events, tutorial services, information about financial assistance opportunities in college, and advice on a range of career options. Students are also provided with an intensive 6-week summer academic residential or nonresidential program at a college campus.

The first comprehensive evaluation of Upward Bound (UB) was done by Burkheimer, Riccobono, and Wisenbaker (1979). This evaluation investigated the high school retention rates of UB students, the rate of entry of UB students into postsecondary institutions, and Upward Bound's effectiveness in helping students to attain skills and motivation necessary for postsecondary success.

The experimental design consisted of matched comparison groups, comparing 3,710 UB students and 2,340 comparison students in the 10th, 11th, and 12th grades who attended the same schools. Students in the two groups were matched on grade level, ethnicity, low-income status, and academic risk status. Data were collected using questionnaires, interviews, and student records.

Based on fall-to-spring high school continuance rates, UB participants remained in high school at a rate slightly higher than that of the comparison group students. The difference was significant in the 10th and 11th grades, but not 12th. Evidence also suggested that the longer the students were involved in the program, the higher was their rate of school continuance. Fall-to-fall high school continuance rates were lower for both groups, but the UB students still showed a higher continuation rate in Grade 10, but not in Grade 11 or 12.

The UB students entered institutions of postsecondary education (PSE) at a higher rate than the comparison students. UB had a greater percentage of high school graduates who were eligible to attend college (71%) than did the comparison group (47%), and 65% of the college-eligible UB students attended PSE institutions versus 43% of the control group.

UB students involved in the program the longest benefited the most from the program. Students who had participated in UB for 3 years had a 78% college attendance rate; those who had participated in UB for 2 years had a 69% college attendance rate; and those who had participated for 1 year had a 68% college attendance rate.

The most recent evaluation of Upward Bound was done by Mathematica Policy Research, Inc. (Myers & Schirm, 1999). This evaluation produced an initial report focusing on the short-term academic impact of UB on students. Secondary questions answered by the evaluation included the length of students' participation in UB, attrition rates in UB, reasons for leaving the program, what types of students benefited from UB services, and the types of services provided by UB.

A pool of potential participants was collected by asking students across the country to complete UB applications and also to complete a questionnaire that asked about family background, attitudes and expectations, and school experiences. A follow-up survey updated their school-related experiences, attitudes, and expectations. Data from high school transcripts were also used in the selection process. Eligible participants from 67 sites participating in UB were then selected and randomly assigned to an Upward Bound group (1,481 students) or a control group (1,266 students).

Overall, the students in this study were mostly female (70%) and African American (53%). Latinos (25%) made up 25% of the sample; other participants included Caucasian (20%), Asian (5%), and Native American (5%) students.

Of the students invited to participate in Upward Bound, 18% chose not to join. Many students did not participate in the program because they had taken jobs, had problems with transportation or family issues, or had time conflicts. Latino and Asian students were more likely to participate when invited than were African American students, and younger students were also more likely to participate than were older students.

Of the students who joined the program, about 35% left during the first year and 55% were estimated to have dropped out by senior year. Students who planned to complete less than a baccalaureate degree were more likely to drop out of the program, as were students who took jobs. African American students were more likely to leave UB than members of other ethnic groups.

Analyses of UB showed that the UB participants earned more academic credits in math and social studies than the control group. Of the students who remained in the study, UB participants received considerably more academic preparation and support for college than did students in the control group. They were also more likely to take courses such as English, mathematics, and science. Overall, Upward Bound had no significant impacts on students' in-school behavior, grade-point averages, or credits earned in English or science, and it did not reduce dropout rates. However, for Latino students, UB did have a positive effect on dropout, credits earned, and enrollment in 4-year colleges (discussed later).

As in the previous study (Burkheimer et al., 1979), length of time in the program was an important factor. Participants who had been involved in UB for more than 2 years earned more credits in high school than did other students and were significantly more likely to go to 4-year colleges.

The impact of UB was greater for Latino and White students than for African Americans. Latino and White UB participants increased their academic coursework by 2 credits each year; African American students increased their academic loads by less than 0.5 credits. Latino and White students in UB had lower dropout rates than corresponding control students, but this was not true for African Americans. Latinos and Whites who participated in UB were significantly more likely than controls to attend 4-year colleges.

Overall, one of the main limitations of this study was the UB attrition problem (which the program acknowledges). As noted earlier, 18% of the students selected did not enter the program, and another 55% of those who entered dropped out of it. This means that of the students evaluated, only about 27% of the students received the entire 4-year program.

Another limitation of the study is its difficulty in identifying a truly untreated control group. Some of the control group students may still have had access to the same or similar types of services as the UB students. The authors state that more than 40% of the students in the control group received similar services, such as Talent Search (which is another TRIO program).

Although Upward Bound is funded federally, it is operated at local public and private institutions of higher education, 2-year as well as 4-year. The funding cycle for Upward Bound programs is generally 3 years, although the program is usually continuous at any given site. Upward Bound began in 1967, and now it serves about 44,000 precollegiate students in 563 programs.

SCORE

SCORE (Johnson, 1983) is a dropout prevention/college preparatory program that was initially developed as a partnership between the Orange County (CA) Department of Education and the University of California at Irvine. This program targets at-risk students in Grades 9–12 whose likelihood of graduating from high school or enrolling in college is felt to be low by their teachers. SCORE equips its student participants with the tools that they need to stay in high school and to attend college by providing them with a set of comprehensive services. These services can be separated into five components, which are adapted to the needs of each school.

First, students receive professional career counseling from a SCORE guidance counselor, who helps work through any obstacles preventing them from meeting their professional goals. Second, students receive tutoring in various subjects and instruction in study skills from SCORE teachers. The third component of SCORE focuses on motivation. SCORE students are given opportunities to join various clubs, in which they work together and provide one another with motivational support. Fourth is a parent program that helps parents to support their children's academic success. The final component is a summer academic program, in which students take courses ranging from college preparatory courses to actual college courses to remedial courses. For Latino and other students with limited English proficiency, SCORE focuses on moving students out of separate English as a second language (ESL) classes into the mainstream.

Schools that initially intend to implement SCORE attend a 3-day workshop to discuss schoolwide changes that will need to be in place for implementation. Next, study skills teachers are chosen, and they participate in a 2-day workshop, after which the program is adapted to fit the needs of the specific school. At the end of the implementation year, the program is reevaluated to see whatever changes (if any) need to be made for the following year.

The first evaluations of SCORE (Wells, 1981) involved comparing University of California eligibility rates of the first group of SCORE students with those of the state of California. University of California eligibility rates for SCORE students were 40%, compared to a random sample of high school African American and Latino graduate students surveyed by the California Post-Secondary Education Council (CPEC) of 5.2%. SCORE students also enrolled at a higher rate (41%) in 4-year colleges than did a selected comparison group of minority high school graduates, also surveyed by CPEC (11%). The next portion of this evaluation compared the effects of partial implementation of SCORE to full implementation. Students who received less than all five components of SCORE had a 32% college enrollment rate, whereas those who had had all five components and attended all sessions (especially including the summer institute) had a 56% college enrollment rate. The last part of this comparison included matching 99 SCORE seniors from a school that was 43% Latino with 112 students from a matched control school that also had a 43% Latino population. All (100%) of the SCORE students completed their college requirements, compared to 52% of the students in the comparison sample.

The SCORE program published anecdotal reports on four schools with substantial but varying proportions of Latino students (SCORE, 1994).

The first school, in Gonzales, California, consisted of 1,200 students, of whom 45% were migrant. Prior to adopting SCORE in 1983, 3% of the high school graduates had completed the requirements to enroll in a university. With the adoption of SCORE, the figures steadily increased until they reached 28% in 1990. Migrant students from Gonzales High School enrolled in 4-year colleges and universities at a much higher rate (51%) than the national migrant average (5%). The number of SCORE students enrolled in intermediate algebra also rose from 42 to 119 and from 12 to 63 in other mathematics courses. Chemistry and physics enrollment also increased from 60 in 1987 to 175 in 1992.

The second school, in Madera, California, was 100% Latino, and all of the students were involved in migrant education. When they initially entered the school, many of the students were limited English proficient. Upon graduation, 93% of the LEP students tested as fully English proficient. After participating in SCORE, 90% of the migrant students who participated attended college; 100% of the students who graduated attended either 4- or 2-year colleges. Some of the students dropped out as a result of financial issues, but none because of academic problems.

Students in a school in Buena Park, California, who had been selected into SCORE were those who had scored in the bottom quartile on the CTBS and therefore qualified as Title I students. This group made up 69% of the total freshman class. The percentage of graduates who attended 4-year colleges went up from 22% to 31%. While in college, all of the SCORE graduates maintained a 2.8 grade-point average (GPA) in their college prep curriculum during their freshman year. All limited English proficient students were also fully English proficient at the end of the freshman year, and maintained a B GPA through their senior year in high school. Buena Park High School eliminated remedial mathematics, instituted algebra for most ninth-grade students, and then heterogeneously grouped all social science classes. The dropout rate decreased from 3.3 to 2.3.

The final school, in Stockton, California, had a heterogeneous mix of students. Here SCORE is mainly an after-school tutorial program, using teachers who tutor in their classrooms 1 to 4 days per week. Since the adoption of SCORE, elective enrollment in college preparatory classes increased 84% from the previous year. The number of students who took the SAT also increased from 11 in 1982 to 110 in 1993. The number of Advanced Placement English classes also increased from one to six, and most recently, the school has adopted an international baccalaureate program. The number of students who dropped out decreased from 141 in 1988 to 71 in 1992.

The evaluations of SCORE are far from ideal in experimental design. Most of the statistics presented for SCORE students are anecdotal; different outcomes, presumably those showing the most impressive gains, are reported for each school. The first study compared SCORE students to California averages for minority students, without any evidence that the SCORE students were similar in other ways to California averages. However, the changes over time in dropout and college enrollment rates are large, and have been shown in many schools. It seems likely that SCORE is in fact having an important impact on the graduation and college enrollment rates of Latino as well as non-Latino students.

SCORE is currently used in over 250 schools throughout California and seven other states. K–12 programs have also been initiated on the islands of Palau and Saipan. Additional programs are expanding through a process of training trainers in new schools and districts, enabling schools to tailor a program that best serves the needs of its students.

Project AVID

Project Advancement Via Individual Determination, Project AVID (Mehan et al., 1992; Swanson, Mehan, & Hubbard, 1995), is a high school dropout prevention/college enrollment program that began in San Diego County, California, in 1981. In AVID, low-achieving students felt to have good academic potential are placed in rigorous college prep courses and are taught to excel academically. The program began as a means of improving the academic achievement of minority students who were being bussed into a predominantly White suburban high school in San Diego County.

When schools initially agree to become AVID schools, a leadership team made up of the school principal, head counselor, AVID teacher, and the leaders in English, foreign languages, history, science, and mathematics attend a week-long summer training institute. Follow-up training is also provided in the form of monthly workshops by the AVID lead teachers, semiannual site team meetings and site visitations by the AVID county staff, and quarterly tutor and parent workshops.

The main backbone of the AVID program is the lead teacher/coordinator. She or he acts as a coach, constantly expecting the best academic performances from both the teachers and the students. The AVID lead teacher/coordinator is also responsible for training and hiring professionals and paraprofessionals such as tutors to work with the students in the program. The lead teachers raise funds for the program, and are involved in the coordination and planning of field trips.

Students who participate in AVID are selected into the program by AVID coordinators. Eligibility requirements include average to high CTBS scores, but low junior high school grades, and parental consent.

Once the students enter the program they enroll in AVID classes, where they are taught such strategies as inquiry, writing, and higher order thinking skills. They are also provided academic assistance and tutoring in their regular subjects during the AVID class hours. Sometimes, some of the AVID students themselves are the tutors.

Students participate in AVID activities during lunch, recess, elective periods, and after school. They may be given AVID notebooks, which are used to take "AVID style notes," and AVID badges or ribbons. Some schools engage students in printing a special AVID newspaper that discusses AVID student successes.

In the most recent evaluation of AVID, Mehan, Villanueva, Hubbard, and Lintz (1996) compared the school records of 248 students who had participated in AVID for 3 years (AVID3) in 1990–1992 with those of 146 students who had also met the criteria for AVID and initially participated in the program for a year, but then dropped out (AVID1). Students' records were from 14 AVID schools in San Diego County, with Latino compositions ranging from 8% to 37%. The original number of students in each group was 353 for the AVID3 students and 288 for the AVID1 students, and the number of Latino students who participated in the follow-up interviews was 102 in the AVID3 group and 40 for the AVID1 group. The two groups were fairly equal in socioeconomic status. Among AVID3 students, 71% came from homes whose families made under $40,000 per annum, as opposed to 65% of the AVID1 students.

Analyses comparing AVID3 and AVID1 divided students into three groups. The first group (high) consisted of students who had high CTBS scores and high grades, or middle CTBS scores and high grades. In this group, there were 37 (25%) AVID1 students, and 72 (29%) AVID3 students. The second group (middle) consisted of students who had high CTBS scores and middle-level grades, or middle-level scores and middle-level grades. The middle group consisted of 77 (53%) AVID1 students and 140 (56%) AVID3 students. The final group (low) consisted of students who had both low grades and low CTBS scores. This group consisted of 32 (22%) AVID1 and 36 (15%) AVID3 students.

The college enrollment rates of the two AVID groups were compared to those of the San Diego County high school population, and to those of the U.S. population. Comparisons of these four groups showed that AVID students had a greater rate of attending 4-year institutions, followed by AVID1 students. Looking specifically at the Latino students, who comprised the majority of the students in the study, 43% attended 4-year institutions, compared to the San Diego County rate of 25%, and the AVID1 rate of 20%. Interestingly, 43% of the AVID3 graduates attended 2-year colleges, compared to 40% of the AVID1 students, and 37% of the county population, and 14% of the AVID3 students were engaged in work right after high school, compared to 38% of the county population and 40% of the AVID1 population. Comparing the AVID1 and AVID3 groups on attempting and actually completing college preparation classes to make them eligible for the University of California or the California State University system, the differences favored the AVID3 group. In the high AVID1 group, 78% of the students attempted college preparation courses and 62% of them completed these courses, compared to the AVID3 group, where 85% of the students attempted the courses and 67% completed them. For the middle students, there was a similar pattern. For the AVID1 middle group, 42% of the students attempted the courses, and 14% of them completed the courses, compared to 68% of the middle AVID3 students who attempted the courses and 23% who actually completed them. The largest impact of participating in this program shows up in the low groups.

For the AVID1 low group, 22% of the students attempted the college-level courses, and none of them completed the courses, compared to 53% of the low AVID3 students who attempted the courses and 11% who actually completed them.

The advantage of AVID3 over AVID1 participants was greatest for students whose parents had not completed high school (44% for AVID3 vs. 17% for AVID1). There was a smaller but still important difference for students whose parents were high school graduates (51% for AVID3 vs. 39% for AVID1) and for students whose parents had a bachelor's degree or more (48% for AVID3 vs. 39% for AVID1).

Overall, these results suggest that AVID had some positive effects on the students who needed it most. It is important to note that the Mehan et al. (1996) study, while it uses a comparison group, still presents issues of concern, and does not meet the standards of this review. First, the AVID1 and AVID3 groups cannot be considered comparable, as the AVID3 students were able to remain in this rigorous program for all 3 years while the AVID1 students dropped out. It is likely that the AVID3 students were therefore more motivated, higher achieving, and better behaved than the AVID1 students. Comparison of both AVID groups to San Diego County and U.S. means are even more susceptible to bias. Students are specially selected for AVID based on high CTBS scores and other indications of promise, and some number of students do not even make it to the end of the first year (and are therefore not included in either group). Still, the college enrollment rates for AVID are impressive, and the program has a good track record in serving Latino as well as non-Latino students throughout the United States, and for these reasons is worthy of consideration by other schools serving many students placed at risk.

The state of California now has over 400 AVID programs serving over 20,000 students. Today, AVID is an international program, adopted by over 700 schools in 13 states as well as by the Department of Defense Schools in Europe and Asia. AVID Summer Institutes, now held throughout the world, provide staff development for nearly 2,000 educators a year.

Project GRAD

Project GRAD (Graduation Really Achieves Dreams) (Ketelsen, 1994) is a comprehensive dropout prevention/college attendance program developed and evaluated at Jefferson Davis High School, which serves a population that is 83% Latino and very low in socioeconomic status. It was begun in 1989 by a former chief executive officer (CEO) of Tenneco, James Ketelsen, in collaboration with the University of Houston. Tenneco and other funders promised any student who graduated on time from Jefferson Davis with a GPA of 2.5 a 4-year, $1,000 per year college scholarship. Students were provided with two 5-week summer academic institutes held at the University of Houston, opportunities to participate in paid internships in local businesses, and interventions to improve schoolwide discipline, parent involvement, and quality of instruction. An evaluation of Project GRAD compared the entire school population in 1989, before the program began, with that in 1993 (Ketelsen, 1994). Over that time period, the percentage of students graduating in 4 years rose from 50% to 78%. College attendance rose from 10% of all graduates to 60%. In 1999, the Davis feeder system has a 68% graduating senior rate and the number of students qualifying for the scholarships has increased 12% from 1992 to 65% of the student body satisfying the requirements. The pass rate on the 11th grade Texas Assessment of Academic Skills (TAAS) increased from 37% to 86% and the number of students enrolled in honors courses doubled.

A later comparison of Project GRAD to a control school (Opuni, 1995) showed less impressive outcomes in terms of graduation rates and academic achievement, but continued to show substantial gains in college attendance. Annual dropout rates at Jefferson Davis dropped from 18% in 1988–1989 to 11.5% in 1994–1995, but similar reductions were also found in the comparison schools and in other Houston high schools. Only small differences (favoring Davis) were found in on-time graduation rates, and there were no differences on academic achievement measures. However, among students who did graduate, college attendance rates increased from 20% in 1988–1989 to 41% who attended college immediately after high school and 56% who eventually did so. This is more impressive as the total population of students graduating was also increasing over this time period. Because of the disappointing findings with respect to achievement and dropout, however, the project is adding interventions relating to achievement, discipline, and attendance in the entire feeder system that leads to Davis High (Ketelson, 1994; McAdoo, 1998).

Currently, Project GRAD is fully implemented within two high school systems in Houston, and is expanding into a third, serving a total of more than 26,000 students. These interventions include Success for All/*Éxito Para Todos* in elementary and middle schools (see chap. 6 in this book), a math program called Move It Math, and a school climate program, Consistency Management/Cooperative Discipline (Freiberg, Stein, & Huang, 1995). It is phasing in programs in Newark and Los Angeles, and has plans to expand into several additional urban districts (see McAdoo, 1998).

CPEC PROGRAM EVALUATIONS

In 1992, the California Post Secondary Education Commission (CPEC) conducted an evaluation of nine college attendance/dropout prevention programs around the state of California (Edgert & Taylor, 1992). The programs reviewed shared a common goal: increasing the number of ethnic minority students enrolling in postsecondary institutions. All of them serve many Latino students. Yet the programs differed in the regions served, specificity of program missions, components and services, demographics of schools served, and administering agencies.

This section provides a brief descriptive analysis of these programs. Some of the programs, such as MESA, are national programs whose California component was evaluated in the CPEC report. Others, such as Cal-SOAP, are local California-created programs that have not been replicated elsewhere. All of the programs serve significant numbers of Latino students.

The evidence of effectiveness provided by the programs reviewed by CPEC did not meet our evaluation criteria. First, although some of the programs had pre–post, experimental–control comparisons, they did not establish the equivalence of the experimental and control group before the treatments were introduced. Most of the programs had selection criteria for entry into the program (e.g., test scores or enrollment in college-preparatory classes), but the comparison groups were not selected in the same way. Some simply compared outcomes to those of "all" high school students across the United States (or all minority students). Second, even in cases where students in a given grade cohort were compared to those in a previous cohort, no evidence was given to show that the two cohorts were initially equivalent. Although we cannot say that the CPEC programs are proven to be effective, they are all used on a fairly broad scale with Latino students, and for this reason we do provide descriptive information about them.

Mathematics Enrichment and Science Achievement (MESA) is a program created by the University of California in 1970, out of concern among educators about the small number of African American and Mexican American college graduates in engineering. The mission of the program is to develop academic and leadership skills, raise educational expectations, and instill confidence in students from backgrounds historically underrepresented in fields such as engineering, physical science, and other math-based fields. MESA strives to accomplish this goal by creating partnerships among staff, advisors, committed middle and high school science and math teachers, school district officials, university professors and administrators, industry members, and parents.

The main component of MESA that focuses on college enrollment is the Mesa Schools Program (MSP). MSP is specially designed to support precollege students by providing them with extra academic assistance in middle and high school to prepare them to succeed in the sciences and in mathematics-related fields in high school and college. The MSP begins in the seventh grade, so students could be involved in the program for as long as 6 years (Grades 7–12).

To be eligible for the MSP middle school program, students must meet certain academic criteria: They must score between the 40th and 90th percentiles on the CTBS, they must be interested in math-based fields, and they must be likely to complete algebra in the ninth grade. To be involved in the MESA senior high school program, students must be involved in college preparatory mathematics or science classes, interested in mathematics-based fields, and able to take the A–F (college preparatory) course pattern.

Students enrolled in MSP are provided with services such as meetings, MESA (MSP) classes, college advising, school course counseling, academic assistance, science workshops, math workshops, PSAT/SAT workshops and preparations, visits to campuses, motivational speeches made by individuals from the private sector and postsecondary educational institutions, participation in science fairs, skill development classes, tutoring, a summer program, recognition awards such as scholarships, and field trips that include visits to business and industry.

Currently there are MESA centers at 48 sites throughout California, which serve over 20,000 students. In California, MESA serves a student population that is 60% Latino. The MSP component of MESA has 20 centers that serve over 250 middle, junior, and senior high schools. Hundreds of MESA and MSP centers also exist elsewhere in the United States.

Alliance for Collaborative Change in Education School Systems (AC-CESS) is a college enrollment program that works with the San Francisco and Berkeley school districts. ACCESS began at the University of California, Berkeley, in 1980, as a Chancellor's initiative to improve neighboring secondary schools' ability to prepare underrepresented students for college. ACCESS strives to improve curricular, instructional, and organizational components of the school, focusing on mathematics, English, and counseling.

Using site-based management in areas such as staff development and technical assistance, teachers are taught to improve their curriculum, instructional standards, counseling expectations, and leadership and school organization. Although ACCESS has specific structural components, it is generally adaptable to the needs of the school.

When enrolled in ACCESS, students receive tutoring, academic/college advising, and in-class instruction in specific curricular areas. ACCESS begins in the 6th grade, and continues until the 12th grade, so students can potentially be involved in ACCESS for 7 years. Middle school participants eligible for ACCESS are all students enrolled in mathematics and English courses. High school students eligible to become ACCESS participants are those enrolled in college preparatory mathematics and/or English courses at sites receiving ACCESS assistance for teachers, counselors, and administrators. ACCESS students are required to complete college preparatory (A–F) course requirements, and are given extra assistance to help them to improve their standardized test performances.

California Academic Partnership Program (CAPP) is a college attendance program administered by the California State University system. The program creates partnerships among school districts, colleges, and universities to improve learning opportunities and academic preparation for middle and high school students, so that they are better prepared to attend and graduate from college. CAPP strives to achieve its goal by providing schools at various levels (colleges, universities, and middle and high schools) with grants that allow them to work together to create academic and professional development opportunities to improve the college preparation of all students.

In order to be involved in CAPP, students must be enrolled in precollege or college preparatory courses in English, mathematics, science, social sciences, or foreign language. They are provided with services such as advising, visits to campuses that they might attend, parental involvement in their education, tutoring, and summer programs. Unlike many of the programs in this report, CAPP exists at a given site for only 3 years, and then the program leaves the site, so students typically participate in CAPP for 2 to 3 years.

CAPP currently exists in 15 school districts in the State of California, on 6 community college campuses, 6 California State University campuses, 3 University of California campuses, and 2 additional independent institutions.

California Student Opportunity and Access Program is a program developed to increase the postsecondary enrollment of minority students by serving as a clearinghouse for educational information, providing academic support for students, and supplementing the school's counseling function.

Prerequisites for student selection into the program are interest in pursuing postsecondary educational goals and likelihood of benefiting from the program services. Students involved in Cal-SOAP are provided with such services as academic and career advising, assistance with college applications, campus visits, skill development classes, summer residential programs, test preparation workshops, and tutoring. Students involved in Cal-SOAP can remain in the program for a maximum of 6 years, but in practice they typically remain for only 2 or 3 years.

Cal-SOAP currently exists in 35 school districts in the state of California, and on 25 community college campuses, 13 California State University campuses, 7 University of California campuses, and 14 additional independent institutions.

The *California Readiness Program* (CRP) is a college preparatory program that is a partnership between the California State University and the California Department of Education. CRP seeks to increase the enrollment and success of African American and Latino students in ninth-grade algebra and college preparatory English courses with eventual hopes of increasing the number of students attending college.

The main prerequisite for selection into CRP is an interest in attending college in the future. Students enrolled in CRP are provided with services such as California State University campus visits, cross-age mentoring and tutoring from CSU interns in mathematics and English, parental activities, problem-solving instruction, and workshops provided to the family about the benefits of college attendance and the availability of financial assistance. This program involves 10 school districts and 5 California State University campuses.

The *California Early Academic Outreach Program* (EAOP) is a college attendance program administered by the University of California, whose goal is to increase the number of minority students (African American, Native American, and Latino) eligible for admission to the University of California system. The program aims to assist individual students to enroll in and complete college preparatory courses of study that eventually lead to eligibility for admission to the University of California by strengthening knowledge, motivation, and preparation for postsecondary education through individual and group activities with students, parents, and schools.

Program participants are middle/junior high school students who have the potential to benefit from services to achieve college eligibility and who are willing to take a prescribed sequence of courses. EAOP students who join the program can be served for a maximum of 6 years (Grades 7 through 12). Some of the services available to the students include academic skills development, administrative and programmatic linkages between schools and the university, dissemination of information, motivational development, and participant identification and referral. EAOP exists in 176 school districts and at 8 University of California campuses in California.

Middle College is a college attendance/high school dropout prevention program that aims to reduce the number of high-risk students with college potential who do not graduate from high school, and increase the number of students from this category who attend college. This program was patterned after a model created by La Guardia Community college in New York (1988). Middle College brings the high schools and the community colleges together to form a partnership through which services are provided to the students.

Students enrolled in Middle College could be involved with the program for a total of 3 to 4 years. Services provided include academic, career, and personal counseling, career internship experience, classroom instruction, staff development, and tutoring. Participants include students with a history of truancy, low academic achievement, and counselor recommendation.

Middle College is administered out of the office of the California Community College Chancellor. California participants involved in MC include the Los Angeles and Richmond Unified school districts, Contra Costa College, and Los Angeles Southwest College.

CATEGORIZATION OF PROGRAMS REVIEWED

As noted earlier, an ideal program for this review would be one that was specifically designed to prevent dropping out of high school among Latino students, had been rigorously evaluated many times in elementary or middle schools serving many Latino students, and had been extensively replicated in such schools. However, few programs would meet all of these criteria. Table 2.1 summarizes the degree to which each of the programs reviewed met the various inclusion criteria. Table 2.1 is only a summary; see the program reviews for more detail on the characteristics, evaluation evidence, and replicability of each program.

CONCLUSION

The six dropout prevention and college attendance programs that met our evaluation criteria, as well as the California Post Secondary Education Commission (CPEC) that did not, are very diverse in their interventions as well as their findings. Yet there are important commonalities among them as well. First, even accounting for mild to serious problems in experimental design (especially relating to problems of selection bias), it is clear that the six main programs reviewed can have a substantial impact on the dropout rates, college attendance rates, and other outcomes for Latino adolescents who are placed at risk. Second, while only four of the six (AVID, SCORE, Upward Bound, and the Coca-Cola Valued Youth Program) have active dissemination programs, there is nothing inherent to any of these programs that would keep them from being disseminated broadly. They are expensive, but well within the means of our society, especially given the immediate costs to our society of high dropout rates and underused talent.

Although the interventions themselves differ considerably, there are some common themes among them. One is personalization, trying to increase the holding power of the school by creating meaningful personal bonds between students and teachers and among students. Most of the programs use some sort of small-group intervention and/or mentoring to enhance individual attachments to school. Another common element involves connecting students to an attainable future. For example, both Project GRAD and Upward Bound give students an experience on a college campus to make college seem more real and attainable. SCORE and AVID, among others, provide counseling to keep students preparing for college and occupations. Another common theme is targeted academic assistance, giving students help with specific courses with which they are struggling as well as more generic study strategies.

Finally, many of the programs attempt to give students status and recognition within the school for academic efforts. For example, the Coca-Cola Valued Youth Program gives at-risk students an opportunity to tutor younger children, a high-status, responsible role. AVID essen-

TABLE 2.1
Categorization of Programs Reviewed

Program Name	Grades Served	Spanish Bilingual Focus	Meets Evaluation Criteria for Achievement	Evaluated With Latinos	Designed Specifically for Latinos	Widely Replicated
ALAS	7–12	Yes	Yes	Yes	Yes	No
AVID	9–12	No	Partially	Yes	No	Yes
Coca-Cola Valued Youth Project (VYP)	7–12	Yes	Yes	Yes	Yes	Yes
GRAD	K–12	No	Partially	Yes	No	No
SCORE	9–12	No	Partially	Yes	No	No
Upward Bound	9–12	No	Yes	Yes	No	Yes
CPEC programs						
Mathematics Enrichment and Science Achievement (MESA)	7–12	No	No	Yes	No	Yes
Alliance for Collaborative Change in Education School Systems (ACCESS)	6–12	No	No	Yes	No	Yes
California Academic Partnership Program	9–12	No	No	Yes	No	Yes
California Student Opportunity Program	7–12	No	No	Yes	No	Yes
California Readiness Program	9–12	No	No	Yes	No	Yes
California Early Academic Outreach Program	7–12	No	No	Yes	No	Yes
Middle College	9–12	No	No	Yes	No	No

tially places promising at-risk students in top track classes, with enough assistance to succeed there. Finally, most programs recognize the importance of families in the school success of their children, and provide activities to engage parents' efforts in support of their children's achievement and school completion.

There is not enough evidence from studies of dropout prevention or college attendance models to indicate which components of these comprehensive models are most effective or cost-effective. Yet it is clear that these are effective approaches to increasing the graduate rates and college attendance of Latino students. The existing successful approaches are intensive, comprehensive, and built around positive expectations for adolescents. They demonstrate that the problem of unacceptably high dropout rates and low college attendance rates among Latino students is one we can solve. There is much more we need to learn about these programs, but we already know enough to take action on this critical problem.

ACKNOWLEDGMENTS

An earlier version of this chapter was written for the Hispanic Dropout Project, and portions of it were adapted from Fashola and Slavin (1998). It was partially supported by a grant from the Office of Educational Research and Improvement, U.S. Department of Education (grant R-117D-40005). However, any opinions expressed do not necessarily represent the positions or policies of the U.S. Department of Education.

APPENDIX: CONTACTS FOR INFORMATION ON PROGRAMS REVIEWED

ALAS
Katherine A. Larson and Russel W. Rumberger
University of California, Santa Barbara
Graduate School of Education
3326 Phelps Hall
Santa Barbara, CA 93106
805-893-4393 or 805-893-3385

AVID
Mary Catherine Swanson
Director, AVID program
San Diego County Office of Education
6401 Linda Vista Road
San Diego, CA 92111-7399
619-292-3500

Coca-Cola Valued Youth Project
Linda Cantu, Project Director
Intercultural Development Research Association
5835 Callaghan, Suite 350
San Antonio, TX 78228-1190
210-684-8180 or 210-684-5389
Fax: 210-444-1714

Project GRAD
J. L. Ketelsen
PO Box 2511
Houston, TX 77001
713-757-3563

SCORE
Sharon Marshall Johnson
Educational Innovations/SCORE
23706 Whale Cove
Laguna Niguel, CA 92677
Voice and Fax: 949-363-6764
E-mail: sharonmarjo@earthlink.net
Web site: www.score-ed.com

Upward Bound
David Goodwin
U.S. Department of Education
600 C. Independence Avenue SW
Washington, DC 20202
202-401-0263

REFERENCES

Burkheimer, G. J., Riccobono, J., & Wisenbaker, J., (1979). *Final Report: Evaluation study of the Upward Bound Program—A second follow-up.* Research Triangle Park, NC: Research Triangle Institute.
Cardenas, J. A., Montecel, M. R., Supik, J. D., & Harris, R. J. (1992). The Coca-Cola Valued Youth Program: Dropout prevention strategies for at-risk students. *Texas Researcher, 3,* 111–130.
Coca-Cola Valued Youth Program. (1991). *Proposal submitted to the Program Effectiveness Panel of the U.S. Department of Education.* Washington, DC: U.S. Department of Education.
Council of Chief State School Officers. (1990). *School success for limited English proficient students: The challenge and state response.* Washington, DC: Author.
Durán, R. P. (1994a). Hispanic student achievement. In M. Justiz, R. Wilson, & L. Bjork (Eds.), *Minorities in higher education* (pp. 111–132). Phoenix, AZ: Oryx Press.
Durán, R. P. (1994b). Cooperative learning for language-minority students. In R. DeVillar, C. Faltis, & J. Cummins (Eds.), *Cultural diversity in schools* (pp. 68–81). Albany, NY: SUNY Press.

Edgert, P., & Taylor, J. W. (1992). *Final report on the effectiveness of intersegmental student preparation programs. The third report to the legislature in response to item 6420-0011-001 of the 1988–89 budget act.* Sacramento, CA: California Post Secondary Commission.

Educational Testing Service. (1996). *Dreams deferred: High school dropouts in the United States.* Princeton, NJ: Author.

Ekstrom, R. B., Goertz, M. E., Pollack, J. M., & Rock, D. A. (1986). Who drops out of high school and why? *Teacher's College Record, 87,* 356–373.

Fashola, O. S. (1998). *Review of extended-day and after-school programs and their effectiveness.* Baltimore, MD: Johns Hopkins University, Center for the Research on the Education of Students Placed at Risk.

Fashola, O. S., & Slavin, R. E. (1998). Effective dropout prevention and college attendance programs for students placed at risk. *Journal of Education for Students Placed at Risk, 3*(2), 159–183.

Fashola, O., Slavin, R., Calderón, M., & Durán, R. (1996). *Effective programs for Latino students in elementary and middle schools.* Baltimore, MD: Johns Hopkins University, Center for Research on the Education of Students Placed at Risk.

Fernández, R. R., & Velez, W. (1989). *Who stays? Who leaves? Findings from the ASPIRA five cities high school dropout study.* Washington, DC: ASPIRA Institute for Policy Research.

Finn, J. D. (1989). Withdrawing from school. *Review of Educational Research, 59,* 117–142.

Freiberg, H. J., Stein, T. A., & Huang, S. (1995). Effects of a classroom management intervention on student achievement in inner-city elementary schools. *Educational Research and Evaluation, 1*(1), 36–66.

General Accounting Office. (1994). *Hispanics' schooling: Risk factors for dropping out and barriers to resuming education.* Washington, DC: Author.

Hayward, B. J., & Tallmadge, G. K. (1995). *Strategies for keeping kids in school: Evaluation of dropout prevention and reentry projects in vocational education.* Washington, DC: U.S. Department of Education.

Howe, C. K. (1994). Improving the achievement of Hispanic students. *Educational Leadership, 51*(8), 42–44.

Johnson, S. G. (1983). *A survey of SCORE for College.* Unpublished masters thesis, California State University, Fullerton.

Ketelsen, J. L. (1994). *Jefferson Davis Feeder School Project.* Houston, TX: Tenneco Corporation, Project GRAD.

Larson, K., & Rumberger, R. (1995). Doubling school success in highest-risk Latino youth: Results from a middle school intervention study. In R. F. Macias & R. Garcia Ramos (Eds.), *Changing schools for changing students* (pp. 157–188). Santa Barbara, CA: University of California at Santa Barbara.

Leighton, M. S., Hightower, A. M., & Wrigley, P. G. (1995). *Model strategies in bilingual education: Professional development.* Washington, DC: U.S. Department of Education.

Lockwood, A. T. (1996). *Caring, community, and personalization: Strategies to combat the Hispanic dropout problem.* Washington, DC: U.S. Department of Education, Hispanic Dropout Project.

Losey, K. M. (1995). Mexican American students and classroom interaction: An overview and critique. *Review of Educational Research, 65,* 283–318.

McArthur, E. K. (1993). *Language characteristics and schooling in the U.S., a changing picture: 1979 and 1989.* Washington, DC: National Center for Education Statistics.

McAdoo, M. (1998). Project GRAD's strength is in the sum of its parts. *Ford Foundation Report, 29*(2), 8–11.

Mehan, H. (1996). *Contextual factors surrounding Hispanic dropouts.* Washington, DC: U.S. Department of Education, Hispanic Dropout Commission.

Mehan, H., Datnow, A., Bratton, E., Tellez, C., Friedlaender, D., & Ngo, T. (1992). *Untracking and college enrollment* (Research Report 4). Santa Cruz, CA: University of California at Santa Cruz, National Center for Research on Cultural Diversity and Second Language Learning.

Mehan, H., Villanueva, I., Hubbard, L., & Lintz, A. (1996). *Constructing school success: The consequences of untracking low-achieving students.* New York: Cambridge University Press.

Myers, D., & Schirm, A. (1999). *The impacts of Upward Bound: Final report for phase I of the national evaluation.* Washington, DC: Mathematica Policy Research, Inc.

National Center for Education Statistics. (1993). *Dropout rates in the U.S.* Washington, DC: U.S. Department of Education.

National Center for Education Statistics. (1995). *The educational progress of Hispanic students.* Washington, DC: U.S. Department of Education.

National Center for Education Statistics. (1996). *Dropout rates in the United States: 1994.* Washington, DC: U.S. Department of Education.

National Diffusion Network. (1995). *Educational programs that work: The catalogue of the National Diffusion Network* (21st ed.). Longmont, CO: Sopris West.

Opuni, K. A. (1995). *Project GRAD: Program evaluation report.* Houston, TX: Houston Independent School District.

Orfield, G., & Monfort, F. (1988). *Racial change and desegregation in large school districts.* Washington, DC: National School Boards Association.

Romo, H. D., & Falbo, T. (1996). *Latino high school graduation: Defying the odds.* Austin: University of Texas Press.

Rumberger, R. W. (1987). High school dropouts: A review of issues and evidence. *Review of Educational Research, 57,* 101–127.

Rumberger, R. W. (1995). Dropping out of middle school: A multilevel analysis of students and schools. *American Educational Research Journal, 32,* 583–625.

Rumberger, R. W., & Larson, K. A. (1994). Keeping high-risk Chicano students in school: Lessons from a Los Angeles middle school dropout prevention program. In R. Rossi (Ed.), *Schools and students at risk* (pp. 93–117). New York: Teachers College Press.

Rumberger, R. W., & Larson, K. A. (1995, April). *Toward explaining differences in school attrition among Latino language minority students.* Paper presented at the annual meeting of the American Educational Research Association, San Francisco.

SCORE. (1994). *Proposal submitted to the Program Effectiveness Panel of the United States Department of Education.* Washington, DC: U.S. Department of Education.

Steinberg, L., Blinde, P. L., & Chan, K. S. (1984). Dropping out among language minority youth. *Review of Educational Research, 54,* 113–132.

Stern, D., Paik, I., Catterall, J. S., & Nakata, Y. (1989). Labor market experience of teenagers with and without high school diplomas. *Economics of Education Review, 8,* 233–246.

Swanson, M. C., Mehan, H., & Hubbard, L. (1995). The AVID classroom: Academic and social support for low-achieving students. In J. Oakes & K. H. Quartz (Eds.), *Creating new educational communities, Ninety-Fourth Yearbook of the National Society for the Study of Education, Part I* (pp. 53–69). Chicago: University of Chicago Press.

Vasquez, J. A. (1993). Teaching to the distinctive traits of minority students. In K. M. Cauley, F. Linder, & J. H. McMillan (Eds.), *Annual editions: Educational psychology 93/94.* Guilford, CT: Dushkin.

Velez, W. (1989). High school attrition among Hispanic and non-Hispanic white youths. *Sociology of Education*, 62, 119–133.

Wells, J. (1981). SCORE. *Final report presented for ESEA Title IVC*. Sacramento: Presented to the California Department of Education.

3

Effective Elementary, Middle, and High School Programs for Latino Youth

Anne Turnbaugh Lockwood
University of Wisconsin–Madison

What do effective programs for Latino youth look like in practice? What practical considerations do school administrators and staff need to confront as they enact programs that meet the special needs of Latino youth? This chapter presents three cases of effective programs at the elementary, middle, and high school level—each with a different focus—and illustrates the range of actions that can be taken at the school site to meet the educational and social needs of Latino youth. These cases feature school staff who have taken leadership roles to implement and maintain programmatic integrity and effectiveness.

SUCCESS FOR ALL: LACKLAND CITY ELEMENTARY SCHOOL

Success for All is a comprehensive schoolwide reform that intends to transform the entire learning environment to achieve academic success. Two overarching beliefs—that children must succeed academically and that it is possible to equip school staff with the skills and strategies to ensure academic success—also distinguish this program.

Early intervention, with plenty of one-on-one tutoring in reading if students show signs of falling behind, is a key program component. Tutors are certified teachers who work one-on-one with individual students experiencing difficulty in their reading groups for 20-minute periods at times other than reading or math instruction.

Because a chief programmatic tenet insists that every child must read at grade level by the end of third grade, Success for All builds in appropriate strategies for instruction, assessment, and meeting students' personal needs so this goal can be realized. A strong emphasis on cooperative learning, regular 8-week assessments of student achievement, and flexible, shifting placements in reading groups also distinguish the reform from other programs—along with an emphasis on attending to the social and personal needs of children.

Success for All uses a beginning reading curriculum, Lee Conmigo (Read With Me), in schools with bilingual programs in Spanish. Lee Conmigo uses instructional strategies similar to those in the English program (Reading Roots) but uses curriculum materials and sequencing appropriate to Latino culture and the Spanish language (Fashola, Slavin, Calderón, & Durán, 1996, p. 11).

Evaluations of Success for All show consistent positive results, with effect sizes that average approximately +0.50 standard of deviation at each grade level. Students in the lowest 25% of their grades show average effect sizes of +1.00 or above—more than a full standard deviation. Differences between Success for All students and control students average 3 months in grade equivalent terms in the first grade, increasing to more than a full grade equivalent by fifth grade (Fashola et al., 1996).

Lackland City Elementary School, located in the Northside Independent School District on the west side of San Antonio, Texas, serves a student population of approximately 600 students whose demographics reveal both poverty and the special needs of a diverse student population. Ninety percent of the student body qualify for free and reduced lunch; 87% are Hispanic, 6% African American, and the remainder Caucasian. Approximately 50% of parents are unemployed and receive some sort of assistance. Lackland City Elementary School has a 35% mobility rate.

Lackland City Elementary made the commitment to schoolwide reform in the 1994–1995 academic year, spurred by the desire to improve student achievement and by the recognition that staff needed to attend to social and personal problems that influenced students' academic performance. As a result of the staff's research on educational strategies and programs—and the belief that both students and teachers could do better—Success for All was implemented at Lackland City in the 1994–1995 academic year.

Staff use Success for All's strong reading component and its math curriculum. In addition, Lackland City made several structural changes recommended by Success for All, invested in staff development and ongoing feedback provided by the program, and adopted a schoolwide, proactive approach to solving students' academic and personal/social problems.

The results have exceeded staff expectations. In 1994, the number of fifth graders at Lackland who passed the Texas Assessment of Academic Skills (TAAS) in reading was a meager 51%. In 1995, after 1 year of Success for All, that percentage jumped to 63 and in 1996 to 84%. In mathematics, the gains were similar. In 1994, 55% of Lackland fifth graders passed the TAAS; in 1996, 86% reached a passing score.

Selecting Success for All: The Beginning

The philosophy that undergirds Success for All is relentlessly positive: Every child must succeed in school, every child must read at grade level or better by the end of third grade, and not only is it possible for school staff to ensure each child's academic and personal success: it is imperative.

Prior to the implementation of Success for All at Lackland City Elementary School, staff were dissatisfied with student achievement—but not unified about a schoolwide strategy to improve outcomes. They had become discouraged by the overwhelming needs of their students that they saw little way to meet.

Yet staff were united in the belief that all children should be served by any school improvement effort they might undertake. "The fact that the program included every single child in the school," says Jerry D. Allen, Lackland City's principal, "was one of its biggest advantages—along with its strong research base and specific instructional strategies."

The choice of Success For All began democratically, with a teacher-led committee that reviewed research on programs that showed success with economically disadvantaged students. Once this committee recommended Success for All to Allen, he reacted promptly. "We visited sites in Houston," he recalls, "and were able to convince our district to free us from our regular program and get involved with Success for All."

The major challenges Lackland City faced, Allen believes, were attitudinal and structural. "We needed to believe in the importance of the children's education—all of us, teachers and families. We also needed to learn good techniques for capturing the students' attention and moving them forward academically. Every single one of us needed to be committed to the belief that learning is important and can be achieved by all children."

The Success for All philosophy and belief that all children must succeed goes far beyond optimistic or dogmatic rhetoric and slogans, Allen points out. "When we say children cannot fail," he observes, "we have to be prepared to give each teacher tremendous support. Many principals simply say: Teachers, this kid can't fail. That's easy—and it doesn't work.

"But in this program, when the teacher experiences a problem with a student, it becomes everyone's responsibility. It becomes the Child Advocacy Committee's responsibility or the Family Support Team Committee's duty to get the child the necessary tutoring, to see if social needs are met, and to relieve worries the child is experiencing."

Allen adds, "We want to be the best neighbor possible to our families and children."

The Success for All Process

Today, Allen points to a faculty charged with a clear focus and crystalline goals. "We reinvented the way we do things," he says. "The first year of Success for All, the most experienced teacher was reduced to the same level of expertise as the new teachers because the program was new to all of us. We have seen enormous gains in the level of communication that has occurred among staff because of the program's structure."

One such structure was implemented the year prior to Success for All. Lackland City formed a Child Advocacy Committee to address the massive personal needs of students in a concerted, focused way. This committee—composed of Allen, the school's social worker, educational psychologist, school nurse, the current Success for All facilitator, special education facilitator, and mathematics facilitator—continues to meet weekly to deal with any problems referred to it by teachers.

"We know," Allen says, "that if a child is involved with social struggles he or she is not here with a full, clear opportunity to learn. If a child has no eyeglasses, no food, no clothing, or utilities are turned off at home, we consider all of these as factors that determine how well the child will learn."

The advent of Success for All, with the attendant schoolwide committee, confirmed that staff had made the right beginning. Allen says, "We have a real community effort now when a child is in trouble. We found that we had been providing services in a somewhat scattered manner from many people—and we hadn't been communicating with each other. The initial purpose of the committee was to improve communication among ourselves about the child and the family. We then began a case approach in which someone takes command of the case. That person follows the family all the way through the process until it is a healthy family again."

Allen points to a previously held schoolwide, pervasive belief that the social and personal issues of students were beyond the capabilities of school staff. "We ignored the social issues. That wasn't our job; that was somebody else's job. We have since had a major philosophical change and have realized amazing results in all areas."

Elma Noyola, Lackland City's Success for All facilitator, provides eloquent testimony about how this process works. "We have a Read and Response program in Success for All," she begins. "Every child in our school has to read for 20 minutes at home, Monday through Thursday, and have their parents sign a form that says they listened to their children read aloud to them."

If a child comes to school and says he or she couldn't do the reading at home because the parent wasn't available, Noyola indicts what would have been her response in the years prior to Success for All. "In the past, I would have said: Right, give me another story."

Today, Noyola and Lackland City's school liaison person, Angie Landeros, go to the home. "We introduce ourselves, tell family members about the program, and tell them how they can help us. Many parents will tell me that they don't read or don't understand English. I tell them: Give the child your time. You can help them with reading at home. We treat parents with respect, and as a result they acknowledge and accept what we want them to do."

Home visits always accentuate the positive, she says, with good news about a child's performance at school first and foremost and with emphasis on building rapport with parents through shared experiences. Noyola explains, "Because Angie Landeros and I are both moms, we can say: We know you are busy, but when you are making dinner, have your child read to you. You can listen while you work."

Lackland City works to support parents with classes that will help build their own language and educational skills. The school's English-as-a-second-language (ESL) classes for parents are held during the day and the evening to accommodate different schedules. A GED class helps parents obtain a high school credential and improve the likelihood of finding better-paying employment.

Even marital and family conflict has become something Lackland City does not ignore. "We had children whose parents were in turmoil," Allen says. "To help them, we work with a United Way mental health community agency. We succeeded in getting a half-day of a family-licensed therapist to work at our campus. She works with our families and our children. We have been able to address these needs, not ignore them."

Ensuring that children's health needs were met with appropriate medical attention also became Lackland City's responsibility. "If you truly make the commitment that every child will succeed," Allen reflects, "it is incumbent upon you to find the resources to make those things happen. Our children weren't getting good medical attention. Some had never had a physical or an inoculation. Instead, we spent time removing children from school because their vaccinations were not current—totally contrary to what we should be doing as a school and a staff."

Today, Lackland City has entered a partnership with Santa Rosa Children's Hospital in San Antonio. "We feel fortunate," Allen reports, "because doctors come to the school to provide early diagnostic and preventive services."

Instruction With Success for All

In addition to the shift to proactive attention to students' personal needs, the face of instruction at Lackland City has changed dramatically. As Daryl Michel, a second-grade teacher, says, "All children used to read the same story at the same time in the regular classroom. Whether you were high or low in reading, you moved at the same rate as everybody else. The only variety was that every week we changed stories."

As part of Success for All's reading component, students are moved into cross-age, cross-grade, achievement-appropriate reading groups. Students are regrouped after regular 8-week assessments, although children are not moved backward. Michel explains, "Every student in my reading group is at approximately the same level as every other student in the group, which works much better. If somebody is really struggling or really excelling, we can move them to different groups. We don't want students going backwards, however. Instead, our emphasis is on pushing those who are excelling into the next level if we think they will succeed. We keep the lower-achieving readers at the same level, without moving them backwards, and gradually build them up until they are at the same level as the other students."

The highly structured reading program appeals to Michel and other teachers. "Students work much of the time with partners, not just by themselves, and there is a lot of group work and cooperative learning. As a result, kids speak out more and do much more with presenting material than they did before. They learn how to speak in front of people."

Lackland City has few monolingual Spanish-speaking students. Instead, it has a sturdy bilingual program in which it uses the Spanish materials provided by Lee Conmigo, the Spanish-language component of Roots and Wings.

"We are all master reading teachers now," Noyola adds. "We no longer can tell the difference between experienced teachers and those who are just starting out. Our attitude used to be: No one is going to teach me how to teach reading because I have been teaching for 20 or 30 years and I know how to do it. The proof for experienced teachers that these strategies work is clear. At the end of a day they can see that 100 percent or even 90 percent of the children understand the concept."

She continues, "Everyone is focused on one goal and it is the success of our reading. From one classroom to the next, you can see the consistency. Teachers still have their individual personalities, but the strategies we use are consistent throughout the entire school, from kindergarten through fifth grade."

Michel acknowledges that cooperative grouping does not come easily at first for all children—due to the tendency of some children to try to dominate the group. However, the program's structure again is the key. "Each student has a role, such as the reader or the recorder, and therefore four students work together to create a product."

As a male teacher in the primary grades, Michel reports that relationships with students meld into a warm, family-like atmosphere in the classroom. "I respect all the children," Michel explains, "and became very attached to last year's class. Many of them come back to see me, to visit after school, to tell me how they are doing. That in itself represents a lot."

The Importance of Professional Feedback

Allen believes that a major reason staff have adjusted to the educational philosophy and instructional strategies offered by Success for All has been the presence of intensive staff development prior to the program's implementation coupled with continued, expert feedback provided by Success for All consultants during the school year.

"In the reading program, we begin with three days of training," Allen explains, "which we hold in the summer. In the week of Thanksgiving, which all children have off, teachers have the first two days of that week as inservice. In November, we have our first implementation check from Success for All consultants. They visit every classroom and observe each teacher during reading instruction."

Consultants provide individual, one-on-one feedback as well as team feedback, Allen says. "New teachers have the opportunity to ask: Is this what you mean? Is this the way I should be doing this? What they want and need, of course, is validation. Not only do they receive that, but they also discover some things they need to concentrate on. That identifies our weaknesses. We have these implementation checks in the fall and in the spring."

Developing Professional Community

An unanticipated benefit for school staff has been the development of professional community through interactions outside the classroom that focus on improving instruction. The difference, Noyola says, can be seen most visibly in the teacher's lounge—traditionally a room where teachers go to escape the demands of the school day.

"When we began Success for All, it was all teachers could talk about," she recalls. "How are you doing this? What is especially successful? Can you help me with this? We were all so involved. The enthusiasm we had engulfed us."

From a school struggling to meet the needs of its students and their families, Lackland City is evolving into a completely different environment, she emphasizes. "We are a service-oriented school. Parents now feel very comfortable coming into the school. They can visit with the staff or with me at any time. They can come to our lending library. They can borrow books. They can watch what goes on in the classroom. There are loads of projects for them.

"Many Hispanics," she concludes, "had a bad experience in school and are turned off by it. We want everybody to feel welcome, and we have witnessed it with our hearts."

THE COCA-COLA VALUED YOUTH PROGRAM: LAJOYA MIDDLE SCHOOL

The Coca-Cola Valued Youth Program is an in-school mentoring program targeted to youth at the middle and high school level who are in danger of dropping out of school or having an unsuccessful and unhappy school experience—due to the usual characteristics that place children at risk. It was developed in 1984 by the Intercultural Development Research Association (IDRA), a nonprofit organization in San Antonio, Texas, with funding from Coca-Cola USA. The Valued Youth Program model has been selected by the Coca-Cola Foundation as its flagship strategy for addressing the excessive dropout rate among minority youth (Intercultural Development Research Association, 1995). It has received special recognition from the Peter F. Drucker Foundation for Nonprofit Management in the foundation's first annual award competition for nonprofit programs of excellence and innovation; it also has been recognized by the National Diffusion Network. In 1992, the Coca-Cola Valued

Youth Program was recognized by the Secretary of Education as a model dropout prevention program (Intercultural Development Research Association, 1995).

Youth who are selected to participate in the program become tutors of elementary school youth, at least four grades their junior. As tutors, they work with their tutees 4 days a week at the elementary school site, under the supervision of both the elementary host teacher and the Valued Youth Program teacher/coordinator. The fifth day, they receive special support in a class that focuses on developing their expertise as tutors, addressing their questions, and boosting their literacy skills.

Students who participate in the program receive a modest stipend for their work. A central tenet of the Coca-Cola Valued Youth Program is that if youth are valued, they will respond with increased bonding to school and to adults.

La Joya Middle School illustrates how the Coca-Cola Valued Youth Program works and achieves its results. Located in La Joya, Texas, La Joya Middle School is part of a rural district spread over 29 square miles. Agriculture provides the main source of steady employment to families in the La Joya district, although migrant labor—much more transitory and less secure—is also a common source of employment. Eight hundred migrant families send their children to school in the district. Approximately 80% of students qualify for free or reduced lunch.

Begun in 1991, the Coca-Cola Valued Youth Program is one key lever that has tilted the school's dropout rate in a much more positive direction. In 1994, the La Joya district's dropout rate at 12th grade was 6.9%. In the 1995–1996 academic year it had decreased to approximately 2.5%.

The first year of the program, La Joya Middle School began with 25 seventh graders, keeping them in the program through eighth grade. The following year, they added another 25 seventh-grade students.

The Intercultural Development Research Association provides intensive training for site participants, monitors their progress, and evaluates their success. In results reported by La Joya Middle School, parents of program participants reported some impressive gains. Most parents (88.6%) reported a positive change in their children's behavior as a result of the tutoring program. Changes reported included increased responsibility and maturity, having a more positive attitude/behavior, and being more respectful. One hundred percent of parents reported that the program helped their children in school.

Most program participants reported that the Coca-Cola Valued Youth Program changed their lives and their attitudes toward school (La Joya

Independent School District, 1994–1995). Their scores on the Quality of School Life Scale (QSL), administered to all tutors on a pretest/posttest basis, reflected their newly positive feelings about school.

La Joya Middle School and the Coca-Cola Valued Youth Program

When Rosario Alaniz volunteered to be the Coca-Cola Valued Youth Coordinator at La Joya Middle School in La Joya, Texas, her attitude toward the program, its goals, and the students she would work with was positive. Coming from a background similar to those of the La Joya School District's students—impoverished and difficult—Alaniz felt considerable empathy toward the students selected for the special experience offered by the Valued Youth Program.

But she was taken aback at the outset. Instead of instant results and plenty of student appreciation for the program, Alaniz ran up against the twin barriers of chaos and resentment. "The kids had lots of energy," she says with obvious understatement. "As I described the program to them, I could see that half were listening and half were not paying attention. We began going to the campus where they would be tutoring younger children—and just walking over there was an experience. They would hit cars to make the alarms go off—and they would hide from me."

But as the program progressed, she began to see small signs of improvement. "The students started to change as they worked in the program. They would talk about the students they were tutoring and ask me for little tokens of appreciation for their students."

How did their attitudes first begin to shift? What were the earliest signs that they were beginning to engage with the program? Alaniz says, "They started to communicate with me. Before, they would not talk to me. They began to ask me how to solve problems with their students, saying: 'Ms. Alaniz, my student doesn't listen to me. What do I do?' Or they would say: 'Sometimes I go there and my student isn't there. What should I do?'"

Today, Alaniz smiles at the obvious irony—and remembers it as the first, tiny sign of positive change. The program served as a mirror held up to students that enabled them to observe themselves through the behaviors and attitudes of their tutees.

Another sign of improvement came when other teachers complained less frequently about students enrolled in the program. "Attendance was improving; I heard fewer complaints from other teachers. Students weren't sent to in-school suspension nearly as frequently—and they were not skipping my class."

As an added bonus, grades began to inch upward. "Not dramatically," Alaniz clarifies, "but they were improving. I would tell teachers who came to complain to me that they needed to look at small things to see improvement. Maybe a student brought a pencil and paper to class today—and maybe that is a huge improvement for that student. Once we started to notice those small things, we knew we needed to focus on whatever the student was doing that was positive.

"If we only deal in the negative," she adds, "we become enmeshed in a power struggle that kids at that age enjoy. I began offering lots of reinforcement such as certificates, photographs, and displays that featured the students—and they were shocked. Suddenly they were becoming 'Student of the Month' or 'Most Improved Student.' That had never, ever happened to them before."

Even with obvious improvement, Alaniz emphasizes that no program can offer an instant miracle—asserting that plenty of time, patience, and creativity must be invested in any fledgling effort. "We started the program in February—and I insisted that I keep them the following year. That next year is the year that we really saw results."

Overcoming Obstacles and Barriers

Filamena Leo, Administrative Assistant for Student Services, remembers the early days of the program. "At the time, I was the principal at La Joya Middle School," she says. "We had large numbers of students dropping out at the eighth grade level—and that concerned me. Our overall dropout rate, at times, was as high as 40 percent. I said that we simply had to do whatever we could, using whatever means available to us to keep as many kids in school as possible."

The Coca-Cola Valued Youth Program came to Leo's attention through one of the directors of the Texas Coca-Cola Valued Youth Program, who suggested it to her because of his familiarity with the needs of her district's student population.

The primary obstacle at the beginning, Leo recollects, was resistance and resentment from teachers who did not understand the program's goals—and were not sympathetic to the idea of singling out "problem students" for special attention. "They thought we were targeting kids who had not been successful in school and were rewarding them with a stipend," Leo states. "Today, there is a much more positive and accepting attitude. Teachers can see the changes in the kids who have gone through the program and recognize that it is a worthwhile activity."

Leo echoes Alaniz's observations about the incremental, positive changes in the students who participated in the Valued Youth Program.

"The first change," she observes, "may not be empirical, but it was obvious. We saw more smiles. There were the students who always went around with slumped shoulders, who would not meet your eye. As a principal, I always stood in the hall during passing periods and spoke to each child. Many would not look at me or would not respond. After some time in the Valued Youth Program, they would smile, meet my eyes, and say: 'Good morning.'"

Other changes, she reports, could be seen when students would say with a newfound sense of purpose: "'I can't be absent today. My tutee is waiting for me.'"

"Teachers noticed that students became more respectful in their classroom responses," she says. "Parents also told us that their children talked more openly to them. They were not as embarrassed about telling their parents things—and they helped out around the house more."

Creating a Sense of Purpose

Leo has no trouble responding to critics of the program. "My response to teachers who don't understand why we target these students for special attention has always been that *everyone* needs to feel valued. Everyone has something to offer.

"Yes," she continues, "there are kids who have had some very bad experiences. These experiences have caused them to develop behaviors that some could say do not entitle them to anything we have to offer.

"But," she emphasizes, "we have to remember that they are seventh and eighth graders who perhaps have never been given the opportunity to demonstrate that they have something to give society. All they need is a chance to demonstrate that they can do it—and adequate support to get them to that point."

Advocating for Students and Developing Trust

Belief in her students spilled over into Alaniz's role as teacher and coordinator, pushing her to become their advocate with other school staff. When students saw that she stood up for them, they began to trust her. "Teachers would come to me and say they didn't want a particular student on field trips because he or she misbehaved. I would point out that the student behaved in *my* class; his work was good, he was taking his job very seriously. I would say: *All* students need to go on this field trip.

"Some of them had never been on a field trip because they were always in trouble," she points out. "We took them on several field trips of our own and suddenly they were able to go on their classroom field trips. This was an enormous boost for them because they were accepted with the other kids."

Attendance on field trips is not inconsequential, Alaniz points out. "These field trips and other activities offer all the social things middle schoolers need. Instead, they were punished—and it became a self-fulfilling prophecy."

At one point near the beginning of the program, Alaniz was especially frustrated. "I talked to Mrs. Leo," she remembers, "and told her: I have all these kids who have problems. All they see is each other. They do not have any role models."

Feeling a different approach was warranted, Alaniz asked permission to bring in five more students who were active in student activities but still had environmental characteristics in common with her students. "Some came from migrant homes or had other difficulties. But they were very well-behaved; they had good grades. The result was almost immediate. Bus trips suddenly became quiet. My students began socializing with these other students. Everything calmed down."

After that, the program's emphasis shifted back to the students considered especially fragile—but with a new mindset. "I changed the emphasis of the program to make these students believe that they *themselves* were role models. We provided lots of opportunities for them to interact with others. For example, we had banquets where they would give speeches. They would talk about their work, their teachers, and their parents. Kids would break down and cry when they talked about how they had let their parents and teachers down. They started to value themselves."

She adds, "They began to develop a conscience."

Achieving Positive Attitude Shifts

To Alaniz, shaping the attitudes of students who have been burned by negative experiences with adults and schools is perhaps the most critical part of any improvement or retention effort. "Many of our students identified as at-risk don't see adults as human beings," she notes. "They see us as tyrants who push them around—tyrants with no feelings of our own. After my own son suffered a serious accident, I began to explain to them what had happened in my family and I broke down.

"When I looked up, I saw that each student was crying. It had clicked that I had emotions, I had feelings—and I was an adult, a teacher. They started to share things with me about themselves that were phenomenal. They began to be willing to show their vulnerability."

Because of events in students' lives—some quite tragic—many of Alaniz's students carried a white-hot anger within them, she says. The close-knit quality of the program allowed them a safe place to ventilate their feelings and seek more positive outcomes for themselves.

Financial Incentives

Students who participate in the Coca-Cola Valued Youth Program receive a modest stipend as payment for tutoring younger students. Alaniz explains how they chose to spend their money. "We had a field trip to a mall. Many had never been to a mall."

"Can you imagine this?" she asks. "It was heartbreaking to see them buying clothes for their sisters and brothers, buying shoes and pants and coming back to school with these bags of clothing. They were excited because they were taking something home for their families. Some of the kids saved their money and gave it to their parents. No one spent the money foolishly."

She adds, "Here were kids who had been identified as hard-core juvenile delinquents who were using their money to buy useful things for their families."

Although the stipend was a key motivator at the beginning of the program, students eventually lost interest in the financial aspect of it. "At first, it was: 'When are we going to get paid?' Now, they don't ask me for their checks. One student from Mexico came to me and said she really didn't need the check. She said: 'Ms. Alaniz, this is too important to me. I am not going to take the money.' And she didn't."

Tutors and Tutees: Building Relationships of Value

The most profound change occurred through the relationships that developed between the tutors and their tutees, Alaniz emphasizes. "The kids become completely different when they work with the little ones," she says softly. "They tuck their shirts in, they take off their earrings. They wash their hands in case they have any markings on them.

"The little kids call them 'Sir' and 'Miss,'" she explains. "When you watch them together, it looks like a brother and sister interacting. Sometimes the little ones will scoot over, put their heads on the shoulder of their tutors, and say: 'I can't do it.' The tutor will put the tutee's little hand in his own hand and help them form the letters."

Gains in English-language proficiency can be seen through the program, with the younger children who are being tutored and with the tutors themselves. "At first we didn't accept students into the program who were classified as Limited English Proficient," she recollects. "But I had five students from Mexico who wanted to be in the program. As I watched my students work with the little kids, I saw that those who spoke English were speaking Spanish because some of the little ones were from Mexico. So I brought the students from Mexico into the program and their vocabulary grew rapidly. Within two months they were speaking English."

Setting Standards for Behavior and Academic Work

Although the Coca-Cola Valued Youth Program offers warmth and support to students considered especially at risk, it also places demands for their behavior and academic performance on them. Participation is not a given; students must meet the program's standards in order to stay in it.

"We had kids who were failing four or five out of their six classes," Leo says. "We saw that failure rate drop to two classes after a semester of being in the program. They knew that maintaining a passing level was a key criterion for staying in the program. They also became more confident in themselves as learners," she points out, "and began to believe in themselves a little bit more."

Students are selected to participate in the program through a combination of teacher recommendations, a review of students' school history, their pattern of attendance over the years, and an assessment of their academic achievement. The Valued Youth teacher/coordinator, along with campus counselor, narrows the pool of students down to the number the program can accept.

How is the program presented to prospective participants? Is there any stigma attached to participation?

Leo sighs. "Some do take offense when told they are considered to be at risk. We begin by having the Valued Youth Program teacher meet with them to explain the program. She presents it in a positive way, saying that they have not had such an opportunity before in school and we want to make sure that they do have it. Most students were receptive to that, but sometimes other students would make comments to them that they were selected to be in this program because they were failures or because they had never done anything in their lives.

"We try to prevent this stigma," she adds, "and we never have had a student who declined to participate. But we have had some question us: 'Why am I here? Am I a bad kid?'"

This clearly pains Leo, who again tries to turn to the positive. "We say: 'Yes, you have had some difficulty but we want to change that for you. Do you want to change? Do you want a shot at turning things around for yourself?'"

She adds, "Who can say no to the chance to have a better life?"

Families are informed about the program, although parental permission to participate is not sought.

Benefits of the Program

Leo's words tumble over themselves when she talks about the benefits of the program. "Kids who never have had an opportunity to show their good side are given a chance to do so. Adults begin to see them in a different light because their behaviors change as a result of seeing that they are important to someone else, to the little kids that they tutor.

"The validation that they receive is a powerful tool for changing human behavior. As they begin to see themselves differently, others do as well: teachers, parents, and siblings. With very few exceptions, there is a positive change in behavior. We have removed a very few youngsters from the program, less than five in the three middle schools that participated in the program last year."

Leo likes to illustrate the program's power by relating the story of one student. "One young woman, as a seventh grader, was in the office an average of three times a week. When she came to middle school, the elementary school counselor who had worked with her a great deal said to me: 'You are getting a student I have tried very hard to keep in school. You'll be lucky if you keep her another six weeks.'

"We worked with her in the program, taking it a day at a time. This year, she will graduate from high school."

Alaniz agrees. "If I won the lottery," she states, "I would teach only in the Valued Youth Program, four classes a day. The program has done as much for me as for the students. I was humbled by it. It made me a better person, it made me more patient, and it made me more understanding."

PROJECT AVID: MAR VISTA HIGH SCHOOL AND MT. PLEASANT HIGH SCHOOL

Project AVID (Advancement Via Individual Determination) is a program designed for secondary-level youth in Grades 6–12 to enhance their likelihood of enrolling in a 4-year college or university. Average students believed to have college potential are placed in college preparatory courses. In addition, in their AVID classes they receive the necessary supports and techniques that will enable them to succeed academically.

AVID was founded in 1980 by two English teachers at Clairemont High School in San Diego, California, with the goal of improving the academic achievement of minority students who did not appear to be preparing adequately—or achieving at sufficiently high enough levels—to gain entrance to 4-year colleges or universities. AVID is carefully structured to include a schoolwide team that is put into place at the outset of a school's decision to embark upon the program. This comprehensive team is composed of the school principal, head counselor, AVID teacher, and teachers in English, foreign languages, history, science, and mathematics. This team receives 1 week of training in the summer; monthly follow-up training is provided by AVID lead teachers and/or regional AVID centers. This schoolwide team is key to the program's success, because teachers in different content areas—along with the principal and counselor—understand AVID's goals and structure.

Specific instructional methodologies are central to AVID. They include collaborative learning groups, the use of inquiry method and Socratic instruction, and using writing to facilitate learning (in the form of note-taking, learning logs, and use of discourse modes in writing).

The AVID teacher/coordinator plays a critical role in the program's success, coaching students and functioning as their advocate, all with the goal of increasing their academic achievement. AVID students are selected by AVID coordinators; criteria include average to high California Test of Basic Skills (CTBS) scores, parental consent, and low or average grades in school. The students AVID targets—that is, students whose grades do not match their potential as evidenced by standardized test scores—are disengaging from school. By showing them that college is a viable option for their future and by making school an integral part of preparing for that future, AVID helps to reconnect these students to school. It also helps to improve their academic achievement so that college entrance is indeed viable.

AVID classes provide strategies such as inquiry, writing, and higher order thinking skills. Tutoring in areas where students experience trouble is also a key component of the program. AVID classes are regularly scheduled classes and are offered in elective periods.

College enrollment rates for AVID students are impressive—especially when one considers that it recruits students who would not normally be placed in the college track of their high schools. In 1996, the program served over 20,000 students—both Hispanic and non-Hispanic—in 134 high schools around the country, including 50 high schools in San Diego County. Since 1990, over 5,000 students have graduated from AVID programs. Over 90% of AVID's graduates enroll in college. AVID graduates persist in college at an 89% rate. Over 60% of AVID graduates enroll in 4-year colleges (AVID, 1996).

AVID's accomplishments have been recognized by awards that include the Salute to Excellence Award for Staff Development and Leadership from the National Council of States on Inservice Education, the Dana Foundation Award for Pioneering Achievement in Education, and the A+ Award from the U.S. Department of Education for Efforts to Reach the National Education Goals.

To tell the story of the AVID experience, we focus on two high schools: Mt. Pleasant High School in the East Side Union High School District in San Jose, California, and Mar Vista High School in Imperial Beach, California. Mt. Pleasant High School has a total student population of approximately 2,000; 90 students are currently enrolled in its AVID program. Approximately 33% of Mt. Pleasant's students are classified as limited English proficient (LEP); approximately 34% receive free or reduced-price lunch. Forty-four percent are Hispanic, 18% are Asian, 18% are White, 14% are Filipino, and 6% are African American.

Mt. Pleasant enjoys some extra support for its AVID program—beyond what typical AVID programs receive. The middle school that feeds into Mt. Pleasant High School also has an AVID program. Typically students who will enter AVID at Mt. Pleasant have some prior experience and familiarity with its goals and structure. Many teachers at Mt. Pleasant High School, in addition to the regular AVID staff and AVID team, have received AVID training and are familiar with and sympathetic to its goals and methods.

Mar Vista High School is located in the most southwestern city of the continental United States: Imperial Beach, California. Its student population numbers approximately 1,700 students. Approximately 63% are Hispanic, mostly Mexican American; 25% are White. Smaller percentages of students are African American, Pacific Islander, and Filipino, respectively. Approximately 30% of the school's Hispanic student population is classified as limited English proficient. Mar Vista High School is in its eighth year of AVID implementation. In this section, we hear from staff at Mt. Pleasant High School and Mar Vista High School.

The Benefits of AVID

"What I love about AVID," Grettel Castro-Stanley says with enthusiasm, "is the way in which it addresses exactly what students are doing in each of their classes. In our AVID classes, we constantly examine each student's progress. We want to know how our students are doing in foreign languages, algebra, science—all of their classes. We then help them with their deficits.

"Not only do we work with students academically," she continues, "but we also examine some of the social issues that may keep them from succeeding. It is an approach that not only focuses on the whole child, but also on the whole realm of academics."

Mt. Pleasant High School is in its third year of AVID implementation, Castro-Stanley explains. "We begin with freshmen, who are AVID I students, move them along as sophomores into AVID II, then as juniors into AVID III, and then as seniors into AVID IV—and then they graduate. Meanwhile, each year we start another AVID class at the freshmen level."

Castro-Stanley's role as the AVID coordinator/teacher illustrates the rigors of the work typical to AVID coordinators/teachers. "I become each student's personal counselor," she explains. "I monitor their progress and their grades, and work as their advocate with other teachers. But our approach is a team approach."

It is typical for AVID teachers to go the extra mile to ensure that students receive any extra help that will ease their chances of attaining academic success. For instance, it is not unusual for these teachers to drive a student to an evening tutoring session that will give that student the extra push to succeed in algebra. "We have one senior in the program who has four brothers and sisters," Castro-Stanley says. "Her mother works very hard and is never home. The daughter takes all the children to school, gets them dressed, and does everything to take care of them because her mom is not home to do it. She is also trying to do the academics she needs in order to get into a four-year college.

"We have lots of students in that boat," she adds. "Lots and lots of them. Sometimes we pick these students up ourselves and take them to an off-campus tutorial. At least this gives them two hours of extra tutoring once a week. But it is a struggle, and it is an individual struggle, one-on-one."

Seeing Progress, Viewing Results

During the 1996–1997 academic year, Castro-Stanley saw the first results with Mt. Pleasant's AVID III class of 10, a mix of juniors and seniors. "Out of ten students," she says, "we will see nine go on to a four-year or a two-year college."

AVID's practicality and low cost appeal to Castro-Stanley, who sees the cost of many programs and the difficulties of implementation as significant barriers for many schools, particularly at the secondary level. "AVID is very inexpensive," she says. "Frequently, there are special monies for special programs, such as limited grants—and when the money is taken away, the program dies."

Another benefit, she believes, is that AVID's goals and aims extend—tentacle-like—into the curriculum of the entire school. This extension of the original program allows other students—especially those who might otherwise drop out—to benefit from the program. "For us, it has become an incredible way of restructuring our school without calling it restructuring. All of our teachers like it so much that they are using a great deal of its philosophy. They see that the methodologies used with AVID students are very well organized and focused. Actually, these are basic skills that should be taught from day one but for some reason, we lose them along the way."

Alice Esparza has similar positive sentiments about AVID, which she has worked with since 1988 at Mar Vista High School. "When we began," she remembers, "we focused on the students in the middle in terms of their grades—since AVID was designed specifically for those students in the middle for whom an adequate amount of support could turn them into students who go on to four-year colleges. Our AVID students were those whose teachers thought they had potential, whose test scores showed potential, but who had average or mediocre grades."

Like all AVID coordinators, Esparza is especially savvy about college entrance requirements. Because Mar Vista is located in California, she is especially aware of the entrance requirements of the University of California system. "Our AVID students suffer from a general lack of preparation—and that could interfere with going on to college. The University of California system, for instance, has a very specific sequence of classes that students must take to be admitted. If they are missing any of them, they will not be accepted."

Academic Demands and Adequate Support

Aren't college preparatory classes too demanding if students lack adequate preparation? How does the AVID program provide adequate support to ensure students' needs are met?

Esparza responds, "Twice a week our students meet with tutors. In our program, these tutors are students at local universities. I prefer that they are graduates of the school because if they are, they know both the teachers and many of the kids in the area."

These students, she adds, are excellent role models who provide a concrete sense of what the future might be for Mar Vista's AVID students if they succeed in the program. "They might live down the street from some of our students. They are familiar with the neighborhoods. In these tutoring groups, our students discuss their classes with the tutors, bringing up the points that they do not understand or that are giving them difficulty. They are grouped by subjects in ratios of seven students to one tutor."

At Mt. Pleasant High School, tutoring is offered in a daily morning period between 8 and 8:30 a.m. "This is open to the entire school," Castro-Stanley observes, "not solely AVID students. But our AVID students must attend it four days a week as part of the contract they sign to be in the program.

"If they are behind in any subject, there are individual teachers who will help them. Most of our AVID students attend all five days of the week. In addition to that, during the AVID period, they receive tutoring two days a week from San Jose State University students. These university-level tutors help them academically and socially."

To provide yet another academic boost, Mt. Pleasant uses a program developed on site by the AVID team. Castro-Stanley calls it *shadowing*. Shadowing, she explains, means that San Jose State tutors follow a student experiencing difficulty in a particular class for a week, listening and observing diagnostically to uncover the reason that the student is faltering academically.

"The tutor goes to the problem class with the student, sits with her, and takes notes alongside the student," Castro-Stanley says. "The tutor tries to figure out what is lacking, where the problem lies. We find out amazing things through the feedback of the tutor. Sometimes we find out that the student falls asleep—and that is why she is failing. Sometimes the fault lies in the teaching, because it is inadequate.

"The shadowing component has provided us with some tremendous insights that we use to make necessary changes. Once we know what is going on, we can come up with a plan."

The Use of Tutors

Because Mar Vista has been working with AVID since 1988, it has been able to see its own graduates return to the program as college tutors. While a senior at the University of California at San Diego, Elizabeth Vega, an AVID graduate from Mar Vista, tutored in her alma mater's AVID program. She brought a special understanding of and empathy for the students enrolled in the AVID program. She also has carried a double major in political science and French literature and a minor in economics.

Vega believes her familiarity with the area and the needs of students is a plus that helps students relate to her and her own academic success. "The neighborhood here is economically disadvantaged," she says. "Sometimes a kid needs to see that there are other things out there. It is good for them to see somebody who came out of the same place, is doing well in college, and who studies with them to help them do it too."

Did she think she would go to college when she was in high school? "It was at the back of my mind," Vega responds thoughtfully, "but AVID gave me the skills, the help, and the information I needed to get into college. One of the main problems for students is not knowing which courses to take or how to prepare for exams. AVID gave me that. AVID also helped me to make my goals very specific and target my activities and classes toward those goals."

Tutoring is tightly structured, Esparza agrees, and needs to be to ensure academic success. "The tutors are trained either by the AVID teacher or by the county office of education. They are trained especially in the Socratic method of instruction, rather than didactic lectures. They dialogue with students."

Keeping a constant eye trained on the future guides their efforts. "We know," Esparza says, "that once they are in college they are going to be on their own. They need to start relying on each other. Twice a week, they work in their discussion groups with their tutors on different subject. The point of that is to improve their grades so they can be admitted to a four-year college.

"The other two days a week we teach an extensive curriculum that deals with college study skills, especially note-taking and writing, and we study for the SAT."

Flexibility and Personalization

Another key to the AVID program lies in its flexibility and personalization to the individual student. "Many things happen that affect achievement," Castro-Stanley says. "I switch students' schedules if there is a real personality conflict with a teacher that cannot be resolved. Or our principal, who is very supportive of the program, intervenes."

Constant, relentless monitoring of individual students—even of the most minute details—is also necessary, she asserts. "We collect all the note-taking that students do in all of their classes on a weekly basis—which they compile in binders. In that way, we can monitor their progress and see if some learning is actually taking place. Some students decide they don't want to be bothered. Maybe they have never had much responsibility and find this difficult."

But there are consequences in the AVID program. "If they don't turn in their binders, I meet with them in a small group. A parent then must check the binder on the day before we collect them and write us a note attesting that the student did his work. That pushes parental involvement."

This type of scrutiny can demand a great deal from AVID teachers, she reports—pointing to one teacher who was determined to get her freshman AVID students on task. "She called 30 sets of parents almost every day for six weeks," Castro-Stanley says. "She gave them good news, bad news, whatever news she could. After six weeks of struggle, the light bulb went on and the kids quit fighting her. They started to say: 'I can do this.'"

Future-Oriented Activities and Field Trips

Keeping a concrete sense of the future visible, immediate, and tangible is a critical component of AVID. Field trips to colleges are planned carefully, Esparza says, "to demystify college. We will go to a college and they will actually attend classes. We have guest speakers from different ethnic groups who come in and talk about their professions, what they do every day on their jobs, what they had to do in terms of education to get that job."

If necessary, AVID teachers will intervene to lessen or mitigate negative peer influences that pull students from their academic goals. "We try to restructure their peer groups," Esparza says. "We emphasize team-building through activities, including role-playing. This is especially important because our kids are dealing with other kids who aren't preparing for college, who aren't going on after high school to anything in particular.

"We get them to focus on how they talk to other adolescents, how they respond to them if their pressure is negative. We encourage them to think a lot about who they are and where they belong. We let them know that if they are going to go to college, they need the support of certain people."

Partnerships with universities help students stay focused on their academic goals, Castro-Stanley believes. "Going to universities and having college students here as tutors and role models really motivates the kids," she points out. "Field trips are also very important. The more we expose them to the future, the more they stay on track. We have taken them to Berkeley, to Santa Barbara, to Santa Clara University, to the University of California at Davis. Eventually we will go on an overnight trip where they will spend the night in a dorm."

Ease of Implementation

One of AVID's unheralded benefits is its ease of implementation. Rather than being opposed to it, teachers welcome it. "We never, ever had to sell the program to our staff," Castro-Stanley maintains. "Of course, you must have the support of your administration, and we have fantastic support from our principal. The teamwork is outstanding. The teachers who work in the program are dedicated to it.

"Programs like these," she says, "can have problems becoming institutionalized in high schools. Our experience, however, with AVID has been that it has become institutionalized through ongoing training for more and more teachers, through its interdisciplinary nature, and through its methodologies—which teachers believe in."

When not only students, but teachers, can benefit from a program, its positive effects are very clear, Castro-Stanley asserts. "Teachers like this program so much that they start using it without knowing it. They see it as a wonderful, powerful tool to affect learning.

"I still teach Spanish, but I use the AVID methodologies with every one of my Spanish students, although they are not in AVID."

She concludes, "As a result, everybody succeeds, and that is exciting."

REFERENCES

Advancement Via Individual Determination (AVID). (1996). *Program literature*. San Diego, CA: Author.

Chávez-Chávez, R. (1996). *Curricular constructs for achieving equity: Implications for teachers when engaged with Latina and Latino students*. (Paper prepared for the Hispanic Dropout Project.) Washington, DC: Office of the Under Secretary, U.S. Department of Education.

Fashola, O. S., & Slavin, R. E. (1996). *Effective dropout prevention programs for Latino students*. (Paper prepared for the Hispanic Dropout Project.) Washington, DC: Office of the Under Secretary, U.S. Department of Education.

Fashola, O. S., Slavin, R. E., Calderón, M., & Duran, R. (1996). *Effective programs for Latino students in elementary and middle schools*. (Paper prepared for the Hispanic Dropout Project.) Washington, DC: Office of the Under Secretary, U.S. Department of Education.

Hispanic Dropout Project. (1996). *Data book*. Washington, DC: Office of the Under Secretary of Education, U.S. Department of Education.

Intercultural Development Research Association. (1995). *Organizational brochure*. San Antonio, TX: Author.

Mehan, H. (1996). *Contextual factors surrounding Hispanic dropouts*. (Paper prepared for the Hispanic Dropout Project.) Washington, DC: U.S. Department of Education.

National Center for Education Statistics. (1994). *The condition of education*. Washington, DC: Office of Educational Research and Improvement, National Center for Education Statistics.

4

A Two-Way Bilingual Program: Promise, Practice, and Precautions

Margarita Calderón
Johns Hopkins University

Argelia Carreón
Success for All Foundation

In spite of political pressure, bilingualism is emerging as a strategy for improving the academic achievement of all students. Even after Proposition 227 in California, major districts such as Los Angeles Unified and San Francisco Unified are now more actively planning to increase their two-way bilingual programs. Two-way bilingual or dual-language programs integrate language-minority and language-majority students for instruction in two languages—the native language of the language minority students and English (August & Hakuta, 1997). These programs are gaining recognition in other parts of the United States as well. "U.S. schools now have clear achievement data that point to the most powerful models of effective schooling for English learners. What is astounding is that these same programs are also dynamic models for school reform for all students" (Collier, 1995). With the renewed emphasis on comprehensive school reform by state educational agencies, and an emerging interest in charter schools, dual-language programs may be the right choice for some schools.

Site-based decision-making has enabled schools in border cities with Mexico to implement two-way bilingual programs in which minority and majority students can become bilingual, biliterate, and bicultural. This more holistic aspect of bilingual program implementation has dropped such problematic notions as "when to transition from one language to the other," "when students should exit the bilingual program," and "how to conform to district policies on curriculum and academic accountability." Teams of teachers and administrators in these progressive schools are looking for ways to develop student-centered programs, which are integrated with whole-school efforts to improve and enrich instruction for all students.

The students that schools are preparing along the U.S. and Mexico border must be able to manage complexity, find and use resources, and continually learn new technologies, approaches and occupations. The need for global and binational educational emphasis has brought out the need for "cultural literacy" and "multiliteracies." In contrast to the low-skilled maquiladoras (twin plants), the border work sites now require employees to frame problems, design their own tasks, use new technologies, evaluate outcomes and cooperate in finding novel solutions to border problems. Because border-city students live in bicultural or binational communities, they must also understand and evaluate multidimensional issues that will continue to impact their bilingual society. As Luke (1995–1996) reminded us, the 21st-century citizen will work in media-, text-, and symbol-saturated environments. For millions of students, these will also be bilingual or multilingual environments.

Complex instruction for the binational context requires that teachers combine a profound knowledge of subject matter with a wide repertoire of teaching strategies, state-of-the-art knowledge about learning theory, cognition, pedagogy, curriculum, technology, and assessment, and ample knowledge of the students' language, sociocultural, and developmental background. The teacher must also be as proficient as possible in two languages. Teaching for such goals goes beyond the standard teacher-proof curriculum for traditional bilingual teaching. Teachers must now undertake tasks they have never before been called to accomplish (Calderón, 1996).

CHALLENGES AND ISSUES

As two-way bilingual or dual-language programs begin to flourish throughout the nation, special care must be taken to give the teachers in such programs profound learning opportunities, support, freedom within a well-structured program, and resources to do their job well. Until now, bilingual teachers have been pretty much left to their own devices when it comes to bilingual instructional practices. Fads come and go and bilingual teachers try them for a year or two, or simply adapt pieces of a model. Accountability has been rare. Bilingual program evaluations, like other kinds of "official knowledge" (Apple, 1993, 1995–1996), have been mediated by a complex political economy and the institutions it serves, and have been influenced to point in only certain directions. Therefore, bilingual teacher classroom performance has rarely been considered, ana-lyzed, or held accountable.

Accountability has also taken a back seat to another sensitive factor in bilingual education—the shortage of bilingual teachers. Because schools are desperate to fill bilingual teaching positions, the selection, on-the-job preparation, and teacher evaluation systems have failed to consider qual-ity and accountability in the practice of teaching and learning. Bilingual teachers still feel segregated from the rest of the schoolwide initiatives and caught in "us versus them" school conflicts. Because teachers have been so isolated, they have settled comfortably into their own ways of teaching. We often hear, "We don't want to do that because . . . ," "—there are no materials in Spanish," "—it's not in our curriculum plan," "—it's not whole language," "—it's too much work!" When we combine all these factors, we begin to see why there is so much student failure and why bilingual programs receive so much criticism. Their im-plementation has been subverted in most schools.

These sensitive issues are confounded with other issues such as the historical politics of identity of minority teachers, the feelings that the words "bilingual education" evoke in the public at large, and the slow start on research on effective instruction for bilingual settings. When we compound all this with the state of the art on professional development and school reform initiatives, it is no wonder that students and teachers fail in many bilingual programs.

Historically, bilingual education has been a sociopolitical issue fueled by theories that seek to explain low academic performance and high dropout rates of minority students, especially for those of Mexican de-scent. The education of language minority students is constantly em-broiled in controversy. The use of languages other than English for in-structional purposes continues to be perceived as a threat to national security or some similar un-American activity (McLaren, 1995). The browning of America and future population projections are often high-lighted in an attempt to bring the need for systemic and attitudinal re-form to the forefront. It is often espoused that such reform must come from within the school and its community and not from the outside. However, most reform projects limit their efforts, budgets, and focus when it comes to language-minority students and their teachers. It is not only a language issue but also a comprehensive approach to bilin-gual/English as a second language (ESL) program implementation and change in attitudes that needs to be found.

The education of language minority students is dependent on the de-gree to which these children have access to instruction that is challeng-

ing yet comprehensible. They need an accepting school and social environment, which promotes academic achievement and values cultural and
language diversity. The *Lau v. Nichols* decision of 1974 affirmed a student's right to educational opportunity via appropriate instructional services. To this day the search for the most effective means of accomplish-
ing this goal continues. On the one hand, earlier studies by Hakuta
(1990), Cummins (1981), Krashen (1982), Ramírez, Yuen, Ramey, and
Pasta (1991), and Collier (1995) concluded that long-term primary language instruction complemented with quality instruction in English is the
most effective means for language minority students to attain academic
success. Later studies by August and Hakuta (1997), Calderón, Hertz-
Lazarowitz, and Slavin (1997), and Slavin and Madden (1996) found
that a comprehensive approach to school reform is necessary to implement quality bilingual or English as a second language programs for language minority students. This chapter focuses on one effort to implement
comprehensive two-way bilingual programs in four schools, their level of
commitment, and how it equates to current status of implementation and
impact on students and teachers.

WHY DUAL-LANGUAGE INSTRUCTION?

Preliminary studies on two-way bilingual or dual language programs (Collier, 1995; Christian, Montone, Lindholm, & Carranza, 1997) showed
great promise. The rationale for these programs is not only academic
achievement in two languages but also cross-cultural understanding as a
benefit of positive interactions in the classroom. In the Lambert and
Cazabon (1994) study of the Amigos Two-Way bilingual program in
Cambridge, Massachusetts, students in the program formed close friendships with members of both their own and the other group. In a national
review of two-way bilingual programs, Mahrer and Christian (1993) also
found that when comparison groups are available, evaluations typically
show that English-language learners in two-way programs outperform
those in other programs.

Despite the fairly elaborate theoretical justification for two-way programs, there has been no uniformity in the programs that have been implemented (August & Hakuta, 1997). There are variations of time on each language: Some start out providing 90% of instruction in Spanish the first year
and gradually add English until both languages are used 50% of classroom
time in third or fourth grades. Other programs call for 50–50% from kindergarten on. Programs vary on their student selection, assessment and placement practices, and their policies for admitting newcomer students. Perhaps

the largest variations exist on the instructional practices for teaching in both languages. These practices go hand-in-hand with the variations of professional development practices that teachers are offered to support the implementation of these programs.

Guadalupe Valdés (1997) raised other issues that might underlie the purposes and impact on the beneficiaries of two-way programs. Contrary to the stated purpose and the perceived benefit for all students, she cautioned that issues of language and power must also be considered. Is language an important tool that can be used by both the powerful and the powerless in their struggle to gain or maintain power as perceived by Fairclough (1989, 1992) and Tollesfson (1991), or a means by which the powerful remain in power? Valdez reported that teachers and administrators of a dual-language immersion program have shared with her concerns about disappointing Spanish-language and reading test scores of Mexican-origin students. If a school's program results indicate that English-dominant students outperform Spanish speakers on Spanish tests or any similar inconsistency, this merits careful analysis so that the issue can be addressed. Educators must continue to pursue quality education so that the beneficiaries of two-way programs are clearly both language groups. Nothing else should be acceptable.

Educators working in the field of bilingual education soon learn that their philosophy and commitment to bilingual education is often questioned and their resolve tested by those in power. They see themselves as the only advocates for students, their culture, and language. The Accelerated Two-Way Bilingual program was designed to provide a better opportunity for equity in education for the language minority student in which both language groups would serve as a resource to one another. It was designed as a win–win, value-added program in which both groups would add a second language in the process of attaining an education. It was also hoped that equity in educational access would lead to equity in power and status and more commitment from mainstream teachers and administrators. The other important factor that the project wanted to address was the roles that the principal and the district administration play in the implementation, support and endorsement of the program.

According to Christian (1996) and Lindholm (1990), eight criteria are essential to the success of two-way bilingual programs:

1. Programs should provide a minimum of 4 to 6 years of bilingual instruction to participating students.
2. The focus of instruction should be the same core academic curriculum that students in other programs experience.

3. Optimal language input (input that is comprehensible, interesting, and of sufficient quantity) as well as opportunities for output should be provided to students, including quality language arts instruction in both languages.

4. The target (non-English) language should be used for instruction a minimum of 50% of the time (to a maximum of 90% in the early grades), and English should be used at least 10% at first, then increased to 50%.

5. The program should provide an additive bilingual environment where all students have the opportunity to learn a second language while continuing to develop their native language proficiency.

6. Classrooms should include a balance of students from the target language and English backgrounds who participate in the instructional activities together.

7. Positive interactions among students should be facilitated by the use of strategies such as cooperative learning.

8. Characteristics of effective schools should be incorporated into programs, such as qualified personnel and home–school collaboration.

One important instructional principle is that lessons are never repeated nor translated in the second language, but concepts taught in one language are reinforced across the two languages in a spiraling curriculum. Teachers might alternate the language of instruction by theme or subject area, by time of day, by day of the week, or by the week. If two teachers are teaching, each teacher represents one language (Ovando & Collier, 1998).

PURPOSES OF THE STUDY

The goals of the multilevel action-research project in the schools were to:

1. Document the program design, implementation and program adjustments of the two-way bilingual program.

2. Analyze teacher performance and professional development in the context of implementing complex change.

3. Identify the pedagogic variables that facilitate or impede learning through two languages simultaneously.

4. Identify the most promising program features and the school structures for program implementation and the role of the principal within these.

This report synthesizes 4 years of formative and summative data on these four topics. The first reporting section describes the program features through their process of development and implementation. The second section discusses pedagogy—the key features that facilitated or obstructed learning and achievement. The third section describes the issues of teachers' transfer of knowledge from the professional development program into the classroom. The fourth section discusses the role of the principal and implementation results. The fifth section concludes with implications and recommendations to schools wishing to implement two-way bilingual programs.

THE CONTEXT OF THE STUDY

The El Paso Independent School District (EPISD), with 64,966 students, is the largest of 12 districts in the city of El Paso, Texas. According to the National Clearinghouse on Bilingual Education, the district ranks 13 in a list of 20 school districts in the nation with the largest numbers of enrolled limited English proficient (LEP) students. EPISD reflects its border location with a student population that is 72% Hispanic. Approximately 15,000 students are served in bilingual education in pre-kindergarten to fifth grades and English as a second language programs in Grades 6–12.

The city has a population of over 700,000 people, making it the largest city on the United States–Mexico border and the fifth largest in the state, but one of the most financially impoverished. With more than a million people living in Juárez, Mexico, the El Paso–Juárez twin cities are the largest on the 2,000-mile border from San Diego, California, to Brownsville, Texas. For 400 years the history of these twin cities has been influenced by the clashing of cultures, the shifting of geographical boundaries, the confrontation of ideologies, and the impact of immigration into the United States, as well as the mixing of languages, the blending of cultures, the settlement of long-term boundary disputes, such as the Chamizal settlement, and the economic interdependence of two vastly disparate financial systems. Two cities so different yet so close, whose people sometimes live in one and work in the other, whose families often branch out on both sides of the border, and whose environment, health, and infrastructure are taxed by the challenges of a growing population and the impact of the North American Free Trade Agreement (NAFTA) are permanently linked (Sharp, 1994). The two must collaborate to profit from the diverse resources of their people and to meet the challenges of the border. The early promises of NAFTA and the increasing need for bilingual skills in the workplace created new interest among anglophone parents for their children to learn Spanish.

The school district had been implementing three other approaches to bilingual education:

1. A traditional transitional model that included language and content instruction in Spanish, as well as English as a second language (ESL).
2. A late exit model that included a native cognitive language development component (NLCD), English language arts, and sheltered English content instruction.
3. A special language immersion program within the monolingual classroom, which provided limited instruction in Spanish, ESL, and content instruction in English in schools with low enrollments of students with limited English proficiency.

Some of these programs included monolingual English students in their bilingual classrooms. However, as with most bilingual programs, it was difficult for one teacher to serve two groups of children with extremely different needs within the same class and provide quality instruction for all. Nevertheless, it was evident that students learning English benefited greatly from a variety of English language models, especially their peers. Unfortunately, they were also learning that Spanish, and the people who spoke Spanish were not held in high regard.

Although El Paso has a Hispanic majority, when the two-way program was initiated, many of the English speakers seeking the program were Hispanics. These were the children of parents who didn't speak Spanish because when they went to the El Paso schools they were punished for speaking Spanish. They grew up convinced that Spanish was a liability rather than a resource. These parents now want their children to regain the Spanish language and cultural pride they once lost. Unfortunately, this sense of shame and loss of language and culture leads other Hispanic parents to fight desperately against bilingual programs. Although two-way bilingual education may not be the solution to a history of social inequalities, it can be a vehicle for reform that individual schools or school districts can implement, study, and continue to improve.

The Initial School Sites

The El Paso Accelerated Two-Way Bilingual program was initially implemented in two elementary schools, K–5. The two-way bilingual classrooms reflect the ethnic and language makeup of the community. One school is predominantly upper middle class with the Hispanic and Anglo populations almost 50% each. The other school is a Chapter 1 school with more than 80% of the students on school lunch. The Hispanic student population is approximately 80%; however, about half of these students are English dominant.

Classes at each grade level include approximately 15 Spanish-proficient and 15 English-proficient students. At each grade level, instruction during the day is to occur 50% of the time in English and 50% in Spanish. Therefore, students are placed in cooperative learning teams of four, where two are the Spanish experts and two are the English experts. A bilingual and a monolingual teacher staff each class.

The Second-Phase Sites

At the third school, only about one fourth of the students are Title I, even though it has an 80% Hispanic population. This school began its two-way bilingual program 2 years later, when the curriculum and the structural components had been completed. The school implemented it for 1 year, then adopted Success for All (SFA; Slavin & Madden, 1996) as its reading/language arts component in the lower grades instead of Bilingual Cooperative Integrated Reading and Composition (BCIRC; Calderón, 1990–1991). The teachers are partnered, but each has her own classroom, and students change classrooms for SFA.

The fourth school is a Title I school with about 90% Hispanic students in a high poverty area. This school began by implementing Success for All the first 2 years, then began implementing the two-way program one grade level per year. Teachers are partnered, but each has her or his classroom, and students change classrooms for SFA.

Methodology

Quantitative and ethnographic data were collected for the 3-year study on teachers and their students. Quantitative data consist of teacher, student, and administrator questionnaires and comparison of baseline data with 3-year results for (a) the students' language development, (b) student achievement, and (c) the teachers' professional accomplishments.

Student Assessments Used.   The Idea Oral Proficiency Test (IPT I) was used to measure oral proficiency in both Spanish and English. The purpose of the test was to designate students as limited English/Spanish speaking (LES/LSS) or fluent English/Spanish speaking (FES/FSS) for placement in the program. The May 1992/1993 results were used as base data. The test was administered yearly.

The Texas Assessment of Academic Skills (TAAS), a criterion-referenced test mandated by the state of Texas, was used to measure academic progress in reading, writing, and math in English for Grades 3 and 5.

Student portfolios were assessed and reviewed on an ongoing basis and were used as a tool for instructional improvement and staff development workshops. The portfolios were used to determine the progress of students on their development of writing skills throughout the year. Student portfolios were transferred with the students from year to year.

Nonproject Comparison Group.   Limited English proficient students (Spanish-dominant students) and Anglo or Hispanic English-dominant students in experimental two-way bilingual classrooms were compared to equivalent students in traditional bilingual control classrooms. In the first 2 years of the study, 250 students in pilot classrooms were compared to 250 students in control classrooms in the same schools. After the program was implemented schoolwide, whole-school academic performance was compared to similar schools in the district. When the program reached implementation in 12 schools, the schools' populations were measured through the Texas Education Agency's rankings according to their performance on TAAS.

Ethnographic Studies.   Ethnographic data, analyzed in light of the talent development perspective (Erickson, 1992; Mehan, 1979; Slavin & Boykin, 1995; Calderón & Carreón, 1994), consisted of field notes, interviews, videotaping of the Teachers Learning Community (TLC) sessions, professional development events, and pre and post video recordings of teachers applying innovations in their classrooms.

The study's framework is ecocultural theory (Tharpe & Gallimore, 1988) and Erickson's interpretative fieldwork approach to understand how meaning is developed and sustained through daily interaction, in which activity setting plays a prominent role in understanding complex ecologies. Activity settings are analyzed through five elements: (a) participants, (b) tasks and activities, (c) scripts for conduct, (d) goals, and (e) beliefs. The separate functions are linked with one another in activity (Vygotsky, 1978). Students and teachers are collaborators in the data gathering by coconstructing the ethnographies of their activity, goals, and beliefs in their teaching and in their collegial teams.

Critical discourse analysis is used to analyze how knowledge, power and identity are constructed (Foucault, 1980) within the TLCs and during the team teachers' instructional activities in the classrooms. The combination of classroom and staff development as integrated units of analysis helped us to study the elementary two-way bilingual and high school classrooms from an etic (pedagogical and sociopolitical) perspective and an emic (the construction of discourse in a teaching or learning situation) perspective.

In the Two-Way Bilingual Elementary study, the discourse analyses were used to bring out the values, beliefs, and social practices of Anglo and Hispanic teachers sharing one classroom. Because discourses can never be "neutral" or value free, they always reflect ideologies, systems of values, beliefs, and social practices (Fairclough, 1989; Foucault, 1972). Taken together, these complementary ways of exploring how instructional knowledge is "talked into being" (Green & Dixon, 1993) helped us to understand the professional growth of teachers.

Questions for the Two-Way Bilingual Study. How do teachers construct "common knowledge" of what a two-way bilingual program should be? What is the valorization of particular discourses, subjectivities, and practices in Spanish and English within each classroom? What are the particular social relationships of power, which are sanctioned and encouraged among students? Does Spanish or English receive more or equal status? How are particular spoken and written practices assembled, ranging from how to divide the day's instructional time into Spanish and English blocks to what types of activities teachers structure during Spanish and/or English blocks?

Questions for the Two-Way Schools' TLC Sessions. What are the particular social relationships of power between mainstream and minority teachers? How do mainstream and bilingual teachers develop long-lasting profound and meaningful partnerships in two-way bilingual contexts? How do teachers contribute to one another's talent and professional growth?

Teacher performance and development were analyzed through researcher–teacher joint ethnographies. The ethnographies focused on ways that teachers learned about their new skills and abilities to construct, control and function within bilingual texts. Text is defined as language in use (Halliday & Hasan, 1985). Texts are moments of intersubjectivity—the social and discursive relations between speakers, readers, and listeners. Readers, listeners, speakers, and writers thus depend on intertextuality, repeated and reiterated wordings, statements, and themes that appear in different texts (Fairclough, 1992). This approach to critical discourse analysis helped teachers generate agency for the program, to acquire a profound sense of ownership and commitment. It also gave teachers the tools to see how texts represent the social environment, the power struggles, and the power of two languages at work.

Participants.   The participants in the 3 years of the study were 24 teachers from two schools, 12 at each school. Half were bilingual and half monolingual. All bilingual teachers were Hispanic; all monolingual teachers were White Anglo. Each year, classroom ethnographies were compiled for the 24 teachers through all-day observations, twice in the fall and twice in the spring, by trained observers. All teachers were arbitrarily videotaped for an hour at randomly selected times during the day. Six of the teachers were observed all day, for a whole week. The teachers also responded to a 20-question essay-type questionnaire asking them to elaborate on their teaching practices, team-teaching experiences, and perceived problems and successes. The group of 24 teachers was also observed and videotaped once a month during their 2-hr Teachers Learning Community (TLC) sessions.

The teachers themselves conducted ethnographies in the second year of the project. They analyzed shifts in use of Spanish and English; instructional patterns for each language; students' social relationships of power; and teacher and student participant structures.

PROGRAM FEATURES
AND IMPLEMENTATION PROCESS

Preimplementation Phase

A meeting was scheduled for the principals and key teachers to meet with the bilingual education program coordinator and the director for curriculum and instruction to discuss a local model that would:

1. Comply with state regulations.
2. Utilize best knowledge and practice.
3. Be designed in collaboration with the school community.
4. Result in reform of the school's organization, curriculum and instruction.
5. Improve teaching practice and promote high student achievement.
6. Be accepted by parents, teachers, and students as an enrichment program.

After studying the latest thinking in the field of bilingual education and prominent models for reform, the group decided to design a two-way bilingual program, which would be an integral part of each school's vision. The final framework of program components became the following:

Accelerated Two-Way Bilingual Education Program Features

• Two-Way, Spanish & English Immersion

The program brings children of two language groups together to learn together in two languages. This is a 50/50 model in which Spanish is used as the language of instruction for 50% of the school day and English the other 50%. The objective is for both groups to become bilingual/biliterate and to attain a high level of multicultural understanding.

• Heterogeneous Grouping

Classes in Grades 1 through 5 include approximately 15 students of each language group. Parents of both groups of children select to have their children in the program. Students of all levels of ability, learning styles, and academic background are included in each class of 30 students per grade.

• Team Teaching

A team of two teachers provides instruction for each class of 30 students. One of the teachers is bilingual and is primarily responsible for instruction in Spanish, and the other is monolingual and is responsible for the English instruction.

• Integrated Curriculum

In order to provide a coherent curriculum that facilitates instruction in a second language and maximizes learning in the first language, the curriculum is integrated. The instructional day is divided into two blocks designed to ensure language separation: Integrated Spanish Instruction (ISI) and Integrated English Instruction (IEI).

• Thematic Units Based on an Inquiry Approach to Learning

The curriculum is organized into interdisciplinary units that focus on real world topics. Each topic is stated as a question and the instruction is based on an Inquiry Approach.

• Cooperative Learning

The makeup of the classes demands a great amount of interactive activities that promote learning and second language acquisition as well as continued development of the first language. The use of cooperative learning is the basis of a two-way program. Cooperative learning is used extensively, and the Bilingual Cooperative Integrated Reading and Composition model is used to develop Spanish and English literacy skills. Group Investigation is used to facilitate inquiry and the integration of math, science, social studies, language arts, and fine arts.

• Teachers' Learning Communities (TLC)

TLCs are opportunities for mainstream-bilingual teacher teams to meet continuously to study their instructional practices, adjust and solve multiple problems, take risks, share student successes, analyze student work, and continue their personal and professional growth.

• Intensive Professional Development

After an extensive initial effort, professional development will be ongoing. Some training will be provided for all teachers, and other training will be based on interest and need.

• Parental Involvement

Parents are key to the success of their child's education. In a two-way program, they are an integral part of the program and the support system for their children's education.

• Excellence for All

An enrichment program utilizing two languages for instruction enhances cognitive development and demonstrates the additive value of bilingualism for all students.

Curriculum Development and Implementation

During the preimplementation phase, training was provided for the teachers in the project schools on curriculum writing. The training culminated with the development of a 2-week unit to use as a minipilot in the spring. This activity served many purposes. First, it allowed the teachers to apply their new learnings and philosophy in practice. Second, it allowed the teachers to test these new learnings and philosophy through ample discussions—probing, questioning, studying more and questioning more. At the end of the pilot phase, students and teachers were able to give concrete examples of the benefits of two-way bilingual education to parents. The instructional products, the comments of students and teachers, and the district support for the program were featured at a parent orientation and student preregistration meeting. Numerous questions from parents were answered during the orientation and new insights for program design were derived. Most important, the parents reiterated their message—the program should be made available to everyone.

Global Educational Perspective. The Accelerated Two-Way Bilingual Education Program for kindergarten through fifth grade was designed to address the demands of a changing world and to profit from the intellectual power of bilingualism. It based its thematic units on the following premise: As education takes a global perspective, it must prepare students to become leaders in a world of increasing knowledge, diversity, and technological advancements. To succeed as contributing members of society, today's youth must be critical thinkers, innovative problem solvers, and collaborative workers. They must also be multilingual and highly literate, well versed in the use of technology, mathematics, science, and the social sciences.

During the summer, curriculum guides for Grades 1–5 were developed. The general theme for the curriculum selected was "Discovery." The teachers as a group selected program and grade-level themes, and each grade level embarked on the 3-year journey to write units of study for its grade level. Figure 4.1 illustrates how the units incorporate the disciplines and corresponding learner outcomes in the process of seeking to answer a central question.

Instruction by Teams. The delivery of instruction in a two-way model requires the balancing of content taught in each language and the careful scheduling and planning of lessons in which concepts and skill taught in one language are applied or extended in the other, but not introduced again. The additional challenge in this balancing feat is that each class has two teachers. The bilingual and monolingual teacher team creates the infrastructure of the instructional design. Each class of 30 students has two teachers who teach as a team and collaborate, so that all students benefit from their collective efforts and individual strengths. One of the teachers must be a bilingual teacher with strong skills in Spanish and well versed in second-language development, cooperative learning, content knowledge, and instructional strategies. The other teacher must be a monolingual teacher who is prepared to teach with the same methodologies and also appreciates the benefits of bilingualism. Both teachers need to be extremely flexible.

The team shares ideas, plans instruction, participates in TLCs and peer coaching, collaborates with parents and other teacher teams, and promotes multicultural understanding. Each teacher is responsible for the primary instruction of the appropriate component, integrated Spanish in-

Schedule A Used During First 1-2 Weeks Of A Unit

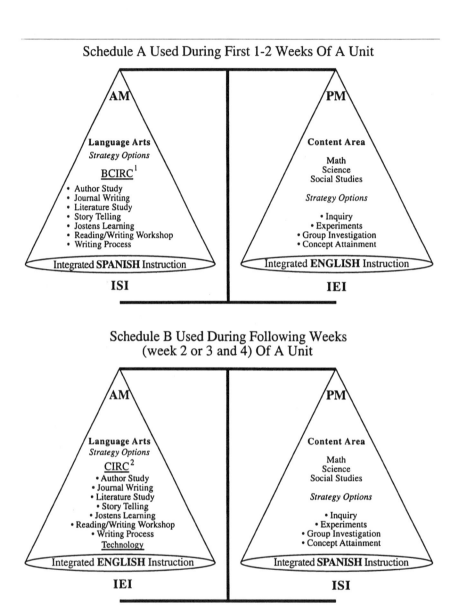

AM

Language Arts
Strategy Options
BCIRC[1]
- Author Study
- Journal Writing
- Literature Study
- Story Telling
- Jostens Learning
- Reading/Writing Workshop
- Writing Process

Integrated **SPANISH** Instruction

ISI

PM

Content Area
Math
Science
Social Studies

Strategy Options
- Inquiry
- Experiments
- Group Investigation
- Concept Attainment

Integrated **ENGLISH** Instruction

IEI

Schedule B Used During Following Weeks (week 2 or 3 and 4) Of A Unit

AM

Language Arts
Strategy Options
CIRC[2]
- Author Study
- Journal Writing
- Literature Study
- Story Telling
- Jostens Learning
- Reading/Writing Workshop
- Writing Process
Technology

Integrated **ENGLISH** Instruction

IEI

PM

Content Area
Math
Science
Social Studies

Strategy Options
- Inquiry
- Experiments
- Group Investigation
- Concept Attainment

Integrated **SPANISH** Instruction

ISI

1. BCIRC = Bilingual Cooperative Integrated Reading and Composition
2. CIRC = Cooperative Integrated Reading and Composition

FIG. 4.1. Two-way bilingual education.

struction or integrated English instruction, but both have mutually supportive roles during the entire instructional process. This organizational structure sends powerful messages to students who see firsthand interaction and collaboration between adults who represent two languages and diverse sociocultural backgrounds. It is also an asset for the teachers, who have an opportunity to learn from each other and collaborate to improve the instructional setting. Training also helps teachers enhance their partnership with parents because all parents (English-speaking and Spanish-speaking) are actively sought and tended to.

Instructional Components and Separation of Languages. The instructional day is divided into two components, integrated Spanish instruction (ISI) and integrated English instruction (IEI). This provides for a 50–50 two-way model in which Spanish and English are utilized for instruction for an equal period of time. This indicates that the languages are valued equally and provides for a clear separation of instructional time in each language. The languages are systematically separated by instructional component, ISI and IEI, as well as by teacher.

Because the curriculum is organized into thematic units, all learning objectives are addressed at separate times in both languages (with the exception of those that are language specific), and materials appropriate for each language are used. To provide for in-depth study and sequential instruction, teachers alternate their schedule so that the content of the unit primarily related to language arts (including literacy and language development) is taught in Spanish BCIRC in the morning during ISI for 1 to 2 weeks and the content related to mathematics, science, and social studies in the afternoon during IEI for the same 1 to 2 weeks. Following that, CIRC (language arts) is scheduled in the morning during IEI and the content area during ISI in the afternoon. Technology, art, music, and drama are integrated throughout ISI and IEI.

Some days, the students spend most of the day in one language, but the percentage evens out as the week progresses. The two teachers use one classroom for teacher-directed instruction and cooperative learning, and the other for computers and learning centers. While one teacher is conducting direct instruction, the other is facilitating group work or monitoring. Figure 4.1 is a schematic representation of the instructional day and indicates how language separation is achieved within the period of a thematic unit.

The purpose of this configuration is to enable the Spanish-proficient students to learn English through extensive interaction with English role models without lagging behind academically. Concomitantly, it is to provide opportunities for native English speakers to learn all subject matter in Spanish, and become proficient in the second language of the community. Students are taught to work together in a mutually supportive environment.

Class Composition.   The 50–50 proportion of English-dominant and Spanish-dominant students in each class promotes the heterogeneous instruction of students who are learning English and those who are fluent speakers of English. Students who qualify for bilingual education due to limited English and native speakers of English who request to participate in the program are placed in the same class, ideally in equal numbers.

Instructional Methods.   The curriculum is delivered through the following instructional models: Team Inquiry, Group Investigation, and the English, Spanish, and ESL versions of Cooperative Integrated Reading and Composition (CIRC and BCIRC) instructional models (Calderón, 1994; Hertz-Lazarowitz & Calderón, 1994; Stevens, Madden, Slavin, & Farnish, 1987). Whole-language approaches (Ada, 1993; Goodman, Goodman, & Flores, 1979) and computer-based instruction in reading (IBM, Jostens) are primarily used in K–1 grades. The whole-language approach consisted of shared reading with big books, interactive reading of trade books or a basal series, centers for student independent learning, and a computer program called Writing to Read.

For second to fifth grades, BCIRC was selected as the instructional approach. Students work in heterogeneous teams of four. First, the teacher introduces a story from a basal text or trade book and introduces vocabulary and background information. Then, students work in their teams on a prescribed series of activities relating to the story, called Treasure Hunts. These include partner reading, in which students take turns reading to each other in pairs; Treasure Hunt activities, in which students work together to identify characters, settings, problems, and problem solutions in narratives; and summarization activities. Students write "meaningful sentences" to show the meaning of new vocabulary words, and write compositions that relate to their reading. The program includes a curriculum for teaching main idea, figurative language, and other comprehension skills, and includes a home reading and book report component. The writing/language arts component of CIRC uses a cooperative writing process approach in which students work together to plan, draft, revise, edit, and publish compositions in a variety of genres. Students master language mechanics and skills in their teams, and these are then added to editing checklists to ensure their continued application in the students' own writing. Teams earn recognition based on the performance of their members on quizzes, compositions, book reports, and other products (Calderón, 1995; Calderón, Hertz-Lazarowitz, & Slavin,

1998; Madden et al., 1996; Slavin & Fashola, 1998). The 5-day cycle of discussion–reading–writing activities is conducted in one language, and then the following week another cycle is conducted in the other language with a different trade book, novel, or basal story. Figure 4.2 depicts the integration of the theme with literature selections, content areas, and skills objectives.

Integrated Curriculum and Discourse. The difference between two-way bilingual and other bilingual/ESL programs is that the learning of English and Spanish is taught throughout the day and not just during language arts/reading or pull out sessions. First and second language are taught throughout the day to reinforce new vocabulary, language, reading,

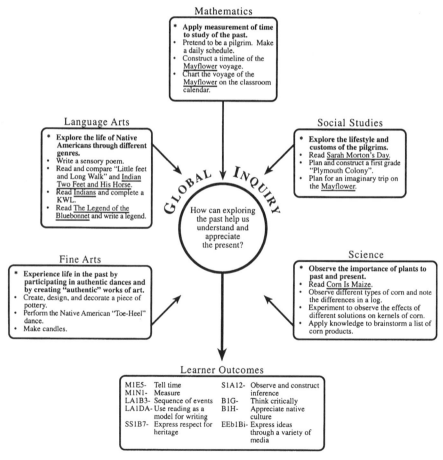

FIG. 4.2. Discover the World, Native Americans, Part I, Grade 1. Any theme-related book may be substituted for literature titles given. *MAJOR LEARNING OBJECTIVE.

and writing skills learned during the specific 90 min of language arts. That is the reason for integrating all subject areas with the reading curriculum.

The use of an integrated curriculum and cooperative learning structures appears to facilitate learning concepts and skills in two languages. Students are grouped in cooperative learning teams and are seated at round tables of four students, two learners of English and two learners of Spanish. This team structure promotes interaction and cooperation among students. Quality discourse organized through the Treasure Hunts promotes second-language development, enhances the student's first language, and accelerates learning in general because students are also reading and writing.

Two-Way Success for All/Éxito Para Todos Instructional Model. The second-phase schools chose to integrate the Success for All/*Éxito Para Todos* program into the two-way bilingual framework used by the other schools. The principle of integrated curriculum also applies in Two-Way SFA programs. Students in Lee Conmigo/Roots and Alas/Wings components are regrouped according to language dominance and continue with the 50–50 content instruction after the 90 min of SFA/EPT. Gradually, the students shift into the other language until all students are learning through alternating weeks of Alas and Wings, about Grade 3 or 4. At this point, all students are proficient bilinguals and can function at high literacy levels in both languages.

Figures 4.3 to 4.6 summarize the configurations for student assessment, placement, teachers' teaming structures, transition from one language to the other, and instructional time distribution within a two-way bilingual program. Figure 4.3 provides guidelines for the half-day and full-day prekindergarten and kindergarten classrooms. Figure 4.4 summarizes recommendations for the Lee Conmigo and Roots classrooms and how to determine which students are immersed in reading in Spanish or English. It also indicates the time allocated to second-language acquisition. Figure 4.5 concentrates on the critical merging of reading in two languages. Finally, Fig. 4.6 sets up the routines for sustaining literacy in both languages.

Several drafts of the SFA two-way bilingual organizational structures were designed and tested. Those of Figs. 4.3 to 4.6 are the ones currently in place. Figure 4.7 illustrates the management of time for each language, and the approximate time of transition from one component to the other.

Staff Development

The preimplementation phase was initially funded by state bilingual education funds. Ninety-nine hours of staff development were conducted by nationally and internationally known experts for the schools' principals,

---

* ASSESSMENT AND PLACEMENT OF STUDENTS
\> TEAM TEACHING CONFIGURATIONS FOR TEACHERS
• INSTRUCTIONAL TIME DISTRIBUTION

PREKINDERGARTEN—*APRENDIZAJE INICIAL*/EARLY LEARNING
* No SFA assessment is necessary. Language proficiency is determined by state/district oral language proficiency assessment guidelines and the Pre-IPT test. This will determine homeroom placement.
\> Each teacher has a heterogeneous classroom of 50% Spanish-proficient and 50% English-proficient students.
• Instruction is 50% Spanish and 50% English.
• The SFA Early Learning/*Aprendizaje Inicial* curriculum will be the core curriculum.
• Spanish and English instruction will be used on alternate weeks. This ensures language separation and full immersion in the language of instruction on an equal basis.

KINDERGARTEN—*APRENDIZAJE INICIAL*/EARLY LEARNING
* No SFA assessment is necessary. Language proficiency needs to be determined through the IPT 1 test. This will determine home-room placement.
\> Each teacher has a heterogeneous classroom of 50% Spanish-proficient and 50% English-proficient students.

First Semester:
• Instruction is 50% English and 50% Spanish.
• The Early Learning/*Aprendizaje Inicial* curriculum and its corresponding components will be implemented via direct instruction in Spanish and English on alternate weeks. However, Spanish dominant children will read with *Deseamos Leer* and English dominant students will read with *Eager to Read*. This requires that teacher(s) group by language for this component for 15 min daily. Letter Investigations activities will also be conducted in the appropriate language during this time and integrated with *Deseamos Leer* or *Eager to Read*.

Second Semester:
• Spanish dominant children move from *Deseamos Leer* to *Kinder Lee Conmigo* (KLC).
• English dominant children move from *Eager to Read* to *Kinder Roots*.
• Instruction continues 50–50. However, students continue reading in their primary language and return to their Spanish or English teacher for 30 min *Kinder Lee Conmigo* or *Kinder Roots*.
  1. In a *half-day* program KLC will be scheduled for 30 min three times per week. In a *full day* program KLC will be provided for 30 min daily.
  2. In a *half-day* program Kinder Roots will be scheduled for 30 min three times per week. In a *full day* program Kinder Roots will be provided for 30 min daily.

FIG. 4.3.   Success for All/*Éxito Para Todos* two-way bilingual program guidelines.

assistant principals, district bilingual coordinator, and teachers. The initial training consisted of the Accelerated Schools model and process, theory and practice for language and literacy, the Bilingual Cooperative Integrated Reading and Composition (BCIRC) model, multiple intelligences, and portfolios for authentic assessment.

* ASSESSMENT AND PLACEMENT OF STUDENTS
> TEAM TEACHING CONFIGURATIONS FOR TEACHERS
• INSTRUCTIONAL TIME DISTRIBUTION

1st–2nd GRADES—LEE CONMIGO/READING ROOTS/WINGS/ALAS
* Students will be assessed first with the IPT 1 to determine language dominance.
* Students will next be assessed with either the SFA Lee Conmigo or SFA Reading Roots
  Initial Assessment, depending on their dominant language.
> Based on numbers of students for each level in each language, SFA classes are formed.
  The team teachers will continue to team and exchange students after the 90-min reading
  block. During the 90-min block, they may need to send their students to other teachers.
  This will create different types of teams, across first and second grades, and perhaps third
  grades.

First Semester.
• Spanish-dominant students will go to Lee Conmigo teachers for the 90-min reading block
  (integrated Spanish instruction time).
• English dominant students will go to Reading Roots teachers for the 90-min reading block
  (integrated English instruction time).

| • Students that test out of Lee Conmigo will be placed in Alas Para Leer for the 90-min block. |

Second Semester.
• Spanish-dominant students will continue with Lee Conmigo teachers for the 90-min read-
  ing block (integrated Spanish instruction time) until they finish book 50. In addition,
  Spanish-dominant students will go to a Reading Roots teacher for 45 min of ESL Reading
  Roots (integrated English instruction time). Students attend ESL and SSL classes as a
  homeroom. They are not regrouped for second-language instruction.
• English-dominant students will go to Reading Roots teachers for the 90-min reading block
  (integrated English instruction time) until they finish book 48. English-dominant students
  will go to a Lee Conmigo teacher for 45 min of SSL Lee Conmigo (integrated Spanish instruction time). Students attend ESL and SSL classes as a homeroom. They are not regrouped for second-language instruction.

| • Students that test out of Lee Conmigo will be placed in Alas Para Leer for the 90-min
  block and a 45-min ESL Reading Roots instructional block later in the day. Students
  that test out of Reading Roots will be placed in Reading Wings for the 90-min block
  and a 45-min SSL Lee Conmigo instructional block later in the day. |

FIG. 4.4.   Success for All/Éxito Para Todos two-way bilingual program guidelines.

Through a subsequent Title VII grant, a stronger staff development
program was implemented the second year. Project teachers, administrators, and district specialists attended a two-semester college course conducted in Spanish and English sessions on BCIRC, cooperative learning
principles and techniques, and the Group Investigation and Inquiry models of teaching. Dealing with Change and peer coaching were also part of
the two courses. As the teachers learned through theory and hands-on

* ASSESSMENT AND PLACEMENT OF STUDENTS
> TEAM TEACHING CONFIGURATIONS FOR TEACHERS
• INSTRUCTIONAL TIME DISTRIBUTION

3rd GRADES—LEE CONMIGO/READING ROOTS or ALAS/WINGS
* All English and Spanish dominant students are assessed with *both Lee Conmigo Initial Assessment* and *Roots Initial Assessment*, and both results are recorded for each child.
> Based on numbers of students for each level in each language, SFA classes are formed. The team teachers will continue to team and exchange students after the 90-min reading block. During the 90-min block, they may need to send their students to other teachers. This will create different types of teams, across first and second grades, and perhaps third grades.

First Semester.
• Spanish dominant students will go to *Lee Conmigo* teachers for the 90-min reading block (integrated Spanish instruction time).
• English dominant students will go to *Reading Roots* teachers for the 90-min reading block (integrated English instruction time).

• Students that test out of *Lee Conmigo* will be placed in *Alas Para Leer* for the 90-min block. Students that test out of *Reading Roots* will be placed in *Reading Wings* for the 90-min block.

Second Semester.
• Spanish-dominant students will continue with *Lee Conmigo* teachers for the 90-min reading block (integrated Spanish instruction time) until they finish book 50. Spanish dominant students will go to a *Reading Roots* ESL certified teacher for 45 min of *ESL Reading Roots* (integrated English instruction time). Students attend ESL and SSL classes as a homeroom. They are not regrouped for second-language instruction.
• English-dominant students will go to *Reading Roots* teachers for the 90-min reading block (integrated English instruction time) until they finish book 48. English-dominant students will go to a *Lee Conmigo* teacher for 45 min of *SSL Lee Conmigo* (integrated Spanish instruction time). Students attend ESL and SSL classes as a homeroom. They are not regrouped for second-language instruction.

• Students who test out of *Lee Conmigo* will be placed in *Alas Para Leer* for the 90-min block and a 45-min *ESL Reading Roots* instructional block later in the day. Students who test out of *Reading Roots* will be placed in *Reading Wings* for the 90-min block and a 45-min *SSL Lee Conmigo* instructional block later in the day.

• Students who tested out of *Roots* and *Lee Conmigo* will continue in *Alas Para Leer* and *Reading Wings* for the 90-min instructional block. Teachers will alternate students between *Alas* and *Wings* either after (1) every 5 day cycle; (2) 2 weeks; or (3) 3 weeks. Second-language instruction is no longer needed.

TAAS NOTE: SFA assessment is to be used, along with district criteria, to determine if students will be tested with Spanish or English TAAS for accountability.

FIG. 4.5. Success for All/*Éxito Para Todos* two-way bilingual program guidelines.

* ASSESSMENT AND PLACEMENT OF STUDENTS
> TEAM TEACHING CONFIGURATIONS FOR TEACHERS
• INSTRUCTIONAL TIME DISTRIBUTION

4th–5th GRADES—ALAS PARA LEER/READING WINGS
* The TAAS in English and TAAS in Spanish Texas Learning Index scores will be the determining factor for assessment and placement of all English and Spanish dominant students.
> Based on numbers of students for each level in each language, SFA classes are formed. The team teachers will continue to team and exchange students after the 90-min reading block. During the 90-min block, they may need to send their students to other teachers. This will create different types of teams, across grade levels.

First Semester.
• Spanish-dominant students will go to *Alas Para Leer* teachers for the 90-min reading block (integrated Spanish instruction time).
• English-dominant students will go to *Reading Wings* teachers for the 90-min reading block (integrated English instruction time).
• Some immigrant students may need *Older Lee Conmigo* instruction for the 90-min block before moving on to *Alas Para Leer*.
• Some students may need *Older Roots* instruction for the 90-min block before moving on to *Reading Wings*.

• Students who test out of *Lee Conmigo and Roots* will be placed in *Alas Para Leer* and *Reading Wings* for the 90-min instructional block. Teachers will alternate students either after (1) every 5 day cycle; (2) 3 weeks; or (3) 3 weeks.

Second Semester.
• Spanish-dominant students will continue with *Alas Para Leer* teachers for the 90-min reading block (integrated Spanish instruction time) for the remainder of the year. Spanish-dominant students will also go to a *Reading Roots* ESL certified teacher for 45 min of *ESL Older Reading Roots* (integrated English instruction time). Students attend ESL and SSL classes as a homeroom. They are not regrouped for second language instruction.
• English-dominant students will go to *Reading Wings* teachers for the 90-min reading block (integrated English instruction time) for the remainder of the year. English-dominant students will also go to a *Lee Conmigo* teacher for 45 min of *SSL Lee Conmigo* (integrated Spanish instruction time).

• Students who tested out of *Roots* and *Lee Conmigo* will continue in *Alas Para Leer* and *Reading Wings* for the 90-min instructional block. Teachers will alternate students between *Wings* and *Alas* either after (1) every 5 day cycle; (2) 2 weeks; or (3) 3 weeks. Second-language instruction is no longer needed

---

TAAS NOTE: SFA assessment is used, along with district criteria, to determine if students will be tested with Spanish or English TAAS for accountability.

FIG. 4.6. Success for All/*Éxito Para Todos* two-way bilingual program guidelines.

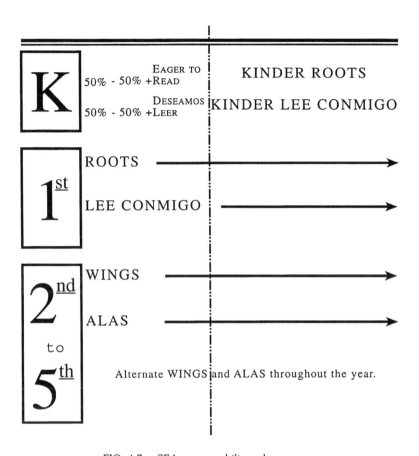

FIG. 4.7. SFA two-way bilingual programs.

activities how to teach students to work in teams, they learned how to work together and build communities of practice. Monthly TLC (Teachers Learning Community) sessions were held at the schools and provided time for teachers to problem solve and share ideas as well as time to ask questions about administrative matters. This course and the TLCs set the foundation for collegiality and continued learning. The TLCs also continued the following years, providing theory, demonstrations in Spanish and English on the teaching models, and computer instruction.

Parental Involvement

Parents became involved in the program from the preimplementation phase. Parent meetings were held in the spring prior to fall implementation to showcase the results of a field test of the curriculum and to provide a general overview. This not only provided background information but also became an incentive for voluntary enrollment of English speakers. All parents in the community were invited, and it was explained that limited English proficient students currently enrolled in bilingual education classes would now be in the new two-way program. For many of the parents of the English speakers, it was an opportunity that they had long awaited. Their children would now have access to quality instruction in Spanish and an enriched curriculum in two languages. The parents of LEP students immediately saw the benefits. No longer would bilingual education be perceived as a remedial program. It was now recognized as an enrichment program for all students.

As a result of the parents' positive responses, classes filled up quickly and some students had to be placed on a waiting list. Each year the list got longer, until the district began implementing the program in other schools.

Activities for parents continued throughout each year. The challenge of working with two language groups of parents and facilitating activities that promote mutual understanding and respect requires sincerity and sensitivity. Teachers conduct discussion groups and structure other opportunities to help parents support their children as they acquire a new language, new friends, and a new culture. Parent–child activities included the publication of a book coauthored by the parent and child. The project included training sessions for parents on reading to children, reading with children, and reading by children as well as writing with children. Child care was provided during which the same reading strategies were used with younger children. The project culminated with an author's "tea" where students displayed their books and received comments on their publication from the audience. Parents reported that their publications became family treasures and heirlooms. The publications typically depicted family members, humor, pets, school, fantasies, and several other topics. Through the efforts of an ongoing learning community of students, teachers, and parents, the goals of the program were implemented and continued to be refined.

Administration and Staffing

Systemic reform incorporates every aspect of schooling, the school community, and the central administration. Site-based management made the school the center of decision making and placed the central office staff in a supportive role, helping to facilitate change behind the scenes. The principal, core teachers, program assistant, and the director for bilingual education also had to learn how to became a team and share the numerous challenges that come with the implementation of a new program.

The first challenge was for each principal to team program teachers, especially because they had to work as partners and share a room. Principals made every effort to encourage teachers to select their teams, but the new experience of working as a team or conducting instruction for half a day in Spanish caused some concern among teachers. Staffing the bilingual position was the most difficult and was done with teachers already on the staff where possible. Mobility and a few teams who found teaming difficult had to be addressed on a yearly basis.

A principal's role in a two-way bilingual school is possibly two times as complex as in regular schools. Unless the staff has been hand picked and is willing to experiment and learn along with the principal, it is a futile effort to even contemplate implementing these programs. Principals must contemplate spending at least a year in preparation for the initial implementation. There are many things to consider: student population; parental and community knowledge and involvement from the start; extensive staff development for processing research-based information; the selection of a two-way model that best fits their needs; staffing; evaluation and assessment; resources and funding; and steps for implementation.

PEDAGOGICAL FEATURES THAT FACILITATED OR OBSTRUCTED LEARNING

Teacher and student development go hand in hand. This section discusses teacher development through peer ethnographies, and the ways teachers learn about their capacities to construct, control, and manipulate bilingual texts. During the TLC sessions, teachers were asked to take on the roles of peer coaches, classroom ethnographers, trainers of other teachers, and curriculum writers. The emphasis on these structures created new tasks and other ways of looking at their daily routines. Peer coaching became a way of doing classroom ethnographies. Simple ethnographic techniques were demonstrated so the teachers could practice and experiment in their classrooms with their peer coaches. Each teacher did a miniethnography while the other was teaching. They scripted a segment, then analyzed and discussed the data together. These instructional events were also videotaped so that the researcher could assist if necessary, and to have a context for discussion at the next TLC meeting.

The following scripts consisted of what occurred during a 30- to 90-min instructional segment. These simple time-dependent observations gave teachers a point of departure for further study and refinement. The scripts were written mostly in English. Monolingual English teachers had no problem identifying participant structures or key events in teaching/learning segments even though the instructional conversations were conducted in Spanish. Next are four examples that teachers brought to the TLC and that generated extensive discussion by the teams of teachers. These were also videotaped in order to conduct a researchers' analysis of the features that facilitated or obstructed student learning and teacher learning.

Two-Way Bilingual Classroom 1—3rd Grade

8:20   (Instruction in Spanish)
        Math review—100s
8:35   Math new instruction—1000s
8:50   Math in Presidential Unit—in teams of four
        —Research questions on presidential facts
9:05   (Instruction in English)
        Explanation of how to work together on these story problems
        —Students begin their work
9:15   Review of organizational strategies for more effective work
9:28   Students begin work again
9:40   Reality check "Who's finished?" "Come help this other team."
        "You have 10 more minutes."
9:50   Students finish, put work away.
Break
(90 min)

During the 22 min of English instruction, students worked with partners on 10 sets of word problems, which integrated social studies and math as follows: Find out who lived the longest: Lincoln or Juárez? How many presidents were there between Washington and Lincoln? Who were they? How many years between their presidencies? Students had readings and Treasure Hunts with some of the information, but other information had to be found in encyclopedias or books on a table.

After a 7-min break, the students came back into the classroom to continue with the presidents' theme. There was a transition activity from English to Spanish in the following manner:

Two-Way Bilingual Classroom 1—3rd Grade

9:55   (Instruction in English)
        Students come back and immediately start reciting English poem from last week with one teacher while the other distributes reading material and questions for next instructional event in Spanish.
        —Students practice choral reading of poem (first boys, then girls, then line by line, then one line soft, one line loud).
        —Teacher asks how students "feel" about this poem. Seven students quickly share.

10:00   (Transition into Spanish)
Students recite last week's Spanish poem. (Students who had memorized the poems received reward points for their team on a wall chart.)

10:05   (Instruction in Spanish)
"Compañeros juntos por favor" sends students to quickly pair up for partner reading in Spanish.
—Following the presidential theme, booklets about Lincoln and Juárez become the reading selection in Spanish. (There's a table with other books, booklets, etc. about U.S. and Mexico's presidents in Spanish.)

10:06   Partner reading is fluent, interactive; students help each other; stay on task and discuss what they read.

10:16   "Un mapa del cuento"
—Students are to map four important events in the presidents' lives.
—Teacher and students discuss some events.
—Teacher explains the task and asks several questions to check for understanding.

10:35   Students begin work.

10:40   Teacher redirects teams by talking about strategies for organization.

10:45   Students go back to work. Some argue about the task, reach agreement, start work.

11:00   Teachers monitor and check work by teams. Bilingual teacher checks sentences to describe each event. Team teacher checks product and process.

11:55   Large maps have been constructed and students are getting ready to present them to the class, after they return from lunch.

(120 min)

In these two examples the teachers are setting the stage for learning by providing the discursive "slots" that enable fluent and limited speakers of two languages, or as Kris Gutierrez (1995) might term, expert and novice learners, to participate in meaningful learning. They involved the students in ways of talking about math, social studies, reading, and writing through negotiation and reasoning. The teachers orchestrated equal status by giving both the English and Spanish speakers a voice in the construction of joint knowledge.

The socially constructed forms of discourse in one language (e.g., organization of team members to complete the assigned task and helping the partners understand in that language) transfer easily into activities in the other language. A systematic program such as BCIRC that uses the same sequence of tasks and patterns for learning helps students transfer knowledge and skills from one language into the other with more ease. These socially constructed forms of discourse are appropriated by students and become a means for restructuring their ways of responding to texts.

Both of the teachers had to interrupt the teams to help them "come up with a better strategy" as soon as they noticed difficulties. Students need time to learn how to learn with peers. Biliteracy implies both literacy in two languages and respect for and the blending of two sociocultural systems of knowledge. This is particularly important for the minority child whose primary discourses may differ from the institutional discourses that are readily acquired by the majority children.

One problem the teachers perceived through the scripts was that the students spent too much time on their maps. "It didn't feel that long" while they were monitoring the students and listening to their discussions. While discussion is critical to learning, the 55 min appeared too long for one task discussion. Too much time on such team products was often a problem in all the classrooms.

The team teachers had been concerned that not enough time was given to Spanish instruction. Their own analysis of their peer coaching scripts reassured them that they were on the right track. Their next step was to continue to do scripts systematically for a whole week to determine the "real time on language" during a week's instructional unit. Unfortunately, the result was that about 65% of time was spent on English versus 35% on Spanish. That information would serve as a next step for improvement. They planned lessons for the following week and used their peer coaching scripts to facilitate further refinement of their teaching and equal time to both languages.

The following two examples illustrate how one team teacher facilitates opportunities for student learning and more peer interaction while the other employs strategies that restrict interaction and learning.

Two-Way Bilingual Classroom 3—4th Grade

8:55   (Instruction in English)
       Teacher reads a poem. Then she says it's really a song and sings it.
       "What character does this remind you of?" Students give opinions
       about other fiction and real life characters.
9:00   How would you read the part about . . . ? Teacher models and then
       helps students get into the rhythm.
       —The teacher reads the poem one more time and the students
       clap when they hear the rhyming words at the end of lines.
9:05   "Lets check for comprehension . . ." The teacher asks the students
       to tell about their own similar experiences.

9:10   "Line up if you can sing the line after my line" The teacher sings
        lines out of sequence. She sings the first line, points to a team, and
        the team has to sing the second line in unison. If they sing it cor-
        rectly, the team lines up to go to PE.

9:15   Students sing themselves out the door. Teachers place materials on
        tables for next activity.

(20 min)

This segment helped students feel and experience phonemic awareness
through rhyme and song in English. The students identify pairs of rhyming words they will later use as a word bank to write their own poems.
When the teacher says "let's check for comprehension," she lets students
give examples of their own experiences similar to the character's dilemma
in the song. The teacher builds interdependence in each team by arbitrarily selecting lines from the song. This means that in each team, all
students must listen attentively and quickly help each other "tune in" to
the sequential line. Furthermore, the two dominant English speakers had
to rush in with a variety of strategies to help the two students who had
not yet memorized the song. This peer assistance was conducted
smoothly and quickly with no trace of the resentment sometimes observed in cooperative teams where the students who "know" do not want
to help those that "don't know."

Although the English segment had several opportunities for minority
and majority students to learn and participate, the Spanish segment that
followed was not as meaningful to the students.

Two-Way Bilingual Classroom 3—4th Grade

10:05   (Instruction in Spanish)
        Morning message: Tengo unos errores aquí, ¿Quién los encuentra?
        (The whole-class attempts to find 5 errors in the teachers' five sen-
        tences.)

10:25   Basado en la canción de esta mañana, ¿qué podría recibir el niño
        para navidad?
        —Students brainstorm and teacher webs students' ideas on the
        chalkboard.

10:30   "These are sentence strips from the story we are going to read to-
        day. Read the sentence strips in pairs and draw a picture about
        what those sentence strips describe." (Students work in pairs to
        draw a picture.)

10:52   Students give pictures to teachers and the teachers post them in se-
        quence on a long bulletin board. The pictures from the book have
        been photocopied and the teachers place them beside the students'

drawings. (Students sit on the floor and chairs facing the bulletin board; 25 students go up, one at a time, to describe what they drew.)

11:08   Teacher reads the story from her trade book.

11:23   Students are asked to write their own song about the same topic when they come back from lunch.

(78 min)

At the beginning of this teaching segment, in what the teacher calls "morning message," 15 min was used to identify five errors. This could have been easily accomplished in 2 to 3 min. During the 78 min, the activity structure was mostly teacher talk, teacher sequencing, teacher reading, and students sitting in pairs but doing independent work (drawing of pictures to depict one or two sentences from the story). The students spent 22 min drawing and 2 min reading, versus the 15 min the teacher took to read. Teacher reading is important for modeling or when it is the type of interactive reading that develops listening comprehension. In this case it was straight reading of the story.

The many typical behaviors of nonlisteners were also evident during that reading segment: restlessness, bothering another student, and other off-task behaviors. The error detection activity was also extremely long and students merely practiced "guessing" strategies. As teachers and ethnographers examined this script, we saw how students had missed out on learning about the story's structure, author's craft, vocabulary in the second or first language, social norms for constructing meaning, or talking about learning. After examining this script, the teacher mentioned that her training on "whole language" had taught her not to impose on the students and to help them out as much as possible. She felt it would take some time to "tighten up [her] technique and not do so much for the students."

Simple scripts such as these helped the teachers begin to analyze how time and quality of learning is distributed throughout each day. They gave a clear yet concise view of time spent on each language; time on subject matter; the time the teacher is on stage versus the time the students are working in teams with partners, or individually; the difference between busy work and learning; and how the team teaching is distributed. It gave teachers some tools with which to step back and generate a set of questions that would serve for analysis, reflection and reorganization of time, language status, and implicit power in the participant structures. After the teachers' group reflection, they synthesized their concerns into the following questions for further analysis:

Teachers' Recommendations After Analysis of Scripts

A. Analyze the academic objective and outcome of the lesson
   1. Does the product reflect ample learning of an academic skill?
   2. What other strategic learning skill have students learned?
   3. What was the linguistic learning? The reading? The writing? The content?
B. How much time do teachers spend on
   1. Explanations of the task and procedures?
   2. Correcting task and procedures or re-explaining?
   3. Doing too much for the students?
C. How much time do students spend
   1. Drawing?
   2. Making products?
   3. Writing?
   4. Reading?
   5. Teaching and learning with partners?
   6. On the computer?
D. What is the status of L_1 and L_2?
   1. How much time is spent in Spanish in a week?
   2. How much time is spent in English in a week?
   3. What is taught in Spanish?
   4. What is taught in English?
   5. How do students react to either one?
   6. How are we improving on a week-by-week basis?
E. How's our team teaching?
   1. How do we orchestrate our roles for each teaching event?
   2. Who was on stage more this week?
   3. How does the team teacher assist?
   4. What does the team teacher really do when the other is on stage?
   5. How can we balance or improve our team teaching?

The list of categories helped the teachers do further inquiry on the quality of student participant structures, the level of quality of learning in one or the other language, and the time and status of each language. With practice, their observations became more focused on the factors that enhanced or restricted learning. The peer ethnographies gave teachers greater insights into their own professional development needs.

By creating a culture of inquiry through ethnography, professional learning was focused and accelerated. With the tools of "teacher ethnography" the teams of monolingual and bilingual teachers drew closer together. They learned about their teaching by observing children and their partner. Their partner provided a mirror for their teaching. Change became meaningful, relevant, and necessary. The teachers' continuous

TABLE 4.1
TAAS (Average Texas Learning Index)

	Reading				Math			
	Two-Way Bilingual				Two-Way Bilingual			
Grade	NonLEP	LEP	Bilingual	District	NonLEP	LEP	Bilingual	District
3	82.0	78.1	70.3	78.3	75.3	73.5	71.0	76.0
4	77.7	73.1	65.4	78.4	77.5	75.3	68.2	75.8
5	79.1	71.0	63.2	80.2	73.3	68.5	64.9	75.3

learning brought about instructional program refinement and impacted student gains as evidenced by the academic and linguistic data compared between experimental and control students.

The academic gains at the end of the 3 years for third, fourth, and fifth graders (Table 4.1) were significantly better for students in the two-way bilingual classrooms than for those in the other three district bilingual programs. Several of students in the fourth and fifth grades had only been in the program one or two years. Nevertheless, their scores from the English Texas Assessment of Academic Skills (TAAS) were relatively at the district's average. Although the LEP students were still behind the nonbilingual students, they were significantly above the other LEP students in the district after the 3 years of simultaneous program development and implementation.

TEACHERS' TRANSFER OF KNOWLEDGE
FROM PROFESSIONAL LEARNING
INTO THE CLASSROOM

Teachers learned through (a) the traditional workshops, (b) becoming ethnographers, (c) practicing peer coaching, (d) their activity in TLCs, and (e) observations and feedback from the bilingual director and the researcher. As coaches, we guided them through their self-discovery by providing feedback after our observations in each context of the four components.

The content imparted in the workshops became the constant variable, which could be observed to measure transfer into the classroom. The observation of transfer focused on four levels: (a) degree of integration of skill or technique into the teacher's instructional repertoire; (b) effect on attitude (toward students and the other teachers); (c) pedagogical contribution (how the teacher enriched the model, taught it); and (d) their collegial relationships and contributions to other teachers. We included collegial relationships because we felt that these were part and parcel of the transfer into a teacher's instructional repertoire.

Teachers were ranked at the beginning and end of each year according to performance levels (1 = exemplary, 2 = average, 3 = needs more assistance). Looking at teachers from the four dimensions of skill, attitude, pedagogical contribution, and collegial contribution helped us find the teachers' strengths. We later borrowed the notion of Talent Development (Boykin, 1996) to build on teachers' strengths. Feedback to the teachers after observations was couched to boost self-esteem while pointing out the three performance ratings for each dimension:

1. Teachers were told how important they were to the project.
2. They were reminded of their influence and that what they do makes a difference: "Here is where you make a difference . . ."
3. "But, there is always room for improvement . . ."
4. "Here are some tools for that . . ."
5. What did we learn from this?

Motivation, Fidelity, TLC

Feedback was appreciated because it was a combination of motivation, tools for adhering fidelity to the goals and program components, and recommendations for joint problem solving and further development in the TLCs. As agents of change, teachers coconstructed an inquiry process based on the data from their and our observations. This was perhaps the greatest motivating factor for the teachers. As long as the TLCs were implemented, teacher agency remained. The knowledge that researchers derived from the teachers about professional development is perhaps one of the greatest contributions of this project. The knowledge of how to structure TLCs in diversity settings has had an international appeal.

Collegial Relationships and Power Struggles

The examples of the ethnographic studies in TLCs allowed teachers to develop meaningful peer relationships and collaborative ways to fashion new knowledge and beliefs about their students, their teaching, and their own learning. Preliminary evidence from the classroom ethnographies indicates that this approach builds texts and contexts for teachers for self-analysis, negotiation, and problem solving. The ethnographies also created a cycle of peer observation for analysis of concrete teaching tasks, joint reflection, and readjustments. The cycle resembled the typical peer coaching cycle of preconference, observation, analysis, and discussion.

The conversational and written texts in the TLCs in most cases established and enhanced social relations and identities as equal peers. Both teacher partners were immersed in the construction of meaning as they sought to understand the teaching and learning processes in their classrooms. This coconstruction also gave equal status to the Hispanic and Anglo teacher. The untapped talents of each teacher were discovered in this joint venture. Each took a turn becoming expert, novice, and equal peer. When this balance is achieved, teachers become empowered. The tensions between official discourses and minority discourses dissipate. The silenced or too often omitted voices of bilingual teachers become an equal contributing factor to school improvement and, more importantly, to student success.

In two cases, however, the teaming did not survive beyond one year. Both teams suffered a difference of ideology. The bilingual teachers felt their partners were either being unfair to minority children, attempted to display superiority in front of the children, or wanted to control every instructional decision. Unfortunately, the teachers felt that they should keep these power struggles private, thus increasing their intensity as time went by. By the time we became aware of their differences, the bilingual teachers had already requested a transfer.

From these two failed relationships, we learned that power relations between monolingual and bilingual teachers need to be addressed from the beginning as part of program implementation. The bilingual and mainstream teachers were in similar stages of their careers but the bilingual teachers had received more preparation and keener insights as to the needs of the Latino children. However, they felt less powerful to make the necessary reforms in their classrooms and in their team relations.

As schools continue to seek schoolwide reform, these issues are bound to occur, regardless of the program. As more students of diverse language backgrounds enter the schools, more mainstream and bilingual teachers will be struggling to change their instructional approaches, attitudes and beliefs. District-wide staff development practices will need to help teachers adapt to social change as well as instructional change.

Staff development for two-way bilingual teachers will certainly need to include issues of power and the type of relationships that are to be encouraged in students and between and among the teachers. More exploration is needed to help mainstream teachers who might feel threatened with bilingual partners with greater expertise. Staff development practices must take special care to note the mainstream teachers' needs. Not all resistance came from racist views; some were merely feelings of inadequacy. Teachers must also be trained to look at the status of each language and how each is encouraged or sanctioned by their everyday instructional decisions, their body language, and the treatment of their partner.

THE ROLE OF THE PRINCIPAL
AND IMPLEMENTATION RESULTS

If strong school-level leadership is important for effective schools (Barth, 1990; Hargreaves, 1997), it is much more important for bilingual schools or schools with large numbers of Latino students (Goldenberg & Sullivan, 1994: Tikunoff et al., 1991). Because of the complexity of two-way program schools, strong leadership from the district and from the principal is critically important. Principals, in particular, must be highly skilled and sensitive to the issues described so far. Principals will need to provide continuous direction and yet work collegially with the bilingual director and district supervisors. A quality collegial relationship at school affords teachers the power to experiment. Yet principals also need to know how to supervise within this context of continuous change and adaptation and a curriculum foreign to everyone. Principals must be well skilled as change agents, instructional leaders, and supervisors. The role of the principal goes beyond the typical expectations of a regular principal because this leader must be highly skilled in human relations, in confronting racial tension, historical inequalities, and ingrained negative attitudes.

> If principals do not adequately monitor the environment and re-examine the customary policies and practices of their schools in response to changing conditions, they risk creating a situation in which teachers become frustrated and demoralized and in which students who differ from the norm are rendered effectively invisible. (Merchant, 1999, p. 153)

The principal of a two-way school cannot be afraid to lead his/her faculty into new territory while ensuring a safe and stimulating environment. It means constant hard work.

The selection of the two-way bilingual programs was partially due to the principals at those schools. Both volunteered to take on and marshal the program. However, only one principal attended all the professional development sessions and the two semesters of coursework. Her school showed the greatest student success and the program persisted, even after she retired during the second year of implementation. Her retirement was unexpected and left everyone speculating as to the reason. An interim principal was appointed the second year and another was hired for the final year. In spite of the turnover, the program persisted because of the initial thrust the first principal gave the program and because the teachers sustained it.

The principal at the second school had been there for many years and continued until the end of the 3-year project. However, by the third year, this school with the lowest socioeconomic status (SES) and highest percentage of Hispanic students was on a downhill spiral in terms of student achievement and unhappy teachers and parents. By not attending the training sessions, the principal had difficulty understanding the components, purpose, and philosophy of the program. The principal, although Hispanic, came from a traditional view of "maintaining peace and the status quo" at all costs.

The school, up to the third year, had implemented the program in only two classrooms per grade level. When the superintendent told the principal to expand it to the whole school, the principal began to plan his retirement. He was certain from the start that all the other teachers would not want to team teach. His expectations were soon reverberating among the teachers. The negative messages from the principal and teachers thereafter reached the parents' ears, and many of them signed waivers to keep their children out of any bilingual intervention at that school.

Hence, the school became divided between those teachers who had already implemented the program and those that were going to do their best to keep it out of their classrooms. Their reasons were that it was too much work and that they didn't like having another teacher with them in the classroom. The principal gave them the option to remain "as they were" and they did. At this particular school, it was also evident that the first and second graders were having many reading problems. The third-grade teachers began asking for easier Treasure Hunts (BCIRC materials) in both Spanish and English. When the faculty had the option to adopt Success for All or a popular worksheets program, the two-way team teachers were outvoted and the faculty opted for the worksheets. The principal and the majority of the teachers (which were Anglo and Hispanic) fought to reenact the former status of the school, the inequalities that had been established years ago in that 80-year-old school.

This school year, their students' scores are among the lowest ranking in the district. Fifty percent of the two-way bilingual teachers have left, and the program has eroded to an unrecognizable stage. The principal retired and a new principal is attempting to pick up the pieces.

SUMMARY AND CONCLUSIONS

The 3-year study documented a process for designing and implementing a two-way bilingual program in two schools. The project had outcomes that can be characterized as successes and some as failures. These served to draw inferences about two-way bilingual program implementation and to make some tentative recommendations for schools planning to develop their own programs and for further research.

The successes hinged on the components carefully orchestrated by the bilingual director and the teachers. The issues of failure appeared to evolve around the principals' and district administrators' lack of leadership. The inferences we can draw here are that:

1. The bilingual educators invested time, energy and commitment to their programs by attempting their best.
2. They used research-based instructional models and expanded the knowledge base.
3. The principals had their own agendas throughout the project.
4. The district administration kept a safe distance.

Successes included the development, piloting, and refinement of a K–5 bilingual interdisciplinary thematic curriculum. The literature-based Bilingual Cooperative Integrated Reading and Composition model of instruction (BCIRC) was combined with math, science, social studies, and multicultural art and music. Each interdisciplinary unit was created around a theme and inquiry question. Each grade-level curriculum consisted of at least 10 themes. The curriculum was so well received by teachers that the following year it was adopted by most of the schools in the district.

A second achievement was the organization of program structures for a 50–50 program. Most two-way bilingual programs in the nation have been organized around a 90–10 instruction formula. That is, 90% of instructional time in kindergarten is given in Spanish and 10% in English. In first grade, it shifts to 80% in Spanish and 20% in English. Then it continues to shift per grade level until it reaches a 50–50 combination. These two schools decided to implement a 50–50 design from kindergarten through fifth grade all at once. The 50–50 program was orchestrated through the units and themes taught weekly, and not necessarily by daily schedules. BCIRC was taught in one language for a 5-day cycle, and then the following cycle was taught in the other language. When there was a need to teach math in one language for a week or two, science would be taught in the other language. Thus, the teachers attempted to adhere to the 50–50 program. The second-phase schools contributed to the experimentation of the organizational structures for a two-way SFA programs.

The program also had great impact on Latino students. Students who had often seen themselves as the ones needing help, or those who did not speak English well, now saw that they were valued by their classmates because they needed their expertise in Spanish. New friendships were made among both language groups, which carried beyond the school grounds. Both groups were succeeding through cooperative learning. For an enthusiastic first grader, class was better than Disneyland. When her family scheduled a trip during school time, she refused to go, because she "might miss something at school."

Student achievement as measured by the state's standardized test scores, and compared to students in the other bilingual programs, was for the most part significantly better for both English monolingual and bilingual students in the two-way schools. Visitors from other Texas districts found their way into the two-way schools, and presentations about the program were in high demand at conferences. Students became so accustomed to visitors that they missed them when no one came to visit for a while. One of the most memorable visitor comments was, "This is better than any gifted and talented program I've ever seen." Due to the students' accomplishments, interest in two-way bilingual education grew in the district, and schools initiated similar programs or used the curriculum.

Teachers became models of cooperation for students as they saw them collaborate and support each other. Students thought it was "exciting" having two teachers in the classroom who taught in different languages. LEP students liked to see the English monolingual teachers supporting Spanish instruction. Limited Spanish proficient students liked how the English teacher was learning Spanish along with them.

Parents also felt the impact of two-way bilingual education. The frequent meetings at the schools kept parents informed and gave them an opportunity to ask questions and make suggestions. Those parents that expressed interest in having their children learn Spanish felt that the school acknowledged their input and thus became avid supporters of the program. Spanish-speaking parents found that Spanish was finally valued and that they and their children brought a special resource to the school. Parents from the two language groups were brought closer together through the activities of parent–child coauthoring, class field trips, and as volunteers in the classrooms. The parents, just as the students, enjoyed learning about each other.

Perhaps the greatest contribution from this project was the implementation and further refinement of the Teachers Learning Communities.

The description of the process and the outcomes for teachers helped advance the concept of a Teachers' Talent Development model of professional development. Even though teachers began at the three levels of adaptability and knowledge base, there were exciting improvements in all the groups. Forty percent of the teachers went on to pursue master's programs. Five became assistant principals and two were promoted this year to principals. Other teachers became teachers of the year or were recognized in some way for their accomplishments. Some became trainers and others curriculum writers for the district. They all created a strong network of learning and sharing, which still continues on an informal basis.

The refinement of TLCs came about through their inventiveness of structures necessary to sustain their experimentation and motivation as they took ownership of the development of the program. The more freedom they were given to add to the curriculum or to the instructional delivery process, the more they got involved. More involvement lead to more learning and utilization of talents that had not been tapped before.

Building on previous studies of TLCs, new TLC activities involved teachers as ethnographers of their and their team teachers' instructional behaviors. Peer coaching also took on new forms as partners experimented with more comfortable processes. Former activities were also confirmed to be useful tools for this project. The activity structure was documented and replicated in new Success for All schools to verify its utility across bilingual settings.

As in most projects, not all was success. One of the most obvious situations was the weakness of the first-grade reading program. It was a combination of "whole-language approaches" and two computer reading–writing programs. The district was very much "into whole language" at that time and refused to look into first-grade reading research-based programs such as Success for All. BCIRC was not designed to be used at first grade, but some teachers attempted to modify it to fit their literature books. The teachers tried their best to invent and put together strategies that mostly avoided phonics.

Among the major failures, we can cite the spiral-down effect of student scores at that school, even after the project. These scores reflected a series of other causal relationships due to weak leadership at the school. The principal felt there was no need for him to participate in the professional development opportunities. He refused to acknowledge that his students needed a strong early reading program. He gave minimal support to the two-way bilingual teachers.

Nevertheless, the program features and key components withstood the test of time and weak leadership. The credit goes to the teachers who became agents within a community of learners. TLC structures helped teachers cope with the lack of school leadership support for the first 2 years of the program. After the second year, the schools were supposed to continue the TLCs while the district supported "refresher" and "new knowledge" workshops. The schools did not sustain the TLCs and during the third year, the quality of implementation eroded and morale deteriorated. In the meantime, a third school that had been watching and learning from this implementation process decided to implement the two-way bilingual program in conjunction with Success for All/*Éxito Para Todos.* The implementation at this new school is helping us make comparisons at different levels and to further the study on two-way bilingual program effects. There is now a fourth school that is taking yet another approach. It implemented Success for All and *Éxito Para Todos* first. Once the teachers became comfortable with SFA/EPT, it began the two-way bilingual program with one grade level per year. This will ease both programs into implementation in the next few years. Thus far, the teachers are comfortable with this plan and the students are doing extremely well.

RECOMMENDATIONS

Two-way bilingual programs are some of the most comprehensive reform initiatives. It is not enough to have the curriculum, well-prepared teachers, and a well-thought-out design. Without the support of the school leadership, the program can still fail. For this reason, in addition to the 11 principles and the 10 goals listed earlier, we make the following recommendations:

1. The programs must be an integral part of the whole school operation—better yet, a whole-school reform initiative where all teachers, administrators, parents, and students are involved.
2. A strong principal must maintain a supportive schoolwide climate and be willing to learn, along with teachers, on a continuous basis, and to supervise/motivate to ensure quality implementation and improvement.
3. The principal must be well skilled in coalition building skills and strong enough to move a faculty beyond political divisions, which are likely to be reflections of the larger community or district ethos.
4. Staff development for teachers and administrators must include ways of addressing and altering power relationships in the school: sociopolitical issues of diversity, difference, ethnicity, equity, bias, power struggles, and, of course, views about bilingual education.

5. Teacher agency and capacity for change, which underlie school reform initiatives such as these, are best enhanced through teachers' learning communities at the school.
6. Staff development, implementation visits, and implementation reports from outside the school are necessary to sustain the quality of the program.
7. The instructional program must be created through a comprehensive balanced curriculum: interdisciplinary learning of both languages through all the content areas articulated with the English and Spanish language arts/reading programs.
8. The instructional program must include explicit skills instruction in reading, higher order skills, and comprehension at all grade levels. Systematic student assessment is necessary to inform instruction and the need for additional interventions.

In essence, we recommend that the school begin by making a commitment to positive working relations, collegial continuous learning, and flexibility in letting go of comfortable routines. Stronger than all other components, the roles and responsibilities of all the stakeholders in the process of change must be made clear. The principal(s) will need to go through intensive retraining in order to develop the new skills that these new programs require. The strong leadership and the climate of positive change are the foundation for a research-based program. The program becomes the basis for everyone's learning and contribution of talent. The comprehensive instructional program must be able to provide teachers with curriculum for the entire day. A program such as Success for All and *Éxito Para Todos* must be integrated with math, science, social studies, and the arts in both languages. Most important, the school leader needs to be well aware and well skilled in the complexities that such exciting programs bring—along with their promise of success.

REFERENCES

Ada, A. F. (1993). Mother-tongue literacy as a bridge tetween home and school cultures. In J. V. Tinajero & A. F. Ada (Eds.), *The power of two languages: Literacy and biliteracy for Spanish-speaking students* (pp. 158–163). New York: McGraw-Hill.

Apple, M. W. (1993). *Official knowledge: Democratic education in a conservative age.* New York: Routledge.

Apple, M. W. (Ed.). (1995–1996). Review of Research in Education No. 21. Washington, DC: American Educational Research Association.

August, D., & Hakuta, K. (Eds.). (1997). *Improving schooling for language-minority children: A research agenda.* Washington, DC: National Academy Press.

Barth, R. (1990). *Improving schools from within.* San Francisco: Jossey-Bass.

Boykin, W. (1996). *Theoretical framework for the talent development model.* Baltimore, MD: Center for Research on the Education of Students Placed at Risk, Johns Hopkins University.

Calderón, M. (1990–1991). Cooperative learning builds communities of teachers. *Journal of Teacher Education and Practice, 6*(2), 75–79.

Calderón, M. (1994). Mentoring, peer-coaching, and support systems for first-year minority/bilingual teachers. In R. A. De Villar, C. J. Faltis, & J. Cummins (Eds.), *Cultural diversity in schools: From rhetoric to practice* (pp. 117–144). New York: SUNY.

Calderón, M. (1995, March). Lecto-Escritura Integrada y Cooperativa. *Revista de Educación, 3*(9), 41–45.

Calderón, M. (1996). Binational cooperative learning communities. In J. D. Flores & E. García (Eds.), *Children of la frontera* (pp.). Charleston, WV: ERIC/CRESS.

Calderón, M., & Carreón, A. (1994). Educators and students use cooperative learning to become biliterate and bicultural. *Cooperative Learning Magazine, 4,* 6–9.

Calderón, M., Hertz-Lazarowitz, R., & Slavin, R. E. (1997). *Effects of Bilingual Cooperative Integrated Reading and Composition on students transitioning from Spanish to English reading* (Report 10). Baltimore, MD: Center for Research on the Education of Students Placed at Risk.

Calderón, M., Hertz-Lazarowitz, R., & Slavin, R. E. (1998). Effects of Bilingual Cooperative Integrated Reading and Composition on students making the transition from Spanish to English reading. *Elementary School Journal, 99*(2), 153–165.

Christian, D. (1996). Two-way immersion education: Students learning through two languages. *Modern Language Journal, 80,* 66–76.

Christian, D., Montone, C., Lindholm, K., & Carranza, I. (1997). *Profiles in two-way immersion education.* Washington, DC: Center for Applied Linguistics.

Collier, V. (1995). *Promoting academic success for ESL students: Understanding second language acquisition for school.* Elizabeth, NJ: NJTESOL-BE.

Cummins, J. (1981). The role of primary language development in promoting educational success for language minority students. In California State Department of Education, Office of Bilingual Bicultural Education (Ed.), *Schooling and language minority students: A theoretical framework* (pp. 3–50). Los Angeles: California State University, Evaluation Dissemination and Assessment Center.

Erickson, F. (1992). Ethnographic microanalysis of interaction. In M. LeCompte, W. Millroy, & J. Preissle (Eds.), *The handbook of qualitative research in education* (pp. 201–225). New York: Academic Press.

Fairclough, N. (1989). *Language and power.* London: Longman.

Fairclough, N. (1992). Discourse and text: Linguistic and intertextual analysis within discourse analysis. *Discourse and Society, 3,* 193–218.

Foucault, M. (1972). *The archaeology of knowledge.* New York: Harper & Row.

Foucault, M. (1980). *Power/knowledge.* New York: Pantheon.

Goldenberg, C., & Sullivan, J. (1994). *Making change happen in a language-minority school: A search for coherence* (EPR No. 13). Washington, DC: Center for Applied Linguistics.

Goodman, K. S., Goodman, Y., & Flores, B. (1979). *Reading in the bilingual classroom: Literacy and biliteracy.* Washington, DC: National Clearinghouse for Bilingual Education.

Green, J. L., & Dixon, C. D. (1993). Talking knowledge into being: Discursive and social practices in classrooms. *Linguistics and Education, 5,* 231–240.

Gutierrez, K. (1995). Unpacking academic discourse. *Discourse Processes, 19,* 21–37.

Hakuta, K. (1986). *Mirror of language: The debate on bilingualism.* New York: Basic Books.

Halliday, M. A. K., & Hasan, R. (1985). *Language, context and text.* Geelong, Australia: Deakin University Press.

Hargreaves, A. (1997). *Rethinking educational change with heart and mind. ASCD Year Book.* Alexandria, VA: Association for Supervision and Curriculum Development.

Hertz-Lazarowitz, R., & Calderón, M. (1994). Facilitating teachers' power through collaboration: Implementing cooperative learning in elementary schools. In S. Sharan (Ed.), *Handbook of cooperative learning methods* (pp.). London: Greenwood Press.

Krashen, S. (1982). *Principles and practice in second language acquisition.* Oxford: Pergamon.

Lambert, W. E., & Cazabon, M. (1994). *Students' view of the Amigos program* (Research Report No. 11). Santa Cruz, CA: National Center for Research on Cultural Diversity and Second Language Learning.

Lindholm, K. J. (1990). Bilingual immersion education: Criteria for program development. In A. M. Padilla, H. H. Fairchild, & C. M. Valadez (Eds.), *Bilingual education: Issues and strategies* (pp. 91–105). Newbury Park, CA: Sage.

Luke, A. (1995–1996). Text and discourse in education: An introduction to critical discourse analysis. In M. W. Apple (Ed.), *Review of research in education* (Vol. 21, pp. 3–48). Washington, DC: American Educational Research Association.

Madden, N. A., Slavin, R. E., Farnish, A. M., Livingston, M. A., Calderón, M., & Stevens, R. J. (1996). *Reading Wings: Teachers' manual.* Baltimore, MD: Johns Hopkins University, Center for Research on the Education of Students Placed at Risk.

Mahrer, C., & Christian, D. (1993). *A review of findings from two-way bilingual education evaluation reports.* Santa Cruz, CA, and Washington, DC: National Center for Research on Cultural Diversity and Second Language Learning.

McLaren, P. (1995). *Critical pedagogy and predatory culture.* New York: Routledge.

Mehan, H. (1979). *Learning lessons: Social organization in the classroom.* Cambridge, MA: Harvard University Press.

Merchant, B. (1999). Ghosts in the classroom: Unavoidable casualties of a principal's commitment to the status quo. *Journal of Education for Students Placed At Risk, 4*(3), 153–172.

Ovando, C., & Collier, V. (1998). *Bilingual and ESL classrooms: Teaching in multicultural contexts.* New York: McGraw-Hill.

Ramirez, D., Yuen, S. D., Ramey, D. R., & Pasta, D. J. (1991). *Longitudinal study of structured English immersion strategy, early-exit, and late exit transitional bilingual education programs for language minority children.* San Mateo, CA: Aguirre International.

Sharp, J. (1994). *Forces of change: Shaping the future of Texas.* Austin: Texas Comptroller of Public Accounts.

Slavin, R. E., & Boykin, H. (1995). *Center for Research on the Education of Students Placed at Risk, Proposal.* Washington, DC: Office of Educational Research and Improvement.

Slavin, R. E., & Fashola, O. S. (1998). *Show me the evidence! Proven and promising programs for America's schools.* Thousand Oaks, CA: Corwin Press.

Slavin, R. E., & Madden, N. (1996, April). *Effects of Success for All on the achievement of English language learners.* Paper presented at the annual meeting of the American Educational Research Association, San Francisco.

Stevens, R. J., Madden, N. A., Slavin, R. E., & Farnish, A. M. (1987). Cooperative integrated reading and composition: Two field experiments. *Reading Research Quarterly, 22,* 433–454.

Tharp, R. G., & Gallimore, R. (1988). *Rousing minds to life: Teaching, learning, and schooling in social context.* New York: Cambridge University Press.

Tikunoff, W. J., Ward, B. A., van Broekhuizen, L. D., Romero, M., Castaneda, L. V., Lucas, T., & Katz, A. (1991). *A descriptive study of significant features of exemplary special alternative instructional programs. Final Report and Vol. 2: Report for practitioners.* Los Alamitos, CA: Southwest Regional Educational Laboratory.

Tollefson, J. (1991). *Planning language, planning inequality.* London: Longman.

Valdés, G. (1997). Dual language immersion programs: A cautionary note concerning the education of language-minority students. *Harvard Educational Review, 67*(3), 391–429.

Vygotsky, L. S. (1978). *Mind in society: The development of higher psychological processes.* Cambridge, MA: Harvard University Press.

5

Improving Literacy Achievement for English Learners in Transitional Bilingual Programs

William M. Saunders
California State University, Long Beach, and
National Center for Research on Education, Diversity, and Excellence,
University of California, Santa Cruz

By the most conservative estimates, no less than 2.8 million children enrolled in U.S. schools are limited English proficient (Crawford, 1997). Although estimates vary, perhaps as many as 50% of these students are in some form of "transitional bilingual education" (August & Hakuta, 1997) where they receive literacy and content area instruction in their first language while learning to speak and comprehend English. Once students have acquired a certain level of first-language literacy and have acquired adequate oral listening and comprehension skills in English, they make the "transition" to English. In other words, they begin receiving formal instruction in English literacy. "Transition" age or grade can vary widely, depending on the program and individual children.

In fact, there are several types of programs that have been designed to address the needs of English learners over the past three decades, most of which vary based on the amount and duration of instruction students receive in their primary language (see Genesee, 1999, for descriptions). At one end of the continuum, students receive no instruction in their primary language: Support is provided through specially designed English instruction. At the other end of the continuum, students receive a true bilingual education: Students are taught and learn in their primary language *and* English at all grades. Transitional bilingual programs fall in the middle of the continuum, using primary language instruction for a period of time and then gradually adding or transitioning students to all English instruction.

Although there is evidence to support the use of transitional bilingual programs (Krashen & Biber, 1988; Willig, 1985), there are widely different views about its effects relative to other programming options for English learners. For example, based on their analysis of several studies that compared the elementary grade effects of transitional bilingual and structured English immersion programs, Rossell and Baker (1996) concluded that English learners are better served by early and intensive exposure to English. In sharp contrast, based on their analysis of the long-term achievement (through high school) of more than 40,000 students from several different programming options, Thomas and Collier (1997) concluded that English learners are best served by true bilingual programs that provide effective, sustained instruction in students' primary language and in English throughout the elementary years.

Despite the complex larger picture, among researchers currently studying transitional bilingual education (Calderón, Hertz-Lazarowitz, & Slavin, 1998; Gersten, 1996; Goldenberg, 1996; Krashen, 1996) there is a growing consensus about two things: (a) The period of transition is pivotal to subsequent achievement, and (b) despite a growing literature that sets forth potential directions, there are few empirical studies of effective transition programs.

Although many educators consider "transition" a positive indication that English learners are entering the mainstream (Gándara & Merino, 1993), transition can be problematic for both students and teachers. First, if transition is handled too abruptly, subsequent achievement tends to stall or decline. In a national evaluation of programs for English learners, Ramirez (1992) found that students from transitional bilingual programs who were abruptly transitioned into all English programs showed a much slower rate of growth in English reading, language, and math than students who were transitioned more gradually and received continued instruction in their primary language throughout the transition period.

Second, even in programs where transition is handled more gradually, the transition period itself typically involves declines in academic challenge and student participation. In a large-scale evaluation of bilingual programs in California, Berman et al. (1992) found what they called the transition "dip." In comparison to earlier grades taught in the primary language or higher grades where students had more experience in English literacy, the transition period was marked by a decrease in the challenge or skill level of curriculum and instruction, less frequent student-initiated interactions during lessons, and lower levels of student participation in class activities.

Third, transition is an enigma for most educators, even for those working in schools and districts with a long history of implementing transitional bilingual programs. Gersten and Woodward (1994) reported that most teachers tend to describe themselves as overwhelmingly uncertain about the appropriate methods to use during transition. Berman et al. (1992) found that few schools in their sample (all of whom had been selected because they had "well-implemented" programs) had specific strategies and curriculum for transition. Moreover, most schools relied on individual teacher judgments to determine student readiness to begin transition, judgments that varied considerably from one teacher to the next. This sense of uncertainty and ambiguity is compounded by an addition finding reported by both Berman et al. (1992) and Gersten (1995, cited in Gersten 1996): Transition classes tend to get assigned to less experienced teachers.

In sum, transition is a crucial period during which many English learners are especially vulnerable to academic underachievement. Unfortunately, educators have little research and few curricular models on which to base policy and practice (Goldenberg, 1996). Gersten (1996) provided a conceptual framework and potential promising practices for transition derived from classroom observations of 27 teachers, some of whom were selected specifically by the researchers as exemplars (see Jiménéz, Gersten, & Rivera, 1996). However, as yet, the framework and practices have not been studied empirically.

Calderón et al. (1998) represent one of the few, if not the only, empirical studies of a program developed specifically for transition: Bilingual Cooperative Integrated Reading and Composition (BCIRC). Although the results of their study are complex, the basic finding is that third-grade students who participated in BCIRC for 2 years significantly outperformed comparable students in the same district who participated in the transition program students normally receive. Aside from their findings regarding BCIRC's specific effects, the broader significance of the Calderón et al. study is that with careful program design and evaluation, the literacy achievement of students in transitional bilingual programs can be substantially improved.

This chapter reports the results of a long-term, ongoing effort involving teachers and researchers in the Southern California area to design, implement, and evaluate an effective transition program for Spanish-speaking students. The goal is to substantially improve students' literacy achievement, in English and Spanish.

THE TRANSITION PROGRAM

As is true in other parts of California (Berman et al., 1992), educators in the Metropolitan School District (a pseudonym) were very concerned about low levels of student achievement as students transitioned from instruction in their home language to instruction in English (Saunders & Lennon, 1993). Our project team (18 teachers, 3 project advisors, 2 researchers) was formed to first examine how transition was operating in the project schools and then research and develop a more successful program. I first describe the program we developed, then report how we evaluated its effects on student learning.

Multiyear Design for Transition

The multiyear design for transition our project team developed optimally spans Grades 2–5. Grades 2 and 3 are referred to as Pre-Transition, Grade 4 is Transition I, Grade 5 is Transition II (see Table 5.1). The multiyear design for transition presumes two things: (a) Students receive effective language arts instruction, and (b) students receive a coherent program of language arts instruction from Grades 2 through 5, from primary language through transitional language arts.

In this district, all Spanish-speaking limited English proficiency (LEP) students enrolled in the bilingual program receive language arts and content area instruction in Spanish while they are acquiring oral English proficiency, addressed primarily through 20–30 min of daily English language

TABLE 5.1
Design and Goals for the Multiyear Transition Program

Phases	Optimal Grades	Goal	Measurable Outcome
	K–1	Initial reading and writing proficiency (Spanish)	Existing norm- or criterion-referenced measures
		Early production II (oral English)	
Pre-Transition	2–3	Grade-appropriate reading and writing achievement (Spanish)	Pass CARE (district transition instrument)
		Speech emergence (oral English)	
Transition I	4	Initial reading and writing proficiency (English)	Existing norm- or criterion-referenced measures
		Academic oral language proficiency (English)	
		Grade-appropriate reading and writing achievement (Spanish)	
Transition II	5	Grade-appropriate reading and writing achievement (English)	Redesignation: LEP to FEP

development instruction (ELD). This program continues until students demonstrate end of second/beginning of third grade level proficiency in Spanish reading and writing and basic oral English proficiency, as measured by district developed assessments. When students demonstrate these proficiencies they qualify to transition and begin English reading and writing instruction, during which time they are to continue receiving Spanish language arts as well. According to district guidelines, transitional language arts should last approximately 3–6 months and concentrate on nontransferable English skills, vocabulary development, oral and reading comprehension, and written language. Subsequent to this period, students enter a mainstream English program. Students are officially redesignated as fluent English proficient when they demonstrate grade-level or close to grade-level reading, writing, and oral language skills on standardized English language achievement tests.

As we began work at the project schools two things were apparent: (a) Students were not being effectively prepared to qualify for transition, and (b) the transitional program students received when they did qualify was, at best, underspecified (Saunders & Lennon, 1993, 1996).

The concept of a Pre-Transition component is designed to emphasize the fundamental role of Spanish reading and writing and oral English development that precedes transition. Large numbers of students were not qualifying to enter transition because they were not functioning at or close to grade level in Spanish literacy, and they were not acquiring oral English skills. The understanding we tried to develop at project schools was that problems with the transition program could not be addressed without devoting serious attention to Spanish language arts and oral English development at the early grades. As part of this effort, we explicitly included Grades 2 and 3 as a Pre-Transition phase in the larger transition program. The thrust of this phase is intensive Spanish reading and writing instruction and extensive oral English development. The Pre-Transition goal is to have all students performing at grade level in Spanish reading and writing, and at the speech emergence level (able to converse) or higher in oral English by the end of third grade. If the goal is achieved, students should have no problem passing the district assessment to qualify for transition.

The problem with transition itself was that schools grossly underestimated the amount of time that should be devoted to it. The district's 3–6 month guidelines encouraged schools to think of transition as a relatively short period of time sandwiched between Spanish and mainstream English language arts, so short as to prohibit any serious attention to curriculum or teacher training.

The concept of Transition I and II was designed to make explicit the need for a concrete transition program of serious substance and duration. By the end of Transition I, students should be able to decode and demonstrate basic understanding of end of third-grade English reading material (within a year of the students' academic grade). They should also increase their academic oral English language proficiency (intermediate fluency), such that they can participate actively in academically oriented discussions. Finally, students should continue to demonstrate grade-level Spanish reading and writing proficiency. We maintain Spanish language arts throughout the entire year of Transition I to support students' Spanish literacy development and draw clear connections between the processes of reading and writing in Spanish and in English.

By the end of Transition II, students should be decoding and comprehending grade-level material in English. The goal is redesignation: Students have transitioned and can perform successfully in a mainstream program when they have grade-level or close to grade-level English skills and can be formally redesignated from limited to fluent English proficient. We do not set forth a Transition II achievement goal for Spanish literacy. During Transition II, teachers promote students' self-selected Spanish reading and writing, but language arts instructional time is devoted exclusively to English reading and writing.

Instructional Components for the Language Arts Program

As part of our work on the transition program, we identified 12 instructional components that seemed most effective in serving the needs of students throughout the three phases of the program (see Table 5.2; see Appendix 1 for descriptions and citations of published literature for each component). Some of these instructional components were intended specifically to address the needs of transition students, but many of the components stand on their own as effective language arts strategies for the middle and upper elementary grades. However, operationalizing these components, integrating them together in a total language arts program, developing management systems, and applying them to programs for LEP students making the transition were essential.

Studying Literature. Across all phases of the program, from Pre-Transition to Transition II—from Spanish to English language arts and from Grade 2 through 5—students study literature. We assumed that stu-

TABLE 5.2
Instructional Components of the Language Arts Program for Grades 2–5

Studying Literature	Skill Building	Other Supporting Components
Literature units (Experience–Text–Relationship)	Comprehension strategies	Pleasure reading
Literature logs	Assigned independent reading	Teacher read-alouds
Instructional conversations	Dictation	Interactive journals
Culminating Writing projects (writing-as-a-process)	Written conventions lessons	
	ELD through Literature	

dents would benefit from more extensive and intensive opportunities to work with text, to study interesting stories under the tutelage of a teacher. Based on research conducted as part of the Kamehameha Elementary Education Program in Hawaii (Au, 1979, 1992; Tharp & Gallimore, 1988) and Spanish-speaking Latino communities in southern California (Goldenberg, 1992/1993), we adapted the Experience–Text–Relationship approach as our framework for literature units. Through ongoing discussions (instructional conversations), writing activities (literature logs and culminating writing projects), and reading, the teacher helps students study the story in relationship to students' own experiences and a central theme. Discussions set up writing assignments, and writings inform subsequent discussions throughout the course of the literature unit. Writing is an individual opportunity for each student to think about and articulate ideas, interpretations, and related experiences. Discussions provide a social opportunity for students and teacher to collaboratively build more elaborated and sophisticated understandings.

Literature units culminate with a written project that serves two goals: (a) developing a deeper understanding of some aspect of the unit (content, themes, related personal experiences), and (b) developing a high-quality piece of writing. Teachers teach writing as a process in the course of these culminating projects. Students share drafts, receive feedback from peers, conference with the teacher, and revise and edit their work. They also receive teacher lessons specific to the kind of writing involved in the project (e.g., narration, persuasion, informational).

In terms of literacy development, we assume that through this recurrent process of individual and social discourse—of reading, writing, and discussing—literature units help students learn to comprehend text, to make connections between the text and their own lives, and develop more fully formed concepts (the themes). Students are learning to engage in meaningful discourse by participating in it (Tharp & Gallimore, 1988). In terms of second-language acquisition (Cummins, 1989; Krashen, 1987), we assume literature units help provide substantial comprehensible input—language that includes slightly more sophisticated structures or vocabulary than the learner can produce on his or her own, but that is understandable within the total context in which it is used. The literature unit becomes a meaningful social context in which words, phrases, language structures, and concepts are used, acquired, and learned (see Saunders, O'Brien, Lennon, & McLean, 1998, for a more detailed explanation of our approach to literature).

Skill-Building Components. As we found throughout our work, studying literature needs to be complemented by additional skill-building components. Students need direct instruction in specific reading comprehension strategies (predicting, summarizing, questioning), and they need daily opportunities to read texts geared to their reading level—assigned independent reading. Comprehension strategies are presented in 2-week modules in the first and fourth quarter of the year. The assigned independent reading center runs throughout the year. Ideally, the center includes materials related to the literature unit; but teachers have used the basal or other reading kits (e.g., SRA, Barnell-Loft) to insure that students have materials they can read independently and can use to practice comprehension strategies. Students need similar study and practice for written language. As part of the weekly dictation program, students study a short but carefully targeted passage from the literature selection. The teacher provides lessons on specific conventions (punctuation, capitalization, grammar), and students practice writing the passage as it is dictated to them by a peer or parent, compose original sentences and paragraphs that include the target conventions, and study words from the passage they have difficulty spelling.

English Language Development (ELD) through Literature (developed by project consultant Dolores Beltran and advisor Gisela O'Brien) is a daily, 45-min oral English program used in the Pre-Transition phases of the program. Instruction is delivered to students in small, homogeneous groups based on students' proficiency level. Lessons and independent activities are all drawn from a particular literature selection (typically one with predictable patterns, language structures, and target vocabulary for various domains). The focus of lessons and the teacher's talk are geared specifically to students' proficiency level. Literature seems to provide a meaningful and motivating context for learning and practicing specifically targeted English oral language skills. It also exposes children to English print well in advance of formal transition to English. ELD through Literature is an integral part of our Pre-Transition program (Grades 2 and 3).

Other Supporting Components.   At all grades, teachers read to students for approximately 20 min at least three times per week. Teacher read-alouds expose students to the language of expert writers and the fluency of an expert reader, engage students in material they may not yet be able to read on their own, and introduce students to new authors and genre. In addition, a portion of time each day is devoted to pleasure reading. Students chose their own books and stories, keep records of their reading, and for those books they find most interesting, they complete short assignments (summaries, synopsis, oral presentations, drawings, etc.). Finally, many Transition I teachers use interactive journals during the first half of the year when students are making their first attempts at English writing. The immediate written response from the teacher provides both emotional support for the students and a highly contextualized and comprehensible English text for students to read.

Theoretical Principles.   Four theoretical principals undergird the program, all of which are assumed to promote first- and second-language acquisition and achievement:

- Challenge: Consistently challenge students academically—challenge them to think, learn, and engage intellectually.
- Continuity: Achieve continuity in curriculum and instruction as students move from primary to middle to upper grades, and from first language (L1) to English language arts.
- Connections: Build on and make explicit connections between students' existing knowledge, skills, and experiences and the academic curriculum to be learned (including language, literacy, and content).
- Comprehensiveness: Address both meaning and skills, both higher level thinking and appropriate drill and practice, and provide complementary portions of student- and teacher-centeredness.

These premises are conditions for learning and achievement, conditions we did not readily find when we began our work at the schools. They are also grounded in the research literature, specifically studies that have tried to identify the characteristics of more and less successful programs for English learners (Berman et al., 1992; Garcia, 1992; Gersten & Jiménez, 1993; Goldenberg, 1991; Ramirez, 1992; Thomas & Collier, 1997).

EVALUATION METHODS

The design of the evaluation study is longitudinal and comparative. We collected data on case study students from project schools ($n = 61$) and case study students from comparable, nonproject schools ($n = 64$). Project students represent the first cohort of students to participate in the multiyear transition program (Pre-Transition through Transition II, across Grades 2–5). Nonproject students participated in the transitional bilingual program students typically receive in the district, which includes a 3- to 6-month transition period. Data were collected on both groups for Grades 1–5. Measures include standardized tests of reading and language; language and literacy assessments used in the district to assess LEP students; and project-developed performance assessments and surveys.

Sampling Procedures and Evaluation Design

Project and Nonproject Case Study Students.   All case study students met the following criteria: (a) They enrolled at their respective school by at least the beginning of first grade and stayed at the same school through Grade 5; (b) their home language was Spanish, and they were classified as limited English proficient when they enrolled; and (c) they participated in a Spanish transitional bilingual program. The two groups of case study students are:

1. *Project*: Students who were enrolled consecutively in the classrooms of project teachers at project schools ($n = 5$) across Grades 2–5.
2. *Nonproject*: Students from comparable neighboring schools ($n = 5$) who completed Grades 2–5 during the same years as the project students.

Ninety project and 90 nonproject case study students (approximately 18 per school) were selected randomly at the beginning of their second-grade year from the pool of students who met the three criteria. Sixty-seven percent of project (61 of 90) and 71% of nonproject students (64 of 90) remained at their respective schools through the end of fifth grade.

Project and Nonproject School Demographics.   Like project schools, all five comparable schools are members of the same school district, located within the same geographic area of southern California, and governed by the same district policies and guidelines regarding bilingual programs. Drawing from a pool of eight neighboring schools that agreed to participate, the five nonproject schools we selected provided us with a nearly exact composite match to our five project schools. Schools were matched based on percentage of LEP students, total enrollment, percentage of students participating in free and reduced-price lunch program, ethnicity, and achievement scores (see Saunders & Lennon, 1996, for details). Project and nonproject schools have the following characteristics: mean enrollment is 880 (range: 478–1295); 96% of the student body is Latino or Hispanic (range: 93–99%); 74% of the students are limited English proficient (range: 65–85%); 95% of students qualify for free or reduced-price lunch (range: 80–100%). Grade 2 Spanish reading median percentiles for the year prior to the project ranged from the 29th to the 48th percentile; 8 of 10 were between the 44th and 48th percentile.

Subgroups Within Project and Nonproject Samples.   Project and nonproject samples are made up of two subgroups:

1. *Transition 4*: Students who qualified for transition at the end of third or the beginning of fourth grade, began transitional English language arts during the first semester of Grade 4, and took standardized tests in Spanish at Grades 1–4 and in English at Grade 5.
2. *Transition 5*: Students who qualified for transition at the end of fourth or the beginning of fifth grade, began transitional English language arts during the first semester of Grade 5, and took standardized tests in Spanish at Grades 1–5.

All project and nonproject students qualified for transition based on the same criteria and instrument used at all district schools (see Instruments: CARE) and were administered standardized tests by school personnel following the same district guidelines and procedures. Students in bilingual programs are eligible to be tested in English three semesters after they qualify for transition. As such, students who qualify for transition at the end of Grade 3 or during the first half of Grade 4 are tested in Spanish at the end of fourth and in English at the end of fifth grade. Students who qualify later than the midpoint of fourth grade are tested in Spanish at the end of fourth and fifth grades.

Drawing Matched Samples.   All comparisons to be reported are based on matched samples of project and nonproject case studies. Drawing from the pool of available project and nonproject case studies remaining at the end of fifth grade, students were randomly selected and matched as closely as possible (within at least 5 percentile points) based

TABLE 5.3
Composition of Matched Project and Nonproject Samples

	Samples			
	1st Project Cohort Case Studies, n = 61; Matched Sample, n = 42		Nonproject Cohort Case Studies, n = 64; Matched Sample, n = 42	
Sample and Subgroup Information	Tran 4	Tran 5	Tran 4	Tran 5
Transition grade	4	5	4	5
Official test Grade 5	Eng	Span	Eng	Span
Number of case studies	39	22	40	24
Percent of case studies	64%	36%	63%	37%
Number in matched sample	28	14	28	14
Percent of matched sample	67%	33%	67%	33%

Note. Tran, Transition; Eng, English; Span, Spanish.

on first-grade Spanish reading and language scores within each subgroup: Transition 4 and Transition 5. First-grade measures were used because project case study students entered project teachers' classrooms beginning in Grade 2 and participated in the Pre-Transition phase of the program across Grades 2 and 3, albeit while the program was in development. In total, we matched 28 Transition 4 pairs and 14 Transition 5 pairs (see Table 5.3). To verify comparability, we conducted statistical tests on first-grade Spanish reading and language scores (NCEs) for each subgroup. No significant differences were found (p values based on t-tests all exceeded .73; means and standard deviations are reported in Table 5.5 of the Results section).

Evaluation Design and Comparisons Available. Table 5.4 shows the measures available for comparisons at each grade for each subgroup. Where it is relevant, the specific language of the measure is specified (English or Spanish; x means data are available). Matching procedures allow for project and nonproject comparisons within each subgroup. Project and nonproject students within each subgroup qualified to begin transition at approximately the same time, were administered standardized tests and performance assessments in the same language from one year to the next, and are matched based on first-grade Spanish literacy measures, measures taken just prior to when project students began participating in the program. Matching procedures also allow for sample-to-sample comparisons, collapsing across subgroups, because the samples are similarly comprised of 28 Transition 4 students and 14 Transition 5 students.

TABLE 5.4
Measures Available for Project and Nonproject Subgroups

| | Project and Nonproject Matched Subgroups | |
| | Transition 4, | Transition 5, |
Grade and Measures	$n = 28$ and 28	$n = 14$ and 14
1, Standardized tests	Spanish	Spanish
2, Standardized tests	Spanish	Spanish
3, Standardized tests	Spanish	Spanish
3, CARE passing (qualify for transition)	x	x
4, Standardized tests	Spanish	Spanish
4, Performance assessment	English	Spanish
4, CARE passing (qualify for transition)	x	x
5, Standardized tests	English	Spanish
5, Performance assessment	English	English
5, Reclassification (LEP → FEP)	x	x
5, Literacy survey	x	x

Note. x, Data are available.

Instruments

Norm-Referenced Achievement Tests. The Comprehensive Test of Basic Skills (CTBS; CTB/McGraw-Hill) was the district-mandated English language standardized achievement test during the years of the study. For those Spanish-speaking LEP students for whom CTBS is not appropriate, district schools use APRENDA (*La prueba de logos en español,* Spanish achievement test; Psychological Corporation, Harcourt Brace Jovanovich, Inc.). Both instruments include subtests of reading and language.

Criteria for Addition of Reading in English (CARE). To formally qualify to begin transition, LEP students must pass the district's CARE assessment, which includes three components: (a) oral English proficiency, (b) Spanish reading, and (c) Spanish writing. Benchmarks for passing are set to reflect end of second/beginning of third grade Spanish literacy skills and speech emergence proficiency in oral English (basically conversant in English). For the purposes of the study, we recorded when students passed CARE and qualified for transition.[1]

---

[1]Oral English proficiency measures should be included in evaluations of transitional bilingual programs. In fact, we collected teacher ratings of oral English proficiency based on the Student Oral Language Observation Matrix (SOLOM), the district-mandated rating scale. Results showed a nonsignificant difference favoring project students. However, we had concerns about the accuracy of ratings for some project and nonproject students and chose not to report the results here. Data are presented and reliability concerns are detailed in Saunders and Lennon (1996).

Performance Assessments: Content. Project-developed perfor-mance assessments measure:

1. Narrative comprehension—students read a portion of a grade level appropriate story, summarize what they read, and then write an end-ing for the story (scored for comprehension of story).
2. Informational comprehension—students read a grade-level appro-priate informational text, describe what they learned, and then re-spond to an inference question (scored for comprehension of text in-formation).
3. Writing communication—students choose a favorite story they have read and summarize it (scored for the clarity with which students convey the content of the story).
4. Writing conventions—students' summaries of their favorite stories are also scored for conventions (spelling, punctuation, capitaliza-tion, usage).
5. Dictation—students take dictation for a grade-level-appropriate text (scored for spelling, punctuation, and capitalization).
6. Independent reading and library use—students list books and stories they have selected and read on their own over the past year; they also indicate if they have been to the public library in the past year and list specific items they checked out.

The assessment is administered in a small-group setting ($n = 6$–10) on 3 consecutive days (60–90 min each day). Students are given as long as they need to complete each task. The small-group setting allows for close proctoring to insure that students understand all tasks. Project teaching assistants administered the assessments to all project and nonproject stu-dents following a manual that details uniform procedures.

Scoring the Performance Assessments. All student work was scored by project staff and teachers under the direction of the author. At each scoring session, "readers" were trained on each task to be scored. Scoring leaders (researchers, project advisors) reviewed the scoring rubric and anchor papers in order to prepare readers to make consistent and ac-curate judgments. Each paper was read and scored blind by two inde-pendent readers (papers were coded with identification numbers). Papers that received two different scores were scored by a third reader, who ad-judicated the discrepancy. Scoring sessions included papers from project and nonproject students and also students from other schools involved in another research study. Papers from each sample of students were randomly distributed in the stacks of papers scored by each reader. Procedures were designed to maintain high levels of reliable, accurate, and unbiased scoring.

Performance Assessment Reliability. The conventional index of reliability for rubric-based scoring is the rate of agreement between readers. Exact agreement is when two independent readers give a paper the same score. Adjacent agreement is when two readers "agree" within one score point (i.e., same score or scores that differ by one point). With a 5-point scale, exact agreement levels above 70% and adjacent agreement levels above 90% are considered strong levels of reliability (Gentile, 1992). Agreement levels averaged across all measures for the 2 years of results to be reported here are: 61% exact and 97% adjacent. Given these levels of agreement and the practice of adjudicating *all* papers, scores should be highly consistent with rubric criteria. (See Saunders & Lennon, 1996, for more reliability data).

Performance Assessment Data. In most cases, results to be reported are based on scores combined across tasks. We averaged students scores for narrative and informational comprehension to generate a single score for Reading. We averaged students scores for written communication, conventions and dictation to generate one score for Writing. Finally, we averaged all five scores to produce a single Combined score. Four statistics are reported: means, standard deviations, and the percentage of students averaging "4.0 or better" and "3.0 or better." All tasks are scored on a 5-point scale. A score of 4 indicates students are meeting challenging grade-level standards. A score of 3 means students are approaching those standards and have demonstrated at least basic competence for that grade level. Scoring rubrics were developed based on national and state models (National Assessment of Educational Progress, California Learning Assessment System).

Literacy-Related Practices. Measures are based on the fifth-grade performance assessments. First, we tallied the items students listed on their reading inventories that were identifiable middle and upper grade stories and books (i.e., age appropriate). The kind of items we did not count include primers (Spot), familiar fairy tales (*Little Red Riding Hood;* *La Caperucita Roja*), Disney titles (*Lion King*), nondescript categories (book about dogs), and periodicals (*T.V. Guide*). Tallies were coded into three categories: 8 or more, 4–7, and 0–3 middle and upper grade stories and books. Results focus on the percent of students listing 8 or more. Second, responses to the question regarding library use were coded into one of three categories: No, Yes, and Yes + Titles (reported going to public library and listed specific items checked out). Results compare the percent of students in the third category (Yes + Titles), the best available indicator of actual library use, self-report notwithstanding. Third, the "favorite" story students chose to write about was coded into one of three categories: (a) middle/upper grade story; (b) primary grade story (*The Hungry Caterpillar*); and (c) familiar fairy tales (*Three Little Pigs*). These codings provide an indication of the quality and sophistication of students' reading experiences. Results compare the percent of students who chose to write about middle or upper grade stories (age appropriate).

Literacy-Related Attitudes. Students completed a questionnaire at the end of fifth grade that asked about their attitudes toward reading and writing in their first language and in English. Questions regarding primary-language reading and writing appear first, and then the same questions are repeated with respect to English. Questions include: Do you like to read and write (. . . in your first language . . . in English)? Do you want to continue learning how to read and write better (. . . in your first language . . . in English)? Response items are: *not at all, not too much, pretty much, very much*. Data to be reported are the percent of students who responded positively to each item (*pretty much* or *very much*).

Data Analysis

Analysis of variance or *t*-tests were conducted on all continuous data (normal curve equivalents [NCEs] for standardized tests and combined scores for the performance assessment). Effect sizes (proportion of a standard deviation separating project and nonproject means) were calculated by subtracting the nonproject mean from the project mean and dividing by the nonproject standard deviation. Chi-square tests were conducted on categorical or coded data. Significance level is .05.

RESULTS

Spanish and English Literacy Achievement

The project's multiyear transition program does a better job of cultivating literacy than the transition program students typically receive in the Metropolitan School District. Across Grades 2–4, project students scored higher than nonproject students on both standardized tests and performance assessments, most of which were taken in Spanish. At Grade 5, when most students took English standardized tests and all students took English performance assessments, project students scored significantly higher than nonproject students on almost every measure taken. Project and nonproject sample differences are detailed first, followed by a synthesis of subsample results.

Standardized Test Results.   Table 5.5 reports grade-by-grade NCE means and standard deviations in reading and language. On both measures, project students increasingly outperformed nonproject students from one grade to the next, with statistically significant differences evident at Grade 5, when most students were tested in English. Effect sizes for reading across Grades 2 through 5 are, respectively, +.26, +.38, +.40, and +.60 (Grade 5 means are 41.90 and 34.51; $p < .01$). Effect sizes for language are +.20, +.27, +.32, and +.59 (Grade 5 means are 45.38 and 37.80; $p < .05$).

TABLE 5.5
Standardized Measures of Reading and Language Achievement,
Grades 1–5 (Mean NCEs and Standard Deviations)

		Subgroups and Test Language						
		Transition 4, Spanish 1–4 English at 5		Transition 5, Spanish 1–5		Samples, All Students		
Domain	Grade	Project (n = 28)	Non (n = 28)	Project (n = 14)	Non (n = 14)	Project (n = 42)	Non (n = 42)	Effect Size
Reading	1	49.12	49.17	28.34	28.15	42.20	42.53	
		19.99	*21.66*	*12.68*	*12.62*	*20.31*	*21.58*	
	2	53.92	50.58	36.54	27.61	48.13	42.93	+.26
		18.12	*19.22*	*15.98*	*11.37*	*19.13*	*20.11*	
	3	59.60	53.66	36.24	27.10	51.81	44.81	+.38
		14.99	*14.91*	*10.21*	*9.61*	*17.47*	*18.34*	
	4	61.81	57.16	45.25	33.21	56.29	49.18	+.40
		17.29	*14.80*	*8.37*	*10.60*	*16.78*	*17.62*	
	5	40.56	33.62	44.56	36.29	41.90*	34.51	+.60
		10.18	*13.85*	*11.41*	*9.04*	*10.64*	*12.40*	
Language	1	51.29	48.96	37.28	36.36	46.62	44.76	
		18.68	*16.97*	*17.80*	*11.55*	*19.37*	*16.37*	
	2	54.43	50.99	32.13	28.23	47.00	43.40	+.20
		15.04	*15.94*	*14.08*	*12.81*	*18.03*	*18.37*	
	3	62.84	56.96	41.46	38.84	55.71	50.92	+.27
		17.34	*16.95*	*13.08*	*13.08*	*18.87*	*17.84*	
	4	64.19	59.18	44.26	35.71	57.54	51.35	+.32
		17.31	*16.47*	*8.72*	*15.78*	*17.66*	*19.57*	
	5	47.33	40.11	41.49	33.18	45.38*	37.80	+.59
		15.63	*12.81*	*8.99*	*12.13*	*13.94*	*12.87*	

Note.   Italicized values are standard deviations. Non, Nonproject.
*$p < .05$.

Performance-Based Assessment Results. Table 5.6 reports mean scores and standard deviations for reading and writing performance assessments conducted at the end of Grades 4 and 5. Differences between project and nonproject samples are significant for both reading and writing at both grades. At Grade 4, when Transition 4 students were assessed in English and Transition 5 students were assessed in Spanish, the effect size for reading is +.48 (project and nonproject means are, respectively, 2.76 and 2.54), and the effect size for writing is +.60 (means are 2.83 and 2.50). Effect sizes are noticeably larger at Grade 5, when all students were assessed in English. The effect size in reading is +1.15 (project and nonproject means are, respectively, 2.79 and 2.25), and the effect size for writing is +.72 (means are 2.87 and 2.37).

Figure 5.1 shows task by task results for the fifth-grade performance assessment. Histograms compare the percentage of project and nonproject students who scored a 3 or better on each task. Project students were significantly more likely than nonproject students to score a 3 or better on three of the four English measures: written communication (74% and 31%, $p < .01$), writing conventions (57% and 38%, $p < .09$), narrative comprehension (64% and 19%, $p < .01$), and informational comprehension (60% and 38%, $p < .05$). In addition, students also completed a task that measured comprehension of an informational text in Spanish. Again, project students were significantly more likely than nonproject students to score a 3 or better, demonstrating at least basic comprehension of a fifth-grade level Spanish-language article (55% and 19%, $p < .01$).

TABLE 5.6
Performance-Based Measures of Reading and Writing Achievement,
Grades 4 and 5 (Mean Scores and Standard Deviations)

		Subgroups and Test Language						
		Transition 4, English		Transition 5, Spanish 4; English 5		Samples, All Students		
Domain	Grade	Project (n = 28)	Non (n = 28)	Project (n = 14)	Non (n = 14)	Project (n = 42)	Non (n = 42)	Effect Size
Reading	4	2.80	2.66	2.68	2.29	2.76*	2.54	+.48
		0.50	0.45	0.50	0.38	0.50	0.46	
	5	3.07	2.39	2.21	1.96	2.79*	2.25	+1.15
		0.60	0.42	0.26	0.46	0.65	0.47	
Writing	4	2.90	2.62	2.67	2.26	2.83*	2.50	+.60
		0.82	0.53	0.64	0.53	0.77	0.55	
	5	3.15	2.67	2.29	1.76	2.87*	2.37	+.72
		0.78	0.60	0.54	0.40	0.81	0.69	

Note. Italicized values are standard deviations. Non, Nonproject.
*$p < .05$.

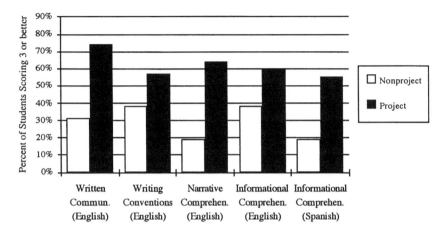

FIG. 5.1. Grade 5 performance assessments results by task. *Note.* All differences except writing conventions are statistically significant ($p < .05$).

Passing CARE (Qualifying for Transition) and Redesignation Rates

Table 5.7 reports the percentage of students who passed the CARE assessment by the end of Grade 3 or during Grade 4 and the number of students who redesignated from limited to fluent English proficient by the end of Grade 5.

First, Grade 3 CARE passing rates for project and nonproject students are 40% and 17% ($p < .05$); cumulative precentages for students passing in third or during the first half of fourth grade are 74% and 60% (ns).[2] Although most project students passed by the end of third grade, most nonproject students passed during the first half of fourth. The higher passing rate at Grade 3 means more project students at an earlier point had the skills necessary to pass CARE and the opportunity to do so: They

---

[2]All project Transition 4 students began Transition I at the beginning of fourth grade. Seventeen students had qualified by passing CARE at the end of third, 7 passed at the beginning of fourth, 3 were expected to pass and did pass CARE shortly after the beginning of the year, and 1 never passed but was included based on the judgment of the school's language appraisal team. All nonproject Transition 4 students began the district's prescribed 3- to 6-month transition program sometime during the first half of fourth grade. Seven qualified by passing CARE at the end of third, 8 passed at the beginning of fourth, 10 passed later in the first semester, and 3 began transition based on the determination of their school's language appraisal team. As such, 100% of project and nonproject Transition 4 began transition during the first semester of Grade 4; the vast majority (96% of project and 89% of nonproject) began transition after passing CARE, but 1 project and 3 nonproject students began transition based on the judgment of the school's language appraisal team.

TABLE 5.7
CARE Passing and Redesignation Rates,
Grades 3, 4, and 5 (Cumulative Percentages)

| | Subgroups | | | | Samples, All Students | |
| | Transition 4 | | Transition 5 | | | |
Indicator and Grade	Project (n = 28)	Non (n = 28)	Project (n = 14)	Non (n = 14)	Project (n = 42)	Non (n = 42)
Percent passing CARE by end of 3rd	61	25	0	0	40*	17
Percent passing CARE during 4th	96	89	29	0	74	60
Percent redesignating by end of 5th, LEP → FEP	57	18	0	0	38*	12

Note. Non, Nonproject.
*$p < .05$.

were properly identified and assessed by their teachers and the school co-ordinator. This is consistent with the conceptualization and goals of the project's multiyear transition program: Improve Spanish language arts and ELD instruction in the pretransition years so more students have the skills necessary to qualify for transition by the end Grade 3 and the opportunity to take part in a full 2 years of transitional language arts. The low third-grade passing rate among nonproject students indicates that more students did not have the skills to pass the assessment, and many who did perhaps were not identified and tested until Grade 4. The prevailing 3- to 6-month guidelines for transition do not encourage schools to recognize that initiating CARE testing in Grade 4 possibly short-changes students from additional time they need in a transitional language arts program.

Second, project students were more than twice as likely as nonproject students to meet the criteria necessary to be redesignated from limited to fluent English proficient by the end of fifth grade, 38% and 12% ($p < .01$).

Literacy Practices and Attitudes

Independent Reading, Library Use, and Favorite Stories. Table 5.8 reports results by subgroup and sample for independent reading, library use, and favorite stories for project and nonproject samples. Differences between project and nonproject students are statistically significant on two of the three measures. Project students were more likely than

TABLE 5.8
Self-Reported Literacy-Related Practices, Grade 5

	Subgroups				Samples, All Students	
	Transition 4		Transition 5			
Indicator	Project (n = 28)	Non (n = 28)	Project (n = 14)	Non (n = 14)	Project (n = 42)	Non (n = 42)
Independent reading, percent with 8 age-appropriate items	43	11	7	7	31*	10
Frequent library use, percent yes and listed items	68	32	29	36	55*	33
Favorite story, percent age appropriate	82	54	36	36	67	48

Note. Non, Nonproject.
*$p < .05$.

nonproject students to: (a) list 8 or more age appropriate books they had selected and read independently over the past year (31% and 10%, $p < .05$), (b) report using the public library and list actual titles checked out over the past year (55% and 33%, $p < .05$), and (c) choose to write about an age-appropriate favorite story (67% and 48%, $p < .08$).

Attitudes Toward Reading and Writing in English and Spanish. Table 5.9 reports results by subgroup and sample for two pairs of survey questions. There are no differences between project and nonproject students in their attitudes toward reading and writing in English: More than 90% of the students in each sample responded positively to the two English survey items. However, there are significant differences between project and nonproject students in their attitudes toward reading and writing in Spanish. Almost all project students but less than two-thirds of the nonproject students said they liked to read and write in Spanish, 95% versus 60% ($p < .01$). Similarly, 86% of project students in comparison to 64% of nonproject students said they wanted to continue to learn how to read and write better in Spanish ($p < .05$).

Synthesis of Sample and Subgroup Results

Table 5.10 synthesizes all results. The organization of the table is designed to reflect the sequential and longitudinal nature of transitional bilingual education. Our premise has been that transition cannot and

TABLE 5.9
Attitudes Toward Reading and Writing in English and Spanish, Grade 5

	Subgroups				Samples, All Students	
	Transition 4		Transition 5			
Survey Questions	Project (n = 28)	Non (n = 28)	Project (n = 14)	Non (n = 14)	Project (n = 42)	Non (n = 42)
Reading/writing in English						
Do you like to . . .						
pretty/very much (%)	93	96	86	86	90	93
Want to continue learning . . .						
pretty/very much (%)	100	100	79	93	93	98
Reading/writing in Spanish						
Do you like to . . .						
pretty/very much (%)	96	50	93	79	95*	60
Want to continue learning . . .						
pretty/very much (%)	86	57	86	79	86*	64

Note. Non, Nonproject.
*$p < .05$.

should not be treated as an isolated, short-term phase in students' elementary school experience. The extent to which transitional bilingual programs help students acquire English literacy is a function of the total program, beginning with Spanish literacy and oral English language development instruction in the primary and middle grades and carrying forth through the transition years. Table 5.10 provides comparisons between project and nonproject students through the various junctures of the transition program: Spanish literacy achievement at Grade 1 and 3; CARE passing rates by the end of third and during fourth grade; Grade 5 redesignation rates; Grade 5 English achievement; and Grade 5 self-reported literacy practices and attitudes.

Data for CARE passing, redesignation rates, and literacy practices and attitudes are the same percentages shown previously. In order to be statistically consistent, achievement indicators are also reported in the form of percentages. For Grade 1 and 3 Spanish literacy achievement, we report the percentage of students scoring at or above the 50th national percentile in Spanish reading and language. For Grade 5 English achievement, we report the percentage of students averaging 3.00 or better across all reading and writing performance assessment tasks (approaching or meeting challenging grade-level standards on all tasks). English achievement is also reflected in the redesignation rates: percent of stu-

TABLE 5.10

Synthesis of Sample and Subgroup Results for Project and Nonproject (Non) Students

| | Subgroups | | | | Samples, All Students | |
| | Transition 4 | | Transition 5 | | | |
Indicator	Project (n = 28)	Non (n = 28)	Project (n = 14)	Non (n = 14)	Project (n = 42)	Non (n = 42)
Grade 1 Spanish achievement, 50th NP reading and language (%)	43	43	7	7	31	31
Grade 3 Spanish achievement, 50th NP reading and language (%)	71	54	0	0	48	36
Qualify for transition						
Passing CARE by end of 3rd (%)	61	25	0	0	40*	17
Passing CARE by end 3rd or during 4th (%)	96	89	29	0	74	60
Redesignation (LEP → RFEP), 36th NP English reading and language by end of 5th (%)	57	18	0	0	38*	12
Grade 5 English achievement, 3.00 on performance assessment (%)	68	18	0	0	45*	12
Grade 5 practices and attitudes						
Reporting 8 age-appropriate books (%)	43	11	7	7	31*	10
Wrote about age-appropriate story (%)	68	32	29	36	55*	33
Reporting library use and items (%)	82	54	36	36	67*	47
Like reading and writing in English (%)	93	96	86	86	90	93
Continue learning reading and writing in English (%)	100	100	79	93	93	98
Like reading and writing in Spanish (%)	96	50	93	79	95*	60
Continue learning reading and writing in Spanish (%)	86	57	86	79	86*	64

*$p < .05$.

193

dents scoring at or above the 36th national percentile in reading and language on English standardized tests. We discuss the synthesis of results briefly for the two samples, and then within each subgroup.

Overall Results: Sample Differences.   The program more than doubled the percentage of students who qualified for transition by the end of Grade 3 (40% vs. 17%) and tripled the percentage of students who reclassified by the end of Grade 5 (38% vs. 12%). What contributed to these overall results and/or limited them is evident in the synthesis of results for each subgroup.

Transition 4 Students.   Results for the Transition 4 subgroup present a strong case for the project's multiyear transition program. The evidence runs from the top of Table 5.10 to the bottom. At the end of first grade 43% of the students in each sample were performing at or above national norms in Spanish reading and language (50th percentile). By the end of third grade and the Pre-Transition phase of the program, percentages rose to 71% among project and 54% among nonproject students—a 65% increase for project students in contrast to a 26% increase for nonproject students. The achievement gains together with timely assessment and identification procedures combined to yield a 61% CARE passing rate among project students by the end of third grade. The lack of comparable achievement gains and likely less attention to timely assessment are probably the reasons for the substantially lower 25% third-grade passing rate among nonproject students.

Ultimately, all project and nonproject Transition 4 students began transition during the first half of Grade 4. Nonproject students received 3 to 6 months of transitional language arts and then entered mainstream English shortly thereafter. In contrast, all project students participated in the Transition I and II phases of the program across Grades 4 and 5. By the end of Grade 5, English achievement levels were markedly different: 68% of project but only 18% of nonproject students averaged 3.00 or better on the performance assessment; and 57% of project but only 18% nonproject students redesignated by the end of fifth grade.

Among Transition 4 students, then, the project's program yielded a 144% increase in the percentage of students who qualified for transition by the end of Grade 3 (61% vs. 25%) and a 217% increase in the percentage of students who redesignated from limited to fluent English proficient by the end of Grade 5 (57% vs. 18%).

Moreover, program effects were not confined to achievement alone. The percentage of Transition 4 students showing evidence of broader literacy practices was substantially higher for project than nonproject students on every measure taken: age-appropriate independent reading (43% vs. 11%), library use (82% and 54%), and age-appropriate favorite stories (68% vs. 32%). In addition, although all students reported positive attitudes toward English, considerably larger percentages of project students reported positive attitudes toward their first language (like to read and write in Spanish: 96% vs. 50%; continue learning to read and write in Spanish: 86% vs. 57%). This is likely a reflection of the project's emphasis on a strong Spanish literacy program prior to transition and maintaining Spanish language arts during transition. In the project's program, Spanish language arts instruction continues throughout the Transition I year, and students are explicitly encouraged and supported to continue reading and writing in Spanish during the Transition II year. In contrast, under district guidelines, Spanish maintenance is confined solely to the short and ambiguous 3- to 6-month period prescribed for transition.

Transition 5 Students. Project Transition 5 students made substantial Spanish literacy gains across Grades 1–4. By Grade 4, project students were scoring significantly higher than nonproject students on standardized and performance-based assessments of Spanish reading, language, and writing. As shown in Table 5.10, however, these gains were not enough to make it possible for most students to met any of the successive criteria that characterize a successful transition: on grade level in Spanish reading and language at Grade 1, 7% and 7%; on grade level in Spanish reading and language at Grade 3, 0% and 0%; passing CARE by Grade 3, 0% and 0%; passing CARE during Grade 4, 29% and 0%; reclassifying by Grade 5, 0% and 0%; scoring 3.00 or better on the Grade 5 English assessment, 0% and 0%.

It seems clear that the program does not have the capacity to fully address the needs of very low-achieving students. During Grade 4, project Transition 5 students continued in a Spanish (Pre-Transition) program. In fact, the additional year of Spanish proved beneficial for most students, as reflected in the Spanish achievement gains at the end of Grade 4 (see Table 5.5, shown earlier). Students then received 1 year of transition instruction. At the end of Grade 5, however, although they averaged significantly higher than nonproject students on English performance assessments, project students evidenced very low levels of achievement. As such, by the end of their elementary years, project Transition 5 students had acquired only modest levels of Spanish literacy and minimal levels of English literacy. Moreover, project Transition 5 students apparently did not acquire the same kind of literacy practices evident among Transition

4 project students. For example, in comparison to project Transition 4 students, project Transition 5 students were far less likely to independently select and read age-appropriate stories (respectively, 43% vs. 7%), visit and check out books from the library (68% vs. 29%), or have favorite age-appropriate stories to write about (82% vs. 36%).

There might be modifications that can be made in the program to better address the needs of very low achieving students during the pretransition years. However, most likely the problem has to be addressed earlier than Grades 2 or 3. Most Transition 5 students showed little evidence of literacy achievement by the end of Grade 1. As other research projects have shown (Slavin, Madden, Dolan, & Wasik, 1996), literacy difficulties must be addressed in the earliest grades in order for students to achieve success throughout their elementary years. There were gains among project Transition 5 students, and those should not go unrecognized. But more has to be done to make it possible for these students to succeed, especially in a transitional bilingual program where grade-by-grade progress is so critical.

DISCUSSION

Importance of the Study

A Promising Program and the Potential of Transitional Bilingual Programs. Results indicate the multiyear transition program is demonstrably more effective than the program students typically receive, producing higher levels of Spanish literacy, significantly higher levels of English literacy, and important literacy-related practices and attitudes for significantly larger numbers of students. In fact, results reported here likely provide a conservative estimate of program effects because students participated in the program as it was being developed. Similar to Calderón et al. (1998), this study demonstrates that with careful program design and evaluation, transitional bilingual programs can be improved. There seems to be more potential in these programs than many schools achieve.

Identification of Implementation Problems That Limit Transitional Programs. Transitional bilingual programs depend on successive grade-by-grade achievement. Careful program oversight, high-quality primary-language literacy and oral English instruction in Grades K–3, and a transitional language arts program of serious substance and duration are important and interdependent. These are the needs we identified and tried to address. Our experiences at other sites suggest these same needs are widespread but often go unrecognized (see also Berman et al., 1992). Educators and parents tend to assume that low English achievement at the upper grades is evidence that bilingual education per se does not work. But they often fail to scrutinize the quality of primary-language and ELD instruction, and they have little information and few models to develop informed expectations about transition itself.

Implications for Improving Transitional Bilingual Programs. Results reported here have direct implications for educators seeking to improve transitional programs. Without adopting our specific program, results suggest significant payoffs might be had by (a) focusing attention on the *quality* of L1 language arts and oral English language development in the early grades, (b) adopting a longer term approach to transition, (c) establishing an actual curriculum for the transition period, and (d) maintaining L1 language arts instruction during at least the first year when English literacy is introduced. (See Appendix 2: Questions to Guide Schools Seeking to Improve Transitional Bilingual Programs.)

Evidence for Theoretical Principles.   Although we have not yet established empirically the individual merit and manifestation of our theoretical principles, the results support them, overall. Challenge, comprehensiveness, continuity, and connections have had a certain utility in our project because, as several studies have documented (cited earlier) and we observed, they are often lacking in transitional programs for English learners. But we suspect the principles will have similar utility for other educators seeking to improve transitional bilingual and other kinds of programs. All four principles resonate strongly with project teachers (Saunders & Goldenberg, 1997). In addition, we are identifying and in some cases confirming the merit of specific principles in the research and development of other teams (see Calderón et al., 1998, specifically for continuity; Jiménez et al., 1996, for comprehensiveness; Thomas & Collier, 1997, for challenge).

Continuing Questions

To What Extent Are Program Effects Teacher/Project Effects? The teachers who helped develop, implement, and test the program are all very dedicated practitioners. They became interested in the project early on and remained involved over the entire 5 years. They opened up their classrooms to project advisors, and consistently tried to learn and implement new strategies and approaches. Some were veterans, and some were brand new teachers. Some had traditional programs, and others had been experimenting with language arts reforms for quite some time. Some were deeply committed to bilingual education, and others were not. As the project evolved, so did each member of the project team. No doubt, at least some portion of program effects is teacher/project effects—effects achieved by conscientious teachers participating in and supported by a long-term research and development project. Replication studies are needed to produce better estimates of program effects (see Saunders & Goldenberg, 1999b, for initial replication efforts).

Can Program Effects Be Replicated on a Large Scale? Project teachers learned to study literary selections carefully, identify major themes, divide books into manageable and meaningful portions of reading, develop literature log topics, conduct challenging but non-threatening instructional conversations, design engaging writing projects, locate and organize related materials for independent centers, and coordinate a classroom system that cultivated high levels of student responsibility and allowed for extensive small-group instruction. We would like to assume that all teachers have or can develop these skills, but we have not yet demonstrated it. Some teachers at project schools openly commented that what they saw project teachers doing was impressive, but they could not imagine investing so much time and effort into their program. It is probably a mistake, therefore, to underestimate the challenge involved in implementing the program with large numbers of teachers.

What Are the Specific Effects of Individual Program Components? The program was developed as the project team analyzed student needs, examined existing classroom practices, and drew on the research literature. As a total package, the program seems to produce superior literacy results relative to what students in neighboring schools typically receive. However, the language arts program is a fairly complex integration of 12 different components. At this point, it is unclear which components or which combination of program components make the strongest contribute to students' literacy development. Such work is needed. Teachers need reliable information about component effects in order to prioritize, plan and organize instruction (see Saunders & Goldenberg, 1999a).

How Should Schools Address the Issue of Newcomers and Transiency? Evaluation results are based on students who remained enrolled at their schools across Grades 1–5. This sample is representative of about two-thirds of the students at project and nonproject schools. The program we developed puts a premium on careful monitoring of student progress and placement and continuity of instruction at least across Grades 2 through 5. We have not worked out specific strategies for effectively accommodating new students entering the program at Grades 3 and up, especially students enrolling at the middle and upper grades with very low levels of achievement in their first language. As Berman et al. (1992) found, the issues of newcomers and transiency are major impediments to the effectiveness of transitional bilingual programs and must be taken very seriously.

Have We Reached the Limits of Transitional Bilingual Programs? The program we developed emphasizes the importance of primary language instruction through Grade 3 and maintenance of primary language literacy instruction during Grade 4. In Grade 5, students are encouraged to continue self-selected reading and writing in their primary language, but instruction is delivered exclusively in English. Thomas and Collier's (1997) longitudinal study of academic achievement spanning 1st through 12th grade seems to indicate that transitional bilingual programs—even those bolstered by a great emphasis on primary language instruction, a more gradual approach to transition, and more effective pedagogy—are less successful in the long run than "true" bilingual programs that make English *and* primary-language achievement complementary goals throughout the elementary grades. The results we have produced so far are in the same range as those reported by Thomas and Collier for "best case" well-implemented transitional bilingual programs. Because the vast majority of bilingual programs are transitional, one of our goals is to make them as effective as possible. Nevertheless, we have to face the prospect that there may be inherent limitations to transitional designs.

ACKNOWLEDGMENTS

This chapter was adapted from Saunders (1999). Thanks to the students, parents, and administrators at the project schools and the teachers and advisors who comprised the research and development team, including the directors of the team Deborah Lennon and Gisela O'Brien; advisors Tina Saldivar, Leticia Villa, and Sally Wong; project teachers Abbey Alessi, Kris Bullivant, Victor Chavira, Rafael Delgado, Susan Dickson, Gary DiPierro, Melissa Dodd, Teresa Franco, Mae Hom, Cindy Kim, Hillary Long-Villa, Gerardo López, Albert Martínez, Celia Mata, Jerry

McLean, Estella Mercado, Lydia Moreno, Sylvia Salazar, Liz Salcido, Susan Sandberg, Imelda Valencia, Anita Winter, and Rossana Yñiguez; and project consultants Dolores Beltrán and Claude Goldenberg. Thanks also to Claude Goldenberg and the anonymous reviewers for their helpful comments on this chapter. The project described here was supported by a Title VII grant from the U.S. Department of Education, Office of Bilingual Education and Minority Languages Affairs. Additional research support was provided by the Spencer Foundation; the National Center for Research on Cultural Diversity and Second Language Learning, University of California, Santa Cruz; the Urban Education Studies Center, University of California, Los Angeles; and the National Center for Research on Education, Diversity, and Excellence, University of California, Santa Cruz. No endorsement from any source should be inferred.

APPENDIX 1: LANGUAGE ARTS
PROGRAM COMPONENTS

Literature Units (Experience–Text–Relationship Approach). On average, students engage in four literature units across the year. Titles are chosen to fit the students' grade level and language proficiency (in particular across Transition I and II). The literature unit is propelled by an ongoing process of reading, writing (literature logs), and discussion (instructional conversations). Discussions are conducted in small groups of 6–10 students and managed through a specifically designed rotation system (teacher-specific). The instructional framework for the literature units is called Experience–Text–Relationship (Mason & Au, 1986): Throughout the course of the unit, the teacher tries to help students understand the relationship between their own experiences, the content of the literary selection, and one or more major themes that apply to the selection (e.g., friendship, sacrifice, perseverance, commitment, justice, cultural identity). In addition to those three critical elements (experience, text, theme), the teacher enriches the unit with lessons, activities, and supplementary readings that build background knowledge necessary for developing a deeper understanding of the selection and theme(s). Typically, units culminate with a writing project (see Culminating Writing Projects) through which students elaborate on some aspect of the literature unit.

Literature Logs. Teachers divide the literary selection into "chunks" (manageable portions of reading) and assign a literature log entry for each chunk. Students complete the log entry at an independent center, and typically small-group discussions begin with some or all students sharing their logs. Literature log prompts might ask students to (a) write about a personal experience (related to the story), (b) elaborate on something that has happened in the story (e.g., assume the role of the character), or (c) analyze/interpret some aspect of the story or theme. In preparing a literature unit, teachers develop specific log prompts for each chunk, but often prompts emerge naturally from small group discussions.

Instructional Conversations (Small-Group Discussions). Throughout the course of the literature unit, teacher and students meet in small groups to discuss the story, log entries, related personal experiences, and the theme(s) for the unit. The amount of time allotted to the discussion segment and frequency vary from teacher to teacher, but on average students spend at least 45 min per week engaged in discussion. The discussion provides the teacher with the opportunity to (a) hear students articulate their understanding of the story, theme(s) and related personal experiences, and (b) in the process of facilitating the discussion, challenge but also help students to enrich and deepen their understandings. Facilitated by the teacher, the small-group discussions, also referred to as Instructional Conversations (Goldenberg, 1992/1993), allow students to hear, appreciate, and build on each others' experiences, knowledge, and understandings.

Culminating Writing Projects (Writing-as-a-Process Approach). On average, students complete four major writing projects across the year, taking the pieces through the entire process of writing: prewriting, drafting, sharing, receiving feedback, revising, editing, and preparing a final, polished piece of work (Calkins, 1986, 1991; Graves, 1983, 1991). Typically these projects are directly related to the literature units, which conclude with a culminating writing (e.g., fully developing a literature log, or a writing assignment tailored to the themes and content of the literature study). The key to this process is revision. Three things seem to promote meaningful revision: (a) helping students learn to share and receive/provide feedback, (b) discussing examples (student or published) of the kind of writing students are working on, highlighting for students things they might incorporate in their own pieces when they revise, and (c) one-on-one conferences with the teacher.

Comprehension Strategies. Students are taught specific strategies to use while they are reading in order to monitor their own comprehension (McNeil, 1984; Palinscar & Brown, 1985). The two essential strategies are pausing intermittently during reading (a) to summarize what they've read and (b) to formulate and answer test-like questions about the reading material. Strategies are introduced during 2-week training modules provided at the beginning and middle of the year. Students practice the strategies in pairs at the assigned independent reading center.

Assigned Independent Reading. Students are regularly assigned reading selections from available materials (basals, literature titles, and any other sources) to read independently. Optimally, selections are related to the themes and topics being discussed in the Literature Units. Students complete various accompanying assignments to promote comprehension and hold the students accountable for what they read (summaries, comprehension questions, graphic organizers, paired and group activities). Readings and assignments are completed in class as part of an independent center and/or for homework.

Dictation. The most extensive dictation program (Seeds University Elementary School, 1992) includes: Students engage in dictation exercises weekly, taking a cold dictation of a grade-level-appropriate passage (at the beginning of the week), studying the features of that particular passage and practicing the dictation (throughout the week), and then completing a final dictation (at the end of the week). But as we've found, even a less extensive dictation program (two times per week) is beneficial. Two elements are critical for successful dictation: (a) explanations from the teacher about language and punctuation items featured in the dictation passage, and (b) opportunities for the students to proofread and check their dictation against the actual passage.

Written Conventions Lessons. Students receive directed lessons about the conventions of written language (punctuation, capitalization, grammar, word usage). Lessons include a presentation from the teacher, opportunities for guided and independent practice, and then application to writings the students are working on (e.g., literature logs, writing projects, even dictation passages). The key is connecting what is studied in the lessons to the actual writing students are doing.

Oral English Language Development Through Literature. Used in Grades K–3, the ELD program is based on a natural-language approach and children's literature (Beltran & O'Brien, 1993). Literature provides a meaningful, motivational, and enjoyable context for learning and practicing specifically targeted English oral language skills. It also exposes children to English print well in advance of formal transition to

English reading. On average, students receive 30 min of ELD per day. Lessons are conducted in small groups organized by English language production level. Organizing groups by production level allows the teacher to focus more successfully on students' specific needs.

Pleasure Reading. A portion of time each day, or at the upper grades as part of a weekly system, is scheduled for students to select and read things on their own for pleasure and interest. Students keep and review with the teacher a record of their ongoing readings (reading inventory), and often complete assignments related to their readings: preparing summaries and synopses, oral presentations for book sharing time, drawings, and so on. Three things help promote pleasure reading:

1. Teachers introduce students to numerous selections (trips to library, a full classroom library, lending read-aloud selections, making recommendations).
2. Teachers explicitly teach students how to choose and try out books (reading the cover synopsis, reading a portion of the book, reading various books from the same author).
3. Students have a chance to share and discuss with each other and teacher what they are reading.

Teacher Read-Alouds. At least three times per week, teachers read to students for approximately 20 min. Read-alouds (Trelease, 1985) serve various purposes: promote pleasure reading; expose students to the language of expert writers and the fluency of an expert reader; engage students in reading material they may not yet be able to read themselves; and increase students' familiarity with different genres of writing.

Interactive Journals. Used primarily in Grades K–2 and at the beginning of transition, interactive journals provide students with regular, nonthreatening opportunities to write about topics of their own choice and participate in a written dialogue with the teacher (Flores et al., 1991). Teacher response occurs as often as possible and provides students with examples of conventional writing. Interactive journals help Grade K and 1 students break the written language code; later, in Grade 1 and 2, they help students develop initial writing fluency. Transition teachers use interactive journals during the first semester of transition when students are making their first attempts at English writing. The immediate response from the teacher provides both emotional support for students and a highly contextualized and therefore comprehensible English text for students to read.

APPENDIX 2: QUESTIONS TO GUIDE SCHOOLS SEEKING TO IMPROVE TRANSITIONAL BILINGUAL PROGRAMS

1. Are students achieving L1 literacy in the early grades (first, second, third)? Are we emphasizing the fundamental importance of L1 language arts in the early grades?
2. Are students achieving oral English language proficiency in the early grades? Are we emphasizing the fundamental importance of oral English language development while students are receiving language arts instruction in L1?
3. Do we have criteria and an instrument for identifying students prepared to add transitional language arts (i.e., add English reading & writing instruction)? Are we emphasizing the importance of teaching to those criteria?
4. Do we have a transitional language arts program (e.g., stated goals, curriculum, reading series, assessments of progress, designated timeframe)? Are we emphasizing the importance of transitional language arts (e.g., assignment of teachers and teaching assistants, professional development, program materials)?
5. Do we continue to teach and promote L1 literacy during transition? Are we emphasizing the importance of ongoing L1 literacy achievement as we teach students how to read and write in English?
6. Do we have criteria and an instrument for identifying students prepared for mainstream language arts? Are we emphasizing the importance of teaching toward those criteria?

REFERENCES

Au, K. H. (1979). Using the experience-text-relationship method with minority children. *Reading Teacher, 32,* 677–679.
Au, K. H. (1992). Constructing the theme of a story. *Language Arts, 69,* 106–111.
August, D., & Hakuta, K. (Eds.). (1997). *Improving schooling for language minority children: A research agenda.* Washington, DC: National Academy Press.
Beltran, D., & O'Brien, G. (1993). *English language development through literature.* Workshop and documentation presented at the annual conference of the California Association for Bilingual Education, Anaheim, CA, February.

Berman, P., Chambers, J., Gandara, P., McLaughlin, B., Minicucci, C., Nelson, B., Olson, L., & Parrish, T. (1992). *Meeting the challenge of language diversity: An evaluation of programs for pupils with limited English proficiency* (Executive summary, Vol. I). Berkeley, CA: BW Associates.

Calderón, M., Hertz-Lazarowitz, R., & Slavin, R. (1998). Effects of bilingual cooperative integrated reading and composition on students making the transition from Spanish to English reading. *Elementary School Journal, 99*(2), 153–165.

Calkins, L. M. (1986). *The art of teaching writing.* Portsmouth, NH: Heinemann.

Calkins, L. M. (1991). *Living between the lines.* Portsmouth, NH: Heinemann.

Crawford, J. (1997). *Best evidence: Research foundations of the Bilingual Education Act.* Washington, DC: National Clearinghouse for Bilingual Education.

Cummins, J. (1989). *Empowering minority students.* Sacramento, CA: California Association for Bilingual Education.

Flores, B., Garcia, E., Gonzalez, S., Hidalgo, G., Kaczmarek, K., & Romero, T. (1991). *Bilingual holistic instructional strategies.* Unpublished manuscript.

Gándara, P., & Merino, B. (1993). Measuring the outcomes of LEP programs: Test scores, exit rates, and other mythological data. *Educational Evaluation and Policy Analysis, 15,* 320–338.

García, E. (1992). Effective instruction for language minority students: The teacher. *Journal of Education, 173*(2), 130–141.

Genesee, F. (Ed.). (1999). *Program alternatives for linguistically diverse students* (Educational Practice Report No. 1). Santa Cruz, CA: Center for Research on Education, Diversity and Excellence.

Gentile, C. (1992). *Exploring new methods for collecting students' school-based writing: NAEP's 1990 portfolio study.* Washington, DC: National Center for Education Statistics.

Gersten, R. (1996). Literacy instruction for language minority students: The Transition years. *Elementary School Journal, 96*(3), 227–244.

Gersten, R., & Jiménez, R. (1993, April). *Language minority students in transition.* Symposium presented at the annual conference of the American Educational Research Association, Atlanta, GA.

Gersten, R., & Woodward, J. (1994). The language minority student and special education: Issues, themes, and paradoxes. *Exceptional Children, 60*(4), 310–322.

Goldenberg, C. (1991). Learning to read in New Zealand: The balance of skills and meaning. *Language Arts, 68,* 555–562.

Goldenberg, C. (1992/1993). Instructional conversations: Promoting comprehension through discussion. *Reading Teacher, 46,* 316–326.

Goldenberg, C. (1996). Commentary: The education of language-minority students: Where are we, and where do we need to go? *Elementary School Journal, 96*(3), 353–361.

Graves, D. H. (1983). *Writing: Teachers and children at work.* Portsmouth, NH: Heinemann.

Graves, D. H. (1991). *Build a literate classroom.* Portsmouth, NH: Heinemann.

Jimenéz, R., Gersten, R., & Rivera, A. (1996). Conversations with a Chicana teacher: Supporting students transition from native to English language instruction. *Elementary School Journal, 96*(3), 333–341.

Krashen, S. (1987). *Principles and practice in second language acquisition.* New York: Prentice Hall.

Krashen, S. (1996). A gradual exit, variable threshold model for limited English proficient children. *National Association of Bilingual Education News, 19*(17), 1, 15–18.

Krashen, S., & Biber, D. (1988). *On course: Bilingual education's success in California.* Sacramento, CA: California Association of Bilingual Education.

Mason, J. M., & Au, K. H. (1986). *Reading instruction for today.* Glenview, IL: Scott, Foresman.

McNeil, J. D. (1984). *Reading comprehension: New directions for classroom practice.* Glenview, IL: Scott, Foresman.

Palinscar, A., & Brown, A. (1985). Reciprocal teaching: A means to a meaningful end. In J. Osborn, P. Wilson, & R. C. Anderson (Eds.), *Reading education: Foundations for a literate America* (pp. 299–310). Lexington, MA: D. C. Heath.

Ramirez, J. D. (1992). Longitudinal study of structured English immersion strategy, early-exit and late-exit transitional bilingual education programs for language minority children (Executive summary). *Bilingual Research Journal, 16*(1 & 2), 1–62.

Rossell, C. H., & Baker, K. (1996). The educational effectiveness of bilingual education. *Research in the Teaching of English, 30*(1), 7–74.

Saunders, W. (1999). Improving literacy achievement for English learners in transitional bilingual programs. *Educational Research and Evaluation, 5*(4), 345–381.

Saunders, W., & Goldenberg, C. (1997, April). *Identifying salient elements of a successful transition program for English language learners.* Paper presented at the annual meeting of the American Educational Research Association, Chicago.

Saunders, W., & Goldenberg, C. (1999a). Effects of instructional conversations and literature logs on limited- and fluent-English proficient students' story comprehension and thematic understanding. *Elementary School Journal, 99*(4), 277–301.

Saunders, W., & Goldenberg, C. (1999b). *The effects of a comprehensive Language Arts/Transition Program on the literacy development of English learners* (Technical Report.) Santa Cruz, CA: Center for Research on Education, Diversity and Excellence.

Saunders, W., & Lennon, D. (1993). *Developing academic literacy in English through a program of integrated language arts: Year 3 evaluation* (Project T003A00185). Washington, DC: Office of Bilingual Education and Minority Affairs, U.S. Department of Education.

Saunders, W., & Lennon, D. (1996). *Developing academic literacy in English through a program of integrated language arts: Year 5 evaluation* (Project T003A00185). Washington, DC: Office of Bilingual Education and Minority Affairs, U.S. Department of Education.

Saunders, W., O'Brien, G., Lennon, D., & McLean, J. (1998). Making the transition to English literacy successful: Effective strategies for studying literature with transition students. In R. Gersten & R. Jiménez (Eds.), *Promoting learning for culturally and linguistically diverse students* (pp. 99–132). New York: Wadsworth.

Seeds University Elementary School. (1992). *Dictation program: An approach to written language development.* Los Angeles, CA: Seeds University Elementary School, University of California, Los Angeles.

Slavin, R., Madden, N., Dolan, L., & Wasik, B. (1996). *Every child, every school: Success for All.* Newbury Park, CA: Corwin.

Tharp, R., & Gallimore, R. (1988). *Rousing minds to life.* Cambridge, England: Cambridge University Press.

Thomas, W. P., & Collier, V. (1997). *School effectiveness for language minority students.* Washington, DC: National Clearinghouse for Bilingual Education.

Trelease, J. (1985). *The read-aloud handbook.* New York: Penguin.

Willig, A. (1985). A meta-analysis of selected studies on the effectiveness of bilingual education. *Review of Educational Research, 55*(3), 269–317.

6

Effects of Bilingual and English-as-a-Second-Language Adaptations of Success for All on the Reading Achievement of Students Acquiring English

Robert E. Slavin
Johns Hopkins University

Nancy Madden
Success for All Foundation

Students who enter school with limited English proficiency are among the most likely of all students to be at risk for school failure (August & Hakuta, 1997). These students score substantially worse than other language minority students in schools of equal levels of poverty in both reading and mathematics at third grade (Moss & Puma, 1995). They are retained far more often, and have many other difficulties. Ultimately, limited English proficient (LEP) students are substantially more likely than other students to drop out of school; dropout rates average 42% for these students, compared to 10.5% for students who were never limited in English proficiency (McArthur, 1993). The educational difficulties of limited English proficient students are not entirely due to difficulties with English. These students are typically children of recent immigrants who suffer from the effects of poverty, mobility, limited capacity of parents to support their children's success in school, and underfunded, overcrowded schools (August & Hakuta, 1997). Even after limited English proficient students become fully proficient in English, their school performance remains substantially lower than that of other students (McArthur, 1993).

For many years, debates about the education of limited English proficient children have focused on the question of language of instruction. While children are acquiring sufficient English language skills to function well in all-English instruction, should they be taught in their native language or in English? If they are taught in their native language, should they be transitioned as soon as possible, or maintained in native language instruction until their English proficiency is at a very high level? Reviews of research on this topic generally find benefits for native language instruction, followed by a gradual transition to English (e.g., Garcia, 1994; Meyer & Fienberg, 1992; Ramirez, Yuen, & Ramey, 1991). Although there is considerable debate about this research, almost all investigators have found such bilingual programs to be at least as effective as, or more effective than, English-only instruction from the outset (August & Hakuta, 1997; National Academy of Sciences, 1998). Despite this research consensus, bilingual programs are under considerable assault at the political level, particularly with the 1998 passage of Proposition 227 in California banning most types of bilingual programs.

In recent years, there has been an increasing focus on the *quality* of instruction received by students acquiring English, in whatever language they are being taught. Among children receiving native language instruction, those who succeed in that instruction ultimately perform substantially better in English than those who do not (Garcia, 1991, 1994). Whether students are taught in English or in their native language, their success in learning to read is the most important factor in their long-term success in school. This is not to diminish the importance of native-language instruction, but simply to note that although the language-of-instruction issue is being fought out on largely political terms, it is incumbent on educators to develop, evaluate, and disseminate effective strategies for bilingual as well as English-only instruction for students acquiring English. As a practical matter, a very large proportion of English language learners will always be taught in English (if only because of shortages of teachers proficient in other languages, especially non-Spanish languages), and hopefully there will always be many English language learners being taught in their native language. We need effective strategies for both situations.

The renewed focus since the late 1980s on the quality of bilingual and ESL programs has led to numerous observational and descriptive studies of effective education for English language learners (see, e.g., Fleischman & Hopstock, 1993; Garcia, 1987; Leighton, Hightower, Wrigley, Pechman, & McCollum, 1993; Tikunoff et al., 1991). However, few studies have directly compared outcomes of innovative bilingual or ESL programs to traditional programs (see Ramirez, 1986).

There is remarkably little research evaluating programs designed to increase the Spanish reading performance of students in bilingual programs. Calderón, Hertz-Lazarowitz, and Slavin (1998) evaluated a bilingual adaptation of Cooperative Integrated Reading and Composition (BCIRC) in El Paso elementary schools starting in second grade. This program, based on a successful program originally developed in English for English proficient students (Stevens, Madden, Slavin, & Farnish, 1987; Stevens & Slavin, 1995), involves having students work in small cooperative groups. Students read to each other, work together to identify characters, settings, problems, and problem solutions in narratives, summarize stories to each other, and work together on writing, reading comprehension, and vocabulary activities. Students in BCIRC classes scored significantly better than control students on the Spanish Texas Assessment of Academic Skills (TAAS) at the end of second grade, and as they transitioned to English in third and fourth grades they performed significantly better than control students on TAAS reading tests given in English.

Although it is important to improve the outcomes of bilingual and English-only reading instruction for English language learners at all grade levels, there is a particular need to see that students are successful in beginning to read in the early elementary grades. Many students fail to read adequately by third grade and are then at risk for being retained in grade or assigned to special education or long-term remedial services, all of which are key predictors of ultimate dropout (Lloyd, 1978). Latino students, with one of the highest dropout rates of all ethnic groups (General Accounting Office, 1994; National Center for Educational Statistics, 1993), are particularly at risk if they do not read well.

If all students are to achieve their potential in school, all must begin with success in reading in the early grades. One program that has achieved a great deal of success in meeting this goal is called Success for All, a comprehensive model for restructuring elementary schools that focuses on prevention and early, intensive intervention. The program's philosophy is that learning problems must first be prevented by providing students with high-quality instruction from prekindergarten or kindergarten onward, improving school–family links, and assessing student progress on a regular basis. When problems appear despite effective preventive measures, interventions must be applied immediately and intensively to solve them before they become serious. In particular, one-to-one tutoring is provided to first graders who are failing to read well. The English version of Success for All has been evaluated in comparison to matched control schools in nine school districts throughout the United States and has been found to be consistently effective on measures of reading, reductions in retention and special education placements, and other outcomes (Slavin & Madden, in press; Slavin, Madden, Dolan, & Wasik, 1996; Slavin, Madden, Dolan, Wasik, Ross, Smith, & Dianda, 1996).

The first application of Success for All (SFA) to English language learners began in Philadelphia's Francis Scott Key School, which serves a high-poverty neighborhood in which more than 60% of students enter the schools speaking Cambodian or other Southeast Asian languages. An adaptation of Success for All was designed to meet the needs of these children. This adaptation focused on integrating the work of English as a second language (ESL) teachers and reading teachers, so that ESL teachers taught an SFA reading class and then helped limited English proficient students with the specific language and reading skills needed to succeed in the school's (English) reading program. In addition, a cross-age tutoring program enabled fifth graders, now fully bilingual in English and Cambodian, to help kindergartners succeed in the English program. The performance of students at Francis Scott Key has been compared to that of students in a matched comparison school each year, and the results have consistently favored Success for All for Asian as well as non-Asian students (Slavin & Yampolsky, 1991). This chapter reports the reading performance of the English language learners at Key and its comparison school as of spring 1995, the end of the seventh year of program implementation.

In 1992, a Spanish adaptation of Success for All called *Éxito Para Todos* ("Success for All" in Spanish) was developed for use in Spanish bilingual programs. During the 1992–1993 school year, *Éxito Para Todos* (EPT) was implemented in one Philadelphia school serving a predominately Latino (mostly Puerto Rican) student body. The first year results showed the Spanish bilingual students to be performing substantially better than controls on individually administered tests of Spanish (Slavin & Madden, 1994). This chapter reports the results for the third graders who completed their third year in *Éxito Para Todos* in 1996.

A third evaluation of Success for All with English language learners was carried out by WestEd, an educational laboratory in southern California (Dianda, 1995; Livingston & Flaherty, 1997; Slavin & Madden, 1995). This study involved three schools. Fremont Elementary in Riverside, California, and Orville Wright Elementary in Modesto, California, are schools with substantial Spanish bilingual programs, and implemented *Éxito Para Todos*. The third, El Vista Elementary, also in Modesto, serves a highly diverse student body speaking 17 languages using an ESL approach. Students in all three schools were compared to matched students in matched schools. In each case, students are assessed in the language of instruction (English or Spanish).

An Arizona study compared first graders in two Success for All schools to those in three locally developed Title I schoolwide projects and one

Reading Recovery school (Ross, Nunnery, & Smith, 1996). Finally, the largest study of *Éxito Para Todos*, in the Houston Independent School District, produced data both on the overall effects of the Spanish adaptation of SFA/EPT and on the effects of the degree of implementation of the model (Nunnery, Slavin, Madden, Ross, Smith, Hunter, & Stubbs, in press).

This chapter summarizes experimental research on the three studies of *Éxito Para Todos* and the three studies of the English-as-a-second-language adaptations of Success for All, with a focus on effects of these programs on the academic achievement of English language learners.

SUCCESS FOR ALL AND *ÉXITO PARA TODOS*: PROGRAM DESCRIPTION

Success for All is a comprehensive reform program for elementary schools, especially those serving many students placed at risk. It restructures Title I staff and resources, plus any other available resources (e.g., bilingual, ESL, special education, or state compensatory education), to focus on prevention, early intervention, and long-term professional development, instead of remediation. With students acquiring English, two adaptatons of Success for All are used. One, *Éxito Para Todos*, used in Spanish bilingual programs, initially teaches reading in Spanish and then transitions children to English reading according to district policies and timetables. The other, used with speakers of many languages, incorporates research-based English-as-a-second-language strategies in the English curriculum. Specific elements of both program adaptations are described in the following sections.

Reading Tutors

One of the most important elements of the Success for All and *Éxito Para Todos* model is the use of tutors to support students' success in reading. One-to-one tutoring is the most effective form of instruction known (see Wasik & Slavin, 1993). The tutors at Fairhill, Fremont, and Wright, the schools using *Éxito Para Todos*, were Spanish bilingual teachers. At the schools using the ESL adaptation of Success for All, tutors were certified teachers paid for by Title I funds, plus ESL teachers from the schools' staffs. Tutors worked one-to-one with students who were having difficulties keeping up with their reading groups. Students were taken from their homeroom classes by the tutors for 20-min sessions during times other than reading or math periods. In general, tutors supported students' success in the regular reading curriculum, rather than teaching different objectives. For example, if the regular reading teacher was working on stories with long vowels or was teaching comprehension monitoring strategies, so did the tutor. However, tutors identified learning deficits and used different strategies to teach the same skills.

During daily 90-min reading periods, tutors served as additional reading teachers to reduce class size for reading. Information on students' specific deficits and needs passed between reading teachers and tutors on brief forms, and reading teachers and tutors were given regular times to meet to coordinate their approaches with individual children.

Initial decisions about reading group placement and need for tutoring were made based on informal reading inventories given to each child by the tutors. After this, reading group placements and tutoring assignments were made based on 8-week assessments, which included teacher judgments as well as the program's formal assessments. First graders received first priority for tutoring, on the assumption that the primary function of the tutors is to help all students be successful in reading the first time, before they become remedial readers.

Reading Program

Students in Grades 1–5 were regrouped for reading. That is, students were assigned to heterogeneous, age-grouped classes with class sizes of about 25 most of the day, but during a regular 90-min reading period they were regrouped according to reading performance levels into reading classes of about 15 students all at the same level. For example, a 2–1 (second grade, first semester) reading class might contain first-, second-, and third-grade students all reading at the same level. At the bilingual schools this regrouping was done separately for Spanish-dominant and English-dominant students; at Key and El Vista, the schools using the ESL adaptation, all students were regrouped according to reading level, regardless of language background. Regrouping allows teachers to teach the whole reading class without having to break the class into reading groups. It is a form of the Joplin Plan, which has been found to increase reading achievement in the elementary grades (Slavin, 1987).

The reading program emphasizes development of basic language skills and sound and letter recognition skills in kindergarten, and uses an approach based on sound blending and phonics starting in first grade. The K–1 reading program used in *Éxito Para Todos*, called *Lee Conmigo* ("Read with Me"), uses a series of "shared stories," minibooks that gradually introduce syllables, letter sounds, and sound-blending strategies in stories originally written in Spanish for the program. English-dominant students in all schools experienced Reading Roots, which uses the same instructional methods, but in English. *Lee Conmigo* and Reading Roots emphasize oral reading to partners as well as to the teacher, instruction in story structure and specific comprehension skills, and integration of reading and writing. They provide a rapidly paced, engaging set of routines that involve students in group response games that develop auditory discrimination skills, letter name and letter sound recognition, and sound blending strategies based on the sounds and words used in the books. When they reach the second-grade reading level, students use a form of Cooperative Integrated Reading and Composition (CIRC) with Spanish or English novels and basals. CIRC uses cooperative learning activities built around story structure, prediction, summarization, vocabulary building, decoding practice, writing, and direct instruction in reading comprehension skills. Research on CIRC has found it to significantly increase students' reading comprehension and language skills in English (Stevens et al., 1987) and in Spanish (Calderón et al., 1998). The upper elementary reading program is called Reading Wings in Success for All and *Alas Para Leer* in *Éxito Para Todos*.

Eight-Week Reading Assessments

Every 8 weeks, reading teachers assessed student progress through the reading program. The results of the assessments were used to determine who is to receive tutoring, to suggest other adaptations in students' programs, and to identify students who need other types of assistance, such as family interventions or vision/hearing screening.

English as a Second Language

All schools had instruction in English as a second language (ESL). In the schools using the ESL adaptation, ESL teachers taught regular SFA reading classes during a common regrouped reading period. In general, LEP children were integrated with non-LEP children in reading classes, and experienced the same instruction. After reading period, ESL teachers tutored individual students one-to-one or worked with groups of limited English proficient students. The emphasis of the ESL program in Success for All was on giving students assistance that is directly tied to success in the English curriculum. For example, ESL teachers used the same reading materials used in the classroom reading program. All reading teachers (not just ESL teachers) received manuals and training in ESL strategies, such as Total Physical Response, which they used in all classes containing ESL (and non-ESL) students.

In schools using *Éxito Para Todos*, ESL instruction was also closely connected to instruction in subjects in which students were being taught in English.

Kindergarten

All schools provided a full-day kindergarten for all eligible students. The kindergarten program provided a balanced and developmentally appropriate learning experience for young children. The curriculum emphasizes the development and use of language in the first language (L1) and second language (L2). It provided a balance of academic readiness and nonacademic music, art, and movement activities. Readiness activities included use of integrated thematic units, and a program called Story Telling and Retelling (STaR) or CyReC (*Contar y Recontar el Cuento*), in which students retell stories read by the teachers.

Family Support Team

A Family Support Team in each school provided parenting education and worked preventively to involve parents in support of their children's success in school. For example, schools implement a program called Raising Readers/*Creando Lectores*, which gives parents strategies for reading with their children. Also, family support staff provided assistance when there were indications that students were not working up to their full potential because of problems at home. For example, families of students who are not receiving adequate sleep or nutrition, need glasses, are not attending school regularly, or are exhibiting serious behavior problems receive family support assistance. Links with appropriate community service agencies were made to provide as much focused service as possible for parents and children.

Program Facilitator

A program facilitator worked at each school full time to oversee (with the principal) the operation of the Success for All and *Éxito Para Todos* models. Facilitators helped plan the program, helped the principal with scheduling, and visited classes and tutoring sessions frequently to help teachers and tutors with individual problems. They helped teachers and tutors deal with any behavior problems or other special problems, and coordinated the activities of the classroom teachers, tutors, Family Support

Team, ESL teachers, and others. They organized data from regular 8-week assessments to help teachers make decisions about grouping and about needs for tutoring and other accommodations to students' needs, and to check on the overall success of the implementation.

Teachers and Teacher Training

The teachers and tutors were regular classroom teachers, bilingual teachers, or ESL teachers. They received detailed teacher's manuals supplemented by 2 days of inservice at the beginning of the school year and several inservice sessions throughout the year on such topics as classroom management, instructional pace, and implementation of the curriculum.

PROGRAM EVALUATIONS: *ÉXITO PARA TODOS*

Philadelphia—Bilingual Versus ESL

The bilingual version of Success for All, *Éxito Para Todos*, was first implemented at Fairhill Elementary School, a school in inner-city Philadelphia, starting in 1992. Fairhill serves a student body of 694 students, of whom 78% are Hispanic (primarily from Puerto Rico) and 22% are African American. A matched comparison school was also selected. Table 6.1 shows data on the two schools. From the table it is clear that the two schools were very similar in total enrollment, percent Hispanic and African American, and historical achievement levels (from district records). The schools were also similar in the percent of students receiving bilingual instruction. In both schools about half of all students were in the bilingual program in first grade. Nearly all students in both schools qualified for free lunches. Both schools were Title I schoolwide projects, which

TABLE 6.1
Characteristics of Fairhill and Comparison School

	SFA	Comparison
Total enrollment	694	706
Hispanic (%)	78%	76%
African American (%)	22%	24%
In Bilingual Programs (%)	17%	21%
Free Lunch (%)	93%	99%
Mean percentile, reading (K–5)	30	32
Mean percentile, math (K–5)	53	52

means that both had high (and roughly equivalent) allocations of Title I funds that they could use flexibly to meet student needs.

A misconception about the instruction provided by the control group changed the meaning of this experiment from its original intention. The control group's reading program was described by the district as a bilingual model emphasizing native-language instruction. However, on closer examination, the control group's "bilingual" approach turned out to be more of a sheltered English model, with very little instruction in Spanish. This made the Fairhill experiment a comparison of *Éxito Para Todos* (in Spanish) to a sheltered English control group, mixing language of instruction with method of instruction.

Measures

All students defined by district criteria as LEP at Fairhill and its control school were pretested at the beginning of first grade on the Spanish Peabody Picture Vocabulary Test (PPVT). Each following May, these students were tested by native language speakers on three scales of the Spanish Woodcock (*Bateria Woodcock de Proficiencia en el Idioma*): Letter/Word Identification (*Identificacion de Letras y Palabras*), Word Attack (*Analisis de Palabras*), and Passage Comprehension (*Comprension de Textos*). Starting in third grade, almost all children had transitioned to English instruction, so students were assessed on the corresponding English Woodcock scales as well.

Results

A check for pretest differences on the Spanish PPVT found that there were differences in favor of the experimental group ($p < .03$). PPVT scores were therefore used as covariates in all analyses of covariance (ANCOVA). As shown in Table 6.2, Fairhill students performed far better than control students on all three Spanish measures ($p < .001$). Given that they were taught to read in Spanish and the control group was not, this is hardly surprising. More significant, however, were the differences in English reading performance. Fairhill students scored higher than control students on all three English reading measures. The differences were only statistically significant on Word Attack ($p < .05$; ES = +0.65). However, this finding is of considerable interest, as it shows that third graders taught well in Spanish were performing at least as well and often better in English than were students only taught in English. Of course, these students then had the substantial bonus of the ability to read well in Spanish. The small sample size and significant pretest differ-

TABLE 6.2
Fairhill (Bilingual) Versus Control (ESL), Grade 3

	Spanish		English	
	SFA	Control	SFA	Control
Word Identification				
Adjusted mean	40.75	10.74	43.79	42.77
(SD)	(5.51)	(10.33)	(20.61)	(16.35)
N	21	29	21	29
ES	+2.91		+0.06	
F	133.99***		<1	
Word Attack				
Adjusted mean	21.12	5.01	20.62	13.41
(SD)	(4.87)	(6.36)	(10.67)	(11.08)
N	21	29	21	29
ES	+2.53		+0.65	
F	81.50***		6.42**	
Passage Comprehension				
Adjusted mean	6.13	1.29	17.58	18.20
(SD)	(2.09)	(2.00)	(7.45)	(9.34)
N	21	29	21	29
ES	+2.42		−0.07	
F	65.72***		<1	
Median ES	+2.62		+0.21	

*$p < .05$. **$p < .01$. ***$p < .001$.

ences make these results speculative rather than conclusive, but they are worthy of further investigation.

California Bilingual Schools

Data from first, second, and third graders in the three California Success for All schools were analyzed together by Livingston and Flaherty (1997), pooling data across schools in four categories: English-dominant students, Spanish-dominant students taught in Spanish (*Éxito Para Todos*), Spanish-dominant students taught in English, and speakers of languages other than English or Spanish taught in English. Three cohorts were followed. Data for a 1992 cohort are available for Grades 1, 2, and 3; for 1993, Grades 1 and 2; and for 1994, Grade 1 only. The pooled results for the Spanish bilingual program are summarized in Fig. 6.1 (adapted from Livingston & Flaherty, 1997).

Students in the two *Éxito Para Todos* schools in California scored higher than controls at every grade level in all three cohorts, as shown in Fig. 6.1. Effect sizes across cohorts averaged +1.03 for first graders, +.44

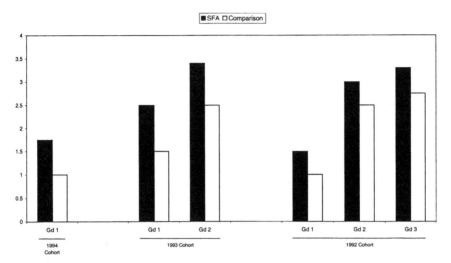

FIG. 6.1.   Grade equivalents for Spanish ESL students, California bilingual schools. Adapted from Livingston and Flaherty (1997).

for second graders, and +.23 for third graders. The analyses for second and third graders probably understate the magnitude of the differences. In line with district and program policies, students are transitioned into English instruction as soon as they demonstrate an ability to excel in English. Because of their success in Spanish reading, many more *Éxito Para Todos* than control students were transitioned during second and third grades. Therefore, the highest achieving experimental students were being removed from the Spanish sample, making the performance of this group look lower than it was.

Houston (Bilingual)

The largest study of *Éxito Para Todos*, the Spanish bilingual adaptation of Success for All, took place in the Houston Independent School District (HISD). Both Spanish and English forms of the program were being studied; only the Spanish results are presented here (see Nunnery et al., in press, for a report of the full study).

The Houston study was unusual in several ways. In contrast to other studies (and to standard practice in implementing Success for All in dissemination sites), schools were allowed to choose how completely to implement the program. They could choose to implement all program elements, the reading program and tutoring without other elements, or just the reading program. The intention was to compare outcomes according to degree of implementation.

Measures

The study compared first graders in 20 schools implementing *Éxito Para Todos* to those in 10 matched schools also using Spanish bilingual instruction. Children were assessed on three scales from the Spanish Woodcock: Word Identification, Word Attack, and Passage Comprehension. Ten children were selected at random to be assessed in each school; after missing data were removed, there was a total of 298 Spanish-dominant students across the 30 schools with bilingual programs.

Results

The Success for All schools were grouped into three categories of implementation—high, medium, or low—based on such implementation categories as whether the school had a full-time, part-time, or no facilitator, the number and certification status of tutors, and the existence of a family support team. Among the bilingual schools, no school fell into the "high" category, primarily because few had certified teachers working as bilingual tutors. The medium-implementation schools, however, had many more paraprofessional tutors and were much more likely to have a full-time facilitator and a family support team than were the low-implementation schools. Otherwise, both sets of schools were very similar to each other and to bilingual programs in comparison schools. The Spanish-dominant SFA students were somewhat more impoverished than those in comparison schools, and had somewhat higher mobility.

Table 6.3 summarizes outcome data for the three sets of schools. Directionally, medium implementers scored higher than low implementers,

TABLE 6.3
Reading Posttests and Effect Sizes, First Graders,
Houston Bilingual Schools, 1996

		Medium Implementation (n = 99)	Low Implementation (n = 102)	Comparison (n = 102)
Word	x	30.18	31.21	27.36
Identification	ES	+0.20*	+0.27*	
Word Attack	x	18.29	17.54	15.48
	ES	+0.30*	+0.22*	
Passage	x	5.05	4.11	4.00
Comprehension	ES	+0.22[a]	+0.02	
Mean ES		+0.24	+0.17	

Note. Adapted from Nunnery et al. (in press).
[a]Marginally significant, $p < .06$.
*$p < .05$.

who scored higher than controls. School-level comparisons showed significant differences ($p < .05$) between both categories of SFA/EPT schools and comparison schools on Word Identification and Word Attack, and a marginally significant difference ($p < .06$) between medium implementation schools and controls on Passage Comprehension. Overall, effect sizes in comparison to controls averaged +0.24 for medium implementers, +0.17 for low implementers.

These results, emphasizing the importance of completeness of implementation, mirror the results found for the English-dominant students in the Houston study (see Nunnery et al., in press).

PROGRAM EVALUATIONS:
ENGLISH-AS-A-SECOND-LANGUAGE ADAPTATIONS

Philadelphia (ESL)

Beginning in September 1988, researchers from Johns Hopkins University began working with the staff at Philadelphia's Francis Scott Key Elementary School to implement Success for All in Grades K–5. Sixty-two percent of its students were from Asian backgrounds, primarily Cambodian. Nearly all of these students entered the school in kindergarten with little or no English. The remainder of the school was divided between African American and White students. The school is located in an extremely impoverished neighborhood in South Philadelphia. Ninety-six percent of the students were from low-income families and qualified for free lunch.

Because of the unavailability of Cambodian-speaking teachers, Francis Scott Key used an ESL approach to its LEP students. The only adult in the school who spoke Cambodian was a bilingual counseling assistant.

Evaluation Design

The program at Francis Scott Key was evaluated in comparison to a similar Philadelphia elementary school. Table 6.4 compares the two schools on several variables. As the table shows, the two schools were very similar in overall achievement level and other variables. Thirty-three percent of the comparison school's students were Asian (mostly Cambodian), the highest proportion in the city after Key. The percentage of students receiving free lunch was very high in both schools, although higher at Key (96%) than at the comparison school (84%). A few differences are worthy of note, however. The comparison school was larger than Key, with 1,128 students overall to Key's 622, and the non-Asian students at the comparison school were almost all African American, whereas 21% of Key's students were White.

TABLE 6.4
Characteristics of Francis Scott Key and Comparison School

Characteristics	Key	Comparison
School enrollment	622	1,128
School enrollment, K–3	365	541
Ethnic composition		
Asian	62%	33%
White	21%	0%
African American	15%	65%
Other	3%	2%
National percentile—reading, spring 1988		
K	42	52
1	37	34
2	17	26
3	33	27
Average daily attendance	90%	91%
Percent free lunch	96%	84%

The data reported here are for all students in Grades 4–5 in spring 1995. With the exception of transfers, all students had been in the program since kindergarten.

Measures

At Francis Scott Key and its comparison school, all students in Grades 4–5 were individually administered three scales from the Woodcock Language Proficiency Battery (Woodcock, 1984): Word Identification, Word Attack, and Passage Comprehension. The Word Identification scale was used to assess recognition of common sight words, the Word Attack scale assessed phonetic synthesis skills, and the Passage Comprehension scale assessed students' abilities to read and comprehend meaningful text.

Analyses of variance (ANOVA) were conducted on each outcome separately. Outcomes were characterized in terms of effect sizes, which are the difference between experimental and control means divided by the control group's standard deviation. Grade equivalents were not used in any analyses, but are presented as convenient indicators of students' absolute performance levels.

Results: Asian Students

The results for Asian students are summarized in Tables 6.5 and 6.6. Success for All Asian students at all three grade levels performed far better than control students. Differences between Success for All and control students were statistically significant on every measure at every grade level ($p < .001$). Median grade equivalents and effect sizes were computed

TABLE 6.5
Francis Scott Key (ESL, Philadelphia)
Scores on Woodcock Reading Scales, Grade 4

	Asian		Non-Asian	
	SFA	Control	SFA	Control
Word Identification				
Mean	75.22	53.56	74.65	64.63
(SD)	(9.76)	(14.02)	(14.54)	(15.72)
N	32	18	20	48
GE	5.8	3.1	5.7	4.3
ES	+1.54		+0.64	
F	41.22***		5.99*	
Word Attack				
Mean	37.53	18.06	31.95	26.65
(SD)	(5.36)	(13.09)	(8.87)	(11.37)
N	32	18	20	48
GE	10.0	2.2	6.1	3.4
ES	+1.49		+0.47	
F	55.12***		3.46[a]	
Passage Comprehension				
Mean	37.44	29.83	40.20	36.46
(SD)	(5.75)	(12.32)	(5.97)	(11.22)
N	32	18	20	48
GE	4.1	2.9	5.1	3.9
ES	+0.62		+0.33	
F	8.87**		1.98	
Median GE	5.8	2.9	5.7	3.9
Median ES	+1.49		+0.47	

*$p < .05$.
**$p < .01$.
***$p < .001$.
[a]$p < .10$.

across the three Woodcock scales. On average, Success for All Asian students exceeded control students in reading grade equivalents by 2.9 years in fourth grade (median ES = +1.49) and 2.8 years in fifth grade (median ES = +1.33). Success for All Asian students were reading about a full year above grade level in fourth grade (GE = 5.8) and in fifth grade (GE = 6.8), whereas similar control students averaged 1.9 years below grade reading level in fourth grade and 1.8 years below grade level in fifth grade.

Results: Non-Asian Students

Outcomes of Success for All for non-Asian students, summarized in Tables 6.5 and 6.6 and Fig. 6.2, were also very positive in Grades 4–5. Experimental–control differences were statistically significant ($p < .05$ or

TABLE 6.6
Francis Scott Key (ESL, Philadelphia)
Scores on Woodcock Reading Scales, Grade 5

	Asian		Non-Asian	
	SFA	Control	SFA	Control
Word Identification				
Mean	79.24	62.57	76.38	68.68
(SD)	(13.94)	(11.95)	(14.93)	(11.64)
N	50	23	26	38
GE	6.8	4.0	6.1	4.7
ES	+1.40		+0.66	
F	24.54***		5.36*	
Word Attack				
Mean	35.60	22.00	34.54	26.18
(SD)	(9.35)	(10.23)	(7.66)	(9.05)
N	50	23	26	38
GE	10.0	2.7	8.7	3.3
ES	+1.33		+0.92	
F	31.42***		14.84***	
Passage Comprehension				
Mean	41.98	36.91	41.31	38.34
(SD)	(6.23)	(6.79)	(8.63)	(9.50)
N	50	23	26	38
GE	5.8	4.0	5.5	4.3
ES	+0.75		+0.34	
F	9.86**		1.62	
Median GE	6.8	4.0	6.1	4.3
Median ES	+1.33		+0.66	

*$p < .05$.
**$p < .01$.
***$p < .001$.

better) on every measure at every grade level. Effect sizes were somewhat smaller than for Asian students, but were still quite substantial, averaging +0.47 in Grade 4 and +0.66 in Grade 5. Success for All non-Asian students averaged almost a full year above grade level (GE = 5.7) in fourth grade, and about 3 months above grade level in fifth grade (GE = 6.1); at both grade levels, Success for All non-Asian students scored at least a full grade equivalent higher than non-Asian control students.

California ESL Students

The California study (Livingston & Flaherty, 1997) included data on children who were acquiring English taught in English. These included both students in one Modesto school that did not have a bilingual pro-

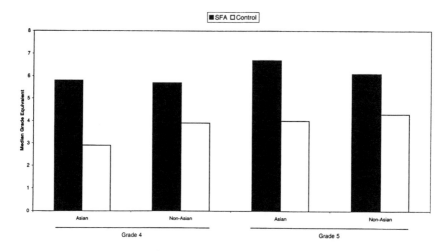

FIG. 6.2. Achievement medians (grade equivalents) for Success for All and control schools, Francis Scott Key (ESL, Philadelphia). Adapted from Slavin and Madden (1999).

gram, as well as LEP students in the two schools (one in Modesto and one in Riverside) who were speakers of languages other than Spanish.

Results for Spanish-dominant students taught in English are shown in Fig. 6.3. Like the results for students taught in Spanish, these comparisons show remarkable impacts for first graders (ES = +1.36), smaller ones for second graders (ES = +.46), and very small differences for third graders (ES = +.09). Again, the successful transitioning of students out of ESL classes reduced the apparent differences by third grade (because the highest achieving students are no longer receiving ESL services).

Other ESL Students

Results for speakers of languages other than English or Spanish (taught in English) are summarized in Fig. 6.4. The patterns for these students are similar to those for Spanish-dominant ESL students, except that there were no differences for the 1994 first-grade cohort. Averaging across cohorts, effect sizes were +.40 for first graders, +.37 for second graders, and +.05 for third graders.

Arizona (ESL)

The most recent study of the ESL adaptation of Success for All in schools serving many students acquiring English is a study in an Arizona school district (Ross, Smith, & Nunnery, 1998). This study compared first grad-

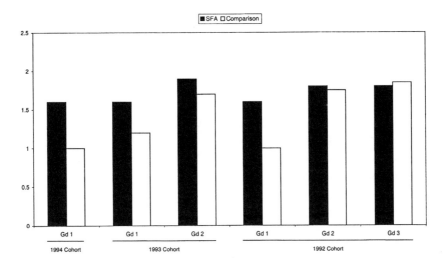

FIG. 6.3.   Grade equivalents for Spanish ESL students, California ESL schools. Adapted from Livingston and Flaherty (1997).

ers in two Success for All schools, three schools using locally developed Title I schoolwide projects, and one school using Reading Recovery, a one-to-one tutoring program for first graders (Lyons, Pinnell, & Deford, 1993). Two strata of schools were compared. Stratum 1 consisted of very impoverished schools, in which 81% of students received free lunch and

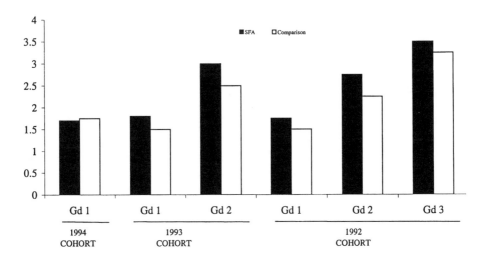

FIG. 6.4.   Grade equivalents and effect size for other ESL students, California ESL schools. Adapted from Livingston and Flaherty, 1997.

50% were Hispanic. Stratum 2 consisted of less impoverished schools, with 53% of students receiving free lunch and 27% Hispanic.

Measures

Students were pretested on the Peabody Picture Vocabulary Test (PPVT) and then posttested on the Woodcock Word Identification, Word Attack, and Passage Comprehension scales, and the Durrell Oral Reading Test. Analyses of covariance compared schools in each stratum to the other two schools in the same stratum, controlling for PPVT pretests.

Results

Table 6.7 (from Ross et al., 1998) summarizes the outcomes for Spanish-dominant students. In the highest-poverty schools (Stratum 1), Success for All students scored higher than the average of the two locally developed schoolwide projects on all measures, but the difference was significant only for Word Attack. Hispanic first graders averaged at grade level (1.8), but the comparison groups were below grade level on all measures (mean = 1.45). Results were similar for the less impoverished schools (Stratum 2); Success for All Spanish-dominant students scored significantly higher than the locally developed schoolwide project and the Reading Recovery school on Word Attack, but there were no significant differences on the other three measures. The Reading Recovery and local schoolwide project schools did not differ on any of the measures.

CONCLUSIONS AND IMPLICATIONS

The effects of Success for All on the achievement of English language learners are not entirely consistent, but in general they are substantially positive. In all schools implementing *Éxito Para Todos*, the Spanish bilingual adaptation of Success for All, effect sizes for first graders on Spanish assessments were very positive. The Houston study showed that this effect was more pronounced when schools were implementing most of the program's elements. The Philadelphia evaluation showed that even after transitioning to English-only instruction, *Éxito Para Todos* third graders performed better on English assessments than control students who were primarily taught in English. For students in the ESL adaptation of Success for All, effect sizes for all comparisons were also positive, especially for Cambodian students in Philadelphia and Mexican-American students in California.

TABLE 6.7

Reading Achievement Test Means, Adjusted Means, and Standard Deviations, Spanish-Dominant Students

School	n	PPVT	Word Identification			Word Attack			Passage Comprehension			Oral Reading		
		M	M	M'	GE	M	M'	GE	M	M'	GE	M	M'	GE
Stratum 1														
1. SFA1	21	65.53 (19.42)	32.38 (17.53)	29.53	1.8	13.24 (10.24)	12.01[2]	1.8	16.13 (10.13)	14.37	1.8	4.38 (4.55)	3.73	1.6
2. LSW1A	39	48.88 (14.10)	18.06 (16.22)	21.96	1.4	3.67 (6.73)	5.36	1.2	8.36 (7.99)	10.78	1.3	1.61 (2.94)	2.49	1.1
3. LSW1B	42	59.64 (16.92)	29.38 (17.18)	28.33	1.7	9.41 (9.69)	8.95	1.5	14.33 (8.46)	13.68	1.7	4.91 (4.51)	4.67	1.7
Stratum 2														
4. SFA2	24	60.91 (14.61)	36.91 (15.53)	37.51	2.0	16.52 (10.89)	16.78[6]	2.1	16.78 (8.72)	17.08	1.8	5.57 (3.71)	5.71	1.8
5. LSW2	22	55.27 (28.79)	34.91 (20.26)	38.10	1.9	11.27 (10.24)	12.64	1.7	16.59 (10.90)	18.17	1.8	7.46 (7.26)	8.24	2.0
6. RR2	28	70.43 (16.84)	33.14 (16.79)	29.36	1.9	9.96 (8.05)	8.35	1.6	17.79 (8.12)	15.91	1.9	6.07 (4.72)	5.14	1.9

Note. Superscripts indicate that the adjusted mean is significantly higher than the mean for the school designated by the superscripted numeral. M, mean; GE, grade equivalent; M', pretest adjusted mean score. Standard deviations are in parentheses. From Ross, Smith, and Nunnery (1998).

The findings of this research suggest many areas in need of further investigation. First, they point to a need for more in-depth qualitative investigations of instructional practices in bilingual Success for All/*Éxito Para Todos* classes as well as in traditional bilingual first grade. A preliminary ethnography of Success for All and control schools has recently been completed (Prado-Olmos & Marquez, chap. 7 in this book), but more work is needed in this area. In addition, it would be important to investigate the effects of the separate components of Success for All in bilingual and ESL classes and to relate these components to student outcomes. This is a component of the Houston study, which contrasted bilingual schools using the *Lee Conmigo* reading curriculum alone, schools using *Lee Conmigo* plus tutoring for first graders, schools using all components of *Éxito Para Todos*, and traditional bilingual control schools, but more research along these lines is needed.

More research is also needed to determine the effects of *Éxito Para Todos* over a longer time period and in a larger number of schools. However, the studies summarized here show the impact of *Éxito Para Todos* on Spanish reading, and show that these gains generally carry over into English reading. A form of Success for All integrating ESL and classroom instruction for English language learners taught in English was also found to be effective.

Both bilingual and ESL instruction are realities for hundreds of thousands of U.S. students. However the political debate about bilingual education turns out, it is time to begin to investigate instructional strategies able to ensure the success of students in reading, whatever the language of instruction. The research summarized here provides a step in this direction.

ACKNOWLEDGMENTS

Adapted from Slavin and Madden (1999). This research was supported by a grant from the Office of Educational Research and Improvement, U.S. Department of Education (No. OERI-R-117-D40005). However, any opinions expressed are those of the authors and do not represent official positions or policies. We thank Katherine Conner, Allie Mulvihill, MaryLouise de Nicola, Renee Yampolsky, and Norris Eldridge of the Philadelphia Public Schools, Marcie Dianda of the National Education Association, Margaret Livingston and John Flaherty of WestEd, Steven Ross and Lana Smith of the University of Memphis, John Nunnery of the Memphis City Schools, and Margarita Calderón, Renee Kling, Lois Hybl, and Gretta Gordy Holloway of Johns Hopkins University for their help with this research.

REFERENCES

August, D., & Hakuta, K. (1997). *Improving schooling for language-minority children: A research agenda.* Washington, DC: National Research Council.

Calderón, M., Hertz-Lazarowitz, R., & Slavin, R. E. (1998). Effects of Bilingual Cooperative Integrated Reading and Composition on students making the transition from Spanish to English reading. *Elementary School Journal, 99*(2), 153–165.

Dianda, M. (1995, April). *Effects of Success for All on the reading achievement of first graders in California bilingual programs.* Paper presented at the annual meeting of the American Educational Research Association, San Francisco.

Fleischman, H. L., & Hopstock, P. J. (1993). *Descriptive study of services to limited English proficient students.* Arlington, VA: Development Associates.

Garcia, E. E. (1987). *Education of linguistically and culturally diverse students: Effective instructional practices.* Santa Cruz, CA: University of California at Santa Cruz, National Center for Research on Cultural Diversity and Second Language Learning.

Garcia, E. E. (1991). Bilingualism, second language acquisition, and the education of Chicano language minority students. In R. R. Valencia (Ed.), *Chicano school failure and success: Research and policy agendas for the 1990's* (pp. 31–49). New York: Falmer.

Garcia, E. E. (1994, April). *The impact of linguistic and cultural diversity on America's schools: A need for new policy.* Paper presented at the annual meeting of the American Educational Research Association, New Orleans.

General Accounting Office. (1994). *Limited English proficiency: A growing and costly educational challenge facing many school districts.* Washington, DC: U.S. General Accounting Office.

Leighton, M. S., Hightower, A. M, Wrigley, P., Pechman, E. M., & McCollum, H. (1993) *Improving education for language minority students: Promising practices in professional development.* Washington, DC: Policy Studies Associates.

Livingston, M., & Flaherty, J. (1997). *Effects of Success for All on reading achievement in California schools.* Los Alamitos, CA: WestEd.

Lloyd, D. N. (1978). Prediction of school failure from third-grade data. *Educational and Psychological Measurement, 38,* 1193–1200.

Lyons, C. A., Pinnell, G. S., & DeFord, D. E. (1993). *Partners in learning: Teachers and children in Reading Recovery.* New York: Teachers College Press.

McArthur, E. K. (1993). *Language characteristics and schooling in the U.S., A changing picture: 1979 and 1989.* Washington, DC: National Center for Education Statistics.

Meyer, M. M., & Fienberg, S. E. (1992). *Assessing evaluation studies: The case of bilingual education strategies.* Washington, DC: National Academy of Sciences.

Moss, M., & Puma, M. (1995). *Prospects: First year report on language minority and limited English proficient students.* Cambridge, MA: Abt.

National Academy of Sciences. (1998). *The prevention of reading difficulties in young children.* Washington, DC: Author.

National Center for Education Statistics. (1993). *Dropout rates in the U.S.* Washington, DC: U.S. Department of Education.

Nunnery, J. A., Slavin, R. E., Madden, N. A., Ross, S. M., Smith, L. J., Hunter, P., & Stubbs, J. (in press). Effects of full and partial implementations of Success for All on student reading achievement in English and Spanish. *American Educational Research Journal.*

Ramirez, J. D. (1986). Comparing structural English immersion and bilingual education: First year results of a national study. *American Journal of Education, 95*, 122–148.

Ramirez, J. D., Yuen, S. D., & Ramey, D. R. (1991). *Longitudinal study of structured English immersion strategy, early-exit and late-exit transitional bilingual education programs for language-minority children.* San Mateo, CA: Aguirre International.

Ross, S. M., Nunnery, J. A., & Smith, L. J. (1996). *Evaluation of Title I reading programs: Amphitheater Public Schools Year 1: 1995–1996.* Memphis, TN: University of Memphis, Center for Research in Educational Policy.

Ross, S. M., Smith, L. J., & Nunnery, J. A. (1998, April). *Title I as a catalyst for school improvement: Impact of alternative school-wide models on the reading achievement of students at risk.* Paper presented at the Annual Meeting of the American Educational Research Association, San Diego, CA.

Slavin, R. E. (1987). Ability grouping and student achievement in elementary schools: A best-evidence synthesis. *Review of Educational Research, 57*, 347–350.

Slavin, R. E., & Madden, N. A. (1994, April). *Lee Conmigo: Effects of Success for All in bilingual first grades.* Paper presented at the annual meeting of the American Educational Research Association, New Orleans.

Slavin, R. E., & Madden, N. A. (1995, April). *Effects of Success for All on the achievement of English language learners.* Paper presented at the annual meeting of the American Educational Research Association, San Francisco.

Slavin, R. E., & Madden, N. A. (1999). Effects of bilingual and English as a second language adaptations of Success for All on the reading achievement of students acquiring English. *Journal of Education for Students Placed at Risk, 4*(4), 393–416.

Slavin, R. E., & Madden, N. A. (in press). *One million children: Success for All.* Newbury Park, CA: Corwin.

Slavin, R. E., Madden, N. A., Dolan, L. J., & Wasik, B. A. (1996). *Every child, every school: Success for All.* Newbury Park, CA: Corwin.

Slavin, R. E., Madden, N. A., Dolan, L. J., Wasik, B. A., Ross, S., Smith, L., & Dianda, M. (1996). Success for All: A summary of research. *Journal of Education for Students Placed at Risk, 1*, 41–76.

Slavin, R. E., & Yampolsky, R. (1991). *Effects of Success for All on students with limited English proficiency: A three-year evaluation.* Baltimore, MD: Johns Hopkins University, Center for Research on Effective Schooling for Disadvantaged Students.

Stevens, R. J., Madden, N. A., Slavin, R. E., & Farnish, A. M. (1987). Cooperative Integrated Reading and Composition: Two field experiments. *Reading Research Quarterly, 22*, 433–454.

Stevens, R. J., & Slavin, R. E. (1995). The effects of Cooperative Integrated Reading and Composition (CIRC) on academically handicapped and non-handicapped students achievement, attitudes, and metacognition in reading and writing. *Elementary School Journal, 95*(3), 241–261.

Tikunoff, W. J., Ward, B. A., van Broekhuizen, D., Romero, M., Castaneda, L., Lucas, T., & Katz, A. (1991). *A descriptive study of significant features of exemplary special alternative instructional models.* San Francisco: WestEd.

Wasik, B. A., & Slavin, R. E. (1993). Preventing early reading failure with one-to-one tutoring: A review of five programs. *Reading Research Quarterly, 28*, 178–200.

Woodcock, R. W. (1984). *Woodcock Language Proficiency Battery.* Allen, TX: DLM.

7

Ethnographic Studies of *Éxito Para Todos*

Patricia L. Prado-Olmos
California State University, San Marcos

Judith Marquez
University of Houston at Clear Lake

Success for All (SFA) is an elementary school reading program designed to improve the reading achievement of all students, especially those in high-poverty schools. *Éxito Para Todos* (EPT) is a Spanish-language adaptation of Success for All (SFA). The idea behind the programs is to organize resources to ensure that virtually every student will succeed in reading throughout the elementary grades, that no student will be allowed to "fall between the cracks." In SFA/EPT programs, students are regrouped across age lines for 90 min so that each reading class contains students reading at one level. This helps eliminate the need to have reading groups within the class and increases the amount of time for direct teacher instruction. Students in Grades 1–6 are assessed every 8 weeks to determine whether they are making adequate progress in reading. This information is used to assign students to tutoring, to suggest alternative teaching strategies in the regular classroom, and to make changes in reading group placement, family support interventions, or other means of meeting students' needs. A specially trained school facilitator coordinates this process with the active involvement of teachers in grade-level teams.

The positive outcomes of SFA and EPT are well documented (e.g., see chap. 6 of this volume). It is clear that SFA/EPT has enormous potential as a national model. It has been shown to repeatedly produce positive student outcomes and to be replicable in diverse settings. Nonetheless, a piece of the picture remains to be drawn. There has been little ethnographic research on classroom processes in SFA/EPT. Describing these classroom processes is critical to understanding the daily life that teachers and students negotiate in classrooms.

Grounded in sociocultural and psychological theories of learning (e.g., Tharp & Gallimore, 1988) and interactional sociolinguistics (e.g., Gumperz, 1986), ethnographic classroom research has revealed that, for example, low-group students are instructed differently from high-group students (Allington, 1983; Collins, 1986), that linguistic minority students reading in their native language can perform more difficult academic tasks than when reading in their second language (Moll & Diaz, 1987), and that teachers take up and adapt instructional program elements to fit in with their personal philosophies of teaching and learning (Prado-Olmos, 1993). SFA/EPT lacks a "thick" description (Geertz, 1972) that would allow for a similar understanding of the everyday interactional processes that are supported and constrained by the programs. Identification and understanding of these interactional processes would allow for program refinement as well as improvement of teacher training.

This is not to say that SFA/EPT researchers, developers, and trainers do not constantly engage in program refinement and teacher training improvement. The changes occur as a result of the feedback the program's developers at Johns Hopkins University receive from its trainers around the country. Indeed, we have been involved in SFA/EPT training sessions for the past 3 years in a number of places around the country. We can see a streamlining of the training process as well as improved attention to common teacher concerns in the most recent training sessions attended. For example, we have observed that teachers are often concerned about very nuts-and-bolts issues about cooperative learning. A common concern is about the one or two students who simply do not work well in groups. At a recent training session held in California, the trainer seemed to anticipate this concern as well as others and had a specific strategy for responding to the questions. In training sessions 3 years ago the responses were less elegant and less informed. Additionally, when we were first introduced to SFA it consisted of an English program only. As the Spanish program was developed it was referred to as "SFA in Spanish." In 1997 the program acquired its own name, *Éxito Para Todos*, and acronym, EPT. Johns Hopkins has been able to adapt and change the program from an English-only program to include the Spanish-language program on the basis of similar feedback from teachers and principals, as well as intensive research by an expert in bilingual education, Margarita Calderón, and other colleagues.

The system of feedback is largely supported because of the intensive contact between school personnel and SFA/EPT trainers. When a school or school district expresses interest in SFA/EPT, a trainer is sent to the school to provide an overview. A vote is taken by the faculty on whether or not the school should adopt SFA/EPT as its reading program. The vote is a critical component of the process. Johns Hopkins refuses to become involved with schools that lack the critical 80% of teacher support. After a successful vote, an intensive introductory training schedule is developed between the school principal and SFA/EPT trainers. The initial training generally occurs over 2 to 3 days for at least 6–8 hours a day. The trainers remain involved with the school for the next three years or more. A minimum of two refresher training sessions are scheduled over the year as well as at least two 2-day implementation visits. The implementation visits are conducted by SFA/EPT trainers to assess the degree of fidelity to the model by the school's staff. The implementation visits also provide the principals and teachers a chance to talk with trainers about problems specific to their school and to get intensive feedback and assistance. This pattern of contact between SFA/EPT trainers and school personnel has provided a wealth of anecdotal qualitative data. Trainers report that they "know when they've stepped into an SFA classroom." This "knowing" is constructed around a certain look to an SFA classroom as well as the ebb and flow of activity that is reported as "typical" to an SFA classroom. These anecdotal reports provide evidence that there may be a distinctive learning environment created by SFA/EPT. Yet we lack description of exactly what that learning environment is or how that learning environment is created.

The present study is a qualitative exploration of *Éxito Para Todos* in selected bilingual schools in Texas and California. The purpose of the study is to provide a description of EPT in these classrooms. We want to describe what it is the trainers "know" as an SFA/EPT classroom. As is common with ethnographic studies, this study has a guiding question: What does reading instruction in *Éxito Para Todos* look like? This chapter responds to this question at a general level. Beyond the guiding question, the chapter also reports on findings about ways that teachers individualize the generic program, because these data emerged from the observations repeatedly as well as in teacher interviews.

SELECTION AND ENTRY INTO SCHOOLS

This study involved two schools in southern California and three schools in the eastern part of Texas. The two schools in southern California became involved with EPT due to the efforts of the principals. Each principal learned about SFA through literature or a workshop. They believed

SFA held promise as an effective program for their school and pursued additional information. The principals acknowledge that it took a great deal of work on their part over a period of 2 to 3 years to gather all the necessary information and to successfully lobby their teachers in order to bring SFA to their respective campuses. Nonetheless, they each brought SFA in as part of a personal decision and commitment.

In contrast, SFA was introduced to the Texas schools through the efforts of the school district office. The school district sought to use SFA as a programmatic response to reducing early-grade retention levels. The school principals were polled about their willingness to learn more about the program. Over 70 schools expressed interest. An unprecedented and extensive training effort was undertaken by Johns Hopkins. Schools were given the choice to implement one of three forms of SFA. Option A was early grades (K–3) reading only; Option B was K–6 reading only plus tutoring; and Option C was K–6 reading, tutoring and the family support program, or full SFA. Johns Hopkins took the opportunity to engage in extensive data collection in the district, and results of the different program options are reported in Nunnery et al. (1997).

The participation of the schools in the present study was sought by the researchers. We wanted to include schools that were just beginning to implement EPT, that served a majority of second-language learners, and where the principals would be amenable to hosting the research project on a long-term basis. The California schools were recommended to the researchers by Johns Hopkins personnel, and the Texas schools were recommended by school district personnel. All of the schools were in the first 2 years of implementation of EPT.

The first step to gaining entry was to contact the principals. A similar procedure was followed for each school. We telephoned the principal and described what we wanted to do. All of the principals indicated an interest and a willingness to discuss the study with us. We set a date for a meeting. Follow-up letters were sent that described the procedures and purposes of the study in more detail. We met with the principals individually, and all indicated they would support our study efforts. If needed, we sought district approval for the study.

SELECTION AND ENTRY INTO CLASSROOMS

An important part of the entry process into the classrooms was identifying the researchers as part of SFA/EPT. Prior to discussions with the teachers, the researchers joined the implementation check teams from Johns Hopkins and visited all of the schools as part of that team. If possible, the researchers also attended training sessions at the school with all of the teachers.

Two classrooms at each school were involved in the study for a total of 10 classrooms. We requested access to a *Lee Conmigo* (K–2) classroom and an *Alas Para Leer* (2–5) classroom at each school. In all but one school the principals were able to accommodate our request. At the time of the study, one California school did not have an *Alas Para Leer* classroom. The school found itself in the unique situation of having a group of readers in the process of transitioning to English reading but who tested at a *Lee Conmigo* level. The school principal, in conjunction with a Johns Hopkins consultant, designated one classroom as a transition Reading Roots classroom. The teacher was experienced in the transition process from Spanish reading to English reading and conducted Reading Roots lessons in English with a special emphasis on language development.

All of the teachers and classrooms were recommended by the site principals. The principals approached the teachers, and all the teachers agreed to work with the researchers. We made arrangements to do an initial observation and meeting with the teachers. The teachers had numerous questions about our work and our relationship to the Johns Hopkins University staff. The teachers welcomed us into the classroom and regarded us as resources about EPT and teaching in general.

DATA COLLECTION

The primary method of data collection was participant observation. Data were collected over a 2-year period. The data record consists of field notes, audiotapes, and interviews. The observation system used was the Special Strategies Observation System (Schaffer, Nesselrodt, & Stringfield, 1993). This system allows for both quantitative and qualitative data to be collected simultaneously. The data reported here are the qualitative data.

We observed at a school at least once a month for 2 to 3 days at a time. We observed for the full 90 minute reading period. We were forced to work around holiday breaks, assemblies, field trips, teacher illnesses, and other disruptions to the school day. Nevertheless, the schedule allowed us to visit each school at least twice, and sometimes three times, during the academic year to conduct classroom observations. We also returned to the schools on additional implementation checks as well as on teacher inservice days when a Johns Hopkins trainer was present. These refresher courses provided invaluable data as we learned more about the program and its implementation at a schoolwide level.

Interviews were conducted with the school principals and the teachers. Results from the interviews with the school principals are reported in Marquez and Prado-Olmos (1996).

DESCRIPTION OF THE SCHOOLS

The two schools in California are Seaview Elementary and La Serena Elementary.[1] Seaview Elementary is located within 10 miles of the Pacific Ocean in a suburban area. It occupies one city block among a quiet neighborhood of single family homes. There are approximately 520 students in Grades K–4. Despite its location, Seaview serves a relatively at-risk population; 50% of the students are classified as limited English proficient (LEP), and about 70% of the students qualify for free or reduced-price lunches. The principal indicates the school ranks among the lowest in the district in terms of family income level.

The school has an open campus, although visitors are instructed to go to the office prior to entering school grounds. The buildings are one story and house three classrooms in each wing. A number of portable classrooms have been added as the result of California Governor Wilson's initiative to reduce classroom size in Grades 1–3. The school grounds are well kept. A large blacktop area with handball, tetherball, and basketball courts occupies the center of the school grounds. Classrooms are set around this area on three sides. There is a large grassy field on the fourth side of the blacktop area.

La Serena Elementary is one of hundreds of schools that make up a large, urban school district. It is a decidedly urban school that is located at the border of Latino and Korean neighborhoods. La Serena Elementary is a year-round school. There are approximately 1,150 students in the school in three tracks. Eighty percent of the students are classified as LEP, and more than 90% qualify for free or reduced-price lunches.

A busy thoroughfare runs along one side of the campus, and single-family homes and apartments run along the other three sides. Even though the homes are single family dwellings, often more than one family resides in each. The school occupies one city block and is completely fenced. Access to the school campus is strictly controlled. Visitors are directed through a set of gates to the front office and the only way onto the campus is through the office. The classrooms are located in three two-story buildings. The kindergarten classrooms are in a separate

---

[1]All school names are pseudonyms.

one-story building and have their own playground. The school's main playground is a large blacktop area. There is no grass. As at Seaview, portable classrooms have been added in the class-size reduction effort.

The three schools in Texas are also part of a large urban school district. San Jacinto Elementary is situated in the northern part of the city within a largely Latino community. The school is located in a neighborhood surrounded by single-family houses and apartments. The principal of San Jacinto Elementary described the community as an integral part of the school. She believes the community has a strong sense of ownership for the school. The Parent–Teacher Association meetings average 200 parents in attendance.

Approximately 627 students attend San Jacinto Elementary; 98% are Latino and 55% are classified as LEP. Ninety-seven percent of the students qualify for free or reduced-price lunch. Bilingual classrooms are found in kindergarten through fourth grade and English-as-a-second-language (ESL) instruction in fifth grade. There is an emphasis on transitioning the bilingual students to all-English classes by the third grade.

The school consists of an older building, a newer building, and several portable buildings. The fence surrounding the school campus is locked during the school day. Visitors can access the campus through the front entrance to the building where the school office is located.

Bayou Vista Elementary is in the southern section of the city. There is an empty field across the street in the front, single-family homes on two sides, and a middle school on the fourth side. The empty field gives the school a feeling of openness and isolation. As in the other schools, there are portable buildings to house the overflow of classes.

The principal of Bayou Vista Elementary indicated that families have attended the school for two or three generations. Many students are bused 3 or 4 miles every day to the school. The community immediately surrounding the school is a well-established community with only a 20% mobility rate. Many of the homeowners no longer have children attending the school, yet they remain. The school is 28 years old and has had only three principals in that time, although it has undergone radical shifts in the student body. The school was initially all White and "overnight" became all African American. Over the last 8 to 10 years the student body has again shifted. Among 1,000 students in Grades Pre-K to 5, 53% are Hispanic, 44% are African American, 2% are White, and 1% are Asian. Eighty-nine percent of the students qualify for free or reduced-price lunches, and 24% are classified as LEP. Bilingual classrooms can be found in Grades K–3. There is also a combination fourth and fifth grade bilingual class. The emphasis within this school is on a model of bilingual education in which efforts are made to transition students to monolingual English instruction at third grade.

The school offers a variety of extracurricular programs such as karate and adult ESL instruction. Bayou Vista Elementary also has implemented a program to teach the students respect and individual responsibility.

Davis Elementary is located in the eastern part of the city. The school is situated in a community comprised of warehouses, small businesses, single-family homes, and empty lots. Directly across from the school is a large warehouse covered with graffiti. The school is surrounded by a fence, and visitors are directed to report to the office as they enter the building. There are approximately 860 students at Davis Elementary in grades Pre-K to 6. Ninety-nine percent of the students are Latino, 1% are White, and a very small percentage are African American or Asian. Ninety-five percent of the students qualify for free or reduced-price lunches and 49% are classified as LEP. Bilingual classrooms are found at every grade level at Davis Elementary. Davis Elementary also offers literacy classes for adults and Title I parent classes.

ÉXITO PARA TODOS IN THE CLASSROOM

Éxito Para Todos is structured into two programs; Lee Conmigo ("Read with Me") is taught in Grades K–2 and Alas Para Leer (Reading Wings) is taught in Grades 2–6. Each program is based on cooperative learning principles and is a balance between whole-language techniques and phonics-based instruction. Each program utilizes a 90-min time block for reading instruction. The first 20 min is devoted to an activity called Story Telling and Retelling (STaR). The teacher uses literature and reads to students in order to improve their listening comprehension skills. The teacher engages the students in discussion about events in the story, characters, problems, and other story elements. After the initial 20 min the two programs look very different from each other.

Lee Conmigo uses a sequence of phonetically regular stories called Shared Stories as the primary stimulus material. Each story is designed to introduce a set of specific sounds to the students. The schedule of activities for each story can take 2 to 3 days to complete. Teachers generally make the decision about which schedule they choose to follow. Each activity in a Shared Story is designed to take a certain amount of time so that the ninety minutes is used efficiently. For example, Table 7.1 shows a schedule of activities from the first day of a 3-day schedule for a Shared Story. There are five major blocks of activities to be accomplished on the

TABLE 7.1

Schedule of Activities for *Lee Conmigo*—Day 1

A. Showtime (5 min)
   1. Reading rehearsal
   2. Letter and word formation review
B. Setting the Stage (10 min)
   1. Introduction
   2. Background questions
   3. Predictive questions
   4. Teacher script
   5. Story discussion
C. Letter Activities (10 min)
   1. Alphabet song
   2. Letter presentation
      a. Hearing the sound (tongue twister)
      b. Introducing the sound's pictures and objects
      c. Two-picture game
      d. Making the sound
      e. Introducing the shape
      f. Practicing the shape
   3. Letter games
      a. Say-It-Fast (discontinued in Lesson 5 if students have mastered it)
D. Story Activities (20 min)
   1. Word presentation
      a. Stretch and read
      b. Quick erase
      c. Say-spell-say
      d. Using context
   2. Guided group reading
E. Celebration (5 min)
   1. Performance
   2. Letter sound review

first day. The second and third days have four major blocks of activities that repeat the first-day activities with the exception of Setting the Stage. On days 2 and 3 more time is devoted to Story Activities. This sequence and these activities are to be followed for every Shared Story in Levels 1–3. Level 4 is different in that it begins to introduce the activities that make up the bulk of *Alas Para Leer*. Furthermore, *Lee Conmigo* includes a 20 min block of time devoted to the Peabody Language Program.

Alas Para Leer uses pieces of literature or basal stories as the primary reading book. Each story is divided into two parts. A sequence of story-related activities including silent reading, paired reading, reading comprehension questions, and vocabulary practice is contained in material called a Treasure Hunt. Working in pairs, students are responsible for completing a Treasure Hunt for each story. A sequence of activities relat-

TABLE 7.2
Schedule of Activities for *Alas Para Leer*—Day 2

A. Listening Comprehension (20 min)
B. Reading Together
    1. Vocabulary review
        a. Choral response
        b. Rapid review
        c. Review word meanings and context
        d. Student meaningful sentences (oral)
    2. Story discussion—Section 1
        a. Use Treasure Hunt as a guide
        b. Noteworthy questions/Bloom's
        c. Share predictions with evidence
    3. Team practice
        a. Silent reading—Section II
        b. Partner reading—Section II
        c. Treasure Hunt—Section II
            1) Partner discussion
            2) Individually written responses
        d. Begin meaningful sentences
        e. Words out loud practice
    4. Two-minute edit
C. Book Club (15 min)

---

ing to a given story typically takes 5 days to complete. Students receive direct instruction from the teacher and then engage in team practice of the skills taught. Table 7.2 shows the schedule for an *Alas Para Leer* lesson on the second day of a Treasure Hunt cycle. The bulk of the 90 min is devoted to reading comprehension activities, and the last part of the reading time is set aside for students to read stories of their choice. The first day activities differ in that the teacher directed portion of the lesson focuses on introducing vocabulary and the story setting.

OBSERVATIONS

The researchers entered the classroom with the intent to describe what we saw. One theme that immediately surfaced in the observation notes was the sequence of activities that teachers followed on a day-to-day basis. The field notes indicated that identifiable sets of activities occurred regularly, and it was important to compare these identified activities with a standard format. In order to do so, the qualitative observation notes were summarized into structuration (J. Green, personal communication, 1993) maps (see Appendix). These maps allowed the researchers to track activity visually over time. The maps constructed from the observation notes were compared to maps constructed from teacher training manuals that provided guidelines on how each day in a story cycle was supposed to go.

We found that the teachers observed maintained a high degree of fidelity to the model. The classroom activities were readily indentifiable as an EPT activity, and the sequence of activities closely matched that described by Johns Hopkins. For example, data from two classrooms in California reveal an amazing degree of similarity in activity duration and sequence. Close examination of the observation notes reveals that the ways in which the activities were completed closely mirrored each other across the two classrooms also. A typical EPT lesson in each classroom might look something like this. Students entered the classroom and immediately sat on the floor to the side of the room in front of the teacher. The teacher conducted a StaR lesson for 20 min. Then the students and teacher got up and went to another corner of the classroom where they engaged in Showtime (day 1), Letter Activities, and Story Activities. If students were doing Share Sheets, they went to their desks to work with their partners. Students were then grouped in a different area of the room, on the rug, to do Peabody activities. Then they went back to the area where they did the story activities to do Celebration. These two teachers utilized the whole room and had their materials set up in specific areas for specific activities. It may seem as though transitioning from one area to another was rather confusing, but the teachers utilized similar techniques learned from Johns Hopkins to manage the movement. For example, one technique used frequently was a 1–2–3 signal. At 1 students were supposed to stand up, at 2 they were supposed to gather their materials and push in their chairs if necessary, and at 3 they moved. Observation notes indicate that transition times occupied an average of 1–2 min, often less.

A similar flow of movement was also observed in *Alas Para Leer* classrooms. After the STaR activity, a typical *Alas* teacher would direct the students to go back to their groups. Each of the groups had a name, typically that of a sports team. The teacher then led the students in a review of the vocabulary from the story that they were reading. The students read the vocabulary words and repeated the definitions. Then they dictated meaningful sentences to the teacher so that she could write them on the board. This would then help the students to add to their sentences. After the sentences were all written on the board and the students had copied them on their own paper, the class went on to discuss the story using their Treasure Hunt activity. The students then read the appropriate section of the story silently. Silent reading was followed by paired reading and then on to work on the appropriate section of the

Treasure Hunt. The students worked first with their partners to discuss their answers and then the answers were written individually.

The classrooms observed looked alike in terms of the materials needed for EPT. Teachers displayed the materials and items provided by Johns Hopkins University that related to specific activities, cooperative learning rules, team points and awards, and classroom rules in general. The teachers observed also kept all the necessary instructional materials at hand. The teacher script, provided by Johns Hopkins University, was always visible. The teachers seemed to use it more when they were less familiar with the activity.

The teachers observed also used similar cooperative learning strategies. The use of partners was regularly observed. During STaR a teacher would ask a question and direct students to Think, Pair, Share, meaning the student was to spend a moment thinking about a response, talk to their partner about a response, and then be ready to share with the whole group. Teachers also used the same technique to call on individuals. Students' names were written on popsicle sticks placed in a cup. The teacher would pull out a popsicle stick at random and ask that student to provide a response. Thus each student was assured an opportunity to respond to a question.

We also observed deviations from the model. These deviations generally occurred when the teacher was moving into a new phase of EPT. The degree of fidelity to the model began to decrease when teachers moved into a level they were unfamiliar with, most notably when they began teaching Level 4 in *Lee Conmigo*. Level 4 begins to introduce new activities that provide a transition to *Alas Para Leer* activities. The teachers displayed an understanding of the activities, but they began to "have trouble doing everything we're supposed to be doing every day." A couple of teachers reported, "We don't see how it can all be done in the days allotted. I understand it and I can do the *Lee Conmigo* part, but the kids need more time with the new stuff. I need to see it taught in a real classroom. That would help." It should be noted that these remarks and behavior occurred prior to the Level 4 training session the teachers were scheduled to attend.

Thus, in the classrooms observed, EPT became a structured set of activities that teachers and students readily engaged in. Teachers and students became familiar with the activities and the flow of movement and transitioning was very smooth. Disruptions to the routine were observed when a new student entered the classroom. For example, a new student came into a Reading Roots classroom in California. This student had never been part of *Éxito Para Todos*/Success For All and he entered the class late in the academic year. This classroom was beginning to incorporate activities that are part of Reading Wings, so the activities were becoming more student directed. The student followed the routine during the whole-group instruction with little disruption. Indeed, the researcher was unable to identify the student as new until the class separated into pairs to read to each other.

Reading with a partner occurs a particular way according to Johns Hopkins. Students sit facing away from each other in side-by-side chairs. Thus students are sitting closely and in an ear-to-ear fashion that allows them to hear each other reading in soft voices. In this classroom students typically traded turns after reading a page. When the class first separated into pairs nothing seemed out of the ordinary. However, a few minutes into the activity, the student paired with the new student called the teacher over and complained that the new student wasn't "doing it right." "He's not listening and he's not reading," the student told the teacher. The teacher explained to the new student what he needed to do and left them alone. The experienced student resumed reading, finished his turn, and waited for the new student to begin. The new student looked around the room and didn't begin reading. The experienced student looked and him and showed him where to read. The new student still did not comply. The experienced student once again called the teacher and complained. The teacher took over direction of the activity and sat with the pair while each read a page. After the teacher left, the experienced student read his page. The new student did not read his page. At this point the experienced student gave up trying to get the new student to read and finished reading on his own. The teacher later remarked to the researcher that this student was new and was struggling to get used to the routine.

This example illustrates that the SFA routine was well known to the students and they could articulate what was needed to "do it right." In the classooms observed, a maximum amount of time was spent on reading, with very little time spent on transitioning from one activity to another. Students engaged with the teacher and with each other. As a group, the students moved through the assigned readings with alacrity. *Lee Conmigo* groups that started at Level 1 or 2 moved to Level 4 and beyond by the end of the academic year.

TEACHER INDIVIDUALIZATIONS OF EPT

An additional theme that emerged from the field notes was the ways in which teachers individualized or personalized EPT in their classrooms. Without question, when implemented according to the model, EPT results in a readily recognizable pattern of teacher instruction. It has also been shown that teachers pick up and eliminate elements of programs according to what they believe good instruction to be (Prado-Olmos, 1993). We observed that the teachers in this study implemented the program with a high degree of fidelity to the model, but still instituted or inserted their own special brand of instruction. The teachers did not drop or add components to the program. Rather, they instructed EPT within a larger classroom atmosphere of teaching and learning that could be discerned during EPT instruction.

For example, EPT places a strong emphasis on cooperative learning and a student-centered pattern of classroom management signals and techniques. The teachers utilized these techniques but framed them within their own system of classroom management. One California teacher repeatedly used the EPT signals to direct the students' attention or to manage transitions. But she also had her own way to manage student disruptions or inattention. She utilized a theme of "*ser bien educado*" in her classroom. Directly translated this mean "to be well educated," but it means much more than that in a decidedly Latino cultural sense. It means to be respectful, mindful, responsible, and proud, and to engage in socially responsive and appropriate behavior. The teacher would often reprimand students by reminding them that "*así no se portan los estudiantes que son bien educados*" ("This is not how well-educated students are"). Or at the beginning of an event she would ask them to tell her what behaviors were appropriate for well-educated students. The language of "*ser bien educado*" surfaced repeatedly in the classroom, and the students were well aware of the teacher's expectations regarding their behavior and classroom participation.

Another teacher also enhanced the EPT classroom management with her own ideas. She consistently utilized positive reinforcement of students engaging in appropriate behaviors in order to redirect inattentive students. For example, during one observation the students were not transitioning to completing their Share Sheets as quickly as the teacher would have liked. The teachers praised one group of four students who had begun to work on their sheets. She said, "I see that Nancy's group is working on their Share Sheets quietly. I hope other groups do the same." The other groups looked at Nancy's group and got their own groups organized quickly.

A couple of teachers took up specific activities in EPT and used them as opportunities to engage the students in higher order thinking skills. For example, one *Lee Conmigo* teacher focused on opportunities to get the students thinking and talking about their own ideas and about possibilities. During the Story Activities the teacher would respond to any of the students' questions or ideas about the words or the story in a thoughtful and respectful way. He would probe the idea presented and scaffold the students' thinking about the idea. This extended attention to students' ideas sometimes resulted in the lesson taking longer than planned, but the teacher indicated he thought it was important that the students' ideas be acknowledged and their thinking be developed.

An *Alas Para Leer* teacher also focused on questioning and thinking in a similar fashion. When students were composing their meaningful sentences, the teacher was not satisfied with simple, short sentences. If the teacher thought the students could compose longer and more creative sentences, he would ask the students questions about the content. This would provide the scaffolding necessary for the students to develop their thoughts and add them to the sentences. The result was a set of meaningful sentences that not only helped the students comprehend and utilize the vocabulary, but also helped them to develop their writing skills.

This teacher also utilized examples to which the students could relate. For example, when discussing the location of Central America on the map, he compared it to the ham in the sandwich between North and South America. The teacher's enthusiasm for learning was contagious. It was evident that the students in his class were eager to learn and happy to be there.

Another *Alas* teacher emphasized utilization of a Johns Hopkins technique intended to assist in story comprehension. The teacher utilized the metaphor of a mental picture or movie to help the students to visualize the story or the topic being discussed. She told the students, "*vayan haciendo su película mental*" ("picture your mind movie") as she set the scene for a story and began to read it. This teacher also asked probing questions and expected the students to compose longer and more creative meaningful sentences. She used a semantic map to help students come up with terms related to the vocabulary word. For example, when the word *plaza* was being studied, she wrote the word on the board and asked the students to think about what there is at a "plaza." The students listed items such as grass, flowers, people, and vendors, and the teacher wrote the terms on the board with links to the word *plaza*. The students were then able to utilize these terms in their meaningful sentence for the vocabulary word *plaza*. It was evident that visualization was an important part of this teacher's instructional style.

RESISTANCE TO SFA/EPT

Another theme that emerged from the observation notes was resistance. Not all teachers were equally enthusiastic about SFA/EPT. Some teachers were lukewarm and others were highly critical. We came across this resistance at introductory training sessions, at refresher training sessions, during teacher interviews, and during casual conversations with teachers.

Over the course of the study, it became possible to identify those teachers who might be resistant to SFA/EPT at training sessions by their body language. These teachers often sat at the back of the room, brought schoolwork or newspapers, and generally remained disengaged throughout the session. The teachers told us that they believed their school was doing okay in reading and didn't need to change or that they thought something better was out there. Those teachers who were experienced with SFA/EPT said they found the program too rigid and that they were displeased with the assessments. They had students who were repeatedly placed in the same level two or three times and could see no sense in this type of remediation. Another set of comments focused on the materials. We repeatedly heard reports that the materials were late and they had to delay starting SFA/EPT or start with an incomplete set of materials. Teachers were very frustrated because they believed it was impossible to teach a new and unfamiliar program without the proper materials or support.

Frustration and dissatisfaction with the program led to the withdrawal of one school from the study. A teacher phoned one of the researchers during the summer to inform her that the school was not going to be teaching SFA/EPT the following year. When questioned, the teacher reported that the teaching staff had decided that SFA/EPT "wasn't working. The kids aren't reading any better than before." So the teachers voted to start their own program the following year. The program was going to be a blend of some SFA/EPT techniques, literature books, and some elements of other reading programs. This school was one where the principal had run into resistance from the very beginning.

Another school in the study provides a mini case study example of the multiple challenges a school faces when implementing a program like SFA/EPT. The school principal introduced SFA/EPT to the teaching staff. She had learned about the program in graduate school and had kept it in mind. She reported that it took about 2 years of discussion and consideration before the teachers agreed to try the program. The principal said the vote to use SFA/EPT was well over the required 80%.

When the school began implementing SFA/EPT there were problems obtaining the materials. Teachers were reluctant to begin the program without the proper materials. The principal stayed on top of the problem and their materials problems were solved fairly quickly.

There were the usual bumps and bruises during the first year. The principal reported that implementation visits went well and that there was an improvement in reading test scores at the end of the year.

A slightly different view of the implementation arose from discussions with classroom teachers. The teachers observed seemed comfortable with the program, followed a regular sequence of activities, and used SFA/EPT on a daily basis. However, they expressed dissatisfaction with the program and with the way implementation was being managed in the school. They believed the program had potential but that it needed to be implemented in a more complete way than had occurred. They reported they had begun finding books for StaR on they own and developing their own lessons because they didn't have what they needed from Johns Hopkins. The teachers also reported errors in the Shared Stories and said the stories were sometimes very disconnected from the children's lives. They each held a philosophy that classroom learning should value what students bring, and they believed the Shared Stories failed to do that.

Like other teachers, these two teachers expressed dissatisfaction with the assessment procedures. They saw slightly different groups of students every 8 weeks, but did not have any real sense of how individuals were doing in the program as a whole. They seemed to have fewer instances of students repeating the same books as in other schools, but said they did have students like that and that it was very frustrating for the students and the teacher.

These two teachers were also frustrated because they believed the program facilitator did not respond to their needs. Their needs were becoming critical because they were moving into an unfamiliar part of the *Lee Conmigo*/Reading Roots program. The activities they were supposed to accomplish in the 90 min seemed to have doubled and they simply did not understand how everything was to be accomplished. They wanted to attend a training session about this particular part of *Lee Conmigo*/Reading Roots and to perhaps visit a classroom to see it. The teachers indicated they had shared their concerns and frustrations with the Johns Hopkins trainer, but "nothing happened. Nothing changed."

The teachers said they had shared their concerns and frustrations with the principal. The researcher talked to the principal and heard another point of view. The principal said she was well aware of their concerns. She also said she had done an assessment of teacher satisfaction with the program on her own. The principal reported that the assessment showed the teachers were generally very satisfied with the program and that there were just a few teachers who were unsatisfied. The teachers we were working with were doing great jobs in their classroom and were among the dissatisfied but very vocal minority. The principal said she was trying to work with everyone.

In the end, one of the teachers phoned the researcher over the summer and said she had found another job in a district that did not use SFA/EPT.

ANALYSIS

The description presented in this chapter is just the beginning. In a sense, what has been confirmed is that when the trainers say they "know when they are in a SFA/EPT classroom" they are reflecting some clearly identifiable behaviors, a sequence of instructional activities, and a recognizable classroom environment. There is something to be recognized in EPT classrooms across schools.

The teachers were a select group. In their interviews they sometimes expressed doubts about the program, but each was willing to give the program a fair chance, and they were committed to doing the program well because they were committed to teaching their students to read. They were willing to "act as if" the program was a positive addition to the curriculum and that it would work. It may be that their level of commitment influenced the way the program looked in their classrooms.

It cannot be denied that some teachers are resistant to SFA/EPT before, during, and after experience with it. The resistance arises from multiple factors such as philosophical differences in how to teach or how to teach reading, difficulties in implementation, communication problems in schools, and straight personality conflicts. It is a complex issue that cannot be easily addressed by the schools or Johns Hopkins.

Some teachers in the study remarked they felt disconnected from Johns Hopkins. They felt like SFA/EPT was a very top-down program and did not have a way to listen to or use classroom teacher feedback. Developing a system for organized teacher feedback could be done by Johns Hopkins.

Many questions about classroom processes remain. The data presented here reflect the surface interactions in the classroom. The data indicate that students know what they need to do in each activity. They know where they need to be in the classroom, they know the format for each activity, and they know how to be in a cooperative classroom.

The data from Lee Conmigo classrooms and Alas Para Leer classrooms show that the classrooms are qualitatively different. Lee Conmigo classrooms are more teacher-directed and filled with more activities on a daily basis. Alas Para Leer classrooms have teacher-directed activities but also have activities that students accomplish on their own in pairs or small groups. Thus students are given a little more freedom to have discussions on their own or to problem solve on their own.

This study did not address the close, face-to-face interactions between students. Such a study seems to be the next step. It would be a challenge to do because SFA/EPT involves lots of movement around the classroom and trying to remain unobtrusive in the classroom could prove difficult. However, it is a necessary next step if we are to better understand the ways in which students construct meaning about literacy in an SFA/EPT environment.

APPENDIX A:
STRUCTURATION MAP
OF *LEE CONMIGO* CLASSROOM

8:30 am	STaR (Story Telling and Retelling)
8:50 am	Showtime—Reading rehearsal
8:55 am	Showtime—Letter formation review
8:57 am	Setting the Stage
	Story—*El Club de Libros*
9:16 am	Letter Activities—alphabet song
9:19 am	Letter Activities—syllable blends
	Hearing the sound
	Syllable wheels
9:27 am	Story Activities—word presentation—stretch and read
9:32 am	Story Activities—word presentation—quick erase
9:35 am	Story Activities—red words
9:38 am	Story Activities—guided group reading
9:53 am	Celebration
10:00 am	Dismissal

REFERENCES

Allington, R. L. (1983). The reading instruction provided readers of differing reading abilities. *Elementary School Journal, 83*, 548–59.

Collins, J. (1986). Differential instruction in reading groups. In J. Cook-Gumperz (Ed.), *The social construction of literacy* (pp. 117–137). Cambridge: Cambridge University Press.

Geertz, C. (1972). Deep play: Notes on the Balinese cockfight. *Daedalus, 101*, 1(Winter), 181–223.

Gumperz, J. J. (1986). Interactional sociolinguistics in the study of schooling. In J. Cook-Gumperz (Ed.), *The social construction of literacy* (pp. 45–68). Cambridge: Cambridge University Press.

Marquez, J., & Prado-Olmos, P. L. (1996, April). *"Success for All" in the elementary bilingual classroom: An ethnographic perspective.* Paper presented at the Annual Meeting of the American Educational Research Association, New York.

Moll, L. C., & Diaz, S. (1987). Change as the goal of educational research. *Anthropology and Education Quarterly, 18*(4), 300–311.

Nunnery, J., Slavin, R. E., Madden, N. A., Ross, S., Smith, L., Hunter, P., & Stubbs, J. (1997, March). *Effects of full and partial implementations of Success for All on student reading achievement in English and Spanish.* Paper presented at the annual meeting of the American Educational Research Association, Chicago.

Prado-Olmos, P. L. (1993). *Exploring structure and interaction in small groups: An ethnographic study of cooperative group life in a bilingual elementary classroom.* Unpublished doctoral dissertation, University of California, Santa Barbara.

Schaffer, E. C., Nesselrodt, P. S., & Stringfield, S. (1993). *Special strategies observation system. Research Edition.* Baltimore, MD: Center for the Study of Effective Schooling for Disadvantaged Students.

Tharp, R. G. & Gallimore, R. (1988). *Rousing minds to life. Teaching, learning and schooling in social context.* Cambridge: Cambridge University Press.

8

Curricula and Methodologies Used to Teach Spanish-Speaking Limited English Proficient Students to Read English

Margarita Calderón
Johns Hopkins University

The purpose of this chapter is to provide descriptions of curricula and methodologies used to teach Spanish-speaking limited English proficient (LEP) students to read English. Although the review of the literature focused mainly on "reading in English for Spanish-speaking students," it also included areas dealing with learning and teaching English as a second language (ESL), bilingual literacy, sociocultural factors, school and classroom characteristics, and teacher professional development. From a multitude of publications on Latino schooling practices, only a few dealt directly with reading. From those, only a handful appeared to be research-based programs that presented data on their effectiveness. Most publications were *not* based on empirical research, but relied on political voices or were built on past professional intuitions and assumptions.

The few effectiveness studies that were found are indicated by an asterisk in the bibliography. These reading programs have been shown to be effective through rigorous evaluations, with experimental and control student groups, and either have been replicated or appear to be replicable across a broad range of elementary and secondary schools serving Latino students. These are the studies that could further be replicated within new contexts. The criteria that were used to select the studies were:

1. Used reading strategies that were specifically designed for use with Latino students.

2. Presented rigorous evaluation evidence in comparison to control groups showing significant and lasting impacts on the achievement of Latino students.

3. Have been widely replicated in schools serving Latino students and have evidence of effectiveness in dissemination sites.

In addition to the few studies found, there were compendia that were included in this first category, such as "Improving Schooling for Language-Minority Children" (August & Hakuta, 1997) and "Effective Programs for Latino Students in Elementary and Middle Schools" (Fashola, Slavin, Calderón, & Durán, 1997), because the authors applied the same rigorous standards in order to select the best studies in the field. Unfortunately, except for Success for All/Éxito Para Todos, Bilingual Cooperative Integrated Reading and Composition, and Reading Recovery, all other listed programs were not designed to teach reading. Descriptions of these programs are given in the methods sections of the chapter. The section on "What Is Needed" at the end of this chapter also draws from the few studies found under this category.

The second group of articles reviewed contain general principles or hypotheses about how effective reading programs should be designed (Anstrom, 1998; McLaughlin & McLead, 1997; Medina, 1993; National Coalition, 1994; Rodriquez, Ramos, & Ruiz-Escalante, 1994; Berman et al., 1995; Cohen, 1993; Diaz, Moll, & Mehan, 1986; Olsen, 1994; U.C. LMRI, 1997). There are many articles and books on the general principles of effective practice for Latino students and for bilingual education, but these did not apply consistent standards to evaluate the promising practices they proposed. These principles are summarized in the third part of the chapter.

Finally, the third and largest cohort of publications consists of mainly practitioner manuals, university textbooks, basal series, or bilingual program descriptions. These describe the trends in teaching reading, although no research basis is presented. Nevertheless, descriptions of the most popular methods are included in the methods sections. Only a few titles from this cohort were selected to include in the bibliography. As a reviewer of Title VII proposals, the author finds most of these methods and curriculum descriptions in the yearly proposed Title VII projects. However, another study of Office of Bilingual Education and Minority Language Affairs (OBEMLA)-funded projects might give a more accurate analysis of program implementation trends.

The report begins with setting a context for the curricula and methodologies used to teach Spanish-speaking LEP students to read English. The context for Latino failure or success goes beyond instruction and curriculum. There are many factors that impact on the quality or absence of instructional programs. Therefore, the first part of the review begins with schooling factors that impact on the level of success for language minority students. The second part highlights some of the individual student factors that need to be taken into consideration for effective program design, implementation, and evaluation. The third part summarizes some of the basic principles for teaching reading in Spanish before teaching LEP students to read in English and the current practices/research for different grade levels. The fourth part describes the current approaches used to teach reading in Spanish. The fifth part describes the current approaches used to teach English as a second language as a bridge to reading in English. The sixth part shows the emerging studies of programs designed to facilitate the transition from Spanish to English reading. The seventh part looks at the implications from a discipline called "teaching sheltered English." Although this instructional approach was originally used mainly in secondary schools, its theoretical framework and teaching strategies are being employed in elementary schools today. The eighth part looks at findings from another type of program, two-way bilingual or dual language programs. The ninth part touches briefly on home–school literacy connections. The final part brings the main theoretical concepts and research-based practices together to attempt to describe a prototype for a comprehensive program for teaching English language learners (ELLs) to be successful readers in English.

SCHOOLING FACTORS AFFECTING READING

Historical Neglect, Misconceptions, and Low Expectations

García (1998) found in his study of the literature on "best practices" and "reading programs that work" that these programs neglect to mention or address the literacy needs of LEP students. Although they may be effective for some, he questions their effectiveness for all students. Emergent themes such as this in the literature reflect a preoccupation with the educational reform movements that only seek to "Americanize" the students in lieu of providing "equal educational opportunity" (García, 1998). Basterra (1998) asserted that the schools that have focused their efforts mainly on the provision of equal access to educational offerings have paid little or no attention to the inclusion of issues related to the linguistic and cultural backgrounds of their students.

At one end of the continuum, bilingual educators and researchers call for "a responsive pedagogy" that is built upon the cultural strengths, values, and contributions of students and their families. They strongly reject the "one-size-fits-all" programs. At the other end of the continuum, edu-cators argue for general principles of teaching and learning (best prac-tices) that are effective for all students. These contradictions have nega-tively impacted the schools and have torn bilingual educators apart. Although the sparse research-based instructional practices and programs are widely disseminated through state educational agencies, few schools avail themselves of them. Change is difficult for most schools (Fullan & Hargreaves, 1996; Goodlad, 1990; McLaren, 1993). Fewer schools are willing to take one step further and attempt to adjust best practices to La-tino students' needs. It would seem that the answer to the best type of reading program lies in combining both ends of the continuum—some-thing no program has yet attempted or has yet written about. Success for All/*Éxito Para Todos* (SFA/EPT) (Slavin & Madden, chap. 6, this vol-ume; Fashola, Slavin, Calderón, & Durán, 1996; Slavin & Madden, 1995) comes closest to achieving this balance, but it still needs refine-ment and further development before it can accurately address the lin-guistic and diverse cultural backgrounds of Latino students.

One concept seems clear. What worked in the past for a few Latino students does not work now for the much larger numbers of Latinos in our schools. As schools set out to "reform," "restructure," or "transform" their schooling practices, they must consider looking at Latino students in a completely new way. In general, teachers and administrators have low expectations of Latino students, and this translates into wa-tered-down curriculum and laissez-faire instructional time (Ovando & Collier, 1998). Under the guise of "whole language" or "culturally rele-vant" instruction, many curricula and instructional programs have re-moved accountability, thoroughness, and hard-work ethics from bilingual classrooms (Calderón, 1997). There is an understanding between stu-dents and teachers that comfort is better than that which produces too much work. The most frequent reason reported for not adopting compre-hensive programs such as Success for All/*Éxito Para Todos* or Bilingual Cooperative Integrated Reading and Composition is that "it's too much work!" The culture of laissez-faire appears to be too ingrained in schools with large populations of Latino students.

Lack of Whole-School Support for ELL Programs

Perhaps the biggest detriment to ELL success has been the isolated Eng-lish as a second language (ESL) or bilingual program that works sepa-rately from the rest of the school. ESL and bilingual teachers have been left to implement their programs without support from the rest of the school personnel or administration. Teachers are rarely supervised by their administration because the principals rarely know what instruction in those classrooms should be like. Mainstream teachers are not held accountable for ELL failure because they are the responsibility of the ESL/bilingual staff (Calderón, 1997).

Although much of the literature on Latino schooling focused on the negative aspects of schooling, August and Hakuta (1997 & 1998) provided a comprehensive review of effective schools and practices which do cater to Latino students. Their review identified the following attributes of success:

> A supportive school-wide climate, school leadership, a customized learning environment, articulation and coordination within and between schools, use of native language and culture in instruction, a balanced curriculum that includes both basic and higher-order skills, explicit skills instruction, opportunities for student-directed instruction, use of instructional strategies that enhance understanding, opportunities for practice, systematic student assessment, staff development, and home and parent involvement. (p. 171)

Yet a comprehensive program with all of these components is rare. The authors cautioned that although these attributes provide important guidance for developing effective programs and instructional strategies for ELL, they need to be assessed in the context of schools and classrooms in which they are being implemented. Research is needed to determine which kinds of strategies are exportable and which aspects may be influenced by local context. In general, it is easy to agree with Cole (1996) that attributes of schooling practices call for a deeper understanding of the interaction between students' own cultures and the prevailing cultures of the schools they attend.

There is a strong consensus in the field of bilingual education that responsibility for the underachievement of culturally diverse students must be shared by the whole school. Low expectations of students must be replaced by understanding of their linguistic and cultural background. Children's development and learning are best understood as the interaction of linguistic, sociocultural, and cognitive knowledge and experiences. In most schools, there is a mismatch between the culturally diverse Latino student and the monolithic school culture (E. García, 1998; G. García, chap. 9, this volume; Montero-Seiburth, 1999).

Limited Availability of Research-Based Instructional Practices

ESL and bilingual programs have suffered from a lack of research-based instructional practices. Research needs to investigate the optimal English literacy instruction for children of different ages and with different background variables. When should LEP students be taught to read in English? What is the best English literacy development program for those students who already know how to read in their native language? How can high school ELLs master English and content in 4 years? These are but a few questions waiting to be answered.

In our work with schools we have encountered a strong tradition that insists that English skills be taught in a separate sequential order: listening first, then speaking, and once there is "sufficient" oral language, students begin reading, and eventually they will attempt writing. This has resulted in students spending years on listening and speaking with little or no formal instruction in reading. For instance, the Natural Approach to English language acquisition hinges on the fact that language emerges in stages (Krashen, 1986). Typically, the Natural Approach philosophy underlies holistic approaches to instruction in most ESL and bilingual programs. It is a reaction against the other type of English teaching where the separate structures of language, syntactic rules, and/or phonics were taught. Neither type of commonly used program has research that establishes its effectiveness over time. The question still remains, how should listening, speaking, reading and writing be taught in an integrated approach?

Multiple Complex Issues of Assessment

Fifty-six percent of Latino 17-year-olds are classified as functionally illiterate. From the day they enter school, most Spanish-speaking students are classified as "at risk" for failure. This labeling has more to do with issues of race/ethnicity, class, and language status than it does with academic ability or potential (Tinajero & Ada, 1993). For the most part, school districts comply with state mandates for assessing language proficiency through popular assessment instruments. The majority, however, do not finish this process in time for placement into appropriate instruction. Districts will administer the tests the first year of entry, but generally will not assess again until someone "feels" the student is ready to transition into the English mainstream classroom. Students may be mislabeled and misplaced for years. It is believed that these assessment problems are one of the main causes of students dropping out of school (Calderón, 1997). On the other hand, programs that assess students every 8 weeks or so can determine who needs tutoring or whether groups should be changed, and identify students who might need another type of intervention (Slavin, Madden, Dolan, & Wasik, 1996).

Research is needed on how to use assessments to determine levels of proficiency in different aspects and stages of English development. How can these tests inform teaching practices and school accountability? Research is also needed to determine when LEP students are ready to transition into mainstream classrooms and take the "standard" tests proficient English speakers take. We have not yet answered the issue of what type of benchmarks should be used for students learning English.

Insufficient Teacher Preparation

Latino students are likely to be in classrooms with either a bilingual teacher, an ESL teacher, or a mainstream teacher. It is common knowledge that teachers working with Latino students, particularly in high poverty areas, are not well prepared, as evidenced by most state test results. We are finding from our implementation of Success for All/*Éxito Para Todos* (SFA/EPT) programs that the majority of ESL teachers did not learn to teach reading. Most of their university preparation consisted of theory and practice of teaching beginning oral English.

Whole-school implementation studies mention that most teachers do not perceive diversity as an asset to teaching and learning (Basterra, 1998). Although collaboration between teachers has been found to be necessary for teacher learning as well as for student optimal learning, the studies reviewed make no mention of this.

Some of the areas that need to be addressed through inservice staff development programs are: skills for teaching reading; developing high expectations of Latino students; identifying and adjusting instruction for different student levels of English proficiency, academic performance, and recency of immigration; current knowledge of research-based practices; and collegial practices. Additionally, the process of ensuring transfer from training needs to be incorporated in schools. This process includes instituting teachers' learning communities for continuous study of teaching (Calderón, 1998) and implementation visits by peer and expert coaches (Calderón, 1994; Joyce & Showers, 1988).

Research Is Needed to Examine the Influence of Combined Factors

Success in reading in English for ELL students goes beyond a reading program. Researchers need to pull together effective practices to dispel old myths about the students and ineffective instructional practices through extensive teacher professional development, whole-school responsibility for ELL student learning, high expectations, and a comprehensive program that is linguistically and culturally relevant.

MEETING INDIVIDUAL NEEDS

Poverty and Language

"Reading failure is the overwhelming reason that children are retained, assigned to special education, or given long-term remedial services" (Learning First Alliance, 1998, p. 4). Reading failure in the fourth grade occurs about twice as frequently in children of Spanish-speaking background (64%) as compared to Anglo children (31%). The dropout rate among Latino students is extremely high. In 1991, approximately 35% of Latino students were out of school as compared to 8.9% of Anglos and 13.6% of African Americans. Dropout rates for Latino students born outside of the United States are around 43% (National Center for Educational Statistics [NCES], 1993c).

National statistics inform us that Latino students are far more likely than Anglo students to come from homes in poverty and to have parents who have limited education. Forty percent of Latino children are living in poverty, almost twice the rate for all U.S. children (NCES, 1995).

A second factor identified by the NCES as a cause for student failure is language. Of an estimated 2.3 million limited English proficient (LEP) students in Grades K–12, about 75% speak Spanish (U.S. Department of Education, 1992). About half of all LEP students were born outside of the United States. Immigrant status highly correlates with language and is a key predictor of school failure (General Accounting Office, 1994).

A Broad Range of Student Backgrounds

Immigrant students are highly diverse in immigrant status, parents' education, family support or expectations, intergenerational conflict, economic resources, rough or smooth transition into adolescence, and resilience. LEP-labeled students can be first-, second-, or third-generation Latinos or immigrants. At one extreme, Latino children may be from middle-income families with well-educated parents, but even so the schools have often stigmatized them and lumped them into slow-moving tracks. At the other extreme, Latinos may be recent immigrants, uprooted and still suffering from traumatic experiences on their journey to the United States. They may come to school with a sense of loneliness, loss of cultural identity, fear of ridicule, culture shock, and exhaustion. Many have had little or no education in their home countries. Some students come from Latin America and have Latino names, but do not speak Spanish. Their primary language is an American Indian language. These students will probably withdraw and remain nonparticipatory until they are helped to fit in. Without extra help, they may remain behind in the development of their reading skills or opt to leave school altogether (González & Calderón, in press; Lucas, 1993; Ovando & Collier, 1998).

Diverse Patterns of Language Proficiency

The Latino language minority category includes a broad range of patterns of language proficiency. The students labeled as LEP may be essentially monolingual in Spanish or English, or may possess varying degrees and types of bilingualism. Students represent a wide range of variation in their Spanish background also. They may be exposed to a standard or nonstandard form of Spanish in their bilingual classroom that differs markedly from the Spanish they are familiar with at home. Therefore, in getting to know the student's background, the bilingual or ESL teacher is not just dealing with English proficiency but also with students' home language variations (Ovando & Collier, 1998). The variations are summarized in Fig. 8.1 and discussed further to highlight the implications for instructional interventions at the different grade levels.

Prekindergarten to Second Grades

At the prekindergarten to second grade levels, ELLs have a better opportunity to develop English literacy skills early in their school careers if the appropriate programs are offered. Students in categories 2 and 3 will have more probabilities of success because of their background in Spanish literacy. Students in categories 1 and 4 will need additional assistance. They will most likely need tutoring, extra help with oral language devel-

Category		Oral English Proficiency		Literacy in		Grade Span		
				Spanish	English	K-2	3-6	7-12
1		-		-	-	•		
2		•		•	-	•		
3		-		•	-	•		
4		•		-	-	•		
5		-		-	-		•	
6		•		•	-		•	
7		-		•	-		•	
8		•		-	-		•	
9		-		-	-			•
10		•		•	-			•
11		-		•	-			•
12		•		-	-			•

FIG. 8.1.   English and home language proficiency variations in grades K–12.

opment, and background knowledge of content area concept development.

Third to Sixth Grades

Students in Grades 3 to 6 come to the school fitting into any of the categories 5 to 8. They will need variations of assistance that are more intensive and individualized, for it is typically around the third, fourth, or fifth
grades that ELLs are expected to take high-stakes standardized tests in
English. At these grade levels, a large number of immigrant students or
binational migrant students attend school part of the year in Mexico and
part of the year in the United States. Some of these students have a high
literacy background in Spanish but may not be in the United States long
enough to transfer those skills into English. They need a special intervention. Other binational ELLs have not had an opportunity to attend
school in their home country. Their intervention will need to include basic preliteracy skills.

Another facet of language variation at this level is represented by the
students who lack communicative competence and literacy skills in both
languages. For some, teacher and parental pressure to move them quickly
into English has resulted in "subtractive bilingualism" where students lose
skills in Spanish due to an exclusive focus on English in school and still
remain limited in English (California State Department of Education,
1981, pp. 217–218). Other students have been in the schools since kindergarten but have somehow remained limited in both languages.

Grades 7 to 12

By far, the most challenging reading interventions to be developed are for
ELLs in the secondary schools. Within this category of immigrant or migrant students, there are those who come for the first time to the United
States as adolescents. When these students come into middle schools and
high schools, educators do not know how to develop their reading skills.
Teachers are reluctant to use preprimers, although most eventually do, because there are no programs to effectively and efficiently teach reading to
secondary school students (González & Calderón, in press). Although the
catch-up challenge can be great at all grade levels, it becomes even more
critical in middle and high school, which have more structured curricula
with less emphasis on learning by doing and increased emphasis on abstract
language (Ovando & Collier, 1998). At the other end of the spectrum the
schools find the middle-class adolescents who come extremely well educated and ready to accelerate their learning of English. Unfortunately,

they are often placed in the slow-paced, low-level ESL classes along with all the other ELL students. Some fight their way out of these classes with the school system; others lose interest in school (Walki, 1996).

PRIMARY LANGUAGE LITERACY DEVELOPMENT AS A PRECURSOR TO READING IN ENGLISH

Rationale for Reading in the Home Language Before Reading in English

In the literature, we repeatedly find three principles that underlie the rationale for teaching Latino students to read in their primary language before teaching them to read in English (California State Department of Education, 1981, 1986; Collier, 1995; Cummins, 1993; Genesse, 1987; Goldenberg, Reese, & Gallimore, 1992; Mace-Matluck, Alexander-Kasparik, & Queen, 1998; Skutnabb-Kangas & Cummins, 1988; Thomas & Collier, 1997):

- Although conversational abilities may be acquired fairly rapidly in English, upward of 5 years is usually required for second-language learners to attain grade norms in academically related aspects of the second language.
- Literacy-related abilities are interdependent across languages, such that knowledge and skills acquired in one language are potentially available in the other.
- Continued development of both languages enhances children's educational and cognitive development.

A study in progress (Thomas & Collier, 1997) suggests, based on preliminary evidence, that programs that maintain and promote continued use of the home language, rather than having students transition to all-English instruction in elementary school, produce superior academic outcomes in English.

Although these principles are widely used in the development and implementation of bilingual programs, there are only two studies focused on reading that have controlled for interactions among student background (e.g., prior schooling in the native language, age), ways in which the first and second languages are used, and other institutional variables (e.g., overall quality of schooling). Only one was found in the review recently conducted by August and Hakuta (1997). These two studies are described in the sixth part of this chapter.

Thomas and Collier, under the auspices of the Center for Research on Cultural Diversity and Second Language Learning, redesigned their prior analysis of bilingual program effects in order to find causal relationships between reading in the primary language and reading in English. Thus, the issue of Latino student transfer of skills from first to second language still needs to be resolved.

Current Practice in Prekindergarten and Kindergarten Bilingual Classrooms

Beginning readers in kindergarten need exposure to skills that are known to predict future reading achievement (Snow, Burns, & Griffin, 1998). Instruction should be designed to stimulate verbal interaction, to enrich children's vocabulary, to encourage talk about books, to develop knowledge about print, including the production and recognition of letters, and to generate familiarity with the basic purposes and mechanisms of reading. Through the theories of bilingual education we can hypothesize that if these interventions for early reading are provided in the student's primary language, it should make it easier for the students to develop these skills.

Unfortunately, in the schools we have studied, some bilingual programs place Latino students in an all-English kindergarten, let them experience a year of failure, and then place them in Spanish instruction that is seen as remedial in first grade. In essence, many students miss out on learning the conventions of print and the development of a rich vocabulary and discourse for prereading in either language. If students do not attend kindergarten or if the program is not designed to develop the early reading skills, the students may not have the opportunity to develop these skills in the later grades.

Prekindergarten through first-grade curriculum has received very little attention in bilingual reading research. There were no rigorous studies for this particular level. This means that it has left the field wide open for multiple interpretations as to what instruction should look like at the primary levels.

Current Practice in First-Grade Bilingual Classrooms

Because of the rush to move students into English as quickly as possible, another scenario plays out quite frequently in schools serving many Latino children. Students in the first grade are rushed through decoding skills, with little attention paid to phonemic awareness, practice with the sound structure of words, familiarity with spelling–sound correspondences, and common spelling conventions and their use in identifying printed words and "sight" words (Snow et al., 1998). The goal for most teachers is to "get the student reading in Spanish" as quickly as possible so that the second-grade teachers can focus on their transition into English reading. The first-grade teachers' language arts block is typically fragmented because of the pressure to teach English as a second language, language arts in Spanish, and all the other subjects. If a student does not attend kindergarten or has had a nonproductive kindergarten experience, his or her first-grade experience may be worse in a fragmented curricula. Without a comprehensive program for developing decoding and comprehension skills, many students experience failure from the start (Slavin, Madden, Dolan, & Wasik, 1996; Snow et al., 1998).

Beginning in kindergarten and first grade, instruction should promote comprehension by actively building linguistic and conceptual knowledge in a rich variety of domains, as well as through direct instruction about comprehension strategies such as summarizing the main idea, predicting events and outcomes of upcoming text, drawing inferences, and monitoring for coherence and misunderstandings.

Current Practice in Second-Grade Bilingual Classrooms

Vignettes of second-grade bilingual classrooms are presented in the fourth part of this review to describe specific methods for teaching reading in Spanish. These vignettes attempt to portray the discontinuity and limitations of current methods. Borrowing from best practices principles (Slavin & Madden, chap. 6, this volume; Snow, 1998), students at second grade should further their understanding of the story elements, story structure, and the author's craft. In this phase, teachers need to have had ample experiences exploring literary devices and comprehension skill building in two languages. Many bilingual credentialed teachers have not had these experiences. They may lack the discourse in Spanish for taking students through these analyses if their university or staff development programs did not model the discourse. When students are placed in ESL programs during this phase, their limited English may not enable them to comprehend the higher order discourse necessary to analyze all the nuances of an author's craft.

Current Practice in Third-Grade Bilingual Classrooms and Beyond

There has been a great deal of emphasis on the teaching of thinking skills (Jensen, 1998; Palinscar & Brown, 1985). For many second-language learners, however, instruction in the use of cognitive strategies is almost nonexistent (Gersten & Baker, 1999; Waxman, de Felix, Martinez, Knight, & Padrón, 1994). Research identifying cognitive reading strategies used by second language learners revealed a variety of strategies that students use to comprehend text (Padrón, 1992; Warren & Rosebery; 1995). Padrón and associates found that bilingual students use fewer strategies and different types of reading strategies than English monolingual students. They believe that this is due to the assumption that students must demonstrate the ability to learn basic or lower levels of skills before they can be taught higher level skills. LEP students are generally not taught higher level thinking skills until they can speak the language well. Nonetheless, the researchers found that when LEP students were instructed in four specific comprehension monitoring strategies (summarizing, self-questioning, clarifying, and predicting), the use of these strategies improved reading achievement. These strategies are particularly necessary in the upper grades (Padrón, 1992; Simich-Dudgeon, 1998).

Connections to the Report on Preventing Reading Difficulties

In a recent report on prevention of reading difficulties (Snow et al., 1998), the research committee identified three potential stumbling blocks to skilled reading for any student. The first is the difficulty of understanding and using the alphabetic principle (the idea that written spellings systematically represent spoken words). If we apply this notion to LEP students, we can assume that their placement in English reading must be done after the students have an understanding of and practice using the alphabetic principle. It is hard to comprehend connected text if word recognition is inaccurate or laborious (Snow et al., 1998). If children learn the alphabetic principle in their native language, it should not be as laborious as learning the alphabetic principle in their limited English.

Another obstacle that the report mentioned is a failure to transfer the comprehension skills of spoken language to reading and to acquire new strategies that may be specifically needed for reading. ELLs will need a carefully designed program to help them transfer these skills.

The third obstacle to reading that Snow et al. reported, which magnifies the first two, is the absence or loss of initial motivation to read or failure to develop a mature appreciation of the rewards of reading. The majority of reading problems faced by Latino students in 3rd to 12th grades are the result of problems caused by immersion into reading programs in English. August and Hakuta (1997) stated that Latino children have been at risk for many years because they have been placed in language environments with no direct reading instruction.

THE MOST COMMON INSTRUCTIONAL PRACTICES FOR TEACHING SPANISH READING TO LEP STUDENTS

Reading in Spanish in bilingual classrooms appears to fall into two main approaches: eclectic word recognition approaches, and variations of a whole-language approach. A third approach, which is currently only in about 300 schools, is Success for All/*Éxito Para Todos*. The eclectic word recognition approach was promoted through basals up until the late 1980s. The basal publishers then substituted it with a whole-language approach, which focused more on children's literature but removed or deemphasized phonics or decoding from the reading process. The SFA/EPT Spanish, ESL, and English reading programs attempt to provide a more balanced approach to reading by integrating those methods and techniques that have been proven effective through research or component building (Slavin, 1984). The component building for SFA/EPT is different from the eclectic methods commonly used in most classrooms. The eclectic method contains features of other methods but are usually put together without a systematic plan (Freeman & Freeman, 1998). The word recognition, whole language, and EPT/SFA methods are described and presented through classroom vignettes that follow. We have found that bilingual teachers employ the same methods for teaching reading in English as they do for teaching reading in Spanish.

Word Recognition/Traditional Method of Reading in Spanish

The traditional word recognition approach was put together from knowledge about reading methods used in the Spanish-speaking world. These methods were divided into three approaches, synthetic and analytic (Bellenger, 1979; Freeman & Freeman, 1998). In the synthetic approach, children are taught to read by first identifying letters, then syllables, then isolated words, then phrases, and finally short texts—usually one or two sentences. Recitation, memorization, and careful pronunciation are the important main tasks. In the analytic approach, children began with whole words and then broke the words into parts to be analyzed. This also became the *método global* that taught reading beginning with the sentence or phrase and moving to the word, then the syllable, and finally the letter.

The traditional word recognition approach limits the scope of reading, as Freeman and Freeman (1997) described in a U.S. second-grade bilingual classroom:

> The twenty-seven children in the bilingual class are divided into five groups, three for Spanish reading and two for English. Four groups are busy at centers doing various activities while one group of four children are in a small circle reading with the teachers. The centers consist of: (1) finishing pages in a take-home book which consists of pictures of animals that come from eggs with the name of the animal labeled beneath it. The students color the picture of each animal and copy the text label in their own handwriting on the line underneath the printed text. One group at this center is working with the English version of the book and another is working in Spanish with the bilingual aide. Other children are at the computers working on a program that helps them practice basic vocabulary words in Spanish and English using the CD-ROM program *Lyric Language*. Still others are working on an art project with plastic eggs that nylon stockings come in. They are following a model provided and making a clay duck to go into the egg.
>
> Meanwhile the teacher with the middle Spanish reading group is showing a list of words she has printed on paper: pato (duck), huevo (egg), tiempo (time), pronto (soon), cinco (five), nido (nest) and dijo (said). She reads the words to the students and then asks them some questions about the words such as: What did you notice about these words? (they all end in o) How many syllables are there in each word? (two) What do the words mean? What is a pato (duck)? After they identify all the words, the teacher takes the big book, *El patito feo* (*The Ugly Duckling*) and reads it to them tracking the words with her hand. Then she gives the children little book versions, and they take turns reading the story aloud. If the reader has difficulty with a word, Alicia encourages the student to sound it out. If this strategy fails, Alicia or one of the other children says the word aloud for the reader. After they have read the story again, the teacher asks questions about the story: Which animals come from eggs in this story? (the ducks) And, which other animal? (the ugly duckling) And, what is the other name of this animal? (pp. 27–28)

The description of this classroom depicts this still popular approach to reading in bilingual classrooms. The focus for learning to read is mainly on word recognition, recall questions, and follow-up individual seat work. Many bilingual teachers still prefer this method, which is also popular in most Spanish-speaking countries in spite of their whole-language basals. In our studies, we have observed that as teachers experience more and more failure in their students' reading, they tend to return to these more traditional methods.

Whole-Language Approach to Reading in Spanish

The more recent approaches are called the socio-psycholinguistic or constructivist or *método integral* (Dubois, 1995; Ferreiro, 1994; Freeman et al., 1995; Goodman, Goodman, & Flores, 1999; Simich-Dudgeon, 1989). This whole-language approach is the current approach used with Mexico's national texts.

The whole-language or socio-psycholinguistic approach is much more complex. Its purpose is to focus on comprehension or "meaning-making" with a variety of children's literature texts. This very popular approach to reading assumes that "students learn to read by reading . . . as long as the focus is on meaning, [and] we acquire written language in the same way that we acquire oral language" (Freeman & Freeman, 1999, p. 37). This approach is exemplified by a description of another teacher's second grade bilingual classroom working with the same unit as the traditional teacher described by the Freemans earlier:

> In Celia's class, more student work is visible. The egg drawings reveal more individuality; they don't strictly follow a model. The science journal entries include a variety of observations rather than following a uniform pattern. One bulletin board, labeled "What we know about animals that lay eggs" and "What do we wonder about them?" features a list of questions students have generated and written out themselves. The books around the room include trade books in Spanish and English that deal with the theme as well as large class-made books about oviparous animals created by children from previous classes.
>
> Like Alicia, Celia is sitting with a small group of students while the other children work independently. However, while Alicia's children were working on specifically assigned projects at centers or the computer, some of Celia's second graders have paired up and are reading and talking about the books in the reading corner. The story books and content books laid out for them all center on the theme of animals and insects that lay eggs. Other students are at a listening station with their headsets on, following along in books as their story is read on a tape. Some are writing stories, either independently or in pairs. A few students are at the computers typing their stories. Still others are at the incubator making observations and writing them in their science journals.
>
> The students with Celia are discussing a book she has just read to them. The question, "What do you remember?" is used for the discussion. After a few minutes, Celia reminds the children of the questions about animals

that lay eggs that the class had brainstormed after their literature study on *El patito feo* (*The Ugly Duckling*). The children read those questions with her. Two questions were "Which animals lay eggs?" and "How are the eggs same and different?" Celia suggests that the children might list some possible answers from the book they just read. She also encourages the students to keep these questions in mind as they read other books. (pp. 29–31)

Although Celia's approach seems to be much more student centered and more focused on meaning, it is also evident that the students have learned stories not by reading but by listening to the teacher read the stories or from the tapes at the listening center. The discussions center on questions previously posted by other classes and from previous stories the teacher has read to them. As evidenced in many whole-language classrooms, we find that the students remember story details but they cannot read the story with fluency.

Éxito Para Todos Approach to Reading in Spanish

A third approach being used in about 300 schools in the United States and 4 pilot schools in Mexico is the Spanish version of Success for All/ *Éxito Para Todos* (Slavin, Madden, Rice, & Calderón, 1996–1999; Dianda & Flaherty, 1995). If two teachers were teaching students at a 2.1 reading level in Spanish, the following sequence of activities would be observed the first day of a 5-day cycle of activities in an *Alas Para Leer*/Reading Wings classroom in an SFA/EPT school (Slavin, 1999):

During this ninety-minute period, the teacher begins with twenty minutes of reading a story that illustrates "cause and effect." At previously selected pages she stops and asks students to think and then discuss with their partners questions such as: "What is the effect of this character's actions? What is the cause? What would you do if you were in his place? What did I do when I couldn't read that big word? Let me read on so we can find more examples of cause and effect." She continues to model think aloud strategies for comprehension of story elements and decoding unfamiliar words. Before leaving that text, the teacher asks the students to summarize what they have learned about cause and effect and to think of other stories that contained similar examples.

For the next forty minutes students read a different novel and participate in teacher directed, individual, partner and team reading, discussion, and writing activities. First, the teacher sets the purpose for reading a new selection (finding other examples of cause and effect) and shows some objects and a spot on the map to create a context for the story. She does a quick introduction of the new vocabulary words with their "kid friendly" definitions written on a chart paper and another with the word used in the context of meaningful sentences. The teacher models reading with a couple of paragraphs. Then, students read silently before reading the selection one more time with their partners. Afterwards, the partners help each other with "Treasure Hunts," where the "Treasures" are the main elements of each story: characters, settings, problems, and problem solutions. They discuss these as thoroughly as possible because tomorrow they will have an extended discussion with the teacher and the rest of the class. Some students are finished and are helping each other learn the new vocabulary words. During the last fifteen minutes, some students are reading another book of their choice silently, while others are preparing to present book reports on books they've read at home, hoping to entice their classmates to want to take home and read their books. (p. 5)

The students in the *Alas*/Wings classrooms have already learned to read in their first grade *Lee Conmigo*/Roots classrooms. In the *Lee Conmigo* classrooms, we see teachers using a fast-paced, structured curriculum that teaches phonics in the context of meaningful, interesting text:

Children are reading books to each other in pairs, writing their own compositions in teams, retelling stories and predicting outcomes of stories that have been read to them. A puppet named "Alphie" brings out a letter of the day and a silly sentence using that letter: Mimí mira mi moño marrón en mi mesa de muñecas. The children play many games with the "m" sounds, shape and name and then integrate them into words. The teacher's instruction is upbeat, fast-paced, and varied. Students are constantly involved in the lesson, chanting, singing, writing letters in the air and on each other's backs, all responding on cue to teachers' many questions. (Slavin, 1995, p. 4)

EPT uses the same approach and methods as Success for All, with small exceptions due to linguistic differences between English and Spanish. EPT uses more of a whole-language approach with prekindergarten and kindergarten children (centers, emergent writing, teachers reading of big books and trade books, etc.) and also integrates phonemic awareness and the alphabetic principle, and story retell. Kindergarten children begin reading instruction during the second half of the year and continue where they left off in the first grade. First-grade teachers concentrate on word recognition through syllabic segmentation, sound–letter correlation, story retell, comprehension, and story-related writing. Second-grade reading strategies emphasize more comprehension reading strategies, first modeled by teachers reading aloud and then with different texts by students reading individually and with partners. Reading comprehension skills are explicitly taught through additional materials. Writing is taught through story-related activities and composition strategies. Children in Grades 3 to 6 continue to develop reading and writing skills through similar approaches.

Eclectic Approach or Popular Techniques to Reading in Spanish

Some of the reading strategies and techniques most commonly used in the eclectic classrooms are as follows: *método alfabético* (alphabetic method); *método onomatopéyico* (onomatopoeic method); *método fónico o fonético* (the phonics or phonetic method); *método silábico* (syllabic method); *método de palabras generadoras* (generative word method); *método global* (global method); and *el método léxico* (lexical method). Although they are labeled as methods, some or most of these techniques are integrated into the most prevalent methods: *el método ecléctico* (eclectic method); *el lenguage integral o método integral* (whole language); and *Éxito Para Todos* (Success for All). The following are a few examples used to further illustrate how they look within these models.

El Método Alfabético y El Método Onomatopéyico *(Phonemic/Phonological Awareness)*

Eclectic Traditional.   The teacher writes three words on the board, *mamá* (mother), *mano* (hand), and *ama* (he/she loves). Then the teacher reads each word in the following manner and the students repeat as she points to each letter with her finger: "eme" (m) "a" (a) "eme" (m) "a" (a)—"mama." The problem with saying the name of the letter instead of the sound is that the students will soon stumble upon words such as *hijo* (son). The child would pronounce "hache" (h), "i" (i), "jota" (h), "o" (o) which put together would sound "hacheijotao." For phonemic awareness the teacher shows a picture of monkeys in a cage surrounded by a group of laughing people. The teacher asks What are the people doing? (laughing) What sound are the people making? (ja, ja, ja) What sound are the monkeys making (ji, ji, ji).

Eclectic Whole Language.   Rather than learning letter names and sounds by spelling out individual words, students have the alphabet displayed in the room and books about the alphabet are there for students to refer to as they do their own writing (Freeman & Freeman, 1999; pp. 73–75). Children listen to poems and rhymes about the alphabet and look at the illustrations, which depict an object with that beginning sound. Children make up their own alphabet text for each letter and then illustrate the pages. Sometimes a whole class works on a big book and all the children illustrate pages or help cut out pictures from magazines to paste on the letter pages. These pages are then laminated, and the book remains in the classroom for children to refer to as they wish.

The teacher and children read a predictable book about farm animals. The children are encouraged to make the sounds of the farm animals in readers' theatre followed by the writing of their own stories following similar patterns. Rhymes and songs provide additional opportunities to use and listen to the sounds of language.

Same Techniques in Éxito Para Todos.   In pre- and kindergarten grades, children distinguish and identify the letters of the alphabet through phonological awareness (understanding that spoken words are composed of smaller units of sound) through learning poetry, fingerplays, and songs that are alliterative or rhyme; letter investigation, which is finding objects in the classroom whose names begin or end with the same sound or analyzing their names and objects labeled throughout the classroom, then charting their discoveries; doing clapping activities and playing games to identify the syllables in words; singing the alphabet song with accompanying motions; and doing shared reading with the teacher.

Shared reading in EPT/SFA focuses on the reading of rhythmic, repetitious, and enjoyable text. It gives children an opportunity to become the reader very early in their reading process by incorporating rereading, choral responding, and the teacher's demonstration of the conventions of reading.

In the first grade, children continue to sing an alphabet song, which is followed by a series of activities centering on the names and sounds of the letters. *Escuchando el sonido* (listening to the sound) is first introduced with the riddle of the day that utilizes the sound of the letter in various word variations (*Mimí mira mi moño marrón en mi mesa de muñecas*). The new sounds are introduced in two ways: first by saying the word, then by saying the initial syllable several times. The next game is called *Presentación de dibujos y objetos* (presenting pictures and objects), where pictures and objects beginning with the new sound are introduced by the teacher while saying the word and initial syllable. The students practice without the teacher. The game called *Juego de dos dibujos* (two picture game) helps students practice the sound and discriminate that sound from others. The next game, *Haciendo el sonido* (making the sound), shows students how to make a "pure" sound for that letter. Up to now, the name of the letter has not been used, only the sound. The next game, *Presentación de la forma* (presentation of the letter formation), helps students listen to, separate the sounds, and see the formation of the letter and use its name. This is followed by *Practicando la forma* (practicing letter formation) through a chant and multisensory activities that guide the student to form the letter while associating the sound.

Los Métodos Fónetico y Silábico
(The Phonetic and Syllabic Methods)

Eclectic Traditional.   The teacher has a pocket chart with cards. One card has only the letter "a" on it. Some cards have pictures of objects beginning with the letter "a" such as *abeja* (bee), *astronauta* (astronaut), and *avión* (airplane). The teacher introduces the "a" and shows pictures of the words that begin with "a." She asks some of the students to say the name of the pictures and if the name of the picture begins with the sound of the "a" to put the picture on the same line as the "a." A problem with this phonetic method is that words are usually taught in isolation without relevance to what the teacher and students are reading (Freeman & Freeman, 1997, pp. 80–81).

Other teachers prefer to use a syllabic method where the sounds of the five vowels are usually taught first. Then words are learned by teaching syllables and putting the syllables together into words. A letter is joined with the vowels and students repeat ma, me, mi, mo, mu. These syllables are then put into words, such as, mamá, mimo, memo, or mami. Next, these words are put into sentences: *Mi mamá me mima. Mi mamá me ama. Amo a mi mamá* (My mother pampers me. My mother loves me. I love my mother). The syllabic method is taught sequentially. Each lesson builds on the one before by adding a new consonant. For example, the second lesson would add words with both "m" and "p," so that students would read sentences like *Mamá ama a papá* (Mother loves father). The problem with the syllabic method is that there is the danger of mechanical learning, especially if the material is taught too quickly or if it is too easy or too difficult (Freeman & Freeman, 1999, pp. 85–87).

Eclectic Whole Language.   Proponents of the whole-language approach propose a positive alternative to the phonetic method: the use of "a series of little books with colorful pictures closely tied to the texts, repetitive patterns of language, and interesting themes relevant to young learners . . . [so that] students naturally begin to associate letters and sounds as they work with these books." Whole language proponents also suggest that these emergent literacy series books be used as an alternative for the syllabic method "because the pictures and text are so closely aligned, emergent readers could read the book in chorus as a group, in pairs, or even on their own" (Freeman & Freeman, 1997, pp. 82–88).

Sounds and Letters in Éxito Para Todos/*Success for All.* The *Lee Conmigo* lesson has three major parts—a story telling and retelling (STaR) or listening comprehension unit, the shared story lesson, and a Peabody unit. Each day begins with a 20-min STaR lesson in which the teacher reads and discusses a story. The 50-min shared story lesson (description follows) would be followed by a 20-min Peabody lesson on oral language development. Lessons are presented over 2 or 3 days, depending on the levels and abilities of the students.

1. Metacognitive strategies (understanding the purpose for reading, previewing to prepare for reading, monitoring for meaning, and summarization).
2. Showtime (reading rehearsal and letter formation review).
3. Presenting the story (setting the stage; teacher reads the story, adding comments and asking the students questions, requesting predictions and student experiences).
4. Sound, letter, and word development activities.
   - Alphabet song.
   - Letter presentation (two-picture game, hearing the sound, introducing pictures and objects, making the sound, introducing the shape, practicing the shape).
   - Letter games (say-it-fast, students' words, yes-no game, matching games).
   - Story activities (word presentation, stretch and read, quick erase, say-spell-say, using context, guided group reading, partner reading, share sheets, spelling, stretch and count, stretch and spell, celebration).

Lee Conmigo lessons take advantage of the fact that Spanish is highly phonetic, and use stories written by Latino authors that build on letter sound and syllables one at a time, as do the Reading Roots lessons in English. One significant difference between *Lee Conmigo* and Reading Roots lies in the frequent use of syllables (rather than individual letters) as the major unit of sound in *Lee Conmigo*. The stories are enhanced by context provided in a teacher-read portion of the story. *Lee Conmigo* lessons built around these stories teach both metacognitive and word attack skills using the same presentations, games, routines and strategies as Reading Roots (Slavin, Madden, Dolan, & Wasik, 1996). Knowing the routines facilitates the students' transfer from Spanish into English reading.

METHODS FOR TEACHING
ENGLISH-AS-A-SECOND-LANGUAGE READING

Current Practices and Theorics

A proliferation of ESL methods that began in the 1970s and 1980s are still in use. The direct method used by the Army, which is still reflected in most secondary school ESL textbooks, is a combination of dialogs (the Audio-Lingual method) and grammar-based exercises. The Total Physical Response (Asher, 1977), the Natural Approach (Krashen & Terrell, 1983), Suggestopedia (Lozanov, 1978), and the Language Experience Approach (Nessel & Jones, 1981) are all methods very much in vogue.

Effective ESL and bilingual teachers use explicit skills instruction for certain tasks in reading, quality discussions, and writing. They particularly tailor strategies to enhance understanding and for learning to learn. They also supplement explicit skills instruction with student-directed activities such as cooperative learning, partner reading, and collaborative inquiry. They make instruction comprehensible to English language learners by adjusting the level of English vocabulary and structure, and they teach the vocabulary necessary for comprehension of a text (August & Hakuta, 1997; Calderón, 1991; Calderón, Hertz-Lazarowitz, & Slavin, 1998; Chamot, Dale, O'Malley, & Spanos, 1992; Dianda & Flaherty, 1995; Moll, 1988; Saunders, chap. 5, this volume). Adjustments of English to the current level of the students' proficiency includes:

- Using explicit discourse markers such as *first* and *next*.
- Calling attention to the language in the course of using it.
- Using the language in ways that reveal its structure.
- Providing explicit discussion of vocabulary and structure.
- Explaining and in some cases demonstrating what students will be doing or experiencing.
- Providing students with appropriate background knowledge.
- Building on students' previous knowledge and understanding to establish a connection between personal experience and the subject matter they are learning.

- Using manipulatives, pictures, objects, and film related to the subject matter.
- Teaching strategies for reading comprehension.
- Modeling reading aloud for the students.
- Providing opportunities for practice with peers.
- Using cognitive organizers, graphs, semantic maps, word walls, and word banks.
- Using a balance between instruction in basic and higher order skills at all grade levels.

Validating a child's culture and encouraging peer bonding are two ways that have been identified as effective ways of helping children learn (Hamayan & Pfleger; 1987; Ovando & Collier, 1998). Cultural integration of children's literature into daily readings is also a way of validating this child's culture. In order to help a school become more responsive, a new set of educational principles and dimensions is needed.

A line of research by Moll (1988) and associates draws on the principle that parents and community represent a resource of enormous importance for educational change and improvement. Teachers and researchers interview members of Mexican households to identify the funds of knowledge (information and skills) that are available. These funds of knowledge are used to organize their curriculum. This type of ethnographic research that situates the school experiences of language-minority children within the context of culture, community, and society provides rich information that can influence culturally relevant reading programs.

Rigid and Disjointed Methodologies

The problem with the popular ESL methods is that they are either too rigid or one-dimensional in nature, and second-language learning is far too complex a process to be taught using a single method. Second-language learners vary too much from one another to use these linear methods. They all integrate reading at some point in their continuum, but do not deliberately teach reading.

Too Much Time on Listening and Speaking

With the Natural Approach and other philosophies, teachers are told to respect the students' silent period, that time when the students are not yet ready to speak English. Yet this period sometimes turns into a pause in the development of language, cognition, and reading much longer than necessary (Calderón, 1999). Methods need to be found that respect the student's period of getting comfortable with English and still help that student progress through that period in a timely fashion.

Basals

The basal textbook process for reading is probably the most commonly used to teach English reading to ELL students. During the past two textbook adoption cycles, textbook publishers have concentrated on compiling English anthologies of children's literature with activities closely related to whole-language approaches. Most publishers have an ESL version to accompany the Spanish and English series. Some are beginning to emphasize more direct skill instruction in reading, but for the most part, the following sequence of activities appears in most. The process is basically the same for all grade levels, with the expectation that the teacher will conduct most of the reading and writing activities for the students in the lower levels. The basal reading process is usually as follows:

1. Begin each lesson with a piece of literature, asking students to make predictions.
2. Brainstorm what the students know about the theme.
3. Read the book. As you read, stop and ask students to predict what will happen next. Use oral cloze to have students predict what word or phrase will come next.
4. After reading, ask students questions about the story. Use graphic organizers to keep track of the discussion.
5. Reread the selection in a small group session, having the student read the words. Accept all attempts at trying to read the text. Some students will retell the story while others will read it. Use cloze techniques and ask students to track the words while you read. Have students listen to an audio cassette of the selection.
6. A follow-up activity might be an art project related to the selection; flannel-board characters to retell the story; sequencing a set of relevant pictures; dictating or writing a summary of the story; writing a variation of the story, publishing, and illustrating it; holding a literature discussion with a peer; creating a drama; or researching more about the theme.

The follow-up activity for writing instruction is typically described as follows:

7. Brainstorm to create word banks.

8. Brainstorm to create semantic maps.

9. Conduct a Language Experience Approach with wordless books, story summaries, literature, or content logs.

10. Ask students to write in their dialog journals, logs, or writer's workshop.

11. Ask students to draft ideas using their best guesses for spelling, read to peer or teacher for feedback.

12. Edit with the student. Teach one or two writing conventions.

13. Publish the piece by transcribing the student's words into conventional print.

14. Ask student to read the writing.

15. When students are familiar with the story, they can move into decoding and other word-attack skills. Assign students small passages to break into lines and into words. Cutting sentences into words to scramble and unscramble will help students see word divisions. Discuss letter–sound relationships through songs and games.

Whole-Language/Critical Pedagogy

The field is now quite familiar with the drawbacks of whole language. Nevertheless, there are certain principles of whole language that helped teachers become more sensitive to Latino students (Calderón & Carreón, chap. 4, this volume; Ovando & Collier, 1998).

- Introduction to reading and writing must be meaningful.
- Affect plays an invaluable role in reading and writing. A child who enjoys reading is motivated to read, will read more, and by doing so will be a better reader.
- Reading comprehension in a second language, as in the first, is influenced by the background knowledge and the cultural framework that the reader brings to the text.
- It takes into account the whole learner and builds on his or her total array of skills and abilities (Hamayan & Pfleger, 1987).

Another trend in second language teaching is critical pedagogy (Ada, 1993; Cummins, 1993; Freire & Macedo, 1987; Giroux, 1988; McLaren, 1989; Walsh, 1993). Critical pedagogy is a reaction against "transmission models" for educational reform, which break language down to its component parts (e.g., phonics, vocabulary, grammatical rules) and transmit these parts in isolation from each other. In the transmission models, knowledge is viewed as static or inert, to be internalized and reproduced when required (Cummins, 1993). By contrast, the proponents of collaborative critical inquiry encourage the development of student voice through critical reflection on experiential and social issues. Language and meaning are viewed as inseparable, and knowledge is seen as a catalyst for further inquiry and action. Vygotsky's zone of proximal development (ZPD) is the interpersonal space where minds meet and new understandings can arise through collaborative interaction and inquiry. The focus is on generating knowledge rather than transmitting knowledge. An example of this theory in a reading program is Ada's (1993) *creative reading act*, which contains four phases: the descriptive phase, personal interpretive phase, critical analysis phase, and creative action phase. Because the four phases focus on comprehension and interpretation of various texts, it is presumed that the students know how to read. Its purpose is mainly to relate culturally diverse students' experiences to the texts. Through this critical analysis and interactions with the teacher, the students are empowered to form their identity and have opportunities for educational and social advancement.

Critical pedagogy, liberatory education, constructivism, and whole language are sometimes interchangeable in bilingual settings. The bilingual whole-language movement is based on (a) studies of the natural acquisition of second languages and (b) a learning theory called constructivism. Through the study of how people naturally develop a second language came bilingual whole-language pedagogies (Cummins, 1984; Krashen, 1981; Poplin, 1993). Bilingual whole-language classrooms use a variety of activities in reading and writing workshops. They frequently use thematic interdisciplinary units so that meanings can be constructed in large contexts and easily connected by students to their lives. Literature in the primary and second language is widely used. Students work in cooperative groups. Writing tasks include dialogue and dialectic journals, personal journals, letter writing, invented spellings, and reader response narratives. Music, art, and kinesthetic movements are also integrated. Assessment processes generally consist of portfolios, primary language records, and student self-assessments. Students are grouped across grade levels. Specific skills of reading and writing must be broken down by the learners, not the teacher, and learned as skills are needed within the context of real books and stories and writing activities The skills of spelling, word attack, phonics, and so forth are naturally developed as students read the books they chose and care to write about (Tinajero & Ada, 1993).

Perhaps the strongest precept from the critical pedagogy perspective is the concept of liberation of all peoples from oppression (e.g., economic, social, racial, gender, and political). Racism, sexism, monoculturalism, and the unequal distribution of power and wealth are all topics for the classroom. Socially and politically, students must develop their voice in order to know themselves and be able to act in a larger community and society. These activities frequently involve the community by either bringing the community into class or designing real projects to go out.

There are studies of the contexts for learning language, reading, and writing (Gutierrez, Baquedano-Lopez, Alvarez & Chiu, 1999; Rueda, Goldenberg, & Gallimore, 1992; Saunders et al., 1992). They have focused on a discussion format known as instructional conversation that is grounded in the Vygotskian notions of assisted performance. This approach is characterized by a thematic focus, teachers' efforts to build on students' previous verbal contributions and experiences, and direct teaching. Gutierrez's studies on scripts or pedagogical views of reading and writing help teachers provide enriched contexts for literacy learning through assistance and occasions to use and write elaborated and meaningful discourse. Except for the recent Saunders study (chap. 5, this volume), the use of the critical pedagogy, whole-language, and/or constructivist approaches has not been linked to formal assessment of student learning in comparison studies. However, evidence of learning may be gleaned from the ethnographic studies themselves because they describe the students' interactions across time.

The Language Experience Approach (LEA)

The Language Experience Approach (LEA) is often used with ELL students as part of the whole-language approach or as an entity in itself (Simich-Dudgeon, 1989; Timajero & Ada, 1993). LEA is used to activate the students' English language skills and encourages the students to share their experiences with the class. The teacher writes the students' words verbatim and then teaches the students to read what they have said. LEA integrates some decoding skill-building when the teacher asks the students to identify certain letters or patterns in what she/he has written. This process might take up a whole class period. Because the teacher is limited by what the students dictate, their exposure to vocabulary and reading skills remains quite limited. In many bilingual programs, LEA becomes the closest method to a reading program that students receive. In contrast, Success for All uses this activity only in kindergarten and it is only one ninth of the weekly oral language/reading/writing components students experience. An obvious conclusion is that most ELL students have spent a great deal of time developing oral language proficiency, only to be skipped directly into text reading without sufficient instruction in decoding or reading comprehension.

Cooperative Learning

Cooperative learning has been proven to be an effective vehicle for learning content and learning in a second language (Calderón, 1991; Cohen et al., 1999; McGroarty, 1986; Slavin & Madden, 1995). Whether it is called collaborative learning, peer-assisted performance, or cooperative learning, the social context for learning greatly enhances second language learning. In the last 25 years, research has provided significant evidence that collaborative academic talk is at the heart of the learning experience (Simich-Dudgeon, 1998). Cooperative learning is effective when students have an interesting well-structured task such as a set of discussion questions around a story they have just read, producing a cognitive map of the story, or inventing a puppet show to highlight character traits. Cooperative learning gives students opportunities to test their new language, get feedback from peers, prepare for tests, and learn from others. A comprehensive literacy program benefits from the integration of a variety of systematic use of cooperative activities.

In general, students should work in teams of four members (so they can split into partners) that stay together over a period of 6 to 8 weeks. The groups should be able to earn certificates or other recognition based on the degree to which all of their members have mastered the material being presented (Slavin, Madden, Dolan, & Wasik, 1996). Cooperative learning integrated with research-based reading programs such as SFA/EPT and BCIRC has shown significant effects with Latino students.

The Eclectic Approach

Many bilingual educators believe that the instructor ought to select those materials and methods that best fit the needs of the individual learners. Teachers use their judgment to organize instruction by selecting from an ample array of techniques and materials. The danger thus far has been that teachers may not have participated in well-rounded professional development programs to be able to meet the needs of individual learners through eclectic spontaneous methods. Bilingual program descriptions, journal articles, and books on bilingual teaching methodologies describe effective practices that focus on one activity only. One example of this is Story Retell followed by Writing as Reflection and Real-Life Problem Solving. After listening to a story such as *Hansel and Gretel*, students write about the stepmother's behavior or write a letter to the stepmother.

Then children offer practical suggestions to a problem such as how the woodcutter and his wife could avoid starvation. Another popular method is the use of cognitive or semantic maps after reading a story. There are many varied formats to use for mapping out a story plot, the story elements or attributes of the characters, to integrate several points of view, and to learn about students' experiences. However, these methods used in isolation or as the sole method of reading leave gaps in the students' skill development.

ESL Pull-Out Programs Versus a Comprehensive Program

ESL pull-out programs at the elementary schools are the least effective of all programs (Lucas, 1997; Ovando & Collier, 1998; Thomas & Collier, 1997). The 30 min or so a day can in no way begin to develop the myriad skills that LEP students need. Pull-out ESL programs give the message that a school does not want to fully address the needs of the LEP students. Intensive staff development on second-language acquisition and reading for the teachers with the ELL students would be more beneficial than a pull-out ESL teacher.

Although there are emergent methodologies, what is still needed is a program that connects the learning of English communication skills with beginning reading and writing at an appropriate time and sequence. Otherwise, the separation will continue to delay students' access to reading. Of course, learning to speak English should be a priority before being taught to read English. Oral language development provides the foundation in phonological awareness and allows for subsequent learning about the alphabetic structure of English (Snow et al., 1998). However, a closer connection needs to be developed. Thus far, SFA's ESL version of its Reading Roots program has shown significant results for ESL students as compared to students in other ESL or bilingual programs (Slavin & Madden, chap. 6, this volume), even though it is still in the development stages. The researchers attribute the students' success to the connection of language development with reading and writing.

SFA/EPT is a comprehensive reform program instead of a pull-out program. It provides schools with reading curricula and instructional methods in reading, writing, and language arts in Spanish, English as a second language, and English reading. The curriculum emphasizes a balance between phonics and meaning in beginning reading and extensive use of cooperative learning throughout the grades. One-to-one tutoring, usually from certified teachers, is provided to children who are having difficulties in learning to read, with an emphasis on first graders. The family support program focuses on building positive home–school relations and solving problems such as truancy, behavior problems, or needs for eyeglasses or health services. A program facilitator works with all teachers on continuing professional development and coaching, manages an assessment program to keep track of student progress, and ensures close coordination among all program components. Some schools hire an additional bilingual facilitator to work with ESL and bilingual teachers. Extensive staff development and follow-up implementation visits are provided for each school.

Beyond SFA and *Éxito Para Todos*, no other comprehensive whole-school programs were found in the literature. Reading Recovery (Escamilla, 1994), a research-based tutoring program, is also being widely adopted for Latino students. However, it only addresses the needs of a few students. Slavin and Fashola (1998) identified other effective programs for Latino students, but these are not specific to reading development.

THE TRANSITION OF READING IN SPANISH TO READING IN ENGLISH

The transition from Spanish instruction into English instruction has little research on which to base policy and practice (Goldenberg, 1996; Roberts, 1994; Rogers & Carlo, 1991). School policies differ considerably even within each state. There is confusion between transition into English reading and exit out of the bilingual program into an mainstream English classroom. In some cases, instruction in bilingual classrooms means providing LEP students with minimal reading and writing skills in Spanish and oral fluency and comprehension in English before they are transitioned into all-English instruction. Educators consider the transition period a positive indication that English learners are entering the mainstream, but student achievement declines and referrals to special education increase (Saunders, chap. 5, this volume).

The Saunders and Goldenberg study in a large school district used a 3-year transition program with three phases (Saunders, chap. 5, this volume):

Grades K–2
    Goals: Initial reading and writing proficiency in Spanish and early production of oral English.
    Outcome measures: Existing norm- or criterion-referenced measures.

Pretransition in Grade 3

Goals: Grade-appropriate reading and writing achievement in Spanish and speech emergence in English.

Outcome measures: District transition instrument.

Transition 1 in Grade 4

Goals: Initial reading and writing proficiency in English, academic oral language proficiency in English, and grade-appropriate reading and writing achievement in Spanish.

Outcome measures: Existing norm- or criterion-referenced measures.

Transition II in Grade 5

Goals: Grade-appropriate reading and writing achievement in English.

Outcome measures: Reclassification from LEP to fluent English proficiency (FEP).

In this study, students were randomly assigned to one of four treatment conditions: literature logs only, instructional conversations only, literature logs plus instructional conversations, and a control group who continued with traditional basal instruction. LEP students in the instructional conversation and the literature log plus instructional conversations scored significantly higher than those in the control group. However, the combined effects were not significant for the fluent English proficient students. Even though it did not impact the fluent English proficient students, this study demonstrates that through component building, more effective practices for LEP students can be designed and tested.

A 5-year study on transition looked at 500 LEP students in matched experimental and control groups. The experimental group used the Bilingual Cooperative Integrated Reading and Composition (BCIRC) model (Calderón, 1991; Calderón et al., 1998). The control group used the same basal series as the experimental group, but did not use the BCIRC methods. BCIRC teachers used the same teaching strategies to teach Spanish reading and writing, English oral proficiency, and English reading and writing:

- A variety of strategies for building background before listening to the teacher read aloud to students or before their own reading.
- Cooperative team-building activities to explore the theme, topic, and predictions about the story.
- Listening comprehension activities and story retell to develop understanding of story elements and author's technique.

- Teacher modeling of reading, followed by several partner reading strategies and silent reading.
- Partner discussions, team discussions, and teacher-guided discussions focused on story comprehension.
- Cognitive and semantic mapping of story and character analysis.
- Partner story retell.
- Direct instruction in decoding and comprehension strategies.
- Instruction and practice writing meaningful sentences.
- Story-related writing/composition with various genres.
- Extension activities connected to math, science, social studies, and art.
- Student-selected reading.
- Use of Mexican literature and cross-cultural literature.
- Student creative representations of their readings (dramatization, revised stories and publication).
- Tests on meaningful sentences, vocabulary, dictation, and reading comprehension.
- Performance observation of reading fluency, discussion fluency and quality, decoding, and comprehension skills.

Twice as many BCIRC students met the project's and district's criteria to transition into English at the third and fourth grades than in the control group. Students in BCIRC scored significantly higher than the control group on the state's standardized tests in Spanish and English, and on the district's criterion-referenced test. Component building (Slavin, 1984) for CIRC had already proven its effectiveness with English speakers. This 5-year study put together the ESL/Spanish components to test BCIRC's effectiveness with Spanish and ESL readers. BCIRC became the basis for the *Alas/Wings*, the Grades 2–6 Spanish version of Reading Wings for the Success for All/*Éxito Para Todos* program (Madden et al., 1996).

A new study on transition commissioned by the Office of Bilingual Education and Minority Language Affairs is now looking at the specific items that facilitate or impede transfer from Spanish reading into English reading in Success for All/*Éxito Para Todos* bilingual programs. The Center for Applied Linguistics, Harvard, and Johns Hopkins researchers will be studying which skills are learned and how they transfer through experimental and control groups. The skills of bilingual students will also be compared with those of native English proficient students.

Trends to Transition and Exit Students
From Primary Language

Most teachers transition students as prescribed by their textbook series. Others use language proficiency tests or a district's set of criteria. In either case, it has been up to the educators' best guess to decide when students reach a readiness level and the precise time of transition. Until the studies in progress give us more specific information, the schools will continue to transition students mainly based on the number of bilingual teachers available or such other issues unrelated to students' best interests.

TEACHING READING THROUGH CONTENT ESL

Another trend in the field is to teach English as a second language in the context of learning content. In the sheltered English or ESL content approaches, the ESL curriculum is designed around content-area themes with content objectives as well as language objectives. The focus is on teaching and learning content rather than language or reading. Adolescent students lacking literacy skills must develop them as quickly as possible so that they can use reading and writing as learning tools to acquire the concepts and skills they have missed by not having had access to formal schooling in their native countries (Chamot et al., 1999; Echevarria, 1998; Waxman et al., 1994). Although research points to the desirability of developing literacy first in young children's native language so that they can transfer reading and writing skills to English, little is known about the most effective instructional approaches for adolescent students (Chamot et al., 1999; Duran et al., 1995).

Recognizing that English language learners at the secondary level must do more than learn English, many programs go beyond offering ESL classes to include academic content classes taught through specially designed academic instruction in English (Lucas, 1997; Walqui; in press). Terms such as *sheltered instruction, content-based ESL, integrating language and content instruction*, and, in California, Specially Designed Academic Instruction in English (SDAIE), are used to describe these approaches. In such programs, students learn English through content, thus contextualizing language learning, and they learn content through English, thus preventing them from falling further behind in their development of content knowledge than would otherwise be the case, especially for older youths whose U.S.-born peers are already learning complex content in school (Crandall, 1993; Faltis & Arias, 1993; Lucas, 1997; Short, 1993).

The effectiveness of such programs depends on the preparation of teachers to provide instruction in English without oversimplifying the academic content. Few teachers have had this extensive training. There are two projects currently in progress to train teachers on instructional methodologies and curriculum development in order to develop more student-appropriate materials (Chamot et al., 1999; Crandall, 1993). These studies hold great promise for the field of Latino adolescent literacy development.

Once again, the focus is away from direct teaching of reading, although the students are supposed to be learning social studies, science, and math in the process of learning English. A common complication at the secondary school level is that the ESL teachers also need to be well versed in all the content areas in order to effectively teach content and language. This leaves little time to teach the basic reading skills that are most likely missing.

READING DEVELOPMENT IN TWO-WAY BILINGUAL PROGRAMS

Equal Status to Home Language and English

Two-way bilingual or dual-immersion programs integrate language-minority and language-majority students for instruction in Spanish and English. The popularity of two-way bilingual programs is based on the high status it provides for both English-speaking students and Spanish-speaking students. The components typically attributed to two-way bilingual programs are: integrated language and literacy; team teaching by mainstream and bilingual teachers; use of cooperative learning; use of interdisciplinary thematic units; equal status for minority and majority languages; and high level of parental involvement. They are seen as enrichment instead of remedial programs (Christian, 1994; Lindholm, 1994; Pellerano et al., 1998).

Integrated Language and Literacy

The programs also integrate the teaching of language with literacy and content for both languages. Thematic interdisciplinary units are the preferred means to integrate language, culture, content, and students. The result is typically high achievement for both groups of students.

Many programs showed evidence of positive language proficiency and academic achievement outcomes for both native and nonnative English speakers, but most of these studies used designs in which there was no comparison group. When comparison groups are available, evaluations typically show that English-language learners in two-way programs outperform those in other programs (August & Hakuta, 1997; Christian, 1994).

Planned Designs

Despite the popularity and theoretical justification for two-way bilingual programs, there has not been uniformity in the programs that have been implemented. The program designs vary considerably across sites. One variation is called the 90–10 approach because 90% of instruction is provided in the non-English language in the first years of the program. Students from the two language groups are integrated in the same classrooms to receive instruction. Another variation is the 50–50 model where instruction from kindergarten to sixth grade is conducted on a 50–50 percentage of daily instruction by two teachers team teaching. One teacher is bilingual certified and the other monolingual with special training in second-language instruction.

Although flexibility is clearly needed to adapt any program to local conditions, there has been little research directed at understanding the variations and consequences of programmatic decisions. In one study, it was recorded that teachers did not actually adhere to the 90–10 or the 50–50 time frames. The reading strategies in these programs have been scarcely described. More thick descriptions are needed, particularly from those that have sustained positive student outcomes.

More Attention to Teacher Development

Two-way bilingual programs work best when a bilingual and monolingual teacher work together to deliver instruction in both languages (Calderón & Carreón, 1994). For this team teaching to be at its best, extensive staff development is needed throughout the school year. The school's organizational structures for teacher support also need to be in place: principal support, provision of structured time for teacher collegial learning, curriculum development, and adjustments (Joyce & Showers, 1988).

One drawback is that university teacher credentialing programs do not prepare bilingual and monolingual teachers for this type of teaming and knowledge background. Therefore, the schools need to invest considerably to make this program work.

Promise and Problems

Two-way bilingual programs are the most promising programs for ELLs (as well as native English speakers) because they are seen as enrichment programs rather than remedial. This means that they place more importance on excellence in academics and biliteracy. There is equal status for both languages. LEP students are integrated with English speakers; therefore they have more quality interaction with English role models. By the same token, Spanish speakers become the role models for the students learning Spanish as a second language. This reciprocal teaching not only develops learning strategy and rehearsal, but also helps to develop self-esteem. Well-articulated programs such as these foster closer home–school cooperation. Finally, the goal and collective vision of excellence engenders more staff development opportunities.

BUILDING ON HOME LITERACY EXPERIENCES

Research emphasizes the importance and positive effects of Latino parental role in schools (Delgado-Gaitan, 1990; Moll, 1992). These studies and others also remind us that schools value a certain type of parental participation and may unwittingly punish parents who fail to contribute in the culturally prescribed way. Researchers such as Moll and Delgado-Gaitan place the responsibility on the school and describe the role of the school and teacher in building strong school–home relations. However, guidebooks such as "Starting out Right" (National Research Council, 1999) have not existed in Spanish to help parents and teachers connect through literacy.

Books and Breakfast and Xochicalli

The closest to a model for the family literacy workshops such as "Books and Breakfast" and "Chips and Chapters" provided by Success for All's programs (Slavin, Madden, Dolan, & Wasik, 1996). These workshops are designed to bring children, parents, and teachers together to read the books children are currently reading in their classrooms and to model ways of interacting with or listening to children as they read. As part of the Family Support program, these workshops are complemented with other activities that help parents connect with the school, such as "A Second Cup of Coffee" and a series of family support services that connect parents with social and community services beyond the school. A variation of this is the *Éxito Para Todos* Latino version of the SFA family literacy programs called Xochicalli, which is more in tune with Latino culture (Calderón & Berrúm, 1999). This program also helps parents of adolescents in secondary schools by dealing with other issues such as violence prevention, staying in school, and life aspirations.

HIPPY

The Home Instruction Program for Preschool Youth (HIPPY) has taken literacy training for parents into their homes for years. Their Spanish program has been particularly helpful for Latino parents. The hands-on instruction in the home is a valuable option for many Latino mothers. Unfortunately, the program is not widely implemented in all the states.

Integral Part of the Reading in English Program

The messages from these programs is that parents want to be involved in the literacy development of their children, but appreciate a systematic, comprehensive program that lets them know how valuable they are to the school and their children's learning. Schools need to develop home–school literacy workshops or viable approaches as an integral part of their school's reading program.

COMBINED ELEMENTS OF CURRICULA AND METHODOLOGIES USED TO TEACH READING IN ENGLISH

From the review of the literature one can glean that the best way to ensure reading success for Latino ELLs is through a comprehensive program that combines all the elements listed above. From such benchmark publications as *Preventing Early Reading Difficulties* (Snow et al., 1998), *Starting Out Right* (National Research Council, 1999), and *Every Child Reading: An Action Plan* (Learning First Alliance, 1998), program developers can use guidelines that address reading difficulties for LEP students as well. However, based on the review of reading programs for Latino students, these guidelines must be complimented with the other elements listed next. Without these, the field will be addressing reading for second-language-learning Latino students only partially. These elements from the review are briefly summarized next.

Use of Primary Language

The use of native language was prominent among the rigorous studies of effective projects in this review and in the studies identified by August and Hakuta (1997), Fashola et al. (1997), and Slavin and Fashola (1998). There is enough evidence, and more to come (Thomas & Collier, in progress; August, Carlo, & Calderón, in progress), that will confirm the need for developing a strong reading foundation in Spanish before students transition into all-English reading. When quality instruction in Spanish is not possible, a strong ESL reading program may be the next best thing, if it is comprehensive enough.

Reading Materials

Reading materials should include more Latino literature and be more culturally relevant. If programs are developed, they should be from a Latino student perspective. ELL students will need well-written and engaging texts that include the words they can decipher applying their emerging language and reading skills in English. Engaging books may mean using pictures or "readles" that represent words students cannot yet read. Including teacher text on each page, which tells part of the story but is read by the teacher, can enhance the interest and make simple books more meaningful. Eventually, the teacher text disappears. Some student independent reading books need to be slightly below their reading level in order to avoid frustration and begin to develop confidence and love of reading. Others need more challenging literature to progress at a faster pace.

Literature is one of the best vehicles for learning a language. It can also serve as a cultural bridge between the new and the native language. A variety of ethnic literature can also serve to develop cross-cultural understanding and respect for different talents and ethnic groups. Specific lessons can be written for this purpose.

Teachers need a variety of materials (picture storybooks, big books, novels, etc.) at every grade level for different teaching purposes, such as for concepts of print, some to read aloud by teachers to teach listening comprehension and thinking skills, others for students to develop fluency, and others for pleasure reading. They'll need sets of increasingly complex material. The ESL reading material will need to be adjusted to meet the levels of English proficiency. A balanced literacy program needs a variety of texts.

Background and Vocabulary Building for Beginning Reading

All classrooms should be designed to stimulate verbal interaction, to instruct vocabulary, and to encourage talk about books. Background building of concepts and unfamiliar cultural norms and cultural knowledge should be discussed as part of a prereading, during reading, and after reading activity. Word banks, word walls, and vocabulary games are all part of comprehension.

Developing Listening Comprehension and Higher Order Thinking Skills

Teachers read aloud to students from books that are slightly beyond the students' reading level. Through expressive reading and discussion about characters, plot, setting, themes, and literary devices, students learn comprehension strategies and vocabulary. These discussions facilitate information processing by assisting students in making connections among story elements, genres, content, structure, and author's craft. During 20 min of daily interactive reading, the teachers model word-attack strategies such as sounding out, rereading, reading the whole sentence, predicting, and other think-aloud techniques. After reading, the teacher and students summarize what they learned about the elements of the story and use a variety of means to retell the story.

When students are guided by their teachers through these comprehension activities, they learn how to transfer and use these strategies as they begin to read on their own. By then, they have also developed a rich receptive vocabulary as well as a process for analyzing literature. The transfer will be easier if they first learn the strategies in Spanish.

Phonemic Awareness, Phonics, Decoding, and Word Identification

To read in English, ELLs must know how to blend isolated sounds into words and how to break words into their component sounds. If students in first grade or in the upper grades do not know their letters and sounds, they will need direct instruction on these. Phonemic awareness is a precursor to reading. Phonemes are the basic speech sounds that are represented by letters of the alphabet, several of which are different in Spanish and English. Students need experience with rhyming words to help them distinguish the sounds between one alphabet and the other. Recognition of letters and sounds can be applied by writing simple stories. Just as kindergarten and first-grade monolingual English children practice writing with invented spelling, ELL students also need time to experiment with the new language.

A strong phonemic awareness program must be complemented with a proper balance between phonics and meaning. In the past, LEP students have had little in the way of phonics instruction. Even when students learned to read in their native language, their transition into English reading probably left gaps caused by contrasting phonemics of the two languages. Because failure to learn to use spelling–sound correspondence to read and spell words is shown to be the most frequent and debilitating cause of reading difficulty, we can guess why most Latino students are failing. In addition to elementary programs, special programs for middle and high school LEP students need to be developed that provide a balance between phonics and meaning.

Strategies for Reading Fluency, Comprehension, and Study Skills

Instruction in the use of cognitive reading strategies and study skills will help counter Padrón's finding that students' lack of success causes them to develop a "learned helplessness." That is, low-achieving students often have a low self-concept and therefore believe that they are not capable of learning. Consequently, strategy instruction needs to include techniques that help students learn how to learn, such as strategies to use before reading, while reading, and after reading. These strategies will facilitate their reading process and develop confidence in their ability to learn.

Types of Reading

There are various reading strategies in addition to the commonly used small-group round-robin reading. Round-robin reading or calling on individual students to read out loud for all their peers to hear is probably detrimental for a second-language learner. Strategies that are not threatening enhance self-confidence in reading and help the student learn to read faster. Some of these strategies are as follows:

- Teacher models reading and students track silently.
- Shared reading with big books, where teacher reads, points out conventions of reading, and students join in at certain intervals.
- Interactive reading where teacher reads aloud and discusses the story, and helps students make connections to their experiences.
- Partner reading where students read aloud with a partner, alternating sentence by sentence, and later paragraph by paragraph or page by page.
- Shadow reading, where three students read together; the one who needs the most help initially shadows (repeats) what the other partners are reading.

A variety of reading strategies will give students sufficient practice in reading to achieve fluency with different kinds of texts.

Independent Reading/Pleasure Reading

The program to be developed should promote independent reading during school and outside of school by such means as daily at-home reading assignments, encouraging parent involvement, and having books available that are of interest to the students. Parents can be asked to send in signed forms indicating that children have done their home reading. Many Latino parents do not read in English; therefore, the students can read to them. Schools can have volunteer listeners for the students who cannot get assistance with reading in English in their homes.

A portion of class time should be set aside for students to select and read whatever they chose independently. They can share what they've read through oral presentations, summaries, role plays, or other activities that show their creativity and individual talents.

Related Writing

Creative and expository writing instruction should begin as early as possible. Writing gives second-language learners opportunities to use their new language competence, even if it is barely emerging. Research shows invented spelling to be a powerful means of leading students to internalize phonemic awareness and the alphabetic principle. Students can gradually be taught spelling patterns and frames for rendering final written products. Through our projects, we have found that writing becomes easier for second-language learners when it is connected with story-related writing. That is, after they have read, discussed, and worked with a story, they have sufficient vocabulary and patterns to use to write their own stories. By using patterns from the story, they learn good models for writing.

Types of Writing

After second grade, it is important to teach students to use a variety of writing techniques: descriptive, persuasive, functional, poetry, and so on. The variety of genre can be taught by providing frames with sentence starters and paragraph transition markers such as *afterward, unfortunately,* and *sometimes.*

Learning logs and journals provide students with nonthreatening opportunities to write about topics of their own choice. Team stories or team books also provide a social context for feedback and cooperative construction of creative products. Other techniques such as writing meaningful sentences, 2-minute edits, and short dictations have been found effective.

Integrating Language Arts and Language Learning

In lieu of separating ESL from reading and language arts, all of the skills typically taught in the three separate sections should be integrated into a 90- or 120-min block. Critical skills for listening, speaking, spelling, grammar usage, critical thinking, rich discussions, literature analyses, and comprehension can best be taught through a string of activities around one single storybook. A 5- to 7-day cycle of well-designed components can tap all the skills. As cycles are repeated with other stories, students scaffold information, vocabulary, and skills.

Interdisciplinary and Integrated Reading

Beyond the 90- to 120-min language arts block, thematic interdisciplinary units help second-language learners anchor their new learnings to a greater extent. Through articulation of themes, the sciences and math concepts will relate through a redundant vocabulary and well-crafted sequence of concept development.

Role of Interaction and Peer-Assisted Performance: Cooperative Learning

Cooperative learning is effective when it is embedded in a comprehensive reading program and students have interesting well-structured tasks such as a set of discussion questions around a story they have just read, producing a cognitive map of that story, or inventing a puppet show to highlight character traits. Cooperative learning gives students opportunities to test their new language, get feedback from peers, prepare for tests, and learn from others.

Tutoring

With a quality program, most children can learn to read by the end of first grade in their primary language. Nevertheless, there will be some that need extra help through tutoring. If this is the case for primary-language literacy, then we can expect that for learning to read in a second language, more students will need tutoring. One-to-one tutoring, closely aligned with classroom instruction (not as a separate program), has been found to be effective. Well-trained certified teachers or paraprofessionals can help struggling students through 20-min daily interventions.

Instructional Conversations

The program should provide, throughout the course of a literature unit, opportunities for the teacher and students to discuss the story, log entries, related personal experiences, and the theme for the unit. The frequency of discussions provides the teacher with the opportunity to hear students articulate their understanding of the story, its themes, and their related personal experiences and to challenge students while helping to enrich and deepen their understandings. Facilitated by the teacher, the small-group discussions, referred to as instructional conversations, allow students to hear, appreciate, and build on each others' experiences, knowledge, and understandings.

Print Environment

Second-language classrooms need to be cluttered with print: word walls, cognitive maps, samples of meaningful sentences, writing prompts, writing frames, and displays of students' work. The more vocabulary that is exposed, the more they will borrow to use in their oral and written discourse. Each time a teacher introduces a story, key vocabulary words with the teacher's student-friendly definitions should be posted. Teachers need to model writing as much as possible.

Story Telling and Story Retelling

Second-language learners need practice with speech conventions. They need to learn to structure a speech narrative with a beginning, middle, and ending or conclusion, main point, and so forth. Opportunities for story telling or retelling of a story give students practice with their new vocabulary, thoughts, and organization of the production of that thinking. They can practice with their partner or in the safety of their teams. They can also hold a private conference with the teacher for guidance and feedback.

Celebration of Reading

Motivation for reading can be built in at the end of a week by assigning two to four students to show off their reading skills to the class. The teacher should be careful to let the students know ahead of time so that they will prepare. Another way to celebrate is by inviting parents for refreshments and to listen to their children read.

Frequent Systematic Assessments

Assessment is a key and sensitive issue for educators of Latino and language minority students in general (Thomas & Collier, 1997; O'Malley & Valdez Pierce, 1996). Assessment for Latino students means finding a combination of assessments for the following purposes: placement decisions, ongoing classroom assessments, assessments for exit or reclassification, assessments for bilingual special education, and measuring academic success and linguistic success (Ovando & Collier, 1998).

Assessments in a reading program should be frequent and progressively crafted in order to measure student progress and effectiveness of the instructional practices. Reading tests given at 8-week intervals enable teachers to determine who is to receive tutoring, to change students' reading groups, to suggest other adaptations in students' programs, and to identify students who need other types of assistance. It also helps teachers get together and gauge the effectiveness of their teaching and of the program intervention (Slavin, Madden, Dolan, & Wasik, 1996).

Home–School Literacy

Family literacy programs should expand the scope of literacy beyond the classroom and reach into the homes to provide parents opportunities to learn together with their children. Teachers can model how to employ parent–child interactions that build literacy habits and reinforce what students are learning in the classrooms (Mulhern, Rodriguez-Brown, & Shanahan, 1994).

Technology

A research area of increasing interest has been the use of the computer for the acquisition of a second language and biliteracy. Several studies have attempted to test the possibility of the use of technology-mediated language development (Arias & Bellman, 1994; DeVillar, Faltis, & Cummins, 1994; Gonzalez-Edfelt, 1994; Sayers, 1994; also see work by Mehan and Vazquez). These studies provide practical and theoretical insights into the learning process through technology.

Schoolwide Programs

The research so far offers a variety of venues for addressing the multiple issues of literacy for Latino students. A next step might be to use a strategy Slavin (1984) called *component building*. That means implementing a long program of field experimental research on classroom practices that are or could become components of complete programs, but are separable elements in themselves. They must be evaluated rigorously and systematically in order to determine which produce the strongest and most reliable effects on student learning, which produce negligible effects, and which produce no or even negative effects.

The English literacy program for second-language learners will need to organize and test components that provide a balanced program for developing listening, speaking, and writing skills. Direct instruction and student activities should consist of phonemic awareness, phonics, discourse patterns, comprehension skills, higher order analyses, and writing. These learning opportunities should be structured around Latino literature and culturally relevant materials.

"Giving a child initial reading instruction in a language that he or she does not yet speak can undermine the child's chance to see literacy as a powerful form of communication by knocking the support of meaning out from underneath the process of learning" (Snow et al., 1998, p. 237).

As part of the comprehensive program, supplementary services include tutoring, family support, home literacy component, and a buy-in from the whole school personnel that the education and success of all Latino students are the responsibility of all the teachers and administrators in the school. Therefore, a comprehensive school reform program will most likely be the best recourse. As these programs are designed, they should be tested through rigorous evaluations to ensure program effectiveness.

CONCLUSION AND RECOMMENDATIONS
FOR RESEARCH

Learning to read in English for an ELL is as complex for the student as it is for the teacher and the school system. Many factors come into play: linguistic, cognitive, social, affective, and cultural background. An effective reading program needs to address all factors simultaneously without losing sight of the desired outcomes for the student. This means that the onus of teaching the student to read is not only on the classroom teacher, but also on the school system that selects and implements the reading program, creates other support systems for students and parents, and establishes a quality teacher professional development program.

This chapter has described some of the practices currently in place. Some show great promise; others have not proven to be effective. The science of teaching reading to ELLs is still in its infancy. Some of the questions schools need to ask themselves as they set out to implement a reading program for ELLs are:

1. What instructional methodologies work best for teaching reading to ELLs in bilingual classrooms?
2. What instructional methodologies work best for teaching reading to ELLs in English-only environments?
3. What instructional methodologies work best for teaching reading to ELLs in two-way or dual-language programs?
4. What instructional methodologies work best for teaching reading to older students (4th to 12th grades)?
5. When is it appropriate for ELLs to transfer from native-language instruction in reading into English instruction in reading?
6. How are language development and reading instruction best integrated?
7. How are the rest of the content subject areas integrated or dovetailed with the language/reading development system?
8. In what language should the content subject areas be taught? Until when?
9. What is the best approach and language for teaching early literacy?

These are only a few of the most common questions asked by teachers. As schools discuss reading for ELLs, a discussion of their teachers' development must accompany their new efforts. Some questions schools need to begin with include: What types of professional development do teachers need

1. To develop fluency in the students' native language?
2. To effectively combine language and reading instruction?
3. To effectively combine language, reading and content instruction?
4. To accept responsibility for every student's success?
5. To work in Teachers Learning Communities to improve their practice continuously?
6. To move their schools into compliance, equity and excellence?

As teachers acquire new perspectives, attitudes, and skills, these must be complimented with new attitudes, perspectives, and skills of the school and district administrators. Without a strong staff development program for administrators, we can only hope for the type of administrative support and leadership needed in the schooling of ELLs that will attain success for both ELLs and their teachers.

The effective reading models described in this chapter have been used in a variety of ELLs learning contexts. We know that these models begin to address the questions just posted for both students and teachers. Although there is still ample room for refinement of current models, we also know that schools can obtain great results from them right now—if they want them.

ACKNOWLEDGMENTS

This chapter was originally written for the Southwest Educational Development Laboratory (SEDL) under the auspices of the U.S. Office of Bilingual Education and Minority Language Affairs. The author thanks Wes Hoover, Director of SEDL, for his encouragement and support of this chapter.

REFERENCES

Citations with an asterisk are those articles/studies that met the following criteria:

1. Are English reading strategies that were specifically designed for use with Latino students.
2. Present rigorous evaluation evidence in comparison to control groups showing significant and lasting impacts on the achievement of Latino students.
3. Have evidence of effectiveness in dissemination sites, and replicability.

All others deal with general principles of reading in English for limited English proficient students and/or strategies and promising practices, but lack data and descriptions of rigorous studies to back up assumptions.

Ada, A. F. (1993). Mother-tongue literacy as a bridge between home and school cultures. In J. V. Tinajero, & A. F. Ada (Eds.), *The power of two languages: Literacy and biliteracy for Spanish-speaking students* (pp. 158–163). New York: Macmillan/McGraw-Hill.

Anstrom, K. (1998). *Academic achievement for secondary language minority students: Standards, measures and promising practices.* National Clearinghouse for Bilingual Education. http://www.ncbe.gwu.edu/ncbepubs/reports/acadach.htm.

Arias, A., & Bellman, B. (1994). Pedagogical and research uses of computer-mediated conferencing. In R. De Villar, C. Faltis, & J. P. Cummins (Eds.), *Cultural diversity in schools: From rhetoric to practice* (pp.). New York: SUNY.

*August, D., & Hakuta, K. (Eds.). (1997). *Improving schooling for language-minority children: A research agenda.* Washington, DC: National Academy Press.

*August, D., & Hakuta, K. (Eds.). (1998). *Educating language-minority children.* Washington, DC: National Academy Press.

Basterra, M. del R. (Ed.). (1998). *Excellence and equity for language minority students: Critical issues and promising practices.* Chevy Chase, MD: Mid-Atlantic Equity Consortium.

Bellenger, L. (1979). *Los métodos de la lectura.* Barcelona: Oikos-Tau.

Berman, P., Minicucci, C., McLaughlin, B., Nelson, B., & Woodworth, K. (1995). *School reform and student diversity: Case studies of exemplary practices for LEP students.* Washington, DC: National Clearinghouse for Bilingual Education.

Calderón, M. (1991). Benefits of cooperative learning for Hispanic students. *Texas Research Journal, 2,* 39–57.

Calderón, M. (1994). Mentoring and coaching minority teachers. In R. A. DeVillar, C. J. Faltis, & J. P. Cummins (Eds.), *Cultural diversity in schools: From rhetoric to practice* (pp. 117–144). New York: SUNY.

Calderón, M. (1997). *New insights into staff development for bilingual schools.* Albuquerque, NM: Office of Bilingual Education and Minority Language Affairs' Management Institute.

*Calderón, M. (1998). Adolescent sons and daughters of immigrants: How schools can respond. In K. M. Berman & B. Schneider (Eds.), *The adolescent years: Social influences and educational challenges. Ninety-Seventh Yearbook of the National Society for the Study of Education.* Chicago: University of Chicago Press.

Calderón, M. (1999, March). *Success for Latino students and their teachers.* Keynote speech at the annual meeting of the Teachers of English to Speakers of Other Languages, New York.

Calderón, M., & Berrúm, T. (1999). *Xochicalli: Programa de apoyo familiar en las escuelas.* El Paso, TX: International Academy for Cooperative Learning.

Calderón, M., & Carreón, A. (1994). Educators and students use cooperative learning to become biliterate and bicultural. *Cooperative Learning Magazine, 4,* 6–9.

*Calderón, M., Hertz-Lazarowitz, R., & Slavin, R. (1998). Effects of Bilingual Cooperative Integrated Reading and Composition on students making the transition from Spanish to English reading. *Elementary School Journal, 99*(2), 153–165.

California Department of Education (Ed.). (1981). *Schooling and language minority students: A theoretical framework.* Los Angeles: California State University, Evaluation, Dissemination and Assessment Center.

California Department of Education (Ed.). (1986). *Beyond language: Social and cultural factors in schooling language minority students.* Los Angeles: California State University, Evaluation, Dissemination and Assessment Center.

Chamot, A., Dale, M., O'Malley, M., & Spaos, G. A. (1993). Learning and problem solving strategies of ESL students. *Bilingual Research Journal, 16*(3–4), 1–34.

Chamot, A. U., Keatley, C., & Mazur, A. (1999, April). *Literacy development in adolescent English language learners: Project Accelerated Literacy (PAL).* Paper presented at the Annual Meeting of the American Educational Research Association, Montreal, Canada.

Christian, D. (1994). *Two-way bilingual education: Students learning through two languages.* Washington, DC: Center for Applied Linguistics.

Cohen, A. D. (1993). Researching bilingualism in the classroom. In A. W. Miracle (Ed.), *Bilingualism: Social issues and policy implications.* (pp. 133–148). Athens, GA: University of Georgia Press.

Cohen, E., Lotan, R., Scarloss, B., & Arellano, A. (1999). Complex instruction: Equity in cooperative learning classrooms. In M. Calderón & R. Slavin (Eds.), Building community through cooperative learning. *Theory into Practice, 38*(2), 80–86.

Cole, M. (1996). *Cultural psychology.* Cambridge, MA: Harvard University Press.

Collier, V. P. (1995). *Acquiring a second language for school. Directions in Language & Education # 4:* Washington, DC: National Clearinghouse for Bilingual Education.

Crandall, J. A. (1993). Content-centered learning in the United States. *Annual Review of Applied Linguistics, 13*, 111–126.

Cummins, J. (1984). *Bilingualism and special education: Issues in assessment and pedagogy.* London: Multilingual Matters.

Cummins, J. (1993). Empowerment through biliteracy. In J. V. Tinajero & A. F. Ada (Eds.), *The power of two languages: Literacy and biliteracy for Spanish-speaking students* (pp. 9–25). New York: Macmillan/McGraw-Hill.

Delgado-Gaitan, C. (1990). *Literacy for empowerment: The role of parents in children's education.* Bristol, PA: Falmer Press.

DeVillar, R., Faltis, C., & Cummins, J. (Eds.). (1994). *Cultural diversity in schools: From rhetoric to practice.* Albany: State University of New York Press.

*Dianda, M., & Flaherty, J. (1995, April). *Effects of Success for All on the reading achievement of first graders in California bilingual programs.* Paper presented at the annual meeting of the American Educational Research Association, San Francisco, CA.

Diaz, E., Moll, L., & Mehan, H. (1986). *Bilingual communication skills in classroom context processing.* Washington, DC: National Clearinghouse for Bilingual Education.

Duran, R., Revlin, R., & Havill, D. (1995). *Verbal comprehension and reasoning skills of Latino high school students.* Santa Cruz, CA: National Center for Research on Cultural Diversity and Second Language Learning. http://www.ncbe.gwu.edu/mispubs/ncrcdsll/rr13.htm.

Dubois, M. E. (1995). Lectura, escritura y formación docente. *Lectura y Vida, 16*(2) 5–12.

Echeverria, J. (1998). Preparing text and classroom materials for English-language learners: Curriculum adaptations in secondary school settings. In R. Gersten & R. Jiménez (Eds.), *Promoting learning for culturally and linguistically diverse students: Classroom applications from contemporary research* (pp. 210–229). Pacific Grove, CA: Brooks/Cole.

*Escamilla, K. (1994). Descubriendo La Lectura: An early intervention literacy program in Spanish. *Literacy, Teaching, and Learning, 1*(1), 57–70.

Faltis, C. J., & Arias, M. B. (1993). Speakers of language other than English in the secondary school: Accomplishments and struggles. *Peabody Journal of Education, 69*(1), 6–29.

*Fashola, O. S., Slavin, R. E., Calderón, M., & Duran, R. (1996). *Effective programs for Latino students in elementary and middle schools. Hispanic Dropout Project.* Washington, DC: U.S. Department of Education, Office of Educational Research and Improvement.

*Fashola, O. S., Slavin, R. S., Calderón, M., & Durán, R. (1997). *Effective programs for Latino students in elementary and middle schools* (Report No. 11). Baltimore, MD: Johns Hopkins University, Center for Research on the Education of Students Placed at Risk.

Ferreiro, E. (1994). Diversidad y proceso de alfabetización: De la celebración a la toma de conciencia. *Lectura y Vida, 15*(3), 5–14.

Freeman, Y. S., & Freeman, D. E. (1998). *ESL/EFL teaching: Principles for success.* Portsmouth, NH: Heinemann.

Freire, P., & Macedo, D. (1987). *Literacy: Reading the word and the world.* South Hadley, MA: Bergin & Garvey.

Fullan, M., & Hargreaves, A. (1996). *What's worth fighting for in your school.* New York: Teachers College Press.

García, E. (1998). School reform in the context of linguistic and cultural diversity: Issues of equity and excellence. In M. del R. Basterra (Ed.), *Excellence and equity for language minority students: Critical issues and promising practices* (pp. 1–26). Chevy Chase, MD: Mid-Atlantic Equity Consortium.

General Accounting Office. (1994). *Limited English proficiency: A growing and costly educational challenge facing many school districts.* Washington, DC: Author.

Genesse, F. (1987). *Learning through two languages.* New York: Newbury House.

*Gersten, R., & Baker, S. (1999, April). *Effective instruction for English-language learners: A multi-vocal approach toward research synthesis.* Paper presented at the annual meeting of the American Educational Research Association, Montreal.

Giroux, H. A. (1988). *Teachers as intellectuals: Toward a critical pedagogy of learning.* Granby, MA: Bergin & Garvey.

Goldenberg, C. (1996). The education of language-minority students: Where are we, and where do we need to go? *Elementary School Journal, 96*(3), 361–363.

Goldenberg C., Reese, L., & Gallimore, R. (1992). Effects of literacy materials from school on Latino children's home experiences and early reading achievement. *American Journal of Education, 100*(4), 497–536.

Gonzalez, J., & Calderón, M. (in press). *Mexican pedagogy: The vies of Mexican scholars, practitioners, and intellectuals on the education of Mexican immigrant children in the United States.* Phoenix, AZ: Arizona State University Press.

Goodlad, J. I. (1990). *Teachers for our nation's schools.* San Francisco: Jossey-Bass.

Goodman, K., Goodman, Y., & Flores, B. (1999). Reading in the bilingual classroom: Literacy and biliteracy. http://www.ncbe.gwu.edu/ncbepubs/classics/reading/index.htm. (Original work published 1979)

Gonzalez-Edefeldt, N. (1994). A communicative computer environment for the acquisition of ESL. In R. De Villar, C. Faltis, & J. P. Cummins (Eds.), *Cultural diversity in schools: From rhetoric to practice* (pp. 263–298). New York: SUNY.

Gutierrez, K., Baquedano-Lopez, P., Alvarez, H. H., & Chiu, M. M. (1999). Building a culture of collaboration through hybrid language practices. *Theory Into Practice, 38*(2), 87–93.

Hamayan, E., & Pfleger, M. (1987). *Developing literacy in English as a second language: Guidelines for teachers of young children from non-literate backgrounds.* Silver Spring, MD: National Clearinghouse for Bilingual Education.

Hudelson, S. (Ed.). (1993). *English as a second language: Curriculum resource handbook.* Millwood, NY: Kraus International.

Jensen, E. (1998). *Teaching with the brain in mind.* Alexandria, VA: Association for Supervision and Curriculum Development.

Joyce, B., & Showers, B. (1988). *Student achievement through staff development.* New York: Longman.

Krashen, S. D. (1981). Bilingual education and second language acquisition theory. In California State Department of Education (Ed.), *Schooling and language minority students: A theoretical framework* (pp. 51–82). Los Angeles, CA: Evaluation, Dissemination, and Assessment Center.

Krashen, S. D. (1986). Bilingual education and second language acquisition theory. In California State Department of Education (Eds.), *Schooling and language minority students. A theoretical framework* (pp. 51–82). Los Angeles: California State University, Evaluation, Dissemination and Assessment Center.

Learning First Alliance. (1998). *Every child reading: An action plan.* Washington, DC: Author.

Lindholm, K. (1994). Promoting positive cross-cultural attitudes and perceived competence in culturally and linguistically diverse classrooms. In R. De Villar, C. Faltis, & J. P. Cummins (Eds.), *Cultural diversity in schools: From rhetoric to practice* (pp.). New York: SUNY.

Lucas, T. (1993). What have we learned from research on successful secondary programs for LEP students? *Proceedings of the Third National Research Symposium on Limited English*

Proficient Student Issues: Focus on middle and high school issues. Washington, DC: U.S. Department of Education, Office of Bilingual Education and Minority Languages Affairs.

Lucas, T. (1997). *Into, through, and beyond secondary school: Critical transitions for immigrant youths.* Washington, DC: Center for Applied Linguistics.

Mace-Matluck, B. J., Alexander-Kasparik, R., & Queen, R. M. (1998). *Through the golden door: Educational approaches for immigrant adolescents with limited schooling.* Washington, DC: Center for Applied Linguistics.

*Madden, N., Slavin, R., Farnish, A. M., Livingston, M., Calderón, M., & Stevenson, R. (1996). *Reading Wings: Teacher's manual.* Baltimore, MD: Johns Hopkins University, Center for Research on the Education of Students Placed at Risk.

McGroarty, M. (1986). Educators' responses to sociocultural diversity: Implications for practice. In California State Department of Education (Ed.), *Beyond language: Social & cultural factors in schooling language minority students* (pp. 299–344). Los Angeles, CA: Evaluation, Dissemination and Assessment Center.

McGroarty, M. (1989). The benefits of cooperative learning arrangements in second language instruction. *NABE Journal, 13*(2), 127–143.

McLaren, P. (1993). *Schooling as a ritual performance: Toward a political economy of educational symbols and gestures.* New York: Routledge.

McLaughlin, B., & McLeod, B. (1997). *Educating all our students: Improving education for children from culturally and linguistically diverse backgrounds.* Final Report for the National Center for Research on Cultural Diversity and Second Language Learning, Vol. I. Washington, DC: Center for Applied Linguistics.

*Medina, M. (1993). Spanish achievement in a maintenance bilingual education program: Language proficiency, grade and gender comparisons. *Bilingual Research Journal, 17*(1&2), 57–82.

Moll, L. C. (1988). Educating Latino students. *Language Arts, 64,* 315–324.

Moll, L. C. (1992). Funds of knowledge for teaching: Using a qualitative approach to connect homes and classrooms. *Theory Into Practice, 31*(2), 132–141.

Montero-Seiburth, M. (1999, April). *Review of the literature on Latino academic achievement from secondary to post-secondary education: Policies and trend into the new millennium.* Paper presented at the annual meeting of the American Educational Research Association, Montreal.

National Center for Education Statistics. (1993a). *Language characteristics and schooling in the United States, a challenging picture: 1979 and 1989.* Washington, DC: Government Printing Office.

National Center for Education Statistics. (1993b). *The educational progress of Hispanic students.* Washington, DC: U.S. Department of Education.

National Center for Education Statistics. (1993c). *Dropout rates in the U.S.* Washington, DC: U.S. Department of Education.

National Coalition of Advocates for Students. (1994). *Delivering the promise: Positive practices for immigrant students.* Boston: Author.

National Research Council. (1999). *Starting out right: A guide to promoting children's reading success.* Washington, DC: National Research Council.

Olsen, L. (1994). *The unfinished journey: Restructuring schools in a diverse society.* San Francisco: California Tomorrow.

O'Malley, J. M., & Valdez Pierce, L. (1996). *Authentic assessment for English language learners: Practical approaches for teachers.* Reading, MA: Addison-Wesley.

Ovando, C., & Collier, V. (1998). *Bilingual and ESL classrooms: Teaching in multicultural contexts.* New York: McGraw-Hill.

*Padrón, Y. N. (1992). The effect of strategy instruction on bilingual students' cognitive strategy use in reading. *Bilingual Research Journal, 16*(3&4), 35–52.

Pellerano, C., Fradd, S., & Rovira, L. (1998). *Coral Way Elementary School: A success story in bilingualism and biliteracy.* National Clearinghouse for Bilingual Education. http://www.ncbe.gwu.edu/ncbepubs/discover/discover3.htm.

Poplin, M. S. (1993). Making our whole-language bilingual classrooms also liberatory. In J. V. Tinajero & A. F. Ada (Eds.), *The power of two languages: Literacy and biliteracy for Spanish-speaking students* (pp. 58–70). New York: Macmillan/McGraw-Hill.

Roberts, C. A. (1994). Transferring literacy skills from L1 to L2. *Journal of Educational Issues of Language Minority Students, 13,* 209–221.

Rodriguez, R., Ramos, N., & Ruiz-Escalante, J. (Eds.). (1994). *Compendium of readings in bilingual education: Issues and practices.* San Antonio: Texas Association for Bilingual Education.

Royer, J. M., & Carlo, M. S. (1991). Using the sentence verification technique to measure transfer of comprehension skills from native to second language. *Journal of Reading, 34*(6), 450–455.

Rueda, R., Goldenberg, C., & Gallimore, R. (1992). *Rating instructional conversations: A guide* (Educational Practice Report No. 4). Washington, DC: Center for Applied Linguistics.

Sayers, D. (1994). Bilingual team-teaching partnerships over long distances: A technology-mediated context for intragroup language attitude change. In R. De Villar, C. Faltis, & J. P. Cummins (Eds.), *Cultural diversity in schools: From rhetoric to practice* (pp.). New York: SUNY.

Short, D. J. (1993). *Integrating language and culture in middle school American history classes.* Washington, DC: Center for Applied Linguistics.

Simich-Dudgeon, C. (1998, Summer). *Classroom strategies for encouraging collaborative discussion. Directions in Language and Education* (No. 12). Washington, DC: National Clearinghouse for Bilingual Education.

Simich-Dudgeon, C. (1989). *English literacy development: Approaches and strategies that work with limited English proficient children and adults. Occasional Papers in Bilingual Education* (No. 12). Washington, DC: National Clearinghouse for Bilingual Education.

Skutnabb-Kangas, T., & Cummins, J. (1988). *Minority education: From shame to struggle.* Clevedon, England: Multilingual Matters.

Slavin, R. E. (1984). Component building: A strategy for research-based instructional improvement. *Elementary School Journal, 84,* 225–269.

Slavin, R. E. (1999, April). *How replicable reform models can save America's schools.* Paper presented at the annual meeting of the American Educational Research Association, Montreal.

*Slavin, R. E., & Fashola, O. S. (1998). *Show me the evidence! Proven and promising programs for America's schools.* Thousand Oaks, CA: Corwin.

*Slavin, R. E., & Madden, N. A. (1995, April). *Effects of Success for All on the achievement of English language learners.* Paper presented at the annual meeting of the American Educational Research Association, San Francisco.

*Slavin, R. E., Madden, N. A., Dolan, L. J., & Wasik, B. A. (1996). *Every child, every school: Success for All.* New York: Corwin.

Slavin, R. E., Madden, N., Rice, L., & Calderón, M. (1996–1999). *Success for All Lee Conmigo: Manual del maestro edición en español* (Vol. I–IV). Baltimore, MD: Success for All Foundation.

*Snow, C., Burns, S., & Griffin, P. (Eds.). (1998). *Preventing reading difficulties in young children.* Washington, DC: Committee on the Prevention of Reading Difficulties in Young Children, National Academy Press.

Thomas, W. P. & Collier, V. (1997). *School effectiveness for language minority students.* Washington, DC: National Clearinghouse for Bilingual Education.

Tinajero, J. V. & Ada, A. F. (Eds.). (1993). *The power of two languages: Literacy and biliteracy for Spanish-speaking students.* New York: Macmillan/McGraw-Hill.

University of California Linguistic Minority Research Institute Education Policy Center. (1997). *Review of research on instruction of limited English proficient students.* University of California, Davis. http://lmrinet.ucsb.edu/old/lepexecsum/execsumback.htm.

Walqui, A. (in press.) *Assessment of culturally and linguistically diverse students: Considerations for the twenty-first century.* Aurora, CO: Mid-Continent Regional Educational Laboratory.

U.S. Department of Education. (1992). *The condition of bilingual education in the nation.* Washington, DC: Author.

Walsh, C. (1993). Becoming critical: Rethinking literacy, language, and teaching. In J. V. Tinajero & A. F. Ada (Eds.), *The power of two languages: Literacy and biliteracy for Spanish-speaking students* (pp. 49–57). New York: Macmillan/McGraw-Hill.

Walki, A. (1996). *Access and engagement: Program design and instructional approaches for immigrant students in secondary school.* Washington, DC: Center for Applied Linguistics.

Warren, B., & Rosenbery, A. S. (1995). *"This questions is too easy!" Perspectives from the classroom on accountability in science.* Santa Cruz, CA: National Center for Research on Cultural Diversity and Second Language Learning.

*Waxman, H. C., de Felix, J. W., Martinez, A., Knight, S. L., & Padrón, Y. (1994). Effects of implementing classroom instructional models on English language learners' cognitive and affective outcomes. *Bilingual Research Journal, 18*(3–4), 1–22.

9

The Factors That Place Latino Children and Youth at Risk of Educational Failure

Gilbert Narro Garcia
Office of Educational Research and Improvement
U.S. Department of Education

The American classroom landscape has changed dramatically over the past decade, in large part as a consequence of the increasing diversity among the nation's growing population. There is every indication that student as well as teacher demographics will continue to change well into the 21st century.

Three key developments appear to be of great concern to policymakers and school administrators at both state and local levels: (a) the growing number of students who arrive at school at the beginning and during the year, but are ill-prepared to learn; (b) the growing number of non-native born children and youth who enroll in schools across all grade levels; and (c) the large number of native and foreign-born students who are limited-English proficient (LEP).

Many LEP students grow up speaking languages other than English at home; others grow up in multilingual households; and still others grow up speaking mostly English. Very few children from these households grow up speaking English fluently. Most of them are not proficient enough in English to participate fully in mainstream all-English classrooms; consequently, many of them fail to succeed in school and large numbers of them drop out of school. Furthermore, a high proportion of these students live in high-poverty neighborhoods and attend schools with high concentrations of other poor students.

Although some school districts have addressed these issues and the factors that place children and youth at risk of educational failure head on, there are many others that are still struggling in their efforts to serve LEP students equitably and effectively. The purpose of this chapter is to describe the factors that place LEP students at risk of educational failure. The particular focus is on the subgroup of these students who are Hispanic or Latino.[1] The discussion is especially timely, given the number of state and local school districts engaged in systemic educational reform efforts that are focusing on students who are placed at risk, including those who have limited proficiency in English.

There were approximately 46.8 million students in public schools in grades Pre-K to 12 in 1998. An additional 5.9 million students attended private or parochial elementary and secondary schools. In 1995, 35% of students enrolled in grades 1–12 in public schools were considered to be part of a minority group. Hispanic students represented 14% of the total public school student population and 7% of the total private school student population. The largest number of Hispanic students attended central-city public schools (24.3%). By the year 2020, more than 20% of the children and youth in the United States are projected to be Hispanic.

There is a great deal of variability within the population of children and school-age youth who are categorized as Hispanic or Latino. In short, there is no *typical* Latino child! One feature that describes their heterogeneity is where they are born—some are foreign-born and others are native-born Americans. For example, approximately 45% of the current LEP school-aged student population—Latino and otherwise—are foreign-born immigrants. Some are recent immigrants who grew up speaking a non-English language at home and continue to do the same when they arrive at school in this country. Often, their parents emigrated to the United States when these children were very young. Many others arrive at school as teenagers and young adults. An additional factor to consider is the growing number of immigrant students who have had limited educational experiences in their native countries; consequently, many arrive at school particularly ill-prepared to learn.

Other immigrant youth and children—Latinos included—arrive at school with extensive schooling experiences in their native countries. Their records imply high levels of native language skills and (at least) an acquaintance with English. However, depending on their age of arrival, even these advantaged LEP students have to face the difficult transition

---

[1]For purposes of this discussion, a Latino/Hispanic person is one whose family and home background includes native speakers of Spanish. Their ancestors might have immigrated to the United States from Mexico, South America, or the Caribbean, including Puerto Rico and the Dominican Republic. Latinos: (a) may be of any race, (b) may or may not be limited English proficient and, (c) may or may not be American born.

to new school settings and schooling routines that many native-born students already know. Immigrant students also face a new language of instruction—English—as well as coursework that can be very different from what they studied in their native countries. Many newcomers immigrated to the United States from the most rural parts of their native countries. This is especially the case for Latinos from Central America. Others are from large metropolitan areas, although the probabilities that they lived in poor neighborhoods are high. Lastly, their arrival at school in this country during the normal academic year is difficult for them and for the receiving schools to predict. They may or may not be ready to enroll in school at the beginning of the school year.

Approximately 55% of the school-age LEP students are born in the United States. Latinos represent the majority of this subgroup of language minority children and youth. Like their foreign-born peers, they are unevenly distributed across geographic areas and even within school districts. For example, the highest concentration of LEP and non-LEP Hispanics is found in the West, followed by the Northeast. Furthermore, Hispanics are more likely to live in the central cities of metropolitan areas. Depending on the characteristics of their households, some of them enter school speaking mostly Spanish or a dialect of Spanish. Few of them are literate in Spanish.

Others in this subgroup of Latino children and youth are monolingual English speakers, but they are apt to speak distinct social dialects of English that are influenced by their cultural backgrounds, by their poverty, and by the Spanish language and its dialect spoken by adults at home or in the surrounding community. Consequently, their dialect of English might not sufficiently complement the academic English dialect(s) they encounter in school. Many of these children and youth arrive at school with poorly developed literacy skills in either their native language or English or both languages. In short, many native-born Latinos are limited English proficient, but not in the same ways or degrees that their foreign-born peers are. The likelihood that both of these subgroups of foreign- and native-born Latino students will encounter an array of very demanding and novel social, academic, and linguistic situations at school is great.

However extensive their differences, Latino students share several features. The first is the language domains in which they are limited in proficiency. Many of them exhibit low levels of skills in the four English language arts domains (listening, speaking, reading, and writing) in relation to their typical English-proficient peers. The second is their inadequate preparation to start school ready to learn. Many Latino children start school with severe disadvantages. For example, they are unlikely to be taught many of the early pre-reading skills that their English proficient or middle-class peers normally receive at home. Furthermore, many Latino students do not have access to preschool experiences. The research evidence supports the assertion that when students are not provided with high quality daycare and early childhood services, once in school, their academic achievement and limited-language proficiencies get cumulatively worse over time, grade levels, and all subject matter. Consequently, it becomes increasingly difficult for them to participate in school as equal learning partners with most of their more advantaged and typical English proficient peers.

Latino students, as a whole, share other features. For example, many of them live in households and neighborhoods with high and sustained poverty—sometimes over several generations. Getting to and from school safely for some is a daily trial. Receiving regular and nutritious meals is an equally daunting struggle. Others attend schools with many other poor children, whether they be in rural areas or inner cities. Schools with high concentrations of poor students tend to be poorly maintained, structurally unsound, fiscally underfunded, and staffed with large numbers of minimally prepared and unlicensed or uncertified staff. Furthermore, their families are more likely to move at least once during the school year from one school to another within the same school district, if not to another school district, thus further disrupting their already fragile educational opportunities.

To compound the schooling problems of these students, many of their teachers tend to focus mostly on basic skills and repetitive drills, rather than on higher level content, English language, and comprehension skills that help students build on what they know. The research literature suggests that higher order skills are most likely to hold students' attention, motivate them to learn, and guide them to use lessons learned across multiple subjects. Schools with large numbers of poor students also have limited access to educational technologies. Their teachers tend to use computers and other technologies minimally for instructional purposes. When they do use them, they are more likely to use technologies to teach basic rather than higher order skills, and to drill rather than to engage students in modeling and simulations carried out in cooperative learning settings.

In addition, most high-poverty schools serving Latino students offer limited or no early childhood and preschool programs. Few of them offer comprehensive health and social services to students or their families. Furthermore, communities in which these schools are do not generally support the development of high levels of literacy (in English or Spanish) or to build on linguistic and cultural resources of the students, parents, and other adults.

The probabilities are high that most of the Latino students in these schools will be exposed to a broad array of other significant factors that place them at risk of educational failure throughout their preschool, elementary, and high school years. Most of the risk factors, moreover, negatively impact on each Latino student's readiness to learn in general, learn English in particular, learn grade-appropriate subject matter, stay in school, and go on to college and secure meaningful careers. These students represent a schooling dilemma of national proportions.

The research literature on teaching and learning establishes that all learners are diverse in many respects and that the attainment of high levels of school success—especially literacy skills—requires the long-term and consistent attention of the school, the teacher, the learner, the parent, and the larger community. It also supports the belief that models of foreign language teaching and learning for adults do not easily apply to children and youth, especially to at-risk Latino children and youth who are limited English proficient. In circumstances where school-aged learners are highly proficient in their first or native language (i.e., English or Spanish), these students are more likely to acquire a foreign or second language with relative ease and in short periods of time. However, the acquisition of English (second) language arts skills, especially reading, is a struggle for the majority of Latino students. In summary, students whose native language arts skills are not adequately developed by the time they enter school and are not developed and used while in school would appear to face long odds against success.

There is every reason to be concerned about the needs of Latino students. They need to learn English and subject matter as effectively and efficiently as possible and on par with their English-proficient peers. The consideration of appropriate educational theory and the system-wide implementation of research-based practice should be one of the first steps taken toward meeting this goal. Given that education policies are the domains of state education agencies and local school districts, the burden of developing and assertively implementing sound policies and practices that ensure the success of *all* students in school would appear to rest on those agencies. This burden is no less imperative for Latino students!

FACTORS THAT PLACE LATINO CHILDREN AT RISK

The purpose of this chapter is to describe the factors that place Latino students at risk of educational failure, as well as the factors that place schools at risk of failing these students. Individually and collectively, the factors help us to understand the range of resources (categorized as students' resilience or funds of knowledge) that students bring to school, and help us understand the impediments that particular children and youth face, regardless of the episodic or persistent nature of the factors. Finally, these factors provide a framework for explaining the nature and correlates of the academic and social progress that students make.

Federal education legislation and the research literature include four factors that identify children and youth who are at risk of educational failure. The factors are: poverty, limited English proficiency, race/ethnicity, and geographic location. Unfortunately, these four factors alone offer a limited basis for understanding the resources and deficits that particular students represent; for making decisions about the problems that students face at school; or, for defining the school's educational responses to documented needs or to perceived problems.

The factors that place children at risk can be grouped into three major categories, which are derived from diverse educational, social sciences, and health literatures. They point to a complex interplay of factors that begin to reveal the conditions that impact on learning in general and school success in particular.

- *Category I* factors are personally focused. That is, they define most of the personal features and characteristics of a child or youth. Many of these factors are not easy to change. They begin to define a child's readiness to learn.
- *Category II* factors are more environmental in nature. Thus, they define the surroundings within which a child is born and grows up. These might change over time, although the typical student has little control over them.
- *Category III* factors are more school and learning-conditions specific. These factors are the least influenced by the student or his or her parents because they are present more within a system or institution. They define a school's readiness to effectively serve students.

Think of the factors as radiating out from the student to the neighborhood and then to the educational system. It is important to realize the potential impact the factors can have on a student's readiness to learn.

The factors share at least five important dimensions:

1. Collectively, they constitute the full complement of factors that have the potential to deflect a student from his or her successful course through the educational system.

2. Equally important, they interact with other factors within an individual or across groups of students to either reduce or increase their effect on learning.
3. They bundle in unique ways to create idiosyncratic profiles of students with seemingly identical characteristics (this point is addressed in the last section of this chapter).
4. Some of the factors might be present at one point in a child's life and not others. For example, poverty might be an episodic event or it might be persistent and long term. Likewise, a student might attend a well-managed school one year and a school in chaos the next.
5. The collective impact of these factors is still only poorly understood.

CATEGORY I FACTORS:
YOUTH AND CHILD-FOCUSED

The factors in this category include those that define the psychological, social, cultural, linguistic, and maturational features of children and youth. In short, they define the child's persona; in this case, as a Latino. Furthermore, if a child represents one or more these factors, he or she is likely to be at risk of educational failure. The key factors under this category are:

- Is limited English-proficient.
- Is limited native language-proficient.
- Is not born in the United States.
- Is a recent immigrant in relation to the length of time spent in school in the United States.
- Is an immigrant with little formal schooling in his or her native country.
- Is a speaker of a nonmainstream dialect of English.
- Did not receive early childhood education services (pre-K).
- Has learning or other disabilities.
- Has a physical or medical condition.
- Has been diagnosed with a developmental delay.
- Is a poor reader.
- Is a poor test-taker.
- Has attention deficit disorder.
- Lives in a poverty household.

- Was in a low-achievement track for at least 1 school year.
- Repeated or was held back at least one grade.
- Is overage for grade/school level.
- Belongs to a gang.
- Has committed a crime.
- Has been physically or emotionally abused.
- Dropped out of and returned to school.
- Has been expelled or suspended.
- Has underachieved in at least one grade level.
- Is pregnant.
- Is an unmarried or married teen parent.
- Is a migrant student.
- Feels psychologically isolated or socially unattached to peers.
- Has a negative relationship with adults and/or teachers.
- Works 20 or more hours per week.

The Evidence

Evidence from a diverse literature establishes the substance of the previous factors. It also establishes their importance to educators who are interested in compiling profiles of students, especially of children and youth who, at various levels, might be at risk of educational failure.

The report issued by the Federal Interagency Forum on Children and Family Statistics titled *America's Children: Key National Indicators of Well-Being* (U.S. Department of Education, 1998) includes statistics that elaborate on several of the previous factors.

Early Childhood Educational Experiences

- In 1996, only 37% of Hispanic children ages 3 to 4 attended an early-childhood center, compared to 54% of White and 63% of non-Hispanic, African-American children.

Language Abilities

- The number of school-age children who spoke a language other than English at home and who had difficulty speaking English was 2.4 million in 1995, up from 1.25 million in 1979. This is 5% of all school-age children in the United States.

- Children of Hispanic or Asian origin are more likely than non-Hispanic White or Black children to have difficulty speaking English because they are more likely to speak another language at home.
- From 1986 to 1993, the number of 5- to 17-year-old LEP students increased from 1.6 million to approximately 3.04 million.
- There is a large population of children ages 5 to 17 who speak a language other than English at home, but who are not limited in their English proficiency. Latinos constitute the majority within this important category. The number of children in this group grew from 6.8 million in 1992 to 7.2 million in 1995. Of these, 73% were born in the United States and 27% were foreign-born.

Reading Abilities

- Comparisons in NAEP 1998 are consistent across all three grades: students who were eligible for the free/reduced-price lunch program demonstrated lower reading performance than did students who were not eligible for the program.
- In NAEP 1998, Hispanics in grades 4, 8, and 12 were outscored by their White and Asian peers. For example, the reading assessment score gaps between White and Hispanic students ranged from 31 points in grade 4 to 23 points in grade 12.

Persistence in School

- The Hispanic high school completion rate was 62% in 1996. For Black non-Hispanics, it was 83% and for White, non-Hispanics, it was 92%.
- First and later-generation Hispanics were more than twice as likely to drop out as their non-Hispanic peers.

Minority Status

In 1995, 35% of students enrolled in grades 1 to 12 in public schools were considered to be part of a minority group, an increase of 11 percentage points from 1976.

Immigrant Status

- In 1996, the status dropout rate for Hispanics ages 16 to 24 who were born outside of the United States was 44%. It was 17 and 22% for first and later generation Hispanics, respectively.

- In 1996, Hispanic immigrants were about seven times more likely than non-Hispanic immigrants to be dropouts and were much less likely to have completed high school than were other immigrants.

Living in Poverty

- Most children in poverty are White and non-Hispanic. However, the proportion of Black or Hispanic children in poverty is much higher than the proportion for White, non-Hispanic children.
- In 1995, one out of five children lived in poverty, although the average ranges widely across racial/ethnic groups. Among Black and White children, for example, the proportions living in poverty were about 42% and 11%, respectively and remained stable or declined since 1980. On the other hand, the number of Latino/Hispanic youth under the age of 18 living below 100% of the poverty line increased from 33% in 1985 to 40% in 1996.
- Children under age 6 are more often found in families with incomes below the poverty line than children ages 6 to 17. In 1996, a family of four with an annual income below $16,036 was below the Federal poverty line (U.S. Department of Commerce, 1995).

Parental Education and Student Achievement

- NAEP 1998 results indicate lower average reading scores for students whose parents did not finish high school. In short, students whose parents attained the highest education levels (i.e., graduated from college) scored higher average reading scores than their peers did with parents who have lower levels of education.

Availability of Food and Nutrition

- In 1996, 15% of children in poor households lived in households reporting that they sometimes or often did not have enough to eat compared to less than 1% of children in households with incomes at or above poverty.

Health Care

- The number of children who had no health insurance at any time during 1996 grew to 10.6 million (15% of all children.).
- Hispanic children are less likely to have health insurance than either White or Black children.

- Children without health insurance were more than six times as likely as those with private insurance to have no usual source of health care in 1995. Furthermore, older children ages 12 to 17 are slightly more likely than younger children to lack usual health care.

Teen Parenthood

- During the 1980 and 1994 period, the birth rate for unmarried women ages 15 to 17 years increased from 21 to 32 per thousand.
- In 1996, 85% of births to females ages 15 to 17 were to unmarried mothers.
- Compared to babies born to older women, babies born to adolescent mothers are at a high risk of being low-birth weight and are more likely to grow up in in homes that offer lower levels of emotional support and cognitive stimulation.

Summary Statement on Category I Factors

Numerous portraits can be drawn from these statistics. Most of them point to profiles typical of poor and minority children and youth. The profiles are especially typical of the majority of Latino children. Although statistical breakouts are not readily available for Hispanic students across all of the previous factors, relationships can still be established by cross-referencing some of what we know about the condition of Latino children and youth. For example, the NAEP 1998 report asserts that there is a consistent relationship between the amount of reading done for school and homework and students' reading scores. Students who reported that they read 11 or more pages each day demonstrated higher reading performance. Hispanic students generally do not report reading much on a daily basis. Likewise, at both 8th and 12th grades, students who reported being asked to explain their understanding or to discuss interpretations of what they read at least once or twice a week had higher average scores than their peers who reported doing so less than weekly. Because large numbers of Hispanic students are in classrooms for low and underachieving students, the likelihood that they engage in in-depth discussions of what they have read in and for class would appear minimal. In short, the impact of the previous factors endangers the chances a child or youth has to be ready to learn at any given time point. The factors do not, on the other hand, imply any type or degree of defect in a child;

rather, they simply define the chief characteristics of large subgroups of Latino children and youth living in America today.

CATEGORY II FACTORS: ENVIRONMENTAL

The factors under this category are related to the home, neighborhood, and community in which children and youth live. Collectively, they define the non-academic environment that shapes their early development and later maturation. The factors also define many of the influences on perceptions of self and of others. The key factors under this category are:

- Lives in a household with periodic or sustained poverty.
- Parents are recent immigrants.
- At least one parent or guardian does not speak English.
- Parents or guardian have low levels of educational attainment in the United States or their native country.
- Adults in household infrequently engage in conversations with the student on school matters, including homework or reading assignments.
- Parents or guardian have little or no connections to school or to the community.
- Child attends a school with a high concentration of poor students.
- House does not include space for studying.
- House does not include books and reading material.
- Adults in the household do not read to their children.
- Family lives in a high-poverty and high-crime neighborhood.
- Child has siblings who are school dropouts.
- Child has many other school-age siblings.
- Mother has received poor or no prenatal care.
- Family is highly mobile within a school district and across districts.
- Family lives in a geographically isolated area (rural/small town or inner/central City).
- Family lives in subsidized housing or in a household receiving welfare assistance.
- Child lives in a single-parent or guardian household.
- Parents are employed full-time and have odd work shifts.

- Parents are unemployed.
- Child lives in a household in which there is drug abuse.
- Child lives in a household with minimal or no health insurance.

The Evidence

The *Condition of Education Report* (U.S. Department of Education, 1998a) includes statistics that elaborate on a large number of the previous factors and support their relationship to students' readiness to learn and to their persistence in educational settings. Chief among them are:

Family, Neighborhood, and Geographic Region Characteristics

- Hispanic and Black children are more likely than White children to live in poverty, live in single-parent households, and live in urban areas.
- In 1997, almost 24% of children lived only with their mothers and 4% lived with neither mother or father.
- In 1997, about 45% of Hispanic mothers and fathers of 15- to 18-year-old children had at least a high diploma or GED. Ninety-two and ninety percent of White mothers and fathers, respectively, had a high school diploma or GED.
- The majority of Hispanic students attending grades 1 to 12 live in central cities.
- In 1995, one out of five children lived in poverty, but the average ranges widely across racial/ethnic groups. Forty-two percent of Black children and 11% of White children lived in poverty in 1995.
- In general, White and Hispanic 25- to 34-year-olds who had dropped out of high school were less likely than their Black counterparts to receive assistance for dependent children (AFDC) or public assistance between 1972 and 1996.
- Black and Hispanic children are less likely than White children to have a parent working full time all year.
- In 1995, 36% of U.S. households with children, both homeowners and renters, had one or more of three housing problems: physically inadequate housing, crowded housing, or housing that cost more than 30% of annual household income.

- Language minorities in the top-income quartile were well over twice as likely to speak English very well as those in the middle-income quartiles. Those in the bottom quartile were the least likely to speak English well.

- In 1990, third-generation Hispanic children were more likely to live in a single-parent household than first- or second-generation children were. (U.S. Bureau of the Census, 1990.)

- Between 1992 and 1996, high school students whose parents did not complete high school were more than twice as likely to drop out of school as students whose parents had at least some college education.

- In 1993–1994 school year, as the percentage of low-income students who received free or reduced-price lunch increased, there was an increase in the percentage of public school teachers who reported that student pregnancy, poor nutrition, and poor health were serious problems.

- In 1998, at all 3 NAEP grades (grades 4, 8, and 12), students who reported discussing their studies and reading assignments at home once or twice a month or less frequently had lower average reading scores than their peers who reported higher frequencies of such discussions. (However, some NAEP findings such as this one are self-reported and, as such, their relationship to student performance should be interpreted cautiously.)

- Comparisons of performance on NAEP 1998 showed that 4th- and 8th-grade students in central cities had lower performance than their peers living in urban fringe/large towns and rural/small towns.

- In 1998, students at all three grades who reported watching 4 or more hours of television a day had lower reading scores on NAEP than their peers who watched 3 or fewer hours.

Early Educational Experiences

- In 1996, similar percentages of White and Black 3- and 4-year-olds (about 40%) were enrolled in center-based pre-primary programs. However, only 22% of Hispanic 3-year-olds were enrolled in such programs. Participation rates were almost identical for 5-year-olds of all groups.

- In 1996, Hispanic children were less likely to have been read to or visited a library than White children.

Persistence and Participation in School

- Between 1972 and 1996, students from low-income families were more likely to drop out of school than were their middle-class counterparts.
- Enrolled students who were 5- to 17-years-old who spoke a language other than English at home were more likely than those speaking only English to report having repeated a grade by 1995. Furthermore, Spanish speakers were found to be more likely to have repeated a grade than those who spoke an Asian language.
- During the same period, high school students whose parents did not complete high school were more than twice as likely to drop out of school as students whose parents had at least some college education.
- In 1992, college-qualified Hispanic high school graduates were less likely than qualified White, Black, and Asian/Pacific Islander graduates to take steps toward college admission.
- Students who were involved in student government, participated in other school activities, or who worked for pay, were more likely to participate in community service than those students who were not so involved.

Post High School Adult Education and Literacy

- In 1995, almost 6 in 10 adults who had a bachelor's degree or higher participated in adult education compared to 3 in 10 adults who had a high school diploma or GED.
- Although the United States has a large percentage of adults scoring at the highest levels of literacy, in comparison to 11 other countries, it also has a large percentage of adults scoring at the lowest levels of literacy across prose, document, and quantitative literacy domains.

Immigration Status and Language(s) Spoken

- In 1996, a greater percentage of Hispanics than non-Hispanics ages 16 to 24 were born outside the 50 states and the District of Columbia. As noted earlier, the status dropout rate among this group was 44%, compared to first and later-generation Hispanics (17% and 22%, respectively). This latter group was more than twice as likely to drop out than their non-Hispanic peers. Hispanic immigrants were seven times more likely than non-Hispanic immigrants to be dropouts.

- In general, 5- to 24-year-olds who reported speaking a language other than English in 1995 were more likely to speak English very well than with difficulty. However, there were differences among the language groups in reported English abilities. For example, youth speaking an Asian language were more likely to experience difficulty with English than youth speaking other European languages (63% vs. 83%, respectively).
- Among speakers of Spanish and Asian languages, the proportion of youth between the ages of 5 and 17 who were reported to speak English with difficulty decreased with age.
- In general, the later a parent entered the United States, the more likely that a child was to report difficulty speaking English. The finding is more evident among children between the ages of 5 to 9 and 10 to 13 than among older youth.
- Roughly two thirds of those entering the United States in 1990 or later spoke English with difficulty, compared with just over one quarter of youth who entered the country prior to 1980.

Summary Statement on Category II Factors

The statistics just discussed are useful in describing general profiles of the home and neighborhood environments in which many Hispanic children and youth grow up. For example, the NAEP 1998 Reading Report references research (Baker, Allen, Shockley, Pellegrini, Galda, & Stahl, 1996; Christenson, 1992) that document the higher achievement of students whose parents have taken an active role in their learning. Because many Hispanic students live in poverty households and have parents who are not schooled beyond high school, the likelihood that their parents are substantively involved in their children's schooling would appear less than for non-Hispanics.

CATEGORY III FACTORS: CONDITIONS CONDUCIVE TO LEARNING

The factors under this category are related to the conditions that are conducive to learning, often called opportunities to learn. The factors range along a continuum from teacher preparation to placement in particular schools and classrooms to overall working conditions for teachers and staff. Collectively, these factors define the early educational and school academic environments that determine, in large part, how ready children are to learn in typical preschool settings; how well students do in school generally; and, how well they are assisted in making effective transitions across disciplines, pre-K to 12 grades, and elementary, middle, and high schools. The factors define the parameters of such issues as access to and full participation in high quality and effective educational services. In short, this collection of factors has the potential of placing many schools and other learning environments at risk of failing students. The key risk factors in this category are:

- School district records indicate a high turnover of key teaching and administrative staff.
- School district records indicate a high number of uncertified or unlicensed teachers.
- The physical conditions of the school buildings are substandard in comparison to others in the district or region.
- Educational services (i.e., academic, social, health, etc.) are too limited in scope, quality, and duration to be effective.
- School does not provide adequate counseling and other social, health, and nutrition services.
- School does not provide adequate access to technology or to the Internet, and teachers do not make use of these tools to supplement or improve core content instruction.
- Social services records, especially for at risk students, are incomplete.
- Service providers (staff, teachers, and administrators) are not adequately trained to provide service(s) or provide services in languages that students can understand.
- School is in a high poverty district or neighborhood.
- Parental involvement in the child's or student's educational and social services is minimal.
- The school district does not have an adequate improvement plan for schools identified as low performing.
- Schools in the district are compartmentalized and inhibit cooperation and collaboration among staff, teachers, and parents and among their district peers.
- Professional development programs are of short duration during the year and address few of the teaching and learning priorities of the school district or the state.
- The curriculum is not adequately aligned with state curriculum and assessment frameworks.

The Evidence

The 1999 report from the National Center for Education Statistics titled, *Teacher Quality: A Report on the Preparation and Qualifications of Public School Teachers* (U.S. Department of Education, 1999) includes statistics and correlations that elaborate on many of the factors just discussed. Furthermore, the research knowledge base supports strong relationships between academic achievement and students' access to high-quality educational and academic services. Supporting evidence is also provided by the statistics reported in the *Condition of Education Report* (U.S. Department of Education, 1998) and in *About Thinking K-16* (The Education Trust, 1999). Chief among the factors are:

In-Field Teaching Assignments

- Research has documented that schools with high concentrations of poverty or location in a central city area are more likely than more affluent or suburban schools to have higher rates of out-of-field teaching (U.S. Department of Education, 1996b).
- In 1996, students at public secondary schools with a high poverty level (defined as schools with more than 40% of students eligible for free or reduced price lunch) were more likely to be taught any of the core subjects by a teacher who had not majored in that subject than were students at schools with a low poverty level (5% or less eligible for free or reduced-price lunch).
- In 1993–1994, English language arts teachers were less likely to be teaching in-field for their main assignment field in schools with the highest concentration of poverty (defined by 60% or more of students eligible for free or reduced price lunch).
- Mathematics teachers in 1993 to 1994 were less likely to be teaching in field in schools with the highest minority enrollment (defined by 50 or more minority students).

Teacher Perceptions of Preparation to Teach

- In 1998, 54% of teachers surveyed reported that they taught limited English proficient or culturally diverse students and 71% reported that they taught students with disabilities. However, only 20% and 21%, respectively, reported being very well prepared to address the needs of each group.

Professional Development

- In 1998, most experienced teachers (20 or more years of teaching) were less likely than all others to participate in professional development addressing the needs of LEP or culturally diverse students.

Class Size and Type

- In 1998, teachers in schools with 50% or more minority enrollment taught larger classes than their counterparts in schools with smaller minority percentages.
- Fourth graders in high-poverty public schools are less likely to be in schools with gifted and talented programs or extended day programs than fourth graders in low-poverty schools.

Parental Support

- In 1990 and 1993, the percentage of teachers who thought that lack of parent involvement or parent alcohol or drug abuse were serious problems increased as the percentage of low-income students who received free or reduced-price lunch increased.
- In 1998, 23% of teachers in schools with 33% to 59% of students eligible for free or reduced-price lunch reported that parents supported their efforts, as compared to 41% of their peers in schools with 15% or fewer poverty students.

Internet Access and Use

- In fall 1997, public schools with high-minority enrollment (50% or more) had a lower rate of Internet access than public schools with low-minority enrollment (under 50%). Moreover, the former had a smaller percentage of instructional rooms with Internet access than the latter.

Capital Investments

- In the 1992–1993 school year, relatively low-wealth school districts (those with a median household income of less than $20,000) spent less per student in general and less on capital investment than districts with more wealth (those with a median income of $35,000 or more).

Summary Statement on Category III Factors

The factors just discussed and the supporting evidence establish a compelling case for well-funded schools that are staffed with well-trained and dedicated educators. Schools can either enhance and sustain every student's opportunity to learn to optimal levels or they can impede the critical chances students need in order to succeed in school. Whether done in a calculated way or through incompetent behavior or because, in fact, adequate fiscal and human resources are genuinely unavailable, the fact remains that students who do not have access to good schools and schooling will not achieve according to common expectations.

General Summary and Recommendations

The previous factors are well supported by research and evaluation evidence. Indeed, the knowledge base establishes their influences on the school success of children and youth, their life-long learning experiences and careers, and the quality of their participation in American life as residents in, and citizens of, the United States.

Equally important, educational improvement strategies take time to plan and to implement and require many resources to sustain. One of the most important lessons learned to date about effective and sustainable educational improvements is that they must be *comprehensive*. This means that educators must address all of the facets of schools and schooling, including working with parents and other community leaders to create communities of learners where everybody is involved in the education of *all* students. This also means that the curriculum must be aligned with state content standards and frameworks and both must be aligned with instruction. Furthermore, all three must be aligned with assessments and adopted accountability structures.

School reforms must also be *systemic*. This means that all parts of the system must be vigorously evaluated and managed over time, including social and health services delivery systems. Even though the focus of this book is on Latino students, the emphasis should be on reforms that enhance opportunities for all students to learn to optimal levels and all teachers to be effective. On the other hand, because Latino children and youth pose such particular demands on community-service providers and on schools, it is important to bear their needs in mind.

Another important educational reform lesson is the realization that children and youth, per se, do not arrive at school as *problems*. Rather, problems arise when there is a distinct mismatch between the resources that the typical student brings to school and the responses that the school delivers in order to help him or her acquire new knowledge and learn how to use it. This is especially the case for Latino students at risk of educational failure.

Not only must educational reforms be *systemic* and *comprehensive*, they should also be *informed*. This means that all improvement measures should be developed and implemented on the basis of expert knowledge about children and youth, their communities, and the readiness of schools to serve them effectively.

The full complement of factors listed in this chapter provides a framework for the scope of the data that should be collected, analyzed, and used to make valid decisions about schools and schooling. The factors, moreover, provide the basis for creating profiles of children and youth, for appreciating their presence and absence in seemingly similar children and youth, and for determining their implications for diagnosis of need and for consequent prescriptions of educational services. The factors are also useful for developing institutional profiles with which to gauge the quality of services provided to students and their families.

Consider the following hypothetical situation concerning two Latino students in the typical classroom, both in the 6th grade. Students A and B attend the same inner city school.

Student A Represents the Following Factors:

- Is not a native speaker of English and speaks mostly Spanish.
- Is a poor test taker.
- Repeated 4th grade.
- Was in a low-achievement track in the 3rd grade.
- Is a migrant student whose parents speak mostly Spanish.
- Comes from an abusive and poor household.

Student B Represents the Following Factors:

- Is a speaker of a nonmainstream English dialect and is not literate in Spanish.
- Did not receive early childhood education services.
- Is a poor reader.
- Is over-age for grade/school level.
- Feels psychologically isolated from peers.
- Parents both speak English and work full time to provide the necessary health and nutrition needs.

Both students represent teaching and schooling challenges. However, the challenges are not the same. Both students might appear to need the same services because they are both Hispanic and are LEP. However, on close inspection of their individual profiles, reasonable educators would deduce that they indeed are different—that the factors bundle differently. This information would translate into the use of different approaches to help each student succeed.

Yet, the evidence suggests that many schools do not take the time to conduct the careful diagnoses needed to minimize assumptions about what each student needs, the intensity of what each student needs, and the motivational techniques that might help turn each student around. If we complicated the matter by stating that one of them is a boy and the other a girl, the dimensions of the problem become yet more complex. If we simplified the example by stating that both of the students were non-LEP, they would each still require individual approaches!

Consider other intervening factors: Although the school that the students attend is well managed and has close links to the community, including a low teacher-turnover rate, Student A is in a classroom with many other migrant students and the teacher is inexperienced. Student B, on the other hand, is in a classroom in which most of the students are reading on grade level and have been together since 2nd grade. Under this hypothetical situation, even if the students enjoyed the same profiles, their classroom environments would exert different influences on their opportunities to learn.

The bottom line is that the risk factors serve the purpose of laying out a framework. However, it takes time and energy to identify the full complement of factors that each student in a particular school or classroom represents. It also takes time to determine how the factors bundle and interact over short and long periods of time. It takes an equal commitment to create the maps that lead to the provision of effective services that ensure the success of each student.

Accordingly, four steps are proposed that educators should take to gain a comprehensive understanding of the issues at hand and of their implications for effective educational responses for Latino children and youth. That is, educators need to:

1. Identify the full complement of factors that define these students, especially those who are at risk of educational failure.
2. Understand how the factors bundle within individual Latino students and across groups of students so as not to overgeneralize across particular student subgroups.

3. Determine what the factors imply for the typical array of educational and related social/health services provided and for professional development.

4. Design appropriate educational and management responses for Latino students that stem from the identification of these factors.

REFERENCES

Bennici, F., & Strang, W. E. (1995). *Special issues Analysis Center, Annual Report, Year 3. Volume V: An analysis of language minority and limited English proficient students from NELS:88*. Rockville, MD: WESTAT, Inc.

Baker, L., Allen, J., Shockley, B., Pellegrini, A., Galda, L., & Stahl, S. (1996). Connecting school and home: Constructing partnerships to foster reading achievement. In P. Baker (Eds.), *Developing engaged readers in home and school communities* (pp. 21–41). Mahwah, NJ: Lawrence Erlbaum Associates.

Christenson, S. L. (1992). Family factors and student achievement: An avenue to increase students' success. *School Psychology Quarterly, 7*(3), 178–206.

The Education Trust. (1999). *Thinking K–16*. Washington, DC: Author.

National Research Council, Committee on Developing a Research Agenda on the Education of Limited English Proficient and Bilingual Students. (1997). *Improving schooling for language-minority children: A research agenda*. Washington, DC: Author.

U.S. Department of Education, National Center for Education Statistics. (1995). *The condition of education*. Washington, DC: U.S. Government Printing Office.

U.S. Department of Education, National Center for Education Statistics. (1998a). *The condition of education 1998*. Washington, DC: U.S. Government Printing Office.

U.S. Department of Education, National Center for Education Statistics.(1998b). *Digest of Education Statistics 1998*. (NCES 1999–036). Washington, DC: U.S. Government Printing Office.

U.S. Department of Education, National Center for Education Statistics. (1999). *NAEP 1998 reading report card for the nation*. Washington, DC: U.S. Government Printing Office.

U.S. Department of Education, National Center for Education Statistics. (1980). *High school and beyond, base year student survey*. Washington, DC: U.S. Government Printing Office.

U.S. Department of Education, Office For Civil Rights. (1984). *Elementary and secondary schools civil rights survey, individual school report (ED 102)*. Washington, DC: Author.

U.S. Department of Education, National Center for Education Statistics. (1999). *Teacher quality: A report on the preparation and qualifications of public school teachers*. Washington, DC: Author.

U.S. Department of Education, National Center for Education Statistics. (1996a). *How safe are the public schools: What do teachers say?* (NCES 96–842). Washington, DC: Author.

U.S. Department of Education, National Center for Education Statistics. (1996b). *Do districts enrolling high percentages of minority students spend less?* (NCES 97–917). Washington, DC: Author.

U.S. Department of Education, National Center for Education Statistics and the Federal Interagency Forum on Child and Family Statistics. (1998). *America's children: Key indicators of well-being*. Washington, DC: U.S. Government Printing Office.

U.S. Department of Commerce, Bureau of the Census, Population Profile of the United States. (1995). *Current populations reports*. Washington, DC: U.S. Government Printing Office.

10

An Overview of the Educational Models Used to Explain the Academic Achievement of Latino Students: Implications for Research and Policies Into the New Millennium

Martha Montero-Sieburth
University of Massachusetts–Boston
with
Michael Christian Batt
University of Massachusetts–Boston

This chapter presents a brief overview of the educational explanations during the past 30 plus years found in the research literature for describing Latino academic achievement at the elementary and secondary levels in the United States (Chapa, 1991).[1] It is not an exhaustive review in that it does not pretend to characterize all of the research which has been conducted on Latino achievement to date, but it is exploratory in highlighting the most salient explanations and analyzing their predictive value in terms of educational policy and research implications.

The review grows out of the concerns that as an educator I often hear professed for explaining why Latinos are failing in education. It attempts to highlight the learning that can be accrued to educational achievement explanations for Latinos, but also presents the limitations and gaps that exist in the research and require further investigation.

Of the many concerns which exist, two are particularly salient. One concern is that the educational problems of Latinos are a consequence of

---

[1]This chapter is dedicated to the memory of my cousin, Eladio Trejos Montero, who in his death taught us a great deal about facing life with dignity and humility. His spirit embodies much of the wisdom found in this text.

their home life and families who don't care about education. In fact, many of the explanations advanced for the achievement of Latinos tend to focus on "failure and disadvantages" of students as impermeable and fixed factors. As Bempechat stated, "we know far more about the factors that foster underachievement and school failure than those that contribute to academic success in poor and minority children" (1998, p. 4). Latino families and communities are often assailed as contributing to their poor academic performance in schools, and because they are out of reach of the school, the problems remain at home. The controllable factors within schools, such as student discipline and classroom behaviors, are the only ways in which students are helped by administrators and teachers to achieve. Thus the syndrome of "blaming the victim" is perpetuated, not necessarily with malice nor malintended but without any understanding of Latino families and without immediate recourse being available.

Investigating how Latino students learn at home, or through their peers, or what types of community funds of knowledge are conducive to their achievement in school, is still limited. Left out of these explanations are descriptions of the type of resilience or resistance that Latinos experience, in particular those of immigrants who, despite the odds, expect to succeed. Only through recent studies by Bempechat (1998, 1999), Alexander-Kasparik, Mace-Matluck, and Queen (1996), Lucas (1997), and Suárez-Orozco (1998), Vernez, Abrahamse, & Quigley (1996), as well as Calderón (1997, 1998), among many other researchers, is first-hand evidence of Latino students' expectations, problem solving, and successes defined on their terms being made known.

Another concern is what a colleague refers to as the use of "epistemological imperialism"—the idea that there is only one way of knowing, which is imposed upon all other forms of knowing. These other forms are considered unauthentic and illegitimate.[2] This has been the lens with which Latinos have been analyzed—from a dominant white Anglo cultural research paradigm based on ideological assumptions that range from "saving students" to providing more "compensatory or remedial educational" opportunities. Both share little faith in the inherent success of students and operate as though they need to acquire a singular type of competence. The former operates from a Eurocentric approach to help those in need learn the "white man's ways," whereas the latter serves to

---

[2]This notion was expressed by Prof. Mariella Bacigalupo of the Harvard Divinity School during her presentation on the Mapuche Indians and their expressions of male/female genders as part of their shaman culture at a presentation at the University of Massachusetts, April 19, 1999.

demand the development of knowledge, skills, and abilities derived from a mainstream position that spells success in terms of English-speaking ability, competitive learning, and specific problem solving. Such a position often rejects the nonmainstream ways of learning.

The application of such paradigms to the achievement of Latinos is contingent on how Latinos are perceived, how they are categorized, and how they are associated with other variables such as poverty and language-speaking abilities, for example (Gray, Rolph, & Melamid, 1996; Heller, 1966). Thus the review attempts to demonstrate what have, in effect, been the trends behind such explanatory models and what have been the solutions within educational reform that make sense.[3] It is clear that the educational solutions proposed for Latino achievement will either demand more of the same dominant mainstream competencies or begin to accept the competencies students bring from home to school.

Yet as much research as has been conducted on Latinos in this century, understanding what the effects of different paradigms may be on the results or outcomes for a given population requires the ideological deconstruction of the underlying assumptions of such paradigms. It is critical that in the new century, the perspectives of dominant/mainstream and subordinate/nonmainstream cultural research perspectives and their subsequent paradigms be clearly identified and understood as to their implications for the types of power relationships that such explanatory models may exert in exploring the complexities inherent in the education of Latinos, including achievement differentials between U.S.-born and immigrant Latinos (Gibson & Ogbu, 1991; Lucas, 1996; McDonnell & Hill, 1993; Mehan, Villanueva, Hubbard, & Lintz, 1996; Merino, 1991).[4]

A caveat in using such explanatory models is in order. Although some authors, like those of the Hispanic dropout report *No More Excuses* (Secada et al., 1998), refer to these descriptions or explanations of Latino academic achievement as *myths*, I refer to them as *educational explanatory models* because the descriptions that have been articulated about the educational achievement of Latinos based on research are proffered as the explanations that describe the achievement of Latinos, and in that re-

---

[3]It should be noted that for each explanatory model, there are many studies supporting the basic ideology. However, for the sake of brevity, only those that are representative have been cited, but this does not mean that the numerous studies in the field are being ignored or not recognized.

[4]The author, who will be teaching a course in the future on the Education of Latinos for the Latino Studies Program at the University of Massachusetts–Boston, needed to understand the complexity with which academic achievement of Latinos, both immigrant and U.S.-born, has been researched.

spect they have gained the status of "truth," irrespective of the researcher's perspective. I also use the definition of *educational achievement* proposed by Duran, Escobar, and Wakin (1997) as the "scores on tests and information obtained from performance assessments [which] reflect what students know and can do based on a sampling of questions and problem-solving situations assumed to be relevant to instruction" (p. 1). This traditional meaning has been offset today by a more constructivist notion that includes, as part of such achievement, the skills and strategies for thinking that are created in interaction between students and that demonstrates a range of skills, abilities, and knowledge building. Nonetheless, the normative meaning of achievement continues to be prevalent, so that "teaching to the test" has become acceptable part of teaching–learning.

The notion of *educational attainment* is determined by years of schooling completed, the scores on standardized achievement tests, and types of academic preparation that a student has, whether it is in vocational high school or college track. Yet it is the combination of poor academic achievement with poor educational attainment, low socioeconomic status, language minority status, and Latino identity that sets Latinos apart as a distinctive group in comparison to others within the general population.

The notion of *achievement motivation* as used by Bemphechat (1998) refers to the variety of beliefs that children hold about their learning and includes their degree of confidence in their abilities to learn, their expectations and opportunities for experiencing success, their own assessments of themselves, and how much and to what degree they are invested in academic tasks.

DATA SOURCES AND METHODOLOGY

The literature review on educational explanatory models is framed by multiple perspectives, which include dominant mainstream Anglo researchers, Latino researchers in the United States, and the emerging perspective of Latin American researchers studying migration patterns to the United States. Without a doubt, the educational issues of Latinos in the United States are inextricably linked to the educational and sociocultural patterns of immigrants from their countries of origin. Research on Latino returnees is now beginning to appear in several Latin American countries as part of economic and educational reports.

In the case of U.S.-born Latinos, several factors were considered, including language use, migratory patterns, and cultural embeddedness within the family during first and second generation (Hernández-Chávez,

1995). In this chapter, the focus is mainly on the perspectives that Anglo mainstream and nonmainstream researchers, including Latino researchers, in the United States share.

The methodology in this literature review used comparative and contrastive methods of analysis. Through content analysis, themes for each research study or document were identified and where possible matched with other data sources to evaluate their consistency and representative value in several studies. The sources for conducting such a review were drawn from extensive research studies from the ERIC databases for those studies conducted in the United States, and included each of the major Latino groups: Mexicans, Cubans, and Puerto Ricans, and, to a lesser degree, Central Americans, South Americans, and Caribbean Latinos (Dominicans) if documentation was available.[5] Thus the data sources herein presented are at different levels of analysis, depending on their availability and degree of completed analysis, so the analysis is not comprehensive, but rather exploratory.

THEORETICAL PERSPECTIVES AND EXPLANATORY MODELS USED FOR LATINO ACADEMIC ACHIEVEMENT

From the research reviewed, more than 20 explanatory models were identified that could be applied to Latino educational achievement. I have chosen those models that embody the paradigm shifts taking place in the 30 plus years and that have been most frequently used to explain the education of Latinos.

Traditionally, the educational achievement of Latinos has been described through a variety of explanations, including a presumed intellectual inferiority among Latinos (Stein, 1985), discriminatory placement of Latino students in the vocational track system (Rodríguez, 1974), differential approaches in bilingual education programs for Latinos (Cummins, 1984; Thomas & Collier, 1999) and overrepresentation of Latinos in basic mathematics placements (Oakes, 1985; Wheelock, 1993). A more

---

[5]Letters to universities where faculty are also doing studies of immigrants along the U.S.–Mexican border have been sent to collect papers and symposia information that address educational and achievement issues that have relevance to this topic. For those studies conducted in Latin America, the Latin American Network in Education (REDUC) and extant studies of Latin American research institutes involved in studies of migrants and immigrants have also been consulted. Some of these materials continue to be obtained directly from several of the Latin American research centers in order to be processed for analysis in subsequent publications.

macro view argues that educational failure among Latinos is related to essential differences in human and social capital (understood as skills and
knowledge passed down through generations) among Latino students as
compared to students from the dominant culture (Lareau, 1987). Yet another more recent perspective within a small but growing research literature is the notion of Bempechat and her associates that irrespective of
ethnicity, students who credit school success with ability are high achievers who share their parents' perceptions about educational beliefs and
practices (Bempechat, 1998). It is the focus on *ability* and not *academic effort* that spells success for such students, said Bempechat. For Latinos,
there is an value added meaning to education or *educación*, which is
about learning not only the content of schooling, but the moral values
that the culture upholds. That is why within-group differences about
child-rearing beliefs in individual cases need to be recognized to ascertain
the type of academic achievement that can be expected.

Still others attribute the problem to the disadvantageous position of
Latinos in the American economy (i.e., low-paying jobs and high rates of
unemployment) (Chapa, 1991; Pollard, 1989). An often-cited explanation for the low rate of transfers from community college is the hesitancy
of Latino students to forego earnings lost while attending college and preparing for higher paying careers (Aguirre & Martinez, 1993). These educational models are clustered around the salient categories of policies and
practices from which they have historically risen.

The Cultural Deprivation or Cultural Deficit Model

During the 1960s, minority groups were deemed to have inherent learning deficiencies labeled as *cultural deprivation or cultural deficits*, which
schools could overcome with intervention strategies like Head Start and
with reading programs that could raise literacy standards at home. It was
believed that minority students lacked the cultural stimuli to prepare
them for academic success (Valentine, 1968). Moreover, their lack of social and cultural capital was attributed to a "culture of poverty" (Lewis,
1965). With regard to the use of this explanation for Latinos, the commonly held assumption has been that the home does not prepare students
for the academic demands of schools and that the need to focus on cultural deficits as assets occurs when Latino students acquire the proper academic socialization for schooling.

Criticisms alleging an approach similar to that offered by the previous
genetic model of superiority and inferiority were leveled against this explanation and in particular against the use of social science research as a

means to encapsulate cultural deficits. Allegations of using the African American family described by Black sociologists in negative terms prevailed, and a move toward understanding the home environment from within was advocated by supporters of the following cultural difference model.

By the 1970s and 1980s, *cultural difference models* replaced these assumptions, proposing instead that minority students did not lack cultural stimuli but rather possessed cultural and linguistic codes and values of their own that were unknown to the school system (Cazden, John, & Steiner, 1972; Erickson, 1987). Issues of cultural and linguistic match and mismatch prevailed, and a series of ethnographic studies depicting different linguistic codes, the use of silence, and differential treatment by teachers were published. The research became caught in a cultural/social tug-of-war between home and school expectations.

The Cultural Difference Model

The shift from quantitative measures to qualitative studies incited by sociolinguists, linguists, anthropologists, and educators began to shed light on classroom culture and the dynamics of classroom interactions. The contributions of sociolinguists and anthropologists such as John Ogbu (1987), Courtney Cazden et al. (1972), Frederick Erickson (1987, 1994), Shirley Brice Heath (1983), Henry Enrique Trueba (1987, 1991), and Evelyn Jacobs and Cathie Jordan (1987), to name just a few, highlighted the need to examine the influence of macrostructural analysis on microethnographic issues of schooling through discourse analysis, classroom interactions, and cultural matches and mismatches—the cultural difference model.[6]

Such a model according to Carter and Segura (1979), pointed out that minorities are not so much "deprived" of important cultural experiences as much as they participate in a different set of experiences, which, although they may be worthy in themselves, do not meet the expectations of U.S. schools. An example can be traced to difference in speech styles and school experiences. The language experiences between the home and school in this model confounds minority students, who are often at a loss for responding in a certain way. This lack of continuity, particularly in the linguistic experiences between home and school, coupled with other cultural differences, can often be blamed for academic failure. In

---

[6]See Jacobs and Jordan (1987) and Gibson (1997) for an extensive review of this issue both nationally and internationally.

fact, as Hugh Mehan (1992) figured out, the linguistic and cultural competencies required to become "a competent student" may not have been gained early on nor acquired for group incorporation. Being a competent student requires that the formal and informal rules of the group be implicitly taught.

Although this model emphasized the importance of linguistic codes and communicative exchanges, it fell short of changing the ways in which teachers and principals perceived their students. In fact, of the criticisms leveled at this model, none is as evident as that of John Ogbu, who considered such analysis to miss out on the structural implications and embeddedness of discourse within the larger macro structures. It was from his criticism during the late 1980s that he presented an alternative explanatory model using initially his notion of caste minorities and voluntary immigrants, which later become voluntary immigrants and involuntary minorities.

The Voluntary Immigrants and Involuntary Minorities Explanation

Cazden and Erickson proposed closer sociolinguistic analysis of classroom discourse, and Trueba focused on the negotiated cultural meanings of success, whereas Ogbu and Matute-Bianchi (1986) and Ogbu (1987, 1991a, 1992) presented ethnographic findings of various minority groups in their attainment of educational academic achievements. Ogbu cited differences between voluntary immigrants and involuntary minorities. *Voluntary immigrants* refer to those immigrants who came to the United States willingly, and *involuntary minorities* refer to minorities who came to the United States under subjugation, particularly through slavery, conquest, or repression.

Immigrants come to the United States with a sense of achieving or "making it" by using the available opportunities that already are present (Suárez-Orozco, 1987a, 1989). The findings suggest that immigrant students fare better than their already established counterparts for the following reasons. They interpret the economic, political, and social barriers they face as temporary problems, which are justifiable as "rites of passage." Most believe they will return home, so that their time in the United States becomes goal-oriented and intensified with striving for success. Furthermore, despite their linguistic and cultural subservience, they view educational success as the most viable option for reaching economic parity and political mobility. These perceptions and interpretations among immigrants give way to a "folk theory" of getting ahead in the dominant society in which education plays a central role. In addition, voluntary immigrants respond strongly to group pressures and loyalties, issues of nationalism, and obligations to those left behind, and thus make concrete commitments on their arrival.

Ogbu contended that the consequences for involuntary minorities foster a perceived undeserved oppression with consequent loss of freedom and identity. The long-term effects of involuntary status result in students having a low ceiling of economic and social opportunity available to them. Students experiencing such conditioning power either give up or simply respond with oppositional and at times self-defeating behaviors.

Involuntary minorities compare their status to that of the dominant group, and recognize that they are worse off than they ought to be for reasons that are out of their control. In contrast to the voluntary immigrants, they do not have a "homeland" from which to compare circumstances and derive opinions. They also experience insurmountable, permanent, and institutionalized discrimination and do not believe that the societal rules for advancement work for them in the same way as for others. They realize that a collective effort is essential to overcome their problems, but this effort does not correspond to the demands made by education. Consequently, education is not perceived in the same manner as it may be by new immigrants.

Further compounding this self-limiting perception is the fact that established or involuntary immigrants perceive that the limitations that they face are only strengthened through a "Euro-Anglo" curriculum to which they are subjected in schools. Schools are viewed as "assimilative agents" whose purpose is to shun their cultural values and steer their children away from their cultural roots. Such distrust leads to skepticism of the dominant group, so that resistance seems to be the appropriate course of action to take for many Latino students.

Because involuntary minorities perceive their cultural frame of reference as being in opposition to that of the dominant group, language and cultural barriers that may be viewed as hindering their children's abilities to acquire an education may not be of great concern. Instead of viewing education as a means for upward social mobility, certain involuntary minorities internalize the schooling experience as one that empowers the oppressor and maintains the status quo.

Qualitative research conducted by Margaret Gibson (1987, 1997) indicated that minority students of involuntary status in general tend to reject what they feel is a "White" educational system. Latinos fall into this category based on the number of generations they have lived in the United States while experiencing conquest or repression. In their attempt to "fit" into the mainstream educational system, Latinos have had to forego in many cases their own language and cultural heritage, and have opted to respond by (a) turning to peer cultures, in which gangs may represent the *familia*, (b) dropping out as a response to low ceiling opportunities, or (c) creating oppositional responses to education such as tuning out, fighting back, or simply forgoing success. For these minority students, dropping out of school and performing poorly in educational institutions logically stems from such rejection (Montero-Sieburth, 1993, 1996).

Although Ogbu's contributions along with Margaret Gibson and Suárez-Orozco have presented more refined explanations, the application of Ogbu's theory to explain similar issues with Indian populations in Mexico was questioned by Maria Bertely, who in her work with the Mazahua tribe found limitations to the concept of involuntary minorities in terms of subjugation. She explained that at least for some groups such as the Mazahua, who historically were subjugated and today participate in Mexico's development of an economic infrastructure and democratization process, the groups are limited in such participation more by the racism they experience cloaked by classism than by economic ceilings. She also questioned, under the definition of Ogbu's category of involuntary minority, whether there is the relative freedom for human agency to emerge as countercultural production (Bertely, personal communication, Mexico City, 1997).

Although the cultural difference model has prevailed despite heavy criticism, following the enactment of bilingual education legislation in 1968, bilingual educators began to use the cultural difference explanation for bilingual education.

The Bilingual Education Model

When this explanatory model was applied to bilingual education research, several issues became evident:

1. Uncovering the issue of basic interaction communicative systems versus the role of cognitive academic language programs.
2. Identifying the question about whether the loss of mother tongue could be attributed to assimilation versus accommodation theories.
3. Identifying language shifts in relation to identity and academic achievement of Latinos.

Within the field of bilingual education, Cummins (1984) explained the differences between the basic communicative competence required for everyday communication and speech, and the more academic and cognitive competence that is required by schools and that demands a different level of linguistic and cultural sophistication (the BICS and CALP models). Such explanation began to expand the notion of linguistic competence from Noam Chomsky into communicative competence, which took into account cultural and social domains in different contexts.

Moreover, this explanation served to identify the importance of native language loss and language retention as issues that have strong political implications. In his seminal work, Rolf Kjolseth (1972) warned against the loss of mother tongue in ethnic communities as a way to become assimilated rather than to be pluralistic. He warned communities to retain their mother tongue as a countermeasure to assimilation that was the result of linguistic co-optation.

Hernández-Chávez (1995) followed in Kjolseth's footsteps by identifying the disparaging trend of native language loss among Hispanic immigrants. He pointed out that arriving immigrants and geographic concentrations within communities provided the resources to develop cultural maintenance institutions, by continued immigration, numbers, concentration of population, and low socioeconomic status, and also provided members of the community with opportunities to interact with each other and maintain native languages. However, as Hernández-Chávez denoted, "in recent years, study after study shows a progressive shift to English in the second and third generations and even in younger first generation immigrants" (p. 64).

To bolster his argument, Hernández-Chávez cited historical documents such as the Nationality Act of 1940, which required English for the first time for naturalization of citizenship, and the Internal Security Act of 1950, which added reading and writing to those requirements. These judicial acts, according to him, "compromised an integral part of Anglo-American principles of cultural hegemony where Non-English speaking peoples are to be subjected to the 'great melting pot,' not so much to create a new and hardened alloy, but to be recast, as English speaking replicas conforming to Anglo cultural molds" (1995, p. 65).

Hernández-Chávez, as well as Ogbu, argued that in today's reality, new Latino immigrants learn English quickly and embrace it, whereas established Latinos (e.g., Mexican Americans and Puerto Ricans) maintain their native language in an effort to gain political power and shun assimilation in a discriminatory society. Central American and South American immigrants strive to learn English at a faster pace than Mexican Americans. Yet Mexican Americans for their part are more resistant to Anglo expectations about learning a second language. This is in part due to their history of conquest, sustained discrimination, and subordination in American society. For Mexican Americans, as is also the case for many Puerto Ricans, the retention of Spanish serves as resistance to assimilation and Anglo mainstream culture, but at the same time, it serves to diminish their entry into the power structure of the Anglo mainstream by their not becoming totally bilingual and bicultural. In this respect, the language analysis of the cultural difference model of explanation surfaces much of the current ambivalence that many Latino students face in schooling (López, 1995).

Such ambivalence is played out in schools with the expectation that Latino students solely learn English, through the more popularized immersion programs, early- or late-exit English as a second language (ESL) programs, or through transitional bilingual 3- to 5-year programs. Yet such learning of English occurs for the most part at a personal cost to mother tongue development, cultural grounding (cultural pride and cultural ethnic affiliations), and identity formation, which are fundamental in the socialization of Latino students. At the political level, this is the same expectation echoed by the English-only movement, which has attempted to block bilingual education teaching through Proposition 227 in California, and by continuous repudiation of native language teaching. Hernández-Chávez contended that fear about the rise of Latino political power, and a desire to control immigration, are at the core of such actions (p. 65). To summarize, the schooling experience of Latinos is segregated in demographics, language, and motivational support.

With such a loss in mother tongue serving in essence to disenfranchise Latinos from their roots, it is no wonder that some Chicano students and parents come to view English as the highly valued language of education and commerce, whereas the retention of Spanish is viewed as a hindrance. The consequences of such beliefs go directly against the grain of all bilingual education research conducted since Modiano's seminal work in the 1970s. Instead of being grounded in their mother tongue, Latino students internalize the use of Spanish as a language that blocks advancement and acceptance by the broader society. As Hernández-Chávez (1995) commented, "Many schoolchildren, experiencing embarrassment and shame in their desire to be accepted, reject the use of their native language and even their ethnicity" (p. 65).

No one doubts that in order to be successful in the United States, Latino students need to learn English and incorporate it into their daily lives, but the issue here is that to do so without retaining their linguistic, cultural, and ethnic pride is detrimental in other ways. Students become pitted against their parents, who may support language retention while their schools promote language assimilation. This discontinuity in linguistic experiences at home and school, coupled with other cultural differences, serves to confound Latino students and diminish their academic aspirations.

Because the research focus of bilingual education has been mostly on *what works*, rather than *what makes sense for students and their families*, much of the research has been in terms of proving the effects of different approaches to language learning. Only recently has there been a focus on schooling efforts that demonstrate success, albeit using traditional criteria for successful schools (Brisk, 1999) and programs (Thomas & Collier, 1999).

Between the 1970s and 1980s, the influence of sociology of education and the "new" sociology of education, fostered by Neo-Marxist and anti-positivist educational proponents, brought forth other explanations based on the interplay of economics with education, the role of cultural capital in educational attainment, and the notion of resistance promulgated by the work of Paul Willis in England.

The Use of Economic Explanatory Models

Under the economic model explanation for achievement, supported through the work of Samuel Bowles and Herbert Gintis (1976), schools function as large sorting and categorizing mechanisms in which "meritocratic" criteria, such as standardized test performances, determine either college-bound curricular instruction or lower curriculum tracks. Once a student has been assigned within a group, the opportunity to move into another track is limited. Thus, even though many students may be qualified to move into the more advanced curricular tasks, they may find themselves tracked in such a way as to not have the opportunities that will prepare them for postsecondary schooling.

Under this system, the economic and social status quo differences between students become accentuated. The "meritocratic" system operates by convincing lower income students that they deserve lower status jobs due to their poor scores and grades from tests and curricula that have been designed to represent the knowledge, skills, and attributes of the middle class and beyond. Oakes (1985) and Wheelock (1993), as well as others, repeatedly pointed out how Latinos are siphoned into lower track mathematics and science courses. In Massachusetts, Wheelock uncovered that close to 60% of Latinos in the Boston public schools had been placed in lower track mathematics. This raises the question of how and why such assignments are made, and in whose best interest?

Major criticism has been leveled against this explanatory model by the "new sociologists of education" who dismiss the economic determinism that such a model suggests, in which students are viewed as passive learners. Henry Giroux and Peter McLaren, as well as other educators, viewed the determinism presented as being inadequate to explain the outliers of such a model and the successes which arise.

The Cultural Capital Sociological Model

Under the cultural capital theory model tied to education, and promoted by Bourdieu and Passeron (1977), Lareau (1987), and Dimaggio (1982), variation in school achievement can be traced to differences in cultural capital. Cultural capital refers to the general cultural background, knowledge, dispositions, and skills that are passed from one generation to another. Because schools are one of the main transmitters of culture, they tend to reward the cultural capital of the dominant classes and devalue that of the lower classes. Thus, lower income communities and minority parents seldom share the same knowledge and dispositions that constitute cultural capital attributes.

The cultural capital premise predetermines minority/immigrant students' educational opportunities by correlating their backgrounds with their academic backgrounds. It is aided by the notion of habitus, which refers to the type of experiences from the home that prepare students for their different "lots in life."

Stanton-Salazar (1997) extended this notion of social capital to one of network analysis framework, in which he attempted to understand the socialization and schooling experiences of working-class racial-minority youth. He focused on the relationships that exist between youth and institutional agents and identified the institutional and ideological forces that make social capital problematic and exclusionary for working-class minority children and adolescents. In his explanation, Stanton-Salazar showed how students draw on community resources and ethnic identities "to immunize immigrants from the worst psychological effects of racism and classism" (1997, p. 32). Yet he proposed that the institutional support from school-based institutional agents that some of the English-proficient immigrant students receive accounts for the social capital that they accumulate and draw from.

Again, the earlier criticisms leveled against this model were similarly related to criticisms of the economic model, which used a dependency relationship of passivity on part of the student to learning. However, in its later use, the notion of cultural and/or social capital shifted from its deterministic stance to present multiple perspectives and even counter-perspectives. Stanton-Salazar (1997) referred to this as the type of socialization that requires students to learn to manage life in multiple worlds. Similarly, James Coleman (1994) used the notion of cultural capital as social capital in his analysis of what makes Catholic schools successful. He emphasized that the currency of social motivation and cultural allegiances that parents and students sustain in keeping a culture of high standards for Catholic schools is not often present in public schools.

The criticism that is often leveled at this explanation are expressed by the following questions: What happens when you do not have the habitus as a precondition to acquiring the social or cultural capital that propels you into higher standing? And can that habitus be socialized early through schooling?

The Theory of Resistance

Stemming from the seminal work of Paul Willis (1977) in his study of the lads in school in Great Britain, who during the school day curse and act out, but at night comply by working and behaving as expected, the notion of resistance provides yet another explanation that presents oppositional stances of human agency that yet give way to institutional demands. Under this model, resistance theorists suggest that people and groups who feel castigated against and feel inferior resist giving in to unfair agendas and intolerable situations. Students in this case prefer to decide their own fate even when it means maintaining poor economic standards and creating a culture of opposition. Yet within their displays of opposition, students succumb to the institutional demands, partly because they have either internalized the oppression, or because in rebelling, they have created a greater adversity to be overcome.

Although the theory of resistance has offered insights into the complexities of student lives and experiences, naming oppositional behavior, and presenting the lived-out contradictions, it also has called into question how institutional cultures prevail and sustain themselves. In this regard, it is the lived contradictions presented by this explanatory model that become useful when applied to Latinos who live at times in opposition to the culture that they must fit yet do not understand, or to Puerto Rican students who learn the required English negotiate within the schools or to avoid detainment by police, yet maintain Spanish as a form of defiance or resistance (Montero-Sieburth, 1981).

One apparent use of this model is its application to studies of the Mexican–American border, which can help explain some of the phenomena that researchers are encountering with Latinos who go between the two worlds of the United States and Mexico and who attempt to make sense of their educational and social currency in both. Although the theory of resistance provides greater in-depth analysis for understanding the concrete experiences of students, the issue is, once the resistance has been identified and named, then what? How does one move beyond resistance to deconstruction and reconstruction? And with what new insights?

Coethnic Peer Communities Explanations

More current studies have focused on the rapid assimilation of immigrant groups into American culture and its subsequent results in disastrous academic experiences (Portes & Rumbaut, 1996; Portes & Zhou, 1993). This latest theoretical trend appears to confirm the work of Ogbu in that it locates the problem of chronic underachievement in Latino groups within the structure of coethnic peer communities that switch Latino students out of the dominant mainstream culture into impoverished groups who are struggling for limited resources at the street level.

In their study, Portes and Zhou (1993) presented ethnographic findings on contemporary second-generation immigrants from post 1965 statistics of Mexican Americans. Using the concept of "segmented assimilation," Portes and Zhou identified color, location, and the absence of mobility leaders as the possible outcomes that impact the social contexts and consequences of assimilation. They contended that these three factors, when coupled with established patterns of vulnerability, accentuated mostly in schools through Eurocentric pedagogy and curricula, create unsurmountable challenges for incoming immigrants. They contended that immigrants respond to assimilation through a variety of approaches:

1. The normative approach calls for immigrants to acculturate and then integrate into the White middle class.
2. The assimilation approach sends immigrants straight to permanent poverty and assimilation into an underclass.
3. The economic approach attaches rapid economic advancement with deliberate preservation of the immigrant's community's values and solidarity.

According to Portes and Zhou, the first generation makes education a pivotal and essential social issue, but by the second generation, in which "as of 1980 ten percent of dependent children in households counted by the Census were second generation immigrants" (p. 75), there are wide differences from person to person in educational, linguistic, and social-psychological outcomes. Assimilation occurs differently for immigrant youth, as many immigrants do not adopt the outlooks and cultural ways of their native-born counterparts. In fact, unlike the previous immigrants at the turn of the century who attempted to assimilate quickly, many find that their experiences may lead them in the exact opposite direction.

In contrast, the immigrant youth who remain ensconced in their respective ethnic groups find educational and economic support within those communities. Such immigrants are more receptive to middle-class expectations, whereas established involuntary or immigrant communities, especially those with histories of subjugation (such as Mexican Americans), tend to be pessimistic about their social status and outcomes.

Coupled with such adjustment is also the emergence of what Portes and Zhou (1993) called occupational segmentation, which further debilitates the mobility available to Latino immigrants. Under this process, the established immigrants are sorted into low-scale job opportunities, with those with greatest necessity adapting readily. The new Latino immigrants, who embrace academic challenges more than their established counterparts, quickly accommodate to low levels of education, accept menial jobs that represent the outcomes of their peer groups, and join the ranks of generations of Chicanos before them. To counter this situation, Portes and Zhou (1993) suggested that a process of selective assimilation be understood by immigrants, which empowers them to conceptualize and substantiate the oppositional forces that they will encounter before they succumb. In school, Portes and Zhou (1993) argued, newly arrived youth encounter the effects of a reactive subculture of youth whose parents resist assimilation. Many of them find themselves assimilated into an ideology of despair. The consequence is that before long, Latino students begin to shun education for the purpose of being accepted by peers in response to lingering family problems. Thus the first-generation model of upward mobility through school achievement and attainment of professional occupations can be readily diverted.

In contrast, Portes and Zhou (1993) found that the children of Mexican immigrants who continued to refer to themselves as "Mexicanos," as opposed to "Chicanos"/"Mexican Americans," and who felt closely linked to the parental culture, were among the most successful. They conclude that "the underachievement of Mexican-American children is contingent upon their allegiances to coethnic peer communities which are tend to absorb succeeding generations of Mexican-origin children away from the mainstream into resistive and adversarial groups at the bottom of the new economic hourglass" (p. 85). Thus Portes and Zhou asserted that rapid assimilation into American culture has disastrous consequences for the children of immigrant minorities.

Across various immigrant groups, those who remain closely allied with the ethnic affiliations of their parents are the most academically successful, whereas those who align with coethnic peer communities can experience a more damaging life than those with no community affiliation at all. Peer associations with students who have adapted an oppositional subculture to school norms and values represent a rejection of ethnic pride, academic intentions, and aspirations. Students in these situations need to find a balance between language/cultural retention and adapting to pedagogical expectations of U.S. schools (First, 1988; Portes & Zhou, 1993). Portes and Zhou's (1993) research resonates with Jorge Chapa's (1996) analysis that Latinos today can experience a two-tiered educational system. Those who have middle-class social and cultural capital will readily assimilate and join the ranks of other middle-class Americans, but those without such privileges are doomed to a second-class status that will have dire consequences for later generations.

The Dual Frame of Reference Explanations

By the end of the 1980s and into the 1990s, the primary focus on Mexicans, Puerto Ricans, and Cubans representing Latinos began to shift to include other newly arrived Latino groups. At the same time, greater numbers of qualitative studies, especially case studies and ethnographies of Latinos, began to appear.

Suárez-Orozco reported on Central Americans in the San Francisco area and pointed out that "education was the single most significant avenue to status mobility in the new land" (1987a, p. 11). According to him, Central Americans view their situations through a cross-cultural viewpoint that favors their present environment in the United States over their prior experiences in their homeland.

In his research, Suárez-Orozco integrated the psychological research models of George De Vos (1992) to illuminate the complex consequences of prolonged exploitation and disparagement that Latino students experience. According to De Vos (1992), continuous depreciation (like that facing established Mexican Americans) has concrete psychosocial consequences in the classroom and set up what he calls "ego rigidification" and the emergence of nonlearning strategies among minority students. With continued depreciation, certain minority students engage in what may he calls "defensive nonlearning" in the classroom (p. 42). In this context, involuntary minorities who experience an atmo-

sphere of discrimination, intolerance, and distrust come to resist the traditional Anglo-run educational system, which they view as a psychological threat to their ethnic belonging. De Vos (1992) further argued that
established minority students who do seek academic success engage in
"affective dissonance," which is a mechanism in which behaviors are created for success and are played out within dangerous parameters. Latino
students who "do the White man's thing" may have to contend with peer
alienation and depreciation.

Suárez-Orozco (1987a, 1989) found that many of the immigrants from
Central America who arrived in the United States escaping war experiences, even though they suffered from posttraumatic syndrome and de-
pression in some cases, were eager to learn and were appreciative, polite,
and expended more "learning energy," studying harder and learning English quickly. A key issue that Suárez-Orozco correlated with Central
American students who achieve despite the obstacles they faced back
home is the idea that their achievement was associated to their wish to
help others—typically, less fortunate members of their families and community. This notion of helping others served to help many of these Central Americans strive to succeed despite their often tenuous existence.

Suárez-Orozco noted that unlike involuntary minorities, such as Mexican Americans, Central Americans invest a great deal in their education
and view their situation through a dual frame of reference not available
to involuntary minorities. Mexican Americans have no dual frame of reference matrix, and view the educational system as an institutional pro-
vider of systematic exploitation, explained Suárez-Orozco (1987b). This
dual frame of reference is a process by which recently arriving immigrants
commonly interpret conditions in the context of comparison with events
they experienced at "home." Through this dual frame of reference, Central American are able to face their situations in the United States, no
matter how difficult their experiences may be, and do so in contrast to
their experiences back home. Despite these drawbacks, social mobility is
forged by Central American students through interpretations of opposition to their native countries. The parents of these students also regard
the Anglo-American world they live in as fairer than what they experience in Latin America, so they are more willing to trust and invest in the
education that the U.S. schools provide their children.

Contributing to maintaining this frame of reference is the social identity of immigrants, which is fostered by their sense of *who they are*, which
they bring with them. During the first generation, they tend to retain this
social identity while they learn the language and the culture of their new
host country. This may explain why recent immigrants from Central

America fare better in school performance than established Mexican Americans.

Suárez-Orozco's findings correlate with and advance the basic tenets of Ogbu, which explain that unlike their established counterparts, Central American immigrants are free from a history of depreciation over generations in their new social environments (De Vos & Suárez-Orozco, 1990). They hold different views about schooling than nonimmigrant working-class Latinos, and such circumstances carry over into classroom performances. However, Suárez-Orozco's theory presents a singular picture of a Latino subgroup—Salvadorans, who share a Central American connection to Guatemalans, Hondurans, Panamanians, Costa Ricans, and Nicaraguans, and whose immigrant experiences, although similar in some instances, include other variables such as indigenous factors, linguistic differences, racial attributes ranging from Indian backgrounds to African roots, and distinctive levels of basic educational experiences from their countries of origin that impact their educational status in the United States. Currently, Suárez-Orozco is expanding his research by conducting a major study of immigrants which include other Latino subgroups (Suárez-Orozco, 1998; Suárez-Orozco & Suárez-Orozco, 1995).

The Academic Failure Explanations of "At-Risk" Studies

One of the more recent explanations that has been directly applied to Latino students is the "at-risk" analysis. Stemming initially from a pathological medical model based on the idea that the problems of potential "at-risk" students could be found in their home environments and their families, for at least one or more "risk" factor—being poor, non-English speaking, in low-track educational programs, doing poorly academically, being disruptive, of single-parent background, and on the verge of dropping out of school—such an explanation was reminiscent of the deprivation explanation model of the 1960s. Today such explanation has given rise to a more social and constructivist model that considers, among other things, the idiosyncratic nature of being labeled as "at risk" and explores the conditions of schooling that place students "at risk."

The more recent explanations presented among several researchers but highlighted by Michelle Fine (1986, 1990, 1995) analyze how structures, particularly institutions, enable students to become "at risk" and how they often provide only partial images of dropouts as a means to strengthen the institutions that do not intervene to connect with students. She refers to "youth at risk" as an ideological and historical construction (1995, p. 90). In a similar vein, Robert Donmoyer and Raylene Kos (1993) argued that one of the fundamental problems for studying "at-risk" students is that their idiosyncracies are not taken into account; that is, Latino students do not fit the ideal type of "at-risk" students that the researchers have, nor are their variations, particularly within group, understood.

Using these explanations, the consequence of failure becomes located not in the student but in the institutional structures, the researchers' ideal archetypes or exemplars who in fact are stereotypes or an "appropriated ideological diversion" (Fine, 1995, p. 90). These explanations, as well as those being proposed by Beth Blue Swadener and Sally Lubeck (1995) in *Children and Families "At Promise,"* Hugh Mehan, Irene Villanueva, Lea Hubbard, and Angela Lintz (1996) in *Constructing School Success,* and by Ralph Rivera and Sonia Nieto (1998) for Latino students in Massachusetts, contribute to a growing understanding of the role of achievement in the lives of students who face policies and practices where failure is symptomatic over success (Montero-Sieburth, 1993).

Several research studies conducted by Frau-Ramos and Nieto (1993) as well as Montero-Sieburth (1993) on potential "at-risk" Latino students contradict the national data analysis depicting low socioeconomic status, lack of English speaking, and being Latino as critical factors contributing to leaving school (Steinberg, Blinde, & Chan, 1984).[7] In fact, Montero-Sieburth (1993) pointed out that even when Latino students speak English well, are in regular classrooms, can navigate the school system's policies and rules, and are able to comprehend what is expected of them by teachers and administrators, they are still potentially "at-risk" students because of other impinging factors. In many cases they are denied opportunities to learn in their own way and to use their own native language even for social reasons, are disregarded for who they are, are disrespected, and experience negative attitudes from administrators, teachers, and staff, who make comparisons about them with other more controllable and docile Latinos.[8]

In this regard, the work of Robert Slavin and colleagues through the Center for Research on the Education of Disadvantaged Students

---

[7]In fact, as the *No More Excuses* report signals, "While accounting for just 56 percent of all U.S. immigrants, Hispanics account for nearly 90 percent of all immigrant dropouts" (Secada et al., 1998, p. 5).

[8]In point of fact, the notion of assimilation used by teachers carries a negative connotation, meaning that the more assimilated the immigrant or Latino student is, the more boisterous, loud-mouthed, disruptive, and rebellious the student becomes, offering a different perspective on assimilation than its democratic one.

(CRESPAR) in a variety of programs and particularly through Success for All and Roots and Wings represents school reform initiatives based on known best policies and practices, which include cooperative learning, small-group clustering, collaborative and critical thinking, and the adaptations being made of such practices at international levels. By using the best available research, identifying ways in which students actually learn, and testing such knowledge in different social and cultural contexts, opportunities for learning by all children are being studied.

The Success Factors Explanation

In past years, research in secondary and higher education and of Latinos shows the successes of those few who manage to break the deadlock of academic underachievement. Foremost among these scholars is Henry (Enrique) Trueba (1987, 1998), and Trueba and Bartolomé (1998) who in his research sought to uncover deep-seated cultural explanations for the success of Latino students, and Patricia Gándara's (1995) *Over the Ivy Walls: The Educational Mobility of Low-Income Chicanos*, which centered around Chicano professionals who, in spite of socioeconomic barriers, managed to graduate from high school and go on to Ivy League schools to pursue professional degrees. Gándara's research showcased factors that foster academic success among Chicanos, instead of the more common approach of examining school failure. In addition, the research of Turner, Laria, Shapiro, and del Carmen Perez (1993) is cited as giving examples of where success through resilience and multiple factors is evident in poor Latino youth. Trueba's (1997) research and that of Turner et al. are used herein as the focus of this explanation.

In his research, Trueba presented a pervasive argument that correlates the traveling patterns of Mexican Americans between Mexico and the United States with success rates in educational retention and participation. Trueba perceived that this trend challenges educational institutions to adapt their curricular and pedagogical ideologies to meet these binational circumstances.

Trueba (1997) enumerated the following among the difficulties that Mexican students face in adapting to U.S. educational standards:

1. Most Mexican immigrant families must face language barriers and a general unfamiliarity with the customs and expectations of the new country they enter.
2. Immigrant families face extreme economic and social hardships upon entering the United States.

3. Because immigrants hold a perception of improvement, they often fail to internalize, as established migrants do, the negative attitudes of the mainstream population. This "naiveté" is exacerbated by their maintenance of the given country of origin through a dual frame of reference.

4. The literacy levels of Mexican immigrants are directly linked to their academic advancement.

5. Mexican immigrant students encounter school systems that lack resources and interest in providing students with special attention. Consequently, many teachers tend to perceive Latino children as low achievers and expect likewise.

6. All of these factors combined create a complex setting in which immigrant students must redefine themselves in the United States by motivating themselves to reject their own family, language, and culture (Trueba, 1997).

Education is deeply cherished by Mexican Americans, said Trueba, but only through proper schooling experiences and cultural adaptations that correlate to Latino recognition. He argued that the best learning experience for Mexican Americans could occur through binational and bicultural pedagogical advances and social benefits, and that the impetus for motivating achievement among Mexican American students comes from the abilities of children to retain a sense of self-identity while at the same time negotiating the demands and expectations of public schools. Students who manage to retain their home language, culture, and their familiar cultural institutions and networks are better adapted to succeed in American schools, said Trueba. This situation is enhanced and better used by the Mexican family that utilizes both foreign and U.S. networks.

In this model, parents, but in particular the mother, can monitor and identify purposeful achievements and can enhance the experiences of their youth through the utilization of binational and bicultural assumptions. Trueba pointed out that the role of women in this model is not to be underestimated, especially in the maintenance of home language and cultural principles. These strong familial circumstances foster a higher degree of organizational support and cultural acceptance within the Mexican American family structure, as Laosa (1978) and Delgado-Gaitan (1991) earlier studied for Chicano families.

A team of researchers who studied academic success among poor Latino youth in Massachusetts found that Latinos' success in school was related to a number of variables, including (a) early exposure to school experiences, (b) psychological factors such as self-esteem and aspirations, (c) familial support, and (d) positive high school experience and enrichment programs (Turner et al., 1993). Thus school achievement cannot be identified simply through one factor but needs to include the integration of development processes, family systems, and the sociopolitical context of education in the United States. More research like that mentioned here is appearing where the promise of success and not failure is the focus.

ANALYSIS OF THE RESEARCH
LITERATURE REVIEW

The research literature review indicates there is a plethora of reports and data on the academic achievement of Latinos in the United States. Over 2,000 citations appear on the topic through the Internet and ERIC files, and the REDUC shows at least some emerging studies about returnees and their effects on the educational and social systems in Latin America. Thus it is impossible to analyze each specific study per se. Instead, this section provides identification of some general trends of each of these explanatory models and the type of understanding that they reflect. At the same time, the limitations that such research presents and the need for further research are highlighted.

Substantive Progression of Research Studies

The review, in general, does show a progression of research over the years indicating basic shifts in the descriptions and analysis of Latino achievement studies. Some of the earlier research studies tend to be heavy on descriptive studies, at times to the point of generalization and creating stereotypic images of Latinos, yet they are landmark studies in identifying educational problems that had been all but invisible or couched within Black and White concerns. The later studies begin to shed light on the complexities of Latino students' lives as they intersect with family, schooling, community, and workplace demands, and these studies present a far more critical and in-depth perspective that demonstrates resilience factors, adaptability, and restructuring of alternative schools.[9]

Intervention-Oriented Studies

The educational models, as a whole, indeed reflect the concerns of the time and in that sense enact interventions that are deemed useful to "remediate, compensate, or fix the problem." Such altruistic interven-

---

[9]See Romero, Hondagneu-Sotelo, and Ortiz (1997) and Darder, Torres, and Gutierrez (1997) as examples of this type of critical research.

tions such as Head Start, Follow Through, Distar, and Teacher Core Programs are all ways in which the lot of poor students is thought to be ameliorated and fixed. The good intentions are evident, and some of the results are indicative of the models' effectiveness for some, but not necessarily for others.

Cumulative Effects

In addition, these educational models begin to demonstrate some cumulative effects over time with enunciations of best pedagogical practices—team teaching, cultural transfers, cooperative learning, and the Kamehameha Project, for example. We have learned about the values of Mexican Americans regarding their cultures and education, and we have gained a great deal from the cultural difference approaches demonstrating the importance of language communication and cross purposes. The 30-year plus span of research has enhanced our understanding of between group differences and their own adaptability to learning. We have gained a great many insights on the cultural transfer models and their need for contextual adaptability. We have also understood the dilemmas faced, for example, by Puerto Ricans in "fitting" as Americans and at the same time as Latinos within U.S. society. Yet is the macroanalysis advanced by Ogbu and others that has propelled us to question why some students do well, whereas others simply drop out of school, and why there are more of those who leave school than those who are retained in school.

Nonetheless, what has been gained in knowledge and understanding also demonstrates what yet needs to be done in expanding these types of studies. The review suffers from some limitations based on: (a) the actual type and use of data sets; (b) the contextual and historical scope and range of the research, between- and within-group analysis, and generic and specific group analysis; (c) and an understanding of the underlying research paradigms from which the studies emanate.

Data Sets. Although there is a great deal of research literature on the topic, it is highly dispersed and does not exist except as aggregate data, used to generalize from one specific group to another Latino sub-group and across different schooling levels so as to not be sequenced in a way to be studied carefully. In addition, there are lacunae in the consistency of research on achievement from elementary to higher education. Much of the research on the achievement of Latinos is readily available for specific areas such as reading and writing, as well as bilingual education at the elementary school level, but as one scans the research for middle school and high school levels, the research tends to be descriptive and limited.

Contextual Limitations. The historical and social context in which some of these studies take place is often ignored, so that factors that may influence achievement opportunities are not fully discussed, raising the question of whether the characterization of achievement may be under-described and poorly situated for Latinos. Clearly, any attempt at understanding achievement and attainment over time is problematic not only from its initial interpretations, but also because understanding achievement in different contexts is highly complex and requires vast knowledge and interpretation of both longitudinal data sets such as the *High School and Beyond* studies and multiple case studies of a qualitative nature, which can demonstrate how achievement is interpreted by its own protagonists, using their own sociocultural norms.

The delimitations for analyzing the academic achievement of Latinos vary according to the contextual data which exists on a given group and the point of entry. While this review is delimited in its analysis by only focusing on the past 30 plus years of research in an overview, the accounts of Latino achievement can be traced historically to the educational records in California and Texas accounting for intellectual differences and criteria between Whites and Chicanos of the past centuries, and more recently with different waves of immigrant Latinos' experiences. The thresholds of achievement—that is, the gatekeeping points at which Latinos either continue or drop out—that correspond to middle and secondary schools have only recently been studies. Yet as Duran, Escobar, and Wakin (1997) pointed out, as early as the fourth grade, data from the National Assessment of Educational Progress indicates that Latino students are behind their White, non-Latino counterparts, a distance that continues to build up through secondary school. Thus the middle school, and Grades 9 and 10 of high school are the levels at which the problems of early schooling either come to a head for many Latino students or are detected, often when it is too late.

Between- and Within-Group Analysis. Although the review collectively demonstrates that a great deal has gone into explaining the academic failure of Latino students, much of the comparisons have either been traditionally between-group analysis, as in the case of Latinos in comparison and contrast to African Americans or Asians, or within-group analysis, where Mexicans are assessed educationally in contrast to Cubans and Puerto Ricans. With the rising numbers of Central and

South Americans, the within-group type of research presents a challenge (Suárez-Orozco, 1987a). A more refined set of factors that enhance and/or impede the attainment of achievement needs to be known for all Latino populations.

Generic to Specific Group Analysis.   The review also shows inconsistencies between research studies based on the categorization that identifies Latinos or Hispanics as a generic or monolithic category, often failing to distinguish between subgroups and advancing propositions from one group to another without regard for their own idiosyncracies, and consequently engendering stereotypes. For example, because Mexican Americans and Chicanos have been extensively studied, implications for other subgroups are made without identifying what is known about each group, because they are obscured by being presented either under one collective umbrella or as a single group. The complexities of national Mexicans as distinct from Mexican Americans, or Chicanos for different generations are not made known; nor are the descriptions of Cubans from first wave to most current wave, including Marielitos; nor the differences between Puerto Ricans in the continental United States and those who are island born or who experience constant circular migration; nor the uniqueness of Caribbeans from Dominicans to Haitians and Puerto Ricans; nor the distinctions among South Americans, such as the differences between Colombians and Argentines; nor the fine-line distinctions among Central Americans between Salvadorans, Hondurans, Guatemalans, Panamanians, Nicaraguans, and Costa Rican; nor the differences for returnees to their countries of origin. In this regard, the indigenous, linguistic, and African-origin factors of these groups remain untapped. Thus, much of the needed within-group analysis with this approach is ignored.

Shifts in Research Paradigms.   The shifts in research paradigms of the past 30-plus years are evident the studies of academic achievement of Latinos. The initial explanatory models from the 1960s on embodied a positivist, Eurocentric, White middle-class mainstream dominant culture perspective, supported mainly through quantitative research. Such research, based on enumerating the number of students who could not read nor write, served to highlight Latino students who lacked the academic preparation for school, based on the assumption that their home environment was not conducive to school learning. Such analysis compared underrepresented students including Latinos to the norm, under the assumption that these students needed to be brought up to par.

From the 1970s to the present, the shift that has occurred has been from a dominant, mainstream cultural perspective to a more inclusive nonmainstream perspective that represents underrepresented researchers from the same communities and recognizes alternative constructions of reality. Using multiple perspectives, nonmainstream researchers are "problematizing" the experiences of Latinos students by analyzing not only the in-school factors, but also the cultural and community factors that appear to influence and affect, where the context of the family and the barrio as well as the relationship to the dominant culture and its response is investigated (Moll, Amnti, Neff, & Gonzalez, 1992; Trueba, 1997). Latino researchers are now able to research their own communities, define their ideologies and perspectives, and use their own unique ways of knowing as relevant. Thus, current research tends to represent some of the residues of a mainstream dominant cultural paradigm, including the language format of the past, in continued usage of "at-risk or disadvantaged populations," while at the same time, a nonmainstream paradigm prevails that is challenged by the opinions that exist about Latinos' readiness or lack of empowerment.

Currently there are two overriding opinions about where Latinos are in their education in the United States. On the one hand, there are scholars who believe that the time is ripe for Latino empowerment and educational development within their communities (Montero-Sieburth & Villarruel, in press; Trueba, 1997), and on the other hand, there are scholars who believe that the reality in education for Latinos is somewhat bleak and stark (Arias, 1986; Portes & Rumbaut, 1996; Suárez-Orozco & Suárez-Orozco, 1995). Those who support the empowerment position of Latinos in education see the focus on their successes and negotiation as being evident (Montero-Sieburth, 1993; Trueba, 1987), yet those who see the likelihood of success in education as being limited contend, as does Arias (1986), that Mexican American and Puerto Rican students have experienced a history of educational dilemmas in the United States based on limited resources and little, if any, positive reinforcement in schools. The resources within the schooling systems of these communities are lacking greatly in comparison to their Anglo counterparts, within wealthy and poorer communities, as this becomes an argument to explain the circumstances for dropout rates among Mexican American and Puerto Rican students as being the highest of all minority groups in the United States (Arias, 1986).

What is clear about the research studies on Latino achievement is that beyond the descriptions that are made of educational issues that Latinos face, how the implications of such research are translated into educational policies and practices into the new century has not been addressed. Although the general tenor by which Latino academic achievement is presented as a "problem" has progressed to the stage in which solutions or actions for change have been advanced, the need to frame such solutions is at hand.

EDUCATIONAL AND POLICY IMPLICATIONS

As can be gleaned from this review, many Latino students are inevitably engaged in a cultural/social tug of war between the assimilative efforts of schools against the resistance sought by their families. Others such as Trueba (1997) theorized that this trend is not conducive to or followed by new Latino immigrants. Migration patterns of Mexican Americans contrast with the very ideal of assimilation. Mexican Americans' closeness to their native land promotes the persistence of ethnic identity. Many Mexican Americans, especially those situated in the southwestern states, frequently migrate back and forth over the American and Mexican borders. This process reinforces their ethnic identities and makes assimilation hard. Puerto Ricans likewise do not readily assimilate, particularly if they experience circular migration to and from the island and receive continuous reinforcement of Spanish language use. A different scenario exists for U.S.-born Puerto Ricans, who face the issue of identity confounded by U.S. status as ambivalent. Even in the case of Cuban students, as Fernandez and Shu (1988) indicated, under the best of circumstances, being in general education classes, with average grades, and of middle-class status, the likelihood of their dropping out is present. This leads one to question: What are the educational responses of schools not only to immigrant students, but for U.S.-born Latinos?

The research of Ogbu, Gibson, Suárez-Orozco, and Jacobs and Jordan has addressed some of the issues faced by U.S.-born Latinos in their educational achievement. However, the research of Tamara Lucas, Henze, and Donato (1990) focused on the responses required by high schools, and in the past 2 years several reports, including the research by Lucas (1997), provided some indicators of the challenges that schools need to address in relation to immigrants (Lucas, 1996). In brief, Lucas (1997) identified:

1. A lack of a clear understanding of the nature of the transition from school to beyond for any students by school personnel.
2. A lack of support/assistance for all students who are not going directly to college.

3. Too few bilingual teachers/counselors who are knowledgeable of other cultures and understand the complexities of the immigrant experience.

4. Too few professional development opportunities for teachers and counselors to become bilingual and knowledgeable of other cultures and their experiences.

5. The impact of poverty and ethnocentrism on immigrant students and their families, which is not effectively internalized.

6. The existence of a political climate that does not support efforts to assist immigrants in any special ways and that engenders mistrust among immigrants of people associated with U.S. institutions.

All of these needs and the responses required are within reach of most public schools and do not require great investments of monies, other than expansion of human resources. Lucas (1997) synthesized these in terms of four general categories:

Understanding of Schools as Contextually Bound Systems.   Educators need to systematically think about schools as context-bound organizations that need to cultivate multiple levels of organizational relationships. This means schools are viewed as integral to a larger social/institutional context that includes the school district, the surrounding business community, health and social service agencies, community-based organizations, youth organizations, adult and higher education institutions, families of school-age children, and area residents without children. It also means, as Brice Heath (1983) pointed out, that schools no longer assume that the traditional family nuclear family prevails, so that its role is altered to provide many of the socialization processes once provided by parents. Schools must harness these social indicators and attract their usefulness. Research can also enhance such attempts by presenting studies that demonstrate a movement away from the traditional blaming the victim or pathological explanations of students and their families to the more current context-based analysis.

Consideration of Taken-for-Granted Issues for Immigrants.   This implies that schools must consider ideals concerning immigrant expectations, procedures, customs, and resources that middle-class U.S. families take for granted. To meet this, schools must provide explicit information regarding U.S. schooling, culture, higher education, and the "working world." Schools need to provide concrete examples of how rules operate, how policies are enacted, and how practices including verbal interactions within classroom settings function to communicate (Tharp, 1994).

The Role of Peer Interaction.   Peer-group interaction plays a large role in educational success. Students need to be supported as distinct cultural groups who can acquire public voices. To support the cultivation of such human relationships, the methods, programs, subject matter, technology, school structures, and decision-making procedures all have roles to be undertaken and implemented by minority/immigrant students. As Lucas pointed out, the need to connect is critical for immigrant youth who experience a great deal of cultural, linguistic, and social isolation. Relationships between educators and families are integral to making this transition between home and school a smooth one.

Provision of Flexible Pathways.   There need to be multiple and flexible pathways provided for immigrant students moving into, through, and beyond secondary school. Education needs to be more personalized so students feel comfortable investing themselves in the curriculum and pedagogy of the classroom. School flexibility and cultural relativity are essential, but innovations, structure, and strategies must be flexible and able to be compromised to assist immigrant students and to spur achievement. There is also need for the training of professionals who, without being Latino, will need to attend to learning variability based on immigrant versus nonimmigrant status, language development, cultural capital of the home with the school, learning style differences, and acculturation factors.

Although, at this first cut of analysis, what the educational policy and research implications outcomes may be for Latinos into the next century cannot be totally ascertained, some suggestions do emerge from this review of research:

1. Educational achievement has value-added meaning that extends beyond the assessment of test measures and that is often left out of the research studies. There is much going on in the noncognitive arenas, which we have begun to collect through several research initiatives such as Luis Moll's community funds of knowledge, which are compiling evidence of a different kind than tests (Moll et al., 1992). As the Hispanic dropout report *No More Excuses* (Secada et al., 1998) pointed out, there is much that can be done using alternative assessment, including portfolios, which are an additional venue that has begun to question the more traditional role of assessment and evaluation measures of Latino students. The Success for

All program initiatives cater to preschool and elementary programs based on community and parental interventions, the use of cooperative learning, and hands-on work with teachers on reading and writing that is adapted to the child's abilities (Calderón, 1997, 1998; Slavin, 1990; Slavin & Madden, 1989; Slavin, Madden, Karweit, Dolan, & Wasik, 1992). There is a necessity for mainstream educators to respond to the demands that such diverse groups will require of schooling and curriculum standards criteria, such as block transitioning, and development of culturally unbiased performance criteria.

2. Much of the research indicates that academic achievement is a cumulative experience, so that failure in early grades or repetition can in effect set up later conditions for predicting poor academic achievement. Grade retention is an issue that readily affects Latinos, particular those who are in special education with no opportunity to have a combined bilingual education/special education program (Rong & Preissle, 1998; Spener, 1988). Educators into the new millennium will need to formulate policies and practices that correspond to the delivery of just and equitable programs of education for all students (Darder, Torres, & Gutiérrez, 1997).

3. There is a strong correlation between academic achievement and poverty and eventual lifetime earnings, so that the relationship of education to economy cannot be dismissed (Schoeni, McCarthy, & Vernez, 1996). Thus, the development of coherent curriculum structures that incorporate the student's learning and academic performances with eventual career paths needs to be envisioned in positive ways.

4. There are multiple explanations for the enhancement or detraction of academic achievement of Latinos that historically present the current political position held about underrepresented groups; thus, a deeper understanding of Latinos is warranted within their social and cultural contexts, a trend characterized by a constructivist perspective. This requires the development of a greater understanding of the diversity and shifting demographics of Latinos in the United States, such as the fact that Mexicans are now becoming one of the fastest growing groups in predominantly Puerto Rican and Dominican areas in the Northeast. At the same time, this also implies the need to encourage closer home-to-school ties between Latino families and school administrators and teachers (Sakash, 1991; So, 1987; Tharp, 1994).

5. The seeds that are being sown throughout U.S. schools for Latino students have implications not only for their learning, but for the types of learning and socialization that they acquire. Witness the case of returning Salvardoran adolescents to schools in El Salvador, where violence and

gang membership, unknown before in the communities, is now becoming commonplace as a consequence of their U.S. experiences (personal communication, Marta Trejos, CEFEMINA, 1998).

6. There is the identification of family resilience as a factor that impacts the learning of Latino students, whether family is constituted in the traditional, nontraditional, or adaptive community pattern. The values and core meanings of familial extensions plus identity factors play a growing and significant role in the lives of Latino students' academic achievement and attainment.

This review does indicate that Latinos will expect more than access and retention in schools in the new century. They will seek the attainment of an equitable, just, and quality value-added education that has been promised by educational reform movements in this country for the past 16 years. Identifying those factors from preschool to high school and beyond that provide those opportunities for academic success and achievement will no doubt be one of the trends that we can expect to find research and policies capitalizing on. Continuing to identify "best practices" and positive learning opportunities is yet another trend that we can support. Linking Latino parents to schooling efforts not as add-ons but as central players is yet another trend that will yield results. Perhaps then we can continue to deconstruct the negative arguments that are currently used to describe the achievement of Latinos in favor of positive, socioculturally adaptable learning and achievement experiences.

REFERENCES

Aguirre, A., & Martinez, R. (1993). *Chicanos in higher education* (Report No. 3). Washington, DC: ERIC Clearinghouse.

Alexander-Kasparik, R., Mace-Matluck, B., & Queen, R. (1996, April). *Through the golden door: Effective educational approaches for immigrant adolescents with limited schooling.* Paper presented at the American Educational Research Association annual meeting, New York.

Arias, B. (1986, November). The context of education for Hispanic students: An overview. *American Journal of Education*, pp. 26–56.

Bempechat, J. (1998). *Against the odds. How "at risk" children exceed expectations.* San Francisco: Jossey-Bass.

Bourdieu, P., & Passeron, J. C. (1977). *Reproduction in education, society and culture.* Beverly Hills, CA: Sage.

Bowles, S., & Gintis, H. (1976, April). *Schooling in capitalist America.* New York: Basic Books.

Brisk, M. (1999). *Facing the needs of bilingual learners: Interfacing research, policy and practices.* Paper presented at *American Educational Research Association* Meeting, Montreal.

Calderón, M. (1997). Improving Latino education: Preparing teachers and administrators to serve the needs of Latino students. *ETS Policy Notes,* 8(1), 1–3.

Calderón, M. (1998). Adolescent sons and daughters of immigrants: How schools can respond. In K. Borman & B. Schneider (Eds.), *Yearbook of the National Society for the Study of Education* (Part I, pp. 65–87). Chicago: University of Chicago Press.

Carter, T., & Segura, R. (1979). *Mexican Americans in school: Decade of change.* New York: College Entrance Examination Board.

Cazden, C., Vera, J., & Steiner, S. (1972). *Functions of language.* Rowley, MA: Newbury Press.

Chapa, J. (1991). Hispanic demographics and educational trends. In D. Carter & R. Wilson (Eds.), *Ninth annual status report on minorities in higher education* (pp. 11–17). Washington, DC: American Council on Education.

Chapa, J. (1996). *Mexican American education: First, second and third generation adaptations.* Cambridge, MA: Current Issues in Educational Research Workshop, Harvard University Graduate School of Education.

Coleman, J. (1994). Quality and equality in American education: Public Catholic schools. In J. Kretovics & E. J. Nussel (Eds.), *Transforming urban education* (pp. 228–238). Boston: Allyn and Bacon.

Cummins, J. (1984). *Bilingualism and special education: Issues in assessment and pedagogy.* Clevedon, England: Multilingual Matters.

Darder, A., Torres, R., & Gutiérrez, H. (Eds.). (1997). *Latinos and education: A critical reader.* New York: Routledge.

Delgado-Gaitan, C. (1991). Involving parents in the schools: A process of empowerment. *American Journal of Education,* 100, 20–46.

De Vos, G. R. (1992). *Social cohesion and alienation: Minorities in the United States and Japan.* Boulder, CO: Westview Press.

De Vos, G., & Suarez-Orozco, M. (1990). *Status inequality: The self in culture.* Newbury Park, CA: Sage.

Dimaggio, P. (1982). Cultural capital and school success: The impact of status culture participation on the grades of U.S. high school students. *American Sociological Review,* 47, 189–201.

Donmoyer, R., & Kos, R. (Eds.). (1993). *At-risk students: Portraits, policies, programs, and practices.* New York: SUNY Press.

Duran, R., Escobar, F., & Wakin, M. (1997). Improving Latino education. Aiming for college: Improving the classroom instruction of elementary school Latino students. *ETS Policy Notes,* 8(1), 1–6.

Erickson, F. (1987). Transformation and school success: The politics and culture of educational achievement. *Anthropology and Education Quarterly,* 18, 335–356.

Erickson, F. (1994). Transformation and school success: The politics and culture of educational achievement. In J. Kretovics & E. J. Nussel (Eds.), *Transforming urban education* (pp. 375–395). Boston: Allyn and Bacon.

Fernández, R. R., & Shu, G. (1988). School dropouts: New approaches to an enduring problem. *Education and Urban Society,* 20(4), 363–386.

Fine, M. (1986). Why urban adolescents drop into and out of public high school. *Teachers College Record,* 87, 393–409.

Fine, M. (1990). Making controversy: Who's at risk? *Journal of Urban and Cultural Studies, 1*(1), 55–68.

Fine, M. (1995). The politics of who's at risk. In B. Blue Swadener & S. Lubeck (Eds.), *Children and families "at promise": Deconstructing the discourse of risk* (pp. 76–96). New York: SUNY Press.

First, J. (1988, November). Immigrant studies in U.S. public schools: Challenges with solutions. *Phi Delta Kappan*, pp. 205–209.

Gándara, P. (1995). *Over the ivory walls: The educational mobility of low income Chicanos.* Albany: State University of New York Press.

Gibson, M. (1987). The school performance of immigrant minorities. A comparative view. *Anthropology and Education Quarterly, 18*(4), 262–275.

Gibson, M. (1997). Theme issue: Ethnicity and school performance: Complicating the immigrant/involuntary minority typology. *Anthropology and Education Quarterly, 28*(3).

Gibson, M. A., & Ogbu, J. U. (Eds.). (1991). *Minority status and schooling: A comparative study of immigrant and involuntary minorities.* New York: Garland.

Gray, M. J., Rolph, E., & Melamid, E. (1996). *Immigration and higher education: Institutional responses to changing demographics.* Santa Monica, CA: Rand.

Heath, S. B. (1983). *Ways with words. Language, life, and work in communities and classrooms.* New York: Cambridge University Press.

Heller, C. S. (1966). *Mexican American youth: Forgotten youth at the crossroads.* New York: Random House.

Hernández-Chávez, E. (1995). Native language loss and its implications for revitalization of Spanish in Chicano communities. *Latino Language and Education*, pp. 24–36.

Jacobs, E., & Jordan, C. (1987). Theme issue: Explaining the school performance of minority students. *Anthropology and Education Quarterly, 18*(4).

Kjolseth, R. (1972). Bilingual education programs in the United States: For assimilation or pluralism? In B. Spolsky (Ed.), *The language education of minority children* (pp. 94–121). Rowley, MA: Newbury House.

Laosa, L. (1978). Maternal teaching strategies in Chicano families of varied educational and socioeconomic levels. *Child Development, 49*, 1129–1135.

Lareau, A. (1987). Social class differences in family–school relationships: The importance of cultural capital. *Sociology of Education, 60*, 73–85.

Lewis, O. (1965). *La vida: A Puerto Rican family in the culture of poverty—San Juan and New York.* New York: Random House.

Lewis, O. (1996). The culture of poverty. *Scientific American, 218*, 19–25.

Lopez, A. S. (Ed.). (1995). *Latino language and education: Communication and the dream deferred.* New York: Garland.

Lucas, T. (1996, April). *Into, through, and beyond secondary school: Critical transitions for immigrant youths.* Paper presented at the American Educational Research Association Meeting, New York.

Lucas, T. (1997). *Into, through, and beyond secondary school. Critical transitions for immigrant youths.* McHenry, IL: Delta Systems, Center for Applied Linguistics.

Lucas, T., Henze, R., & Donato, R. (1990). Promoting the success of Latino language-minority students: An exploratory study of six high schools. *Harvard Educational Review, 60*(3), 315–340.

McDonnell, L. M., & Hill, P. T. (1993). *Newcomers in American schools: Meeting the educational needs of immigrant youth.* Santa Monica, CA: Rand Corporation.

Mehan, H. (1992). Understanding inequality in schools: The contribution of interpretive studies. *Sociology of Education, 65*, 1–20.

Mehan, H., Villanueva, I., Hubbard, L., & Lintz, A. (1996). *Constructing school success: The consequences of untracking low-achieving students.* New York: Cambridge University Press.

Merino, B. (1991). Promoting school success for Chicanos. In R. Valencia (Ed.), *Chicano school failure and success* (pp. 119–149). New York: Palmer.

Moll, L. C., Amnti, C., Neff, D., & Gonzalez, N. (1992). Funds of knowledge: Using a qualitative approach to connect homes and classrooms. *Theory Into Practice, 31*(2), 132–141.

Montero-Sieburth, M. (1981). *Ethnographic Case Studies of Bilingual Teachers's Perspectives: Towards a Theory of Culture and Meaning.* Unpublished Doctoral Dissertation. Boston, MA, Boston University.

Montero-Sieburth, M. (1993). The effects of schooling processes and practices on potential at risk Latino high school students. In R. Rivera & S. Nieto (Eds.), *The education of Latino students in Massachusetts: Issues, research, and policy implications* (pp. 217–242). Amherst, MA: M. Gaston Institute and University of Massachusetts.

Montero-Sieburth, M. (1996). Teachers, administrators, and staff's implicit thinking about "at risk" urban high school Latino students. In F. Rios (Ed.), *Teacher thinking in cultural contexts* (pp. 55–84). Albany, NY: SUNY Press.

Montero-Sieburth, M., & Villarruel, F. (2000). *Latino adolescents: Building upon the strengths of our diversity.* New York: Garland.

Oakes, J. U. (1985). *Keeping track: How schools structure inequality.* New Haven, CT: Yale University Press.

Ogbu, J. U. (1987). Variability in minority school performance. *Anthropology and Educational Quarterly, 18*, 312–334.

Ogbu, J. U. (1991a). Immigrant and involuntary minorities in comparative perspective. In M. Gibson & J. Ogbu (Eds.), *Minority status and schooling* (pp. 3–36). New York: Garland.

Ogbu, J. U. (1992). Understanding cultural diversity and learning. *Educational Researcher, 22*, 5–14.

Ogbu, J. U., & Matute-Bianchi, M. E. (1986). Understanding sociocultural factors: Knowledge, identity and school adjustment. In *Beyond language* (pp. 73–142). Los Angeles: California State University Evaluation, Dissemination and Assessment Center. Bilingual Education Office, California State Dept. of Education, Sacramento, CA.

Pollard, D. S. (1989). Against the odds: A profile of academic achievers from the urban underclass. *Journal of Negro Education, 58*(3), 297–308.

Portes, A., & Rumbaut, R. (1996). *Immigrant America: A portrait* (2nd ed.). Berkeley, CA: University of California Press.

Portes, A., & Zhou, M. (1993). The new second generation: Segmented assimilation and its variants. *Annals, AAPSS, 530*, 75–96.

Rivera, R., & Nieto, S. (1993). *The education of Latino students in Massachusetts: Issues, research, and policy implications.* Amherst, MA: M. Gaston Institute and University of Massachusetts.

Rodríguez, C. (1974). The structure of failure II: A case in point. *Urban Review, 7*, 215–226.

Romero, M., Hondagneu-Sotelo, P., & Ortiz, V. (Eds.). (1997). *Challenging fronteras: Structuring Latina and Latino lives in the U.S.* New York: Routledge.

Rong, X. L., & Preissle, J. (1998). *Educating immigrant students: What we need to know to meet the challenges*. Thousand Oaks, CA: Corwin.

Sakash, K. (1991, April). *The influence of Mexican-American children's socially responsible behaviors on achievement*. Paper presented at the Annual Meeting of the American Educational Research Association, Chicago.

Schoeni, R. F., McCarthy, K. F., & Vernez, G. (1996). *The mixed economic progress of immigrants*. Santa Monica, CA: Rand Corporation.

Secada, W., Chavez-Chavez, R., Garcia, E., Muñoz, C., Oakes, J., Santiago-Santiago, I., & Slavin, R. (1998). *No more excuses. The final report of the Hispanic Dropout Project*. Washington, DC: U.S. Department of Education.

Slavin, R. E. (1990). Achievement effects of ability grouping in secondary schools: A best evidence synthesis. *Review of Educational Research, 60*(3), 471–499.

Slavin, R. E., & Madden, N. (1989). What works for students at risk: A research synthesis. *Educational Leadership, 46*(5), 4–13.

So, A. (1987). High-achieving disadvantaged students: A study of low SES Hispanic language minority youth. *Urban Education, 22*(1), 19–35.

Spener, D. (1988). Transitional bilingual education and the socialization of immigrants. *Harvard Educational Review, 58,* 133–153.

Stanton-Salazar, R. D. (1997). A social capital framework for understanding the socialization of racial minority children and youths. *Harvard Educational Review, 67*(1), 1–40.

Stein, C. B. (1985). Hispanic students in the sink or swim era, 1900–1960. *Urban Education, 20*(2), 189–198.

Steinberg, L., Blinde, P. L., & Chan, K. S. (1984). Dropping out among language minority youth. *Review of Educational Research, 54*(1), 113–132.

Suárez-Orozco, M. (1987a). Becoming somebody: Central American immigrants in U.S. inner city schools. *Anthropology and Education Quarterly, 18*(4), 287–299.

Suárez-Orozco, M. (1987b). Towards a psychosocial understanding of Hispanic adaptation to American schooling. In H. E. Trueba (Ed.), *Success or failure, learning and the language minority student* (pp. 156–168). Cambridge, MA: Newbury House.

Suárez-Orozco, M. (1989). *Central American refugees and U.S. high schools: A psychosocial study of motivation and achievement*. Stanford, CA: Stanford University Press.

Suárez-Orozco, C., & Suárez-Orozco, M. (1995). *Transformations: Migrations, family life, and achievement motivation among Latino adolescents*. Stanford, CA: Stanford University Press.

Suárez-Orozco, M. (Ed.). (1998). *Crossings: Mexican immigration in interdisciplinary perspectives*. Cambridge, MA: Harvard University, David Rockefeller Center for Latin American Studies.

Swadener, B. B., & Lubeck, S. (Eds.). (1995). *Children and families "at promise": Deconstructing the discourse of risk*. Albany, NY: SUNY Press.

Tharp, R. (1994). Research knowledge and policy issues in cultural diversity and education. In R. J. Anson (Ed.), *Systematic reform: Perspectives on personalizing education* (pp. 169–200). Washington, DC: U.S. Department of Education, Office of Educational Research and Improvement.

Thomas, W., & Collier, V. (1999, April). *Evaluation that informs school reform: Study, design and findings from the Thomas and Collier (1998) national school-based collaborative research on school effectiveness for language minority students*. Paper presented at the American Educational Research Association Meeting, Montreal.

Trueba, H. E. (Ed.). (1987). *Success or failure? Learning and the language minority student.* Cambridge, MA: Newbury House.

Trueba, H. E. (1991). Linkages of macro–micro analytical levels. *Journal of Psycho-History,* *18*(4), 457–468.

Trueba, H. E. (1997, April). *Challenges in the education of Mexican immigrant children: Adaptive strategies of families in a binational world.* Paper presented at the Immigration and Socio-Cultural Remaking of the North American Space Conference, David Rockefeller Center for Latin American Studies, Harvard University, Cambridge, MA.

Trueba, H. E. (1998). *Critical ethnographic praxis for the study of immigrants.* Cambridge, MA: Harvard Graduate School of Education, unpublished manuscript.

Trueba, H. E., & Bartolome, L. (1998). *Latinos, the emerging majority in schools: Implications for teacher preparation.* Paper requested by the ERIC Clearinghouse on Urban Education and the Institute for Urban and Minority Education (funded by the U.S. Department of Education) at Teachers College, Columbia University, New York.

Turner, C., Laria, A., Shapiro, E., & del Carmen Perez, M. (1993). Poverty, resilience, and academic achievement among Latino college students and high school dropouts. In R. Rivera & S. Nieto (Eds.), *The education of Latino students in Massachusetts: Issues, research, and policy implications* (pp. 191–216). Amherst: University of Massachusetts Press.

Valentine, C. (1968). *Culture and poverty.* Chicago: University of Chicago Press.

Vernez, G., Abrahamse, A., & Quigley, D. (1996). *How immigrants fare in U.S. education.* Santa Monica, CA: Rand Corporation.

Wheelock, A. (1993). The status of Latino students in Massachusetts public schools. In R. Rivera & S. Nieto (Eds.), *The education of Latino students in Massachusetts: Issues, research, and policy implications* (pp. 11–32). Amherst, MA: M. Gaston Institute and University of Massachusetts.

Willis, P. (1972). *Learning to labour: How working class kids get working class jobs.* Westmead, Farnborough, Hants. England: Saxon House.

Author Index

Subject Index

A

A Second Cup of Coffee, 288

Academic achievement
analysis of research and literature review, 354–359
data sources and methodology, 334–335
educational and policy implications, 359–363
Project AVID, 116–117, 119, 120–121
theoretical perspectives and explanatory models
academic failure explanation of at-risk studies, 350–352
bilingual education, 340–343
coethnic peer communities, 346–348
cultural capital sociological, 344–345
cultural deprivation or cultural deficit, 336–337
cultural difference, 337–338
dual frame of reference, 348–350
economic explanatory, 343–344
success factors model, 352–354
theory of resistance, 345–346
voluntary immigrants and involuntary minorities model, 338–340

Academic Expectations Committee, 16
Academic failure model, 350–352
Academic goals, 41
Academic performance, 102, *see also* Performance
Academic skills, 74, 75, 90
Academic standards, 115
Academic success, 128
Accelerated Schools, 11–12, 145
ACCESS, *see* Alliance for Collaborative Change in Education School Systems
Accountability, 16, 126, 127
Achievement for Latinos through Academic Success (ALAS), 75–79, *see also* Dropout prevention
Achievement
academic, see Academic achievement
bilingual programs, 164, 186–188
dropout rate, 68
literacy, *see* Literacy, achievement
medians and ESL adaptations of Success for All/*Éxito Para Todos*, 224
Administration, bilingual programs, 150–151
Adult education, 321

379